Languages for Specific Purposes in the Digital Era

Educational Linguistics

Volume 15

Educational Linguistics is dedicated to innovative studies of language use and language learning. The series is based on the idea that there is a need for studies that break barriers. Accordingly, it provides a space for research that crosses traditional disciplinary, theoretical, and/or methodological boundaries in ways that advance knowledge about language (in) education. The series focuses on critical and contextualized work that offers alternatives to current approaches as well as practical, substantive ways forward. Contributions explore the dynamic and multi-layered nature of theorypractice relationships, creative applications of linguistic and symbolic resources, individual and societal considerations, and diverse social spaces related to language learning.

The series publishes in-depth studies of educational innovation in contexts throughout the world: issues of linguistic equity and diversity; educational language policy; revalorization of indigenous languages; socially responsible (additional) language teaching; language assessment; fi rst- and additional language literacy; language teacher education; language development and socialization in non-traditional settings; the integration of language across academic subjects; language and technology; and other relevant topics.

The Educational Linguistics series invites authors to contact the general editor with suggestions and/or proposals for new monographs or edited volumes. For more information, please contact the publishing editor: Jolanda Voogd, Asssociate Publishing Editor, Springer, Van Godewijckstraat 30, 3300 AA Dordrecht, The Netherlands.

For further volumes:
http://www.springer.com/series/5894

Elena Bárcena • Timothy Read • Jorge Arús
Editors

Languages for Specific Purposes in the Digital Era

Springer

Editors
Elena Bárcena
Departamento de Filologías Extranjeras y sus Lingüísticas
Universidad Nacional de Educación a Distancia
Madrid, Spain

Timothy Read
Departamento de Lenguajes y Sistemas Informáticos
Universidad Nacional de Educación a Distancia
Madrid, Spain

Jorge Arús
Departamento de Filología Inglesa I
Universidad Complutense de Madrid
Madrid, Spain

ISSN 1572-0292
ISBN 978-3-319-02221-5 ISBN 978-3-319-02222-2 (eBook)
DOI 10.1007/978-3-319-02222-2
Springer Cham Heidelberg New York Dordrecht London

Library of Congress Control Number: 2013955740

Printed on acid-free paper

Springer is part of Springer Science+Business Media (www.springer.com)

On LSPs in the digital era

Research on CALL applications aimed at the teaching and learning of LSPs is a thriving area within the field of linguistics. The enormous social demand for language training in specialized domains has led to the proliferation of flexible technological applications of increasing complexity, which require a forum of their own. This book presents the research and teaching communities a representative state of the art of technological and methodological innovation in the teaching and processing of specialized linguistic domains. The authors are recognized experts in the corresponding fields, who present the results of many years of theoretical and applied research undertaken to improve the way in which language can be learnt, taught and/or processed. This book is not only intended for an essentially academic public, but also for anyone interested in the way in which computers and people work with domain-specific languages.

The content of this book is particularly relevant to anyone working in the area defined by the application of technology to the processing and learning/teaching of natural languages, in restricted or specialized professional and academic contexts. This reflects real world demands and also the need to account for the multiple divergences of such linguistic domains with respect to general or standard languages. One such specificity lies in their terminology, which is not only at least partially closed, but also systematically used by the corresponding specialized community, as a direct reflection of the closure and systematicity of the conceptual world of reference. Due to this and other inherent syntactic, semantic, and pragmatic properties of LSPs, they are seen to require a specific approach for their computer-based teaching and processing. Hence, this book is intended for the diverse range of professionals that populate the computer-based language learning/teaching and processing universe, many of whom come from the field of Language and Linguistics (and its related specializations like Applied Linguistics and Computational Linguistics), and also from neighbouring disciplines, like Applied Computing, Second Language Education and Educational Psychology. The book targets scholars, researchers, postgraduate and graduate students, and faculty in teacher education and applied linguistics programs, teachers, teacher trainers, teacher trainees, curriculum and materials developers, testers and evaluators, and others who are interested or merely curious about the field.

In a nutshell, the readers of this book will find different ways in which computational applications can facilitate the teaching and learning of LSP and related subjects. Instructors and researchers in the area will find a good number of ideas to implement in their classes and/or help them in their investigation. It is not a question of chance that the book covers LSPs and CALL as well as other neighbouring fields, as there is great scope for feedback and reusability of principles, models, techniques and strategies between the different types of systems that involve the computational manipulation of languages or linguistic aspects. This interdisciplinary volume pulls together different strands of research, targeting researchers who work on different aspects of sublanguages and their application to computational linguistics, CALL and corpora. This has the advantage that, while an article on, for example, the analysis of the development of a corpus for a given sublanguage is in principle publishable in a general computational linguistics forum, it would probably fail to be read by researchers who cannot regularly follow the many CL journals and books available.

The 16 chapters in this book bring together a unique broad-based, state-of-the-art coverage of current knowledge and research in the interrelated fields of computer-based learning/teaching and processing of specialized linguistic domains. The motivation comes from the fact that, firstly, there is a direct relation between modern CALL and the different aspects of natural language processing for theoretical and practical applications, and secondly, the real world demands for formal language education and training worldwide that focus on restricted or specialized professional domains. This can be seen for the former by the evolution in the design and development of CALL systems, where advances in Natural Language Processing and other neighbouring fields are gradually occupying a more prominent role. Furthermore, there is great scope for feedback and reusability of principles, models, techniques and strategies between the different types of CALL systems as well as, more generally speaking, those systems involving the computational manipulation of languages or linguistic aspects. Similarly, for the latter, in a goal-oriented and globalized world, people require a second language above all to interact with natives of other languages both at work and in well-defined social situations. This fact implies an individualized treatment of the object of study since the relation between the language of a given specialized domain and both other specialized languages and the general language itself is not merely one of inclusion, but rather one of intersection, so there are deviances and significant preferential phenomena to be accounted for at all linguistic levels. However, once again there is great scope for transportability of principles, models, techniques and strategies between the different languages and domains to make the different studies presented in this volume of general interest.

Some of the chapters contained in this book are insightful high level reflections or analyses of the current state and future directions of one of the topics covered. Many recent key concepts regarding the application of computers to natural languages are brought up, questioned and reflected upon, such as: authenticity, personalization, normalization, evaluation, etc. Other chapters provide fruitful low level research on a number of the major techniques, strategies and methodologies that are currently under focus in international research language projects, both of a basic and an applied nature.

The book is divided into four parts. The first part contains four chapters dealing with general issues about learning languages with computers. The first chapter, Information technology and languages for specific purposes in the EHEA: Options and challenges for the knowledge society by Arnó-Macià, is a thorough and insightful review of the impact of computing technology on LSP (Languages for Specific Purposes), focusing mainly on central questions related to LSP, such as the roles of teachers and learners, authenticity and specificity of materials, genre, and skills development, taking into account the European reform of university education. The second chapter, Gimeno's Fostering learner autonomy in technology-enhanced ESP courses, presents the pedagogical implications of a number of technology-enhanced language learning initiatives aimed at increasing learner autonomy. A modern language classroom is claimed and argued to scaffold the observational, exploratory and productive skills that language students need to develop. The third chapter, The I-AGENT Project: Blended Learning Proposal for Professional English integrating an AI Extended Version of Moodle with Classroom Work for the Practice of Oral Skills by Martín and Talaván, presents an adaptive blended learning approach developed in the I-AGENT project. It details an Artificial Intelligence module for Moodle that provides online student scaffolding to an overall blended learning methodology. The fourth chapter, Student assessment in the online language learning materials developed and delivered through the INGENIO system, by Sevilla, Martínez-Sáez, and de Siqueira, provides an analysis of the assessment process of basic language skills, and explores the flexible way in which an online course contributes to the efficiency of such a process in both student self-assessment and tutor-based assessment.

The second part contains four chapters dealing with computer-assisted experiences for the development of language competences and skills. The first chapter, Internet dictionaries for teaching and learning business English in Spanish universities by Fuertes, defends a lexicographical approach to the study of terminology based upon the function theory of lexicography. Following an analysis of the extra-lexicographical scenario of Spanish students of business English, the author claims that Internet specialized cognitive and communicative dictionaries are potentially efficient pedagogical reference tools for understanding the basics of the subject field and communicating in standard business situations. The second chapter, Breeze's Moodle glossary tasks for teaching legal English, reports on the collaborative creation of an online legal English glossary in Moodle as a study tool integrated in a university ESP (English for Specific Purposes) course. The decisions taken by the students involved in this process are analysed, together with the positive feedback obtained from both teachers and peers. The third chapter, Promoting specialized vocabulary learning through computer-assisted instruction, by Perea and Bocanegra, focuses on computer-supported teaching/learning of Maritime English vocabulary in general, and the use of the glossary tool contained in Moodle in particular. The fourth chapter, A practical application of wikis for learning business English as a second language, by Rodríguez Arancón and Martín Monje, presents a case study for the use of wikis as a tool to reinforce students' second language communicative competences. A pilot study is undertaken for an English course on an Economics Degree, the results of which demonstrate an above average success rate, supporting the efficiency of wikis, while requiring additional effort from the teaching team.

The third part contains four chapters dealing with corpus-based applications for teaching and processing (sub)languages. The first chapter, A genre-based approach to the teaching of legal and business English: The GENTT specialized corpus in the LSP classroom, by Borja, Juste, Ordóñez, and Conde, presents practical learning applications for languages for professional purposes. Specifically, this research is based on a corpus of specialized genres developed by the authors, which provides empirically obtained models and patterns to be used as textual, conceptual, linguistic and terminological references. The second chapter, Innovative methods for LSP-teaching: how we use corpora to teach business Russian, by Wilson, Sharoff, Stevenson and Hartley, presents a corpus-based approach to teaching business Russian, which involves the enhancement of existing corpus-based tools to facilitate vocabulary acquisition and register identification. The third chapter, Automatic specialized vs. non-specialized text differentiation: the usability of grammatical features in a Latin multilingual context, by Cabré, da Cunha, San Juan, Torres-Moreno and Vivaldi, presents a tool for the differentiation between specialized vs. plain texts, which uses corpora and machine learning techniques and association rules based on both lexical and grammatical features. This research has direct applications in the automatic compilation of LSPs and the optimization of search engines. The fourth chapter, Laursen and Arinas' Exploring the potential of corpus use in translation training: new approach for incorporating software in Danish translation course design, discusses how to combine functional translation strategies with the use of concordance software and genre analysis in specialized translation training.

The fourth part contains three chapters dealing with natural language processing. The first chapter, Representing environmental knowledge in EcoLexicon, by Faber, León and Reimerink, presents a multilingual terminological knowledge base on the environment as a rich and internally coherent database covering specialized conceptual and linguistic information. A user-friendly multimodal interface has been developed, where interrelated modules can be accessed in a flexible way according to user needs. In order to avoid information overload, the authors have undertaken a reconceptualization process based on domain membership and semantic role. The second chapter, New approaches to audiovisual translation: the usefulness of corpus-based studies for the teaching of dubbing and subtitling, by Rica, Albarán and García Riaza, reflects upon an interdisciplinary study that blends audiovisual translation and corpus linguistics to show some of the possibilities they offer when applied together. For example, analysis of the translations made of a film show how well they were done and also if they reflect the way in which translations were undertaken at the time. The third chapter, Pareja's The pragmatic level of OntoLingAnnot's ontologies and their use in pragmatic annotation for linguistic applications, presents the pragmatic annotation of the OntoLingAnnot annotation framework. As such, the different units, values, attributes and relations that constitute the pragmatic annotation have been devised for the annotation of dialogues and texts in different contexts, such as the development of corpora or language teaching.

LSPs and Computational Linguistics, notably CALL, are two fields with a long, fruitful history of mutual cross-fertilization and which will no doubt continue to do so for many more years to come. It is, therefore, a very appropriate time for the publication of a book like this.

Departamento de Lenguajes y Sistemas Informáticos Timothy Read
Universidad Nacional de Educación a Distancia, Madrid, Spain

Departamento de Filologías Extranjeras y sus Lingüísticas Elena Bárcena
Universidad Nacional de Educación a Distancia, Madrid, Spain

Departamento de Filología Inglesa I Universidad Complutense Jorge Arús
de Madrid, Madrid, Spain

Acknowledgements

The editors of this book are very grateful to the Spanish Ministry of Science and Innovation for funding the research activities (FFI2008-06030 and FFI2011-29829) undertaken by the ATLAS group that have given rise to this publication.

Contents

Contributors

Reyes Albarrán Martín Departamento de Traducción e Interpretación, Universidad de Salamanca, Salamanca, Spain

Ismael Arinas Pellón Departamento de Lingüística Aplicada a la Ciencia y a la Tecnología, Universidad Politécnica de Madrid, Madrid, Spain

Elisabet Arnó-Macià Departament de Projectes d'Enginyeria, Secció d'Anglès, Universitat Politècnica de Catalunya, Barcelona, Spain

Jorge Arús Departamento de Filología Inglesa I, Universidad Complutense de Madrid, Madrid, Spain

Elena Bárcena Departamento de Filologías extranjeras y sus lingüísticas, Universidad Nacional de Educación a Distancia, Madrid, Spain

Ana Bocanegra-Valle Departamento de Filología Francesa e Inglesa, Universidad de Cádiz, Cádiz, Spain

Anabel Borja Albi Departamento de Traducción y Comunicación, GENTT Research Group, Universitat Jaume I, Castellón, Spain

Ruth Breeze Institute of Modern Languages, University of Navarra, Pamplona, Spain

M. Teresa Cabré Institut Universitari de Lingüística Aplicada, Universidad Pompeu Fabra (UPF), Barcelona, Spain

Cristina Calle-Martínez Departamento de Filología Inglesa I, Universidad Complutense de Madrid, Madrid, Spain

Tomás Conde Departamento de Filología Inglesa y Alemana, Universidad del País Vasco, Vitoria-Gasteiz, Spain

Iria da Cunha Institut Universitari de Lingüística Aplicada, Universidad Pompeu Fabra (UPF), Barcelona, Spain

José Macario De Siqueira Rocha Departamento de Informática, Universidad Carlos III, Colmenarejo (Madrid), Spain

Pamela Faber Departamento de Traducción e interpretación, Universidad de Granada, Granada, Spain

Pedro A. Fuertes-Olivera Departamento de Filología Inglesa, University of Valladolid, Valladolid, Spain

Blanca García Riaza Departamento de Filología Inglesa, Universidad de Salamanca, Salamanca, Spain

Ana María Gimeno Sanz Departamento de Lingüística Aplicada, Universidad Politécnica de Valencia, Valencia, Spain

Anthony Hartley School of Modern Languages and Cultures, University of Leeds, Leeds, UK

Natividad Juste Vidal Departamento de Traducción y Comunicación, GENTT Research Group, Universitat Jaume I, Castellón, Spain

Anne Lise Laursen Department of Business Communication, Aarhus University, Aarhus, Denmark

Pilar León-Araúz Departamento de Traducción e interpretación, Universidad de Granada, Granada, Spain

Elena Martín-Monje Departamento de Filologías Extranjeras y sus Lingüísticas, Universidad Nacional de Educación a Distancia (UNED), Madrid, Spain

Antonio Martínez-Sáez Departamento de Lingüística Aplicada, Universidad Politécnica de Valencia, Valencia, Spain

Pilar Ordóñez López Departamento de Traducción y Comunicación, GENTT Research Group, Universitat Jaume I, Castellón, Spain

Mª Dolores Perea-Barberá Departamento de Filología Francesa e Inglesa, Universidad de Cádiz, Cádiz, Spain

Antonio Pareja-Lora Departamento de Sistemas Informáticos y Computación/ATLAS, Universidad Complutense de Madrid/UNED, Madrid, Spain

Juan Pedro Rica Peromingo Departamento de Filología Inglesa I, Universidad Complutense de Madrid, Madrid, Spain

Timothy Read Departamento de Lenguajes y sistemas informáticos, Universidad Nacional de Educación a Distancia, Madrid, Spain

Arianne Reimerink Departamento de Traducción e interpretación, Universidad de Granada, Granada, Spain

Pilar Rodríguez-Arancón Departamento de Filologías Extranjeras y sus Lingüísticas, Universidad Nacional de Educación a Distancia, Madrid, Spain

Eric SanJuan Departament Statistique et Informatique Décisionnelle, Laboratoire Informatique d'Avignon, Université d'Avignon (UAPV), Avignon, France

Brain and Language Research Institute (BLRI), Avignon, France

Ana Sevilla-Pavón Departamento de Lingüística Aplicada, Universidad Politécnica de Valencia, Valencia, Spain

Serge Sharoff School of Modern Languages and Cultures, University of Leeds, Leeds, UK

Paul Stephenson School of Modern Languages and Cultures, University of Leeds, Leeds, UK

Noa Talaván Departamento de Filologías Extranjeras y sus Lingüísticas, Universidad Nacional de Educación a Distancia (UNED), Madrid, Spain

Juan-Manuel Torres-Moreno Departament Statistique et Informatique Décisionnelle, Laboratoire Informatique d'Avignon, Université d'Avignon (UAPV), Avignon, France

École Polytechnique de Montréal, Montreal, QC, Canada

Brain and Language Research Institute (BLRI), Avignon, France

Jorge Vivaldi Institut Universitari de Lingüística Aplicada, Universidad Pompeu Fabra (UPF), Barcelona, Spain

James Wilson School of Modern Languages and Cultures, University of Leeds, Leeds, UK

Part I
General Issues About Learning Languages with Computers

Chapter 1
Information Technology and Languages for Specific Purposes in the EHEA: Options and Challenges for the Knowledge Society

Elisabet Arnó-Macià

1.1 Introduction

As information technology (IT) pervades our society, it has inevitably contributed to transforming educational practices. Alongside profound social changes and shifting paradigms, technology has played a major role in reshaping education, which has led to a reappraisal of the roles of teachers and learners, in particular considering that younger students are especially adept at new technologies. With the progressive internationalization of academic and professional settings and the growth of computer-based communication, teachers and course designers are faced with a changing scenario, which is why the relationship between IT and languages for specific purposes (LSP) merits detailed analysis (see Arnó et al. 2006; González-Pueyo et al. 2009; Arnó 2012). Traditionally, LSP has been a multidisciplinary activity involving collaboration, engagement with disciplinary knowledge, innovation and flexibility, and interaction in authentic situations with realistic materials. Since LSP aims at helping students communicate successfully in academic and professional settings, it is necessary to explore how IT has affected specialized communication and how its potential can be harnessed for educational purposes.

This paper analyzes how IT can be integrated in LSP, considering the roles of technology in specialized communication, as well as the reform of European higher education, as a result of the Bologna process, which has led to the creation of the European Higher Education Area (EHEA). Different technological applications are analyzed in order to identify how they can be integrated in LSP teaching to help students cope with the demands of academic and professional communication in a globalized context. Thus, the paper begins with a general overview of the role of IT in LSP, based on

E. Arnó-Macià (✉)
Departament de Projectes d'Enginyeria, Secció d'Anglès,
Universitat Politècnica de Catalunya, Barcelona, Spain
e-mail: elisabet.arno@upc.edu

E. Bárcena et al. (eds.), *Languages for Specific Purposes in the Digital Era*,
Educational Linguistics 19, DOI 10.1007/978-3-319-02222-2_1,

the definition of 'languages for specific purposes' and theories of language and learning. These perspectives are then examined in the context of the EHEA, which involves the harmonization of degrees, mobility, and employability, together with a shift in focus towards learning processes and outcomes. These processes in turn need to be situated in the broader framework of the knowledge society. In particular, the role of IT in LSP is analyzed from the perspective different dimensions, such as the new and more complex roles of LSP teachers and learners, the development of online courses and materials, the role of discipline knowledge and its integration with language learning, the development of academic skills, as well as IT applications for specialized communication, collaboration and lifelong learning. Lastly, in order to provide an example of how the general implications derived from these dimensions can be applied to a particular technology-based LSP project, the online learning environment *Quantum LEAP (Learning English for Academic Purposes)* is presented, which addresses some of the challenges and options in this changing context.

1.2 The Relationship Between IT and LSP: An Overview

In order to analyze the role of IT in LSP, it is necessary first to set a definition of 'languages for specific purposes'. Dudley-Evans and St. John (1998) provide a comprehensive definition of English for Specific Purposes, in terms of absolute and variable characteristics.

Absolute characteristics:

- ESP is designed to meet specific needs of the learner;
- ESP makes use of the underlying methodology and activities of the disciplines it serves;
- ESP is centered on the language (grammar, lexis, register), skills, discourse and genres appropriate to these activities.

Variable characteristics:

- ESP may be related to or designed for specific disciplines;
- ESP may use, in specific teaching situations, a different methodology from that of general English;
- ESP is likely to be designed for adult learners, either at a tertiary level institution or in a professional work situation. It could, however, be used for learners at secondary school level;
- ESP is generally designed for intermediate or advanced students. Most ESP courses assume basic knowledge of the language system, but it can be used with beginners.

(Dudley-Evans and St. John 1998: 4–5)

This definition includes some key concepts that lie at the core of LSP (e.g. Johns and Dudley-Evans 1991; Dudley-Evans and St. John 1998; Alcaraz 2000; Belcher 2004). First, LSP activity is driven by the practical need to help students participate in academic and work situations, which means that LSP courses and materials are tailored to suit students' specific needs. In turn, the concept of 'need' is also a central step in LSP course design, whose major goal is to respond adequately to learners' needs, with LSP courses aiming at cost-effectiveness. Other driving forces in LSP are authenticity and motivation. Authenticity involves providing materials and situations related to students' target activities, whereas motivation is regarded from a twofold perspective. On the one hand, the LSP student is characterized as being specially motivated, while LSP courses and materials are aimed at fostering this motivation even further. Since LSP teaching aims at helping students enter particular discourse communities, its methodology draws on relevant activities and practices. For this reason, central LSP concerns include the role of discipline knowledge, specialized discourse, as well as the genres typically used by the discourse communities. From the point of view of methodology, Hutchinson and Waters (1987) define LSP as a "learning-centered approach", which considers students' previous knowledge and skills, uses active learning, takes into account affective factors (e.g. enhancing motivation and promoting collaborative learning), and uses varied input for communicative purposes. The development of the field of LSP (with its origins and main impetus in English for Specific Purposes, or ESP) has been driven by economic trends and the internationalization of science, industry, and business. Nowadays, students and professionals worldwide are immersed in work and study contexts that involve communication and collaboration across borders, a situation which is also largely due to developments in technology. Internationalization processes are particularly apparent in Europe, with current trends towards greater cohesion and mobility. This context provides LSP teachers and students with greater opportunities to access different discourse communities and tailor courses to students' genuine needs and practices. These new opportunities also bring up a number of challenges, related to the reappraisal of teacher and learner roles, new demands of materials and courses, as well as general challenges inherent to the uses of technology in our society.

Developments in IT have influenced LSP, not only in facilitating access to specialized discourse and communication, but also as a result of the evolution of technology as a language learning tool (in turn influenced by evolving educational paradigms). Therefore, LSP draws on the developments of CALL (Computer-Assisted Language Learning) in mainstream language teaching. Regarding the evolution of technology-based approaches to language teaching, Levy (1997) pointed at the transition from the role of the computer as 'tutor' to that of a 'tool'. On the other hand, Warschauer and Kern (2000) extended the notion of CALL to that of network-based language teaching (NBLT). This greater technological interconnection has led to the "second wave of online learning" (Kern et al. 2004), whereby language learning is no longer the sole objective, but there is an important focus on social discourses, identity, collaboration, and electronic literacies. Apart from the evolution of technology itself, in the last decade our society has undergone radical transformations in forms of communication, the access to and management of information, the creation of virtual communities, and immediate availability through portable devices. The shifting perspective of the role of the 'computer' in language education and the proliferation of multiple devices has even led to the questioning of the name of CALL to refer to the applications of technology (Kern 2006).

In this rapidly changing environment, it would be too easy to equate innovation with the use of newer technologies. Technology *per se* does not involve innovation; rather, any approach to technology should be based on a sound pedagogic rationale. As Garrett (2009) points out, a systematic approach to technology-based language education does not involve the mere use of technology, but should be based on the full integration of technology, theory, and pedagogy. Another important dimension of the integration of technology in LSP is a critical perspective, which lies at the root of technology use, language education, and LSP practice. The activities of language teaching—especially English, as the major *lingua franca*—and of using technology cannot be considered neutral in terms of the transmission of values and critical implications, a situation that calls for greater teacher awareness (see Chapelle 2003). This awareness is especially important in LSP, since students aspire to enter specific discourse communities, with established norms and practices. Critical pedagogies have been a concern in the literature on ESP/EAP (English for Academic Purposes), as to whether teaching involves accommodation to dominant discourses or should aim at empowering learners (e.g. Pennycook 1997; Belcher 2004; Benesch 2009). With the use of technology for intercultural communication and for access to specialized discourses, it is more necessary than ever to integrate a critical perspective into the use of language and technology as part of current academic and professional practices, paying special attention to the digital literacies involved. In this sense, Rueda et al. (2007) address the relationship of social and academic Internet-based practices to language and literacy development, and identify the EAP teacher's mediator role in integrating those skills.

As said above, the integration of technology should be inscribed in a broader theoretical framework of language and learning. A relevant theory is socio-constructivism (Wertsch 1985; Mercer 2000), by which learning takes place through interaction and involves the social construction of knowledge, mediated through scaffolding, which is based on the Vygotskyan notion of ZPD (Zone of Proximal Development), i.e. the gap between what a learner can do alone and what is able to achieve with the help of a more capable peer (Vygotsky 1978). Learning is thus viewed from an experiential approach (e.g. Kolb 1984; Kohonen et al. 2001), characterized by a focus on the process and the active involvement of the learner, who brings in previous knowledge and views, which serve as a springboard for reflection and analysis and for the further construction of knowledge in a social context. In line with the view of technology as both a context for academic and professional communication and as a tool for learning (Warschauer 2006), students' engagement in discipline-related practices that involve technology provides them with the opportunity to develop their language, digital, social, and critical skills, through interaction with others for the accomplishment of meaningful tasks.

Therefore, the relationship between IT and LSP seems to be particularly appropriate, and it was specifically addressed by Arnó et al. (2006), who identified the following areas of interest (and which are further discussed in Arnó 2012):

- **The analysis of specialized discourse.** Technology has facilitated the development of corpora and tools for analysis, which has yielded insights into specialized language use and has provided ample opportunity for designing materials suited to very specific needs. LSP researchers and course designers can access large corpora of written and spoken language as well as small specialized ones. In addition, the use of technology has led to the emergence of electronic genres.

- **Online communication.** Computer-based communication is not only a tool for learning but also a learning objective in itself, since academic and professional communication often takes place online. Thus, ranging from email and forums to web 2.0 applications such as social networking sites or wikis, computer-based tools can help in the meaningful construction of knowledge in LSP, while they also exemplify typical target situations that are relevant to students' needs (including the demands posed in terms of social, language, academic, and electronic skills).
- **CALL.** Because of the possibility that technology offers for reaching students with very diverse and specific needs, many computer applications have been designed for academic and professional situations, based on the abovementioned trends of viewing the computer as a tool, engaging in collaboration, and paying attention to socio-cultural concerns (see examples in Arnó et al. 2006).
- **Online learning.** Also in line with the above, there are multiple examples of learning environments for LSP that have been developed for self-access, blended, and distance learning situations (see examples in González-Pueyo et al. 2009).
- **Learner autonomy.** IT has also been associated with autonomy, for the affordances it provides for customized learning, learner choice, and learner control and responsibility. As technology offers the advantage of reaching beyond the classroom, attention needs to be paid to the development of learner awareness and the deployment of appropriate strategies.

The areas above—especially CALL, online learning, and learner autonomy—will be dealt with in more detail in subsequent sections of this paper. From the perspective of the new European framework, characterized by transferability, mobility, and a focus on learning processes and outcomes, this paper analyzes how IT can used to enhance LSP teaching. And in the broader context of a globalized, technological society, it focuses on the implications and challenges related to some key issues in LSP, such as the roles of teachers and learners, online courses, the integration of language and content, the development of broader academic skills, as well as network-based communication and collaboration on meaningful tasks.

1.3 Languages for Specific Purposes in the New European Context

The present European context is characterized by different processes that have reshaped the ways in which we work, study, and communicate. On the one hand, there has been a social and political trend towards greater cohesion, which has involved increased mobility and the breaking down of internal European frontiers. One of the effects of this internationalization process is the role that English has acquired as a *lingua franca* (Kirkpatrick 2007). This situation is reflected in the increased use of English as a medium of instruction in European universities and impinges on the teaching of ESP (English for Specific Purposes), as attested by Fortanet and Räisänen (2008). First, ESP/LSP needs to adapt to the demands of academic and professional communication in a global context. Second, as English has become the language of communication in a growing number of academic and professional settings, the context for ESP teaching is changing from that a foreign language situation to a situation in which it gradually becomes more of a second language (see Dudley-Evans and St. John 1998: 35). This shift in context means that current ESP learning needs are clearly and immediately perceived, as learners are actually involved in academic and professional activities in English.

As part of this European cohesion and the building up of a certain European identity, the university reform resulting from the Bologna process is geared towards the internationalization of universities, the harmonization of degrees, a greater focus on learning outcomes, and promoting the employability of graduates.[1] These changes are of special relevance to LSP teaching as it aims at preparing students to communicate effectively in genuine academic and professional situations.

1.4 The Bologna Process and the Common European Framework of Reference for Languages

One of the main outcomes of the university reform is the creation of the EHEA, which aims at greater convergence and involves the redesign of university curricula for comparability and transferability. Within these broader societal and political movements, the major driving forces of the university reform are the promotion of mobility and employability, from the perspective of an underlying European identity, as reflected in the following quote:

> Building on our rich and diverse European cultural heritage, we are developing an EHEA based on institutional autonomy, academic freedom, equal opportunities and democratic principles that will facilitate mobility, increase employability and strengthen Europe's attractiveness and competitiveness.
>
> Ministers responsible for Higher Education in the countries participating in the Bologna Process, London Communiqué, May 2007.[2]

Such trends towards greater cohesion and harmonization have been accompanied by language policies for the promotion of multilingualism and language learning, which play an important role on the European agenda.[3] In relation to language

[1] For information about the development of the Bologna process and the EHEA over the years, see http://www.ehea.info/

[2] The European Higher Education Area. [Online] Available: http://www.ond.vlaanderen.be/hogeronderwijs/bologna/documents/Bologna_leaflet_web.pdf

[3] For an overview of European language policies and the promotion of language learning, see the section on education and languages from the Council of Europe website: http://www.coe.int/T/DG4/Linguistic/Default_en.asp

learning, two important instruments have been developed, the Common European Framework of Reference for Languages (CEFR) (Council of Europe 2001) and the European Language Portfolio (ELP). Both are intended to facilitate the transparency and transferability of language learning outcomes and to provide evidence of language competence. The CEFR identifies different skills (oral and written, including reception, interaction, and production) and provides a benchmark with different levels of competence and specific descriptors. On the other hand, the European Language Portfolio (ELP) constitutes a tool for motivating and guiding learners, so that they can integrate different experiences and languages, reflect on and monitor their learning, and provide evidence of their competence in a way that is transparent to different stakeholders in an international setting.

Apart from responding to the demands of international work and academic settings, LSP teachers also face the challenge of integrating their teaching into university curricula that are being redesigned on a number of premises: developing competences that go beyond subject-matter expertise, responding to the demands of social and economic contexts, and providing students with a broad education as citizens. In this respect, one of the keys of the Bologna process is a competence-based approach, in which expected learning outcomes are clearly specified and curricula are developed so as to integrate different types of competences, both generic and subject-specific. The latter, related to students' discipline knowledge, resonate with the multidisciplinary nature of LSP. Generic competences, on the other hand, refer to the broader ethical and social concerns pointed out above as well as to language, communication, and lifelong learning skills. In particular, in the *Tuning* project (González and Wagenaar 2003), competences are classified into instrumental (language, communication), interpersonal (social skills, ethical commitment), and systemic, which involve overall understanding, sensitivity, and knowledge. In this scenario, LSP courses play an important role, integrating academic and professional communication skills with the social and critical competences that students need as citizens and professionals participating in society.

1.5 Integration of IT in LSP in the New Context

LSP teachers are faced with a number of challenges, in a situation characterized by increased international communication, the need for lifelong learning, and the development of new curricula that involve subject-matter instruction through the foreign language, as well as the integration of different types of competences (social, personal, and linguistic). Another major challenge has to do with the demands of this globalized society, as there are more and more academic and professional situations in which participants interact in different languages. On the other hand, technology affords numerous possibilities for the integration of technology, theory, and pedagogy. Technology facilitates immersion in the relevant discourse community, providing access to authentic materials and contexts for communication. In turn, the integration of IT also calls for the reappraisal of some central issues in LSP: teacher and learner roles, online courses and materials, the role of discipline knowledge, the development of academic skills, as well as the use of technology for collaboration, communication, and lifelong learning.

1.5.1 Roles of the LSP Teacher and Learner

The LSP teacher has usually been considered innovative and flexible (e.g. Swales 1985; Robinson 1991), performing a number of roles (Hutchinson and Waters 1987; Robinson 1991). Specifically, Dudley-Evans and St. John (1998) have identified the following: teacher, course designer and materials provider, researcher, collaborator, and evaluator. In this international, technological context, the role that comes to the fore is that of collaborator, especially as technology allows communication, collaboration, and exchange among LSP teachers as well as with subject-matter specialists. Revisiting the above LSP teacher roles, Räisänen (2009) expands them, noting that over the past decade LSP teachers have been required to develop greater specialism and carry out more research, which in turn has resulted in an expansion of the field. She also highlights the collaborative dimension of the LSP teacher, both in terms of networking (with electronic resources, journals, and forums) and in terms of the challenges involved in collaboration with discipline teachers, within current trends towards the integration of language and content.

The collaborative dimension of LSP teaching can also be approached from the perspective of the profile of LSP learners, who often have a less asymmetric relationship with the teacher because of the experience and discipline knowledge that they bring into the classroom (Dudley-Evans and St. John 1998). Their special motivation arises from their needs and thus they take on an active role in the control and management of information. To support this role, electronic resources provide opportunities to access and share information at the same time as they become authentic contexts for activities related to target academic and professional practices. Therefore, collaboration between LSP teachers and learners is often prompted by the need to respond to the demands of real-life activities in which students are involved—e.g. project work, academic mobility, English-medium instruction—and lends itself to an experiential learning approach. Given the focus of the EHEA on learning processes and outcomes, IT provides us with new challenges and new roles for LSP teachers and learners. For example, IT resources allow teachers to reach larger numbers of students or design courses catering for very specific needs. At the same time, technology also leads to the reappraisal of teacher and learner roles. For example, online learning requires an active role of the learner, who needs to develop autonomous learning and information management skills. New demands are also made on the teacher, not only to adapt pedagogy to these new environments, but also to cope with an increased workload and to respond to student and institutional expectations (resolving questions such as availability or the performance of different teacher roles related to course design, tuition or correction). In the design of online learning courses within the EHEA, Lankamp (2008) reflects on the notion of 'efficiency', stating that "the very success of online writing courses is seen as a threat to the quality of future courses" (p.112), contrasting institutional perceptions of efficiency (seeing online learning as a low-cost option) with teachers' perceptions (from the perspective of the teaching-learning process). Decisions and consequences that may affect the quality of online learning include numbers of students in programs, the activities that teachers are expected to do, recognition and institutional support for teachers, or teacher recruitment, among others. Further discussions on the challenges posed by this complex scenario can be found in, e.g., Noble (1998), Hailey et al. (2001), and Arnó et al. (2006).

1.5.2 Online Learning

Despite the challenges involved, online learning appears as especially appropriate for LSP teaching because of its flexibility (i.e. with the possibility of offering courses tailored to very specific needs), the absence of time and space constraints, as well as the possibility of providing realistic input and integrating discipline knowledge. Because of its ubiquity, online learning can be used to provide tuition to learners in different academic or professional situations, drawing on actual practices from students' discipline or target activities. Collections such as Arnó et al. (2006) and González-Pueyo et al. (2009) gather examples of online learning applications in different learning contexts and for a variety of learner profiles, both regarding discipline knowledge (e.g. English for medicine, nursing, agriculture) and target activities (e.g. writing research papers or professional documents).

In her review of online learning applications in LSP, Luzón (2009) points out a series of affordances of technology. First, online environments facilitate the delivery and management of content, in spite of the limitations of standard learning management systems (LMS) as far as learner-centeredness is concerned. Second, blended learning is more common in LSP than distance learning. Third, online learning also offers the possibility of customizing materials for LSP—e.g. through authoring tools—as well as of promoting learner autonomy through scaffolding and learner support. As an appropriate framework for online course design, Doughty and Long (2003) propose a task-based approach, with courses and materials based on the following criteria:

- Real-world tasks
- Elaborate and rich input (texts for practical, relevant situations)
- Inductive learning
- Focus on form
- Appropriate correction and intervention
- Collaborative learning
- Individualized instruction

As a result of the application of these criteria, Doughty and Long suggest designing computer-based activities based on simulations, tutorials, corpora and concordancing, discussion and authoring, problem-solving, and adaptivity (i.e. activities that provide feedback and guidance pitched at the learner's level). Both these criteria for course/materials design and the types of activities suggested seem especially appropriate for LSP situations, considering the learner's profile and the focus of LSP on real activities from target academic and workplace situations.

1.5.3 Integrating Language and Content

Technology provides a gateway to specialized discipline knowledge and to students' relevant discourse communities. The immediate availability of IT resources allows teachers and students alike to engage in practices related to specific needs, through realistic and engaging contexts. The Internet contains a vast amount of resources related to students' disciplines that lend themselves to interactive practice. For example, medical students can make decisions in virtual scenarios as they respond to emergencies, engineering students can simulate laboratory practice related to different fields, while other resources allow learners to apply scientific knowledge to a specific project, such as designing a roller coaster based on their knowledge of physics.[4] Using these internet-based interactive resources in the LSP classroom can promote collaboration over relevant content and activities, while students engage in meaningful activities related to their disciplines.

Web-based resources allow students to engage in simulations which, due to advances in technology, have evolved from mazes or graphic adventures to more realistic immersive environments (e.g. 'Second Life'). These newer environments are attracting the attention of researchers, who have pointed out language learning benefits in terms of learner-centeredness, in terms of participation, motivation, and collaboration, together with the development of speaking skills, thus overcoming one of the main challenges in earlier web-based resources (see e.g. Deutschmann and Panichi 2009; Peterson 2010).

The discussion of the integration of language and content should take into account current trends towards CLIL (content and language-integrated learning) in the EHEA and its connection with ESP/LSP. Nowadays, there is a growth in the number of programs that are taught in English, as the major *lingua franca*, both because of increased academic mobility and of the perception of English-medium instruction as a relevant communicative context to improve students' language proficiency. As Räisänen and Fortanet (2008) point out, this situation can put ESP/LSP at a crossroads, with language teachers often being assigned an ancillary role, as support for content teachers. These major changes in curriculum design, methodological paradigms, and the use of the foreign language as a medium of instruction

[4]Examples of these resources can be found in the "moulages" from Trauma.org: (http://www.trauma.org/index.php/main/moulages/), the "Virtual Lab" from the "What's engineering" site of Johns Hopkins University: (http://www.jhu.edu/virtlab/virtual-laboratory/), and the "Annenberg Interactive Exhibits": (http://www.learner.org/interactives/parkphysics/coaster/).

have led to the reappraisal of the relationship between content and language, which can add to the 'fragility' (Swales et al. 2001) that LSP teachers and courses have traditionally suffered.

In this scenario, one can envisage different roles for the LSP teacher to take vis-à-vis the teaching of content. One possibility is collaboration with subject-matter specialists, which can take different forms, ranging from providing support for content teaching to genuine interdisciplinary collaboration, with an equal status for both language and content teachers alike. Considering that the EHEA promotes on the integration of different types of competences, LSP teaching can also be approached from the perspective of the generic competences mentioned above, using humanistic and socially-related content as a point of departure to engage students in critical thinking (i.e. along the lines of 'sustained content', Pally 1997). For example, Arnó and Rueda (2011) propose that ESP teachers can adopt an active role as providers of contents related to science, technology and society for engineering students.

At this point, the question that arises is how technology may be used to enhance the integrated learning of content and language. Both CLIL and technology form part of the European agenda to promote language learning at university (Räisänen and Fortanet 2008). With discipline-specific material only a click away, a common ground can be laid for learners, LSP teachers, and discipline experts to interact and engage in interdisciplinary collaboration. As part of this interaction, a wide range of opportunities open up for LSP teachers to design activities that raise students' awareness of their belonging to a certain discourse community and make them explicitly relate language learning to disciplinary knowledge. For example, as part of an online EAP course based on Internet resources, Barahona and Arnó (2001) propose a task in which students select discipline-specific web resources (not intended for language learning) and analyze them from the point of view of the discipline as well as from the language learning benefits that can be derived from their use.

1.5.4 Developing Academic Skills

Technology has transformed the academic landscape in such a way that concepts like 'information', 'open access', 'knowledge', 'authorship', 'voice', and 'empowerment' have acquired new meanings. The ways we access, publish and exchange information have radically changed in the context of what is often called the 'knowledge society' or the 'information society'. But what do these terms mean? What are the implications of the 'knowledge society' or 'information society'? On the relationship between technology and knowledge, Pierre Lévy (1998) used the analogy of a deluge to describe the information revolution. It can thus be considered a "Second Flood", with "the chaotic overflow of information, a flood of data swept along by the tumultuous, rolling waters of communication".[5] In order to make sense

[5] From the English translation (*Cyberculture* 2001, p. xii).

of this 'overflow of information', it is necessary to build knowledge, based on the notion of 'collective intelligence' and driven by democratic ideals. Lévy compared this revolution to the *Encyclopédie* of the Age of the Enlightenment, which involved the collection and dissemination of Knowledge, based on the principles of democracy and citizenship. The work of the French *encyclopédistes* would thus resemble that of Noah during the Biblical Flood, collecting what needed to be preserved for future generations, canonical Knowledge that is manageable and sealed (like Noah's Ark with the specimens in it). In "the Second Flood", knowledge is too vast and unmanageable to be collected and disseminated. Therefore, instead of a single big "Ark" with the canonical Knowledge that needs to be transmitted, there is a collection of individual meaningful sets of knowledge. In other words, each of us is Noah, constructing small varied arks that are interconnected and constantly changing. Thus, within a socio-constructivist paradigm, learning involves the co-construction and sharing of knowledge, with the concept of 'collective intelligence' becoming central. The approach taken by Lévy is in line with the recommendations of UNESCO (2005) for the construction of "Knowledge Societies", in which technological developments, within the "Third Industrial Revolution", are used for the open access to and dissemination of knowledge, for the benefit of humankind.

> [E]merging societies cannot make do with being mere components of a global information society. To remain human and liveable, knowledge societies will have to be societies of shared knowledge. The plural here sanctions the need for an accepted diversity. (Preface, p. 5)

In terms of knowledge and learning, we have witnessed the transformation from a model based on the Encyclopedia to one based on the "Wikipedia" and open access (e.g. software, learning spaces like *Moodle*, etc.). The Internet has also changed from the Web 1.0, mainly a repository of information, to the Web 2.0, based on user-generated contents through blogs, wikis, and social networking sites. For LSP learning, these changes involve the opportunity to access authentic content and genres related to specific disciplines as well as to actively participate in the discourse community in unprecedented ways. Technology facilitates access to resources with varied, multimodal input, which can promote the integration of language and content, as well as lifelong learning, thanks to open access resources available to any citizen who is motivated to improve his or her education. For example, a corpus such as *MICASE* becomes a powerful tool for LSP teachers and students to learn about authentic American academic speech (Swales 2006). On the other hand, students can access authentic multimedia course materials from a variety of subjects through the *OpenCourseWare* site of the Massachusetts Institute of Technology (MIT)[6]. The philosophy underlying the *OpenCourseWare* site is quite explicit, with the motto "unlocking knowledge, empowering minds", which resonates with the ideals of "Knowledge societies". Thus, new learning opportunities are being created, while open access journals and networked platforms of thematic content allow LSP students, teachers, and researchers to participate in the discourse community at large.

It was already some years ago that teachers and researchers of languages for academic purposes harnessed the potential of technology as a learning tool. The vast

[6] MIT, OpenCourseWare: http://ocw.mit.edu/index.htm. Accessed 31 May 2013.

amount of language learning resources available online has made the Internet a 'virtual self-access center' (Little 1997). The Net was exploited for the transformation of self-access centers, like the EAP center reported by Nesi (1998), taking advantage of new possibilities for ease of access and learner choice. Online self-access centers allow learners to develop academic literacy alongside Internet skills, which can lead to the promotion of (collaborative) autonomy, facilitated by computer-mediated interaction (Ding 2005). Because of its hypertextual structure, the Web provides 'connectivity', through flexible learning paths—rather than the predetermined 'content' of previous multimedia materials—which encourages experiential and socio-constructivist approaches to learning (Felix 2002). In view of the changes brought about by technology, the teaching of language has been reappraised on the basis of an "electronic literacy approach", which includes IT-based research skills, online reading, computer-based communication and collaboration, combining different media, and developing autonomous learning skills (Shetzer and Warschauer 2000). Accordingly, current EAP skills need to include critical skills related to technology, such as the evaluation of websites (Slaouti 2002) or a transformed view of writing skills and processes, based on the use of electronic tools and resources (Stapleton 2010). From the perspective of the EHEA, it has been suggested that new university curricula should include digital literacy instruction (Area 2010), as a basic skill for the student of the twenty-first century, given the "digitalization" of current universities, with the growth of Internet-based research and the increasing use of online learning platforms.

The emergence of Web 2.0 applications and, especially, young students' familiarity with them (often more than that of teachers) may lead us to wonder whether and in what ways these applications should be integrated in the LSP classroom. In this respect, Vie (2008) defends the use of Web 2.0 applications in the classroom, on the grounds that students' familiarity with these tools does not necessarily involve the possession of adequate critical literacy skills for their effective academic use. She terms this situation the "Digital Divide 2.0", thus extending the scope of the term 'digital divide' beyond access or ability to use technology. She suggests taking advantage of students' skills in Web 2.0 tools to approach critical and academic literacy concerns. Along these lines, some EAP researchers have related traditional academic writing issues—i.e. audience awareness, text organization, or the process of essay writing—to applications like wikis (Kuteeva 2011) and blogs (Murray et al. 2007). Academic work through Web 2.0 applications which foster students' creation, discussion, collaboration, and reflection is in line with the tenets of the EHEA and a paradigm based on the learner and learning processes.

1.5.5 *Using Technology for Collaboration, Communication, and Lifelong Learning*

One of the main challenges in current LSP teaching is to prepare students for globalized academic and professional contexts, which require electronic collaboration and communication across borders. To respond to these demands, LSP methodologies should be rooted in how technology is used in real-life professional practices. This philosophy underlies what has been termed 'Globally-Networked Learning Environments' (GNLEs) in the field of technical communication (Starke-Meyering et al. 2007). In GNLEs, technology acts both as a learning tool and as a real context for collaboration and communication with different types of audiences, similar to the globalized workplace. GNLEs are the result of teachers' initiatives to set up international online exchanges to develop the skills that students need to work and study in globalized contexts. These projects are characterized by a focus on intercultural competence, approached from an experiential perspective, given the multicultural nature of the partnership. GNLEs are intended to provide students with international academic experience, which is systematically incorporated into the curriculum, thus relating global with local concerns. There is a tradition of technology-based projects in LSP that share these characteristics, such as the 'telecollaboration' between US and German students (Belz 2001), the e-Tandem project between Spanish and Irish LSP students (Appel and Gilabert 2006), the collaboration between US and European students on technical writing and translation projects (Maylath et al. 2008, 2013), or the content-based approach to interculturality through the collaboration between LSP students from Germany and New Zealand (Walker and vom Brocke 2009). These projects also fall within the scope of the abovementioned notion of the "second wave of online learning", in that they are socially situated and address multiple concerns that cannot be disentangled from language learning, such as (inter-)cultural issues, the building and displaying of identities, or the focus on cross-linguistic features. They are approached from an experiential perspective, in the form of real-life, meaningful projects for students to carry out through varied technological tools and forms of communication, such as pair or group work, by email, chats, or different types of sites for sharing materials. These projects follow a task-based approach with a high-degree of learner choice. For example, students can decide what topics and contents they wish to focus on, and they pay attention to specific language points through the alternation of focus on meaning and focus on form. As many of these projects usually involve the learning of each other's L1, language teaching usually takes the form of peer-teaching. Consequently, such practices entail new, flexible roles for teachers and learners, which resonate with the multifaceted profiles of LSP teachers and students outlined above. The teacher takes on the role of task designer, monitor, and consultant, while the student assumes a great deal of responsibility: for the learning process, language, intercultural issues, and contents (Walker and vom Brocke 2009). GNLEs represent the use of technology to familiarize students with the challenges of international academic and professional contexts, with a focus on mobility, multilingualism, employability, and lifelong learning, which are highly relevant to the current European context.

1.6 *Quantum LEAP*: Development of a Technology-Based LSP Project

Earlier sections of this paper have provided an overview of how technology is being used to address some central concerns in LSP, such as learner need and motivation, teacher roles, efficiency, authenticity of tasks and materials, discipline knowledge, and the use of certain genres associated with target discourse communities. In a scenario characterized by the internationalization of academic and workplace settings, the integration of IT in LSP presents numerous options and challenges. Taking into account the European university reform, LSP teachers can exploit the potential of technology to design courses and materials that promote learner-centered methodologies, the integration of different competences, and learner autonomy. The remaining sections will pull together some central notions that have been discussed above to present an example of their application in the development of a particular technology-based EAP project, the online learning environment *Quantum LEAP (Learning English for Academic Purposes).*[7]

1.6.1 Rationale for Creating an Online Learning Environment for EAP

The online learning environment *Quantum LEAP* was created by a team of ESP lecturers from different universities in Catalonia (Spain) in order to take advantage of the affordances of technology to provide an online learning environment for university students that is flexible enough to be used in a variety of EAP situations, both in the classroom and in self-access, especially considering the transition towards the EHEA. The project resulted from the lecturers' initiative to optimize learning resources and to extend ESP teaching/learning beyond the classroom. The project will only be succinctly described here (see Arnó et al. 2009 for details), as the aim of this section is to discuss how different technological and pedagogic principles are applied to the design of a learning tool that tries to respond to the challenges of LSP in the new European context. *Quantum LEAP* consists of a series of thematic modules dealing with interdisciplinary topics of academic interest that try to promote students' engagement (e.g. Women and Science, Humans and Machines, Globalization and the English-speaking World, etc.). In turn, each module is divided into different sections with activities addressing the skills of reading, writing, listening, and speaking (Fig. 1.1).

This project illustrates some of the options for the integration of IT in LSP that have been discussed in previous sections of this paper, which can be summarized as follows:

- Roles of LSP teachers and students.
- Use of English in academic life.
- The European university context.

---

[7] This project is the result of the initiative of a team of lecturers from three Catalan universities: Universitat Politècnica de Catalunya, Universitat de Lleida, and Universitat Rovira i Virgili (Tarragona). The authors of *Quantum LEAP* are Elisabet Arnó, Carmen Rueda, Antonia Soler, Lurdes Armengol, Enric Llurda, and Joaquín Romero. The project has been funded by the Generalitat de Catalunya and the participating universities. For more information about the project and access to the online learning environment, visit http://www.quantumleap.cat

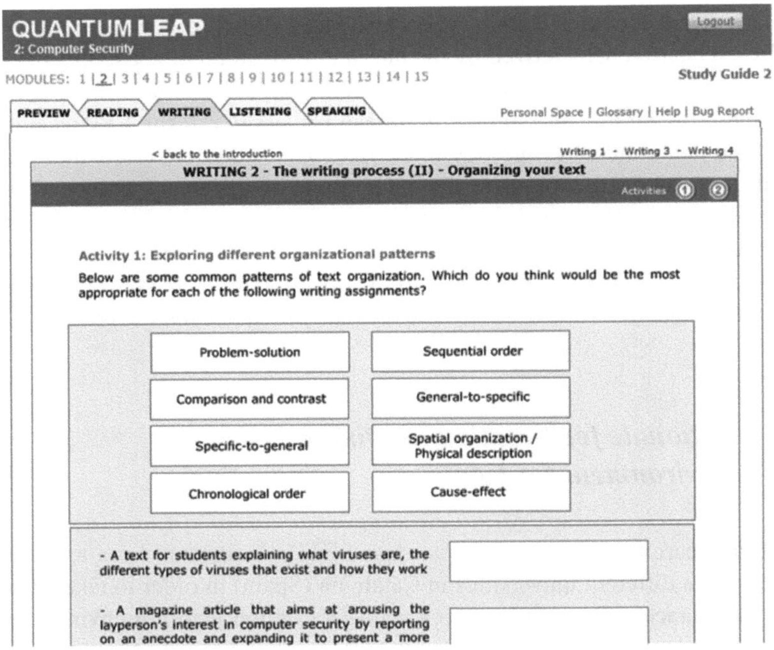

Fig. 1.1 Screenshot from the writing section of Module 2 (Computer Security)

- Integrating content, language, and academic skills.
- Technology for communication, collaboration and lifelong learning.
- Trends towards open access resources.

From the abovementioned roles of the LSP teacher, this project brings to the fore those of collaborator and materials creator, since it basically arose out of the need of a team of LSP teachers to take advantage of the potential of technology in order to create and share materials for EAP students at university. We decided to develop an online environment to help students develop their academic communication skills, both in speech and writing, considering our specific LSP situation: the geographical dispersion of lecturers, the time-consuming nature of the task of developing specific materials that address students' needs, as well as the affordances of technology to reach larger numbers of students. The student role that is envisaged in this project is that of an autonomous learner with high levels of initiative and awareness, taking as the point of departure the central notions of learner choice and responsibility (van Lier 1996). This online learning environment was designed with a high degree of flexibility and interactivity, so that learners can plan, manage, and monitor their own learning process. To achieve this purpose, it contains a series of interactive tools, such as a 'personal log' (to keep track of progress and for self-assessment), 'study guides', and an 'e-portfolio' (to provide evidence of achievement, both in speech and writing). The online learning environment also encourages collaboration and communication—both online and face-to-face—and includes an application that allows students to record and store their own spoken production. Special attention is paid to the spoken language (in terms of reception, interaction, and production, following CEFR guidelines) and a specific pronunciation tutorial is included for practice and awareness-raising (Soler and Romero 2010).

1.6.2 Pedagogic Approach

Taking into account the profile of the LSP learner as a motivated learner who actively participates in the activities of the discipline—in this case, university students from different fields—the learning materials have been designed to engage students in genuine academic work in English, trying to develop critical thinking. In the rationale for the design of *Quantum LEAP* we took into consideration the present European context with increased mobility and the use of English as an academic *lingua franca*, which means that English is increasingly becoming part of students' academic life. This rationale has affected decisions regarding the selection of topics for the thematic modules and the approach that would be adopted to the design of learning activities. On the one hand, the modules deal with contents of academic interest from an interdisciplinary perspective, so that students can express their judgments and make their own contributions, in speech and writing, as part of their academic activity. On the other hand, the materials are based on varied input and relevant academic genres related to the different topics, such as lectures, essays, debates, or different types of articles, for example.

The design of the learning environment has taken into account the new European context, specifically the guidelines of the EHEA and the CEFR. Learning activities have been designed and presented to students on the basis of CEFR descriptors and levels—which, considering the university context in which the project is set, range from B1, independent user, to C1, expert user. Accordingly, the learning objectives and outcomes in the 'study guides', the 'personal log', and the e-portfolio are expressed in terms of the CEFR descriptors, in order to facilitate transparency and transferability, two important principles of the EHEA. Another principle applied to the design of *Quantum LEAP* is that these language learning tools should encourage reflection and the integration of different language learning experiences, as well as provide evidence of competence in the different skills (including student-produced samples in the portfolio). With regard to the integration of competences promoted in the EHEA, *Quantum LEAP* aims at the development of different types of generic competences (language, academic communication, critical thinking, and social responsibility), through the integration of EAP with interdisciplinary content (for a more detailed account of this approach, see Arnó and Rueda 2011). Content is the vehicle for induction into real academic work, as a natural activity, since academic literacy in itself involves engagement with content (see Garner and Borg 2005). Critical thinking is encouraged through students' questioning and reflection on their own values. For example, in the module on 'humans and machines', students explore issues related to the use of technology in our lives, such as social networks or mobile

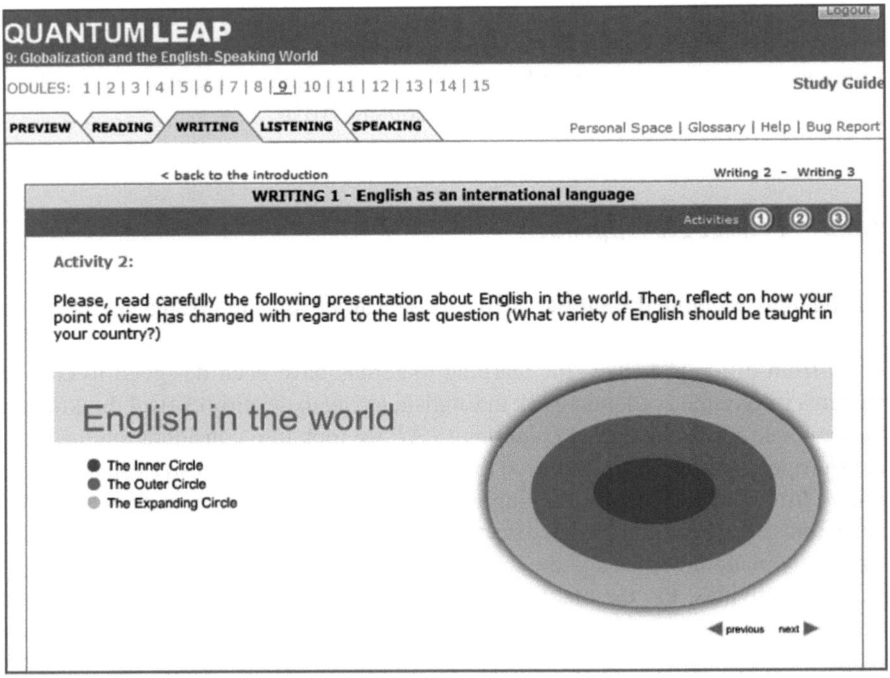

Fig. 1.2 Module on 'Globalization and the English-Speaking World'

devices. These activities are approached from an experiential learning perspective, while providing content input for reflection. Such an approach is exemplified in the module on globalization, in which students are encouraged to reflect on their views of English as an international language, exploring their own uses of the language, and positioning themselves in a scenario characterized by intercultural encounters, while the module provides contents related to current discussions on 'World Englishes' (see Fig. 1.2).

In order to promote academic engagement and critical thinking, *Quantum LEAP* contains a wide range of open-ended activities, which implies that learners are not assessed on their scores or that, often, 'right answers' cannot be provided. Instead, appropriate guidance and feedback are provided in the form of suggestions, models, and step-by-step guides. Scaffolding thus consists of resources that students can use according to their needs, to help them pay attention to both the process and the product as well as to the characteristics of different academic genres. For example, students are provided with guidance and practice on recognizing important features of lectures (such as signposting), on recognizing the structures of essays, and on quoting sources appropriately. Other activities involve, for example, watching a video and taking notes in order to prepare an argument to be developed for its oral presentation at a seminar. Language activities are presented in a broader communication context, from a focus-on-form perspective (Long 1991), to help students understand and produce texts through awareness-raising activities, approached from an experiential perspective. Examples include revising and reflecting on one's own production (both in speech and writing) as well analyzing features of input written and spoken texts to identify certain features. Such activities are in line with the tenets of language awareness (e.g. Carter 1993; Bolitho et al. 2003) in that they aim at engaging students with language by means of a contrastive approach, as an activity of enquiry undertaken by the learner—e.g. to notice salient features in different types of texts or to compare their production with target-like forms. This pedagogic rationale is in line with the abovementioned criteria for the design of online learning materials from a task-based approach (Doughty and Long 2003), which combines real input and tasks with inductive learning, a focus on form, collaborative learning and the possibility of creating personalized learning routes.

In this project, technology plays a multifaceted role, reflecting the technological society that we live in. Apart from being a web-based learning environment with interactive tools for online communication and collaboration, *Quantum LEAP* includes activities focusing on electronic genres and literacies, as these form part of the communicative competence that today's students need to acquire, with activities that involve searching for and comparing information from different sources, or working on the language of email and texting. From the perspective of promoting the broad skills discussed throughout this chapter—the integration of language and content, critical thinking, and social responsibility—emphasis is placed on encouraging reflection on a variety of topics related to our technological society, such as interaction with and through machines, social networking, or science fiction, for example. In keeping with current trends towards open access and the sharing of knowledge, this online learning environment has been made freely available to the academic community at large, also adhering to the notion of lifelong learning, one of the driving forces of the Bologna process.

1.6.3 Evaluation and Further Developments

Quantum LEAP is an ongoing project that is under development, although a beta version is already available. The online learning environment is fully operational, while several pedagogic and technical revisions are being made. Further modifications are being carried out on learner tools such as the 'personal log' and the 'portfolio', in order to improve their ease of use and transferability. Other improvements involve interface design and the creation of mobile applications, to adapt to evolving uses of technology. Evaluation of the project has been carried out both from the technical and pedagogic sides, through usability studies and student evaluation (see Arnó and Rueda 2011). As the project has been gradually implemented in ESP courses at university, students' reactions so far have been highly satisfactory, with course feedback in which students emphasize the variety of academic topics, the integration of content and language, and critical thinking, pointing out that "*it makes you think in English*" and that it contributes to their overall "*education as citizens*".

These student views reinforce the rationale of the project towards a view of LSP that involves the integration of language and broader critical academic skills, within the context of the knowledge society.

1.7 Conclusions

This chapter has analyzed the relationship between IT and LSP in the European university context, given the influence of technology as a learning tool as well as an essential component of today's academic and professional settings. As LSP teachers and course designers strive to help students communicate and collaborate in international settings, we are faced with a number of options and challenges, and the current European framework provides us with an opportunity to reappraise the relationship between IT and LSP. This chapter has discussed the affordances provided by technology to support LSP learning, in terms of online learning applications, the integration of language and content, the development of critical academic skills, as well as online collaboration and communication. Current students need to develop multiple competences to face the demands of academic and professional communication in a globalized knowledge society where technology plays a key role. As an example of the options faced by LSP teachers to integrate IT resources in the EHEA, the project *Quantum LEAP* has been presented. In this project, technology serves multiple aims. It facilitates collaboration among teachers and with learners, it helps to provide an open access learning tool which is flexible and interactive, and it is used as a source of materials, as well as a topic in itself, to encourage the integration of EAP and critical thinking with interdisciplinary content.

In a complex, changing context characterized by globalization, the pervasive presence of technology, greater student and worker mobility (both physical and online), and the use of English as a *lingua franca*, LSP teachers are faced with important challenges. Especially in Europe, with the creation of the EHEA and the trend toward social and political cohesion, we need to address the complex task of preparing students for effective academic and professional communication across borders. Technology can become a powerful tool to provide authentic input, new modes of communication and genres, open access to information, as well as new opportunities for learning and for the development of new literacies. These opportunities are not exempt of challenges, but through collaboration and networking LSP teachers can contribute to building the knowledge societies of the twenty-first century.

References

Alcaraz, E. 2000. *El inglés profesional y académico*. Madrid: Alianza Editorial.

Appel, C., and R. Gilabert. 2006. Finding common ground in LSP: A computer-mediated communication project. In *Information technology in languages for specific purposes. Issues and prospects*, ed. E. Arnó, A. Soler, and C. Rueda, 75–90. New York: Springer.

Area, M. 2010. Why offer information and digital competency training in higher education? In Information and digital competencies in higher education. *Revista de Universidad y Sociedad del Conocimiento (RUSC)* 7(2). http://rusc.uoc.edu/ojs/index.php/rusc/article/view/v7n2-area/v7n2-area-eng. Accessed 24 May 2013.

Arnó, E. 2012. The role of technology in teaching LSP courses. *The Modern Language Journal* 96: 89–104. doi:10.1111/j.1540-4781.2012.01299.x.

Arnó, E., and C. Rueda. 2011. Promoting reflection on science, technology, and society among engineering students through an EAP online learning environment. *Journal of English for Academic Purposes* 10: 19–31.

Arnó, E., A. Soler, and C. Rueda (eds.). 2006. *Information technology in languages for specific purposes. Issues and prospects*. New York: Springer.

Arnó, E., C. Rueda, and A. Soler. 2009. Designing a virtual learning environment for EAP students: Quantum LEAP (Learning English for Academic Purposes). In *Teaching academic and professional English online*, ed. I. González-Pueyo, C. Foz, M. Jaime, and M.J. Luzón, 57–82. Bern: Peter Lang.

Barahona, C., and E. Arnó. 2001. English online: A virtual EAP course@university. In *Methodology and new technologies in LSP*, ed. S. Posteguillo, I. Fortanet, and J.C. Palmer, 181–194. Castelló de la Plana: Publicacions de la Universitat Jaume I.

Belcher, D. 2004. Trends in teaching English for specific purposes. *Annual Review of Applied Linguistics* 24: 165–186.

Belz, J. 2001. Institutional and individual dimensions of transatlantic group work in network-based language teaching. *ReCALL* 13: 213–231.

Benesch, S. 2009. Theorizing and practicing critical English for academic purposes. *Journal of English for Academic Purposes* 8: 81–85.

Bindé, J. 2005. *Towards knowledge societies: UNESCO world report*. Paris: UNESCO Publishing.

Bolitho, R., R. Carter, R. Hughes, R. Ivanic, H. Masuhara, and B. Tomlinson. 2003. Ten questions about language awareness. *ELT Journal* 57(3): 251–259.

Carter, R. 1993. Language awareness and language learning. In *Data, description, discourse*, ed. M. Hoey, 139–150. London: Harper-Collins.

Chapelle, C.A. 2003. *English language teaching and technology*. Amsterdam: John Benjamins.

Council of Europe. 2001. *Common European framework of reference for languages: Learning, teaching, assessment*. Cambridge: Cambridge University Press.

Deutschmann, M., and L. Panichi. 2009. Talking into empty space? Signalling involvement in a virtual language classroom in Second Life. *Language Awareness* 18: 310–328.

Ding, A. 2005. Theoretical and practical issues in the collaborative learner autonomy in a virtual self-access centre. In *Distance education and languages*, ed. B. Holmberg, M. Shelley, and C. White, 40–54. Clevedon: Multilingual Matters.

Doughty, C., and M. Long. 2003. Optimal psycholinguistic environments for distance foreign language learning. *Language Learning and Technology* 7. http://llt.msu.edu/vol7num3/doughty/default.html. Accessed 24 May 2003.

Dudley-Evans, T., and M.J. St. John. 1998. *Developments in ESP. A multi-disciplinary approach*. Cambridge: Cambridge University Press.

Felix, U. 2002. The web as a vehicle for constructivist approaches in language teaching. *ReCALL* 14: 2–15.

Fortanet-Gómez, I., and C. Räisänen (eds.). 2008. *ESP in European higher education. Integrating content and language*. Amsterdam: John Benjamins.

Garner, M., and E. Borg. 2005. An ecological perspective on content-based instruction. *Journal of English for Academic Purposes* 4: 119–134.

Garrett, N. 2009. Computer-assisted language learning trends and issues revisited: Integrating innovation. *The Modern Language Journal* 93(Focus Issue): 719–740. doi:10.1111/j.1540-4781.2009.00969.x.

González, J., and R. Wagenaar (eds.). 2003. *Tuning educational structures in Europe. Final report. Phase one*. Bilbao: Universidad de Deusto.

González-Pueyo, I., C. Foz, M. Jaime, and M.J. Luzón (eds.). 2009. *Teaching academic and professional English online*. Bern: Peter Lang.
Hailey, D., K. Grant-Davie, and C.A. Hult. 2001. Online education horror stories worthy of Halloween: a short list of problems and solutions in online instruction. *Computers and Composition* 18: 387–397.
Hutchinson, T., and A. Waters. 1987. *English for specific purposes: A learning-centred approach*. Cambridge: Cambridge University Press.
Johns, A.M., and T. Dudley-Evans. 1991. English for specific purposes: International in scope, specific in purpose. *TESOL Quarterly* 25: 297–314.
Kern, R. 2006. Perspectives on technology in learning and teaching languages. *TESOL Quarterly* 40: 183–210.
Kern, R., P. Ware, and M. Warschauer. 2004. Crossing frontiers: New directions in online pedagogy and research. *Annual Review of Applied Linguistics* 24: 243–260.
Kirkpatrick, A. 2007. *World Englishes. Implications for international communication and English language teaching*. Cambridge: Cambridge University Press.
Kohonen, V., R. Jaatinen, P. Kaikkonen, and J. Lehtovaara. 2001. *Experiential learning in foreign language education*. London: Pearson Education.
Kolb, D. 1984. *Experiential learning*. Englewood Cliffs: Prentice Hall.
Kuteeva, M. 2011. Wikis and academic writing: Changing the writer-reader relationship. *English for Specific Purposes* 30: 44–57.
Lankamp, R.E. 2008. Curriculum change as a result of the introduction of the masters program: Designing and implementing a European online thesis-training course. In *ESP in European higher education. Integrating content and language*, ed. I. Fortanet-Gómez and C.A. Räisänen, 97–115. Amsterdam: John Benjamins.
Levy, M. 1997. *Computer-assisted language learning: Context and conceptualization*. Oxford: Oxford University Press.
Lévy, P. 1998. *La Cibercultura, el Segon Diluvi?* Trans. M. Llopis, Cyberculture. Barcelona: Edicions de la Universitat Oberta de Catalunya & Edicions Proa.
Little, D. 1997. Responding authentically to authentic texts: A problem for self-access language learning? In *Autonomy and independence in language learning*, ed. P. Benson and P. Voller, 225–236. London: Longman.
Long, M.H. 1991. Focus on form: A design feature in language teaching methodology. In *Foreign language research in cross-cultural perspective*, ed. K. de Bot, R. Ginsberg, and C. Kramsch, 39–52. Amsterdam: John Benjamins.
Luzón, M.J. 2009. Learning academic and professional English online: Integrating technology, language learning and disciplinary knowledge. In *Teaching academic and professional English online*, ed. I. González-Pueyo, C. Foz, M. Jaime, and M.J. Luzón, 11–33. Bern: Peter Lang.
Maylath, B., S. Vandepitte, and B. Mousten. 2008. Growing grassroots partnerships. In *Designing globally networked learning environments*, ed. D. Starke-Meyerring and M. Wilson, 59–66. Rotterdam: Sense Publishers.
Maylath, B., S. Vandepitte, P. Minacori, S. Isohella, B. Mousten, and J. Humbley. 2013. Managing complexity: A technical communication translation case study in multilateral international collaboration. *Technical Communication Quarterly* 22: 67–84.
Mercer, N. 2000. *Words and minds. How we use language to think together*. London: Routledge.
Murray, L., T. Hourigan, and C. Jeanneau. 2007. Blog writing integration for academic language learning purposes: Towards an assessment framework. *Ibérica* 14: 9–32.
Nesi, H. 1998. Using the Internet to teach English for academic purposes. *ReCALL* 10: 109–117.
Noble, D.F. 1998. Digital diploma mills: The automation of higher education. *First Monday* 3(1). http://firstmonday.org/htbin/cgiwrap/bin/ojs/index.php/fm/article/view/569/490. Accessed 31 May 2013.
Pally, M. 1997. Critical thinking in ESL: An argument for sustained content. *Journal of Second Language Writing* 6: 293–311.
Pennycook, A. 1997. Vulgar pragmatism, critical pragmatism, and EAP. *English for Specific Purposes* 16: 253–269.

Peterson, M. 2010. Learner participation patterns and strategy use in second life: An exploratory case study. *ReCALL* 22: 273–292.

Räisänen, C. 2009. Integrating content and language, in theory... In practice: Some reflections. In *Las lenguas para fines específicos ante el reto de la Convergencia Europea. VIII Congreso Internacional AELFE*, ed. E. Caridad de Otto and A.F. López de Vergara Méndez. La Laguna: Servicio de Publicaciones de la Universidad de La Laguna.

Räisänen, C.A., and I. Fortanet-Gómez. 2008. The state of ESP teaching and learning in Western European higher education after Bologna. In *ESP in European higher education. Integrating content and language*, ed. I. Fortanet-Gómez and C.A. Räisänen, 11–51. Amsterdam: John Benjamins.

Robinson, P. 1991. *ESP today: A practitioner's guide*. Hemel Hempstead: Prentice Hall.

Rueda, C., E. Arnó, and A. Soler. 2007. Integrating the Internet into EAP: Developing new literacies and language learning skills. In *The texture of Internet. Netlinguistics in progress*, ed. S. Posteguillo, M.L. Gea-Valor, and M.J. Esteve, 208–229. Newcastle: Cambridge Scholars Publishing.

Shetzer, H., and M. Warschauer. 2000. An electronic literacy approach to network-based language teaching. In *Network-based language teaching: Concepts and practice*, ed. M. Warschauer and R. Kern. Cambridge: Cambridge University Press.

Slaouti, D. 2002. The World Wide Web for academic purposes: Old study skills for new? *English for Specific Purposes* 21: 105–124.

Soler, A., and J. Romero. 2010. Developing pronunciation skills at tertiary level: An online pronunciation tutorial for academic purposes. In *Proceedings of the 9th international AELFE conference*. Tostedt (Hamburg): Attikon.

Stapleton, P. 2010. Writing in an electronic age: A case study of L2 composing processes. *Journal of English for Academic Purposes* 9: 295–307.

Starke-Meyering, D., A.H. Duin, and T. Palvetzian. 2007. Global partnerships: Positioning technical communication programs in the context of globalization. *Technical Communication Quarterly* 16: 139–174.

Swales, J.M. 1985. *Episodes in ESP*. Oxford: Pergamon Press.

Swales, J.M. 2006. Corpus linguistics and English for academic purposes. In *Information technology in languages for specific purposes. Issues and prospects*, ed. E. Arnó, A. Soler, and C. Rueda. New York: Springer.

Swales, J.M., D. Barks, A.C. Ostermann, and R.C. Simpson. 2001. Between critique and accommodation: Reflections on an EAP course for Masters of Architecture students. *English for Specific Purposes* 20: 439–458.

Van Lier, L. 1996. *Interaction in the language curriculum: Awareness, autonomy and authenticity*. London: Longman.

Vie, S. 2008. Digital divide 2.0. *Computers and Composition* 25: 9–23.

Vygotsky, L.S. 1978. *El desarrollo de los procesos psicológicos superiores*. Barcelona: Crítica.

Walker, U., and C. vom Brocke. 2009. Integrating content-based language learning and intercultural learning online: An international eGroups collaboration. In *Proceedings of CLESOL 2008*, ed. A. Brown. http://hdl.handle.net/10179/1591. Accessed 31 May 2013.

Warschauer, M. 2006. Preface. In *Information technology in languages for specific purposes: Issues and prospects*, ed. E. Arnó, A. Soler, and C. Rueda, xiii–xv. New York: Springer.

Warschauer, M., and R. Kern (eds.). 2000. *Network-based language teaching: Concepts and practice*. New York: Cambridge University Press.

Wertsch, J.V. 1985. *Vygotsky and the social formation of mind*. Cambridge, MA: Harvard University Press.

Chapter 2
Fostering Learner Autonomy in Technology-Enhanced ESP Courses

Ana María Gimeno Sanz

2.1 Introduction

Teaching on-line is a rapidly expanding twenty-first century phenomenon in language teaching, and more so as far as teaching English is concerned. Just as an example, the number of entries called up in the Google search engine when the exact string "teaching English online" is typed in calls up a total of 111,000 occurrences ("teach English online" calls up 95,100 results), whereas all other major European languages only call up a few screens of results. The occurrences include sites addressing learners -listing courses, materials, resources, etc.-, as well as tutors and instructors or researchers in the field, but more surprisingly targeting teachers in search of jobs. I came across a YouTube video advertising an eBook on training teachers to teach online to "paying ESL students".[1] In addition, typing in "learning English online" calls up a further 40,800 results and "learn English online", yet a further 187,000, most of which either advertise commercially available online courses or offer free ready-made exercises. If we restrict the search even further and include + beginner level/elementary level/intermediate level/advanced level, we find in both strings that the higher the language level being targeted, the more results appear in increased progression. This may imply that lower levels of proficiency such as beginners and elementary learners prefer face-to-face tuition and classroom contact, whereas intermediate and advanced learners are more willing to explore autonomous learning scenarios; a fact that seems only natural considering that learners who have an intermediate or advanced level of proficiency can to a larger

Parts of this paper have been previously published in Gimeno Sanz (2009a, b), Seiz Ortiz et al. (2010), and Gimeno Sanz et al. (2011).

[1] Retrieved October 22nd, 2010, from http://www.youtube.com/watch?v=rm5G6oZp7Ew

A.M. Gimeno Sanz (✉)
Departamento de Lingüística Aplicada,
Universidad Politécnica de Valencia, Valencia, Spain
e-mail: agimeno@upvnet.upv.es

E. Bárcena et al. (eds.), *Languages for Specific Purposes in the Digital Era*,
Educational Linguistics 19, DOI 10.1007/978-3-319-02222-2_2,

extent become independent learners due to an existing knowledge base and subsequent understanding of the target language, conferring more autonomy on them. This suggests that the Internet is slowly becoming an integral part of our English language teaching practice, especially at levels targeting higher intermediate to advanced learners, that there is an audience for these courses and that learners are increasingly in need of materials and learning scenarios outside the limits of more traditional teaching. However, it does not come as a surprise that when we search for teaching or learning professional or academic English online, there are only two results: one advertising a book published by Peter Lang in 2009 with that very title,[2] and the other is a LinkedIn profile entry.[3] Although there is a large community of language learners who seek to learn languages for specific or academic purposes, there is a very small community of language teachers who are willing to embark in creating tailor-made materials for their learners' specific professional needs; and, understandably so, if we take into account – even today – the amount of time, will and effort that goes into designing interactive multimedia materials for the web.

The determination to change this drove us to design the *InGenio* online authoring shell,[4] an entirely web-based multilingual tool that enables language teachers from around the world to design and publish language learning courseware without having to acquire additional programming skills. The tool was developed within *Proyecto InGenio,* which produced three basic outcomes in addition to the language independent, on-line multimedia authoring shell; (i) an on-line learning environment offering the courseware designed and created within the *InGenio* authoring tool; (ii) a student assessment and on-line tutoring interface; and (iii) a translation tool to adapt the materials into different support languages (Gimeno Sanz 2009a).

Further to creating the authoring shell, we then set out to design an intermediate level online English course intended for learners of English for engineering purposes as a prototype to illustrate some of the things that could be done with the tool. The course is known as *Intermediate Online English.* I shall refer to it below.

2.2 Approaches and Methodology – Independent & Autonomous Learning

When combining the principles underlying teaching languages for professional or academic purposes and e-language learning, one comes to the conclusion that the learning process must foster a number of strategies to ensure deep learning through critical thinking and analysis of new information and ideas, linking these to already known concepts, and leading to understanding and long-term retention of (newly

[2] González-Pueyo, Isabel; Foz Gil, Carmen; Jaime Siso, Mercedes; Luzón Marco, María José (Eds.) (2009). *Teaching Academic and Professional English Online.* Bern: Peter Lang.

[3] Jeanne Farr http://cn.linkedin.com/pub/jeanne-farr/16/277/780

[4] Unlike other platforms such as Moodle or Blackboard/WebCT, *InGenio* is not a Content Management System (CMS).

acquired) knowledge. In addition, the use of Information and Communications Technologies (ICT) in the language curriculum has, to some extent, been responsible for the shift from focusing on the teacher to focusing on the learner when designing web-enhanced materials, and has led courseware designers to adopt a constructivist approach to learning, whereby the student is encouraged to actively construct knowledge and the teacher becomes a guide to support learners through the process of learning. In so doing, students must be equipped with all the necessary tools to become independent learners and take responsibility for their own learning. As pointed out by Blin (2005, p. 33), "Independent language learning environments present language learning opportunities that do not require the constant intervention of a teacher or that can be pursued outside the framework of an educational institution."

Thus, online learning resources such as the ones which can be developed using the *InGenio* platform should ultimately encourage "active learning", that is, a context where the learner is encouraged to write, speak, actively participate, interact with fellow learners, etc. in a resourceful and stimulating learning environment, yet not necessarily under the constant supervision of a teacher. This scenario naturally implies making use of currently available technologies such as video and audio conferencing tools, instant messaging tools, blogs, wikis, etc. The very nature of these tools provide learners with a fair amount of independence which nevertheless also requires guidance by a qualified instructor to help the learner orient his or her activity toward the learning process itself and not deviate attention towards other possible distracting scenarios. Learner autonomy, understood as the capacity to self-manage learning, is also one of the key concepts which has rapidly evolved due to the integration of Computer Assisted Language Learning (CALL) into the language curriculum. As Littlewood (1997, p. 83) points out, "The autonomous learner takes responsibility for his or her own learning, has developed useful and effective learning strategies and is able to work independently." In CALL materials' design, most authors are aware of the fact that a variety of teaching strategies have to be implemented in the courseware in order to facilitate and encourage learners to take up the endeavour of second language acquisition. To this end, the *InGenio* authoring tool has been designed to include, as well as a considerable number of exercise templates, reference materials such as grammar notes, cultural information, multilingual sound-enhanced dictionaries and glossaries, etc. in order to provide learners with all the necessary resources that contribute toward enriching comprehension and understanding of the target language. Another important factor to bear in mind is the need for the inclusion of meaningful corrective feedback on which the learner can rely to support their progress.

In terms of methodology, *InGenio* can be adopted to suit a large number of teaching methodologies, ranging from structural methods to a more communicative approach to language learning. The exercise templates are particularly suitable for designing courses that attempt to acknowledge the fact that a true linguistic competence implies being able to use the language that is appropriate to a given social and cultural context in order to achieve a specific communicative goal. To do this, learners need knowledge of the linguistic forms, meanings and functions for a given context. To achieve this end, *InGenio* provides a variety of goal-oriented learning strategies in a media rich electronic environment that supports the study of the target language. The notion of supporting the study of the language is crucial here. Our objective was not so much the creation of software to "teach" the language, but the construction of learning resources in the shape of an environment that would provide the student with all the tools and information, short of a live teacher, that they might need to undertake a language course.

Because "there are strong arguments to support the notion that students will need higher levels of explicit and implicit assistance in computerised than in face-to-face environments" (Trinder 2006, p. 97), online courseware must replace the absence of face-to-face interaction with techniques and strategies which give the student appropriate support. In order to illustrate this more thoroughly, I would like to illustrate examples from *Intermediate Online English* and from an initiative conducted at UPV called "Docencia en Red" (Networked teaching) to provide ICT-enhanced learning materials.

2.3 Examples of Initiatives Conducted at UPV to Promote Independent Learning

2.3.1 Intermediate Online English

Intermediate Online English was initially designed as a prototype to illustrate the functionality of the *InGenio* authoring tool and delivery platform. Since 2004, however, it has been used as a self-access course by students pursuing to practice English for engineering purposes and seeking to achieve the B2 level of the *Common European Framework of Reference for Languages* (CEFRL)[5] at the Universidad Politécnica de Valencia (UPV). This is the proficiency level required by UPV students in order to be awarded their degree as set forth by internal regulations[6] complying with EU recommendations regarding the Bologna Declaration[7] in general, and the European Commission's "Action Plan for Promoting Language Learning and Linguistic Diversity",[8] in particular. According to the Action Plan, "every European

[5] See Council of Europe (2001). *Common European Framework of Reference for Languages* (CEFRL). Cambridge: Cambridge University Press.

[6] *Diseño de titulaciones. Documento marco UPV.* Approved by the University's Governing Council in February 2008. Retrieved September 18th, 2010, from http://www.upv.es/entidades/VECE/menu_urlc.html?/entidades/VECE/infoweb/vece/info/U0399286.pdf

[7] The Bologna Declaration can be retrieved from http://ec.europa.eu/education/higher-education/doc1290_en.htm. Last accessed 18/09/2010.

[8] "Promoting Language Learning and Language Diversity: An Action Plan 2004-06" (2003), EU policy document available from http://eur-lex.europa.eu/LexUriServ/LexUriServ.do?uri=COM:2003:0449:FIN:EN:PDF. Retrieved 14/11/2009.

citizen should have meaningful communicative competence in at least two other languages in addition to his or her mother tongue." It also sets forth a number of recommendations for universities to follow in order to ensure success of these EU goals. Among them, it states that each university should implement a coherent language policy clarifying its role in promoting language learning and linguistic diversity.

Thus, with respect to language tuition, students enrolling at the UPV on any of the newly regulated degrees[9] will have to prove their language proficiency of level B2 of the CEFRL, which means that they are independent users in the foreign language and…

> Can understand the main ideas of complex text on both concrete and abstract topics, including technical discussions in his/her field of specialisation. Can interact with a degree of fluency and spontaneity that makes regular interaction with native speakers quite possible without strain for either party. Can produce clear, detailed text on a wide range of subjects and explain a viewpoint on a topical issue giving the advantages and disadvantages of various options. (CEFRL, p. 24)

Intermediate Online English is an attempt to aid learners to achieve these can-do statements and, in particular, to support their engagement in technical discussions in their field of engineering. It is currently the foundation for an elective subject delivered at UPV called "*Computer Assisted English*"[10] and is embedded in the *InGenio* Learning Environment, to which registered students have access.

2.3.1.1 Organisation of the Course

Since one of the aims of the course is to reinforce technical English, *Intermediate Online English* has been divided into two distinct parts: one, covering semi-technical topics such as digital devices, the web, electric vehicles, etc., the other, focussing on more general topics such as leisure activities, the Olympic games, theatre-going, film festivals, etc. This division was also implemented in order to balance the intake of formal versus informal language and structures.

The courseware aims to provide an environment in which learners can develop communicative competences at their own pace using different strategies. This is achieved, among other things, by presenting a default route to follow, by offering a large variety of activities, and by developing a progression which moves from

[9]The Spanish Ministry of Education and Science is currently in a process of adapting all of the official university degrees into graduate and postgraduate courses. Further information may be found in Royal Decree 1393/2007 published on 30th October 2007 in the Official State Gazette. Available online from http://www.boe.es/boe/dias/2007/10/30/pdfs/A44037-44048.pdf. Retrieved 15/11/2009.

[10]This is an elective subject worth 4.5 credits (45 h of student workload) open to all UPV students. For further information on this subject, see the Course Study Guide on the UPV website at http://www.upv.es/pls/oalu/sic_asi.Busca_Asi?P_VISTA=&P_IDIOMA=c&p_codi=3235&p_caca=act

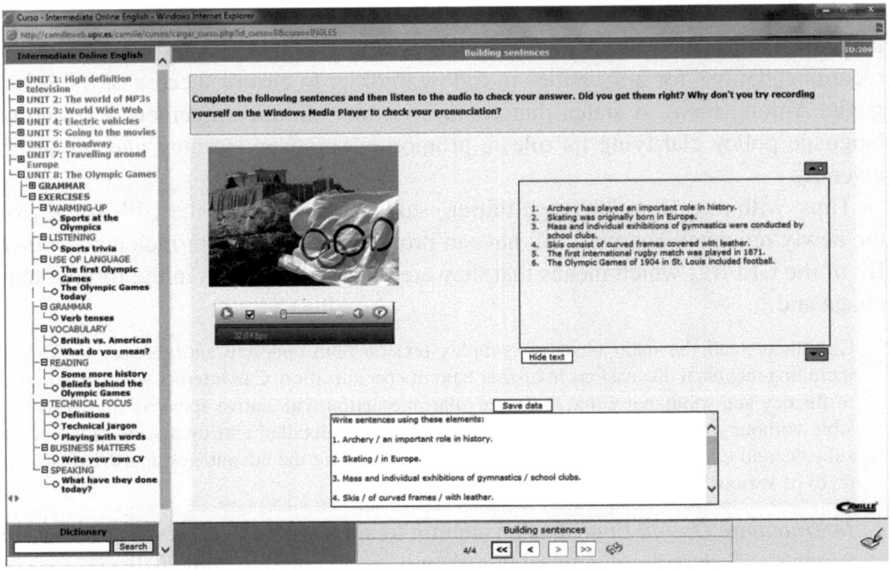

Fig. 2.1 Sample exercise taken from *Intermediate Online English*

receptive to productive skills. Various strategies are used to encourage problem solving and resolution of specific tasks in order to develop use of the target language within specific communicative situations.

Intermediate Online English (Fig. 2.1) contains eight units which are all preceded by a grammar section aimed at revising grammatical points relevant to the course contents. Each unit is divided into ten sub-headings in order to cover practice in all four language skills, in addition to exercising grammatical structures and reinforcing technical vocabulary: warming up, listening comprehension, use of language, grammar, vocabulary, reading comprehension, technical focus, writing, business matters, and speaking, each of which include a number of exercises relating to the section's prime focus. The course itself comprises over 300 exercises and activities that are designed to generate a sound basis for consolidation and acquisition of relevant language skills.

The courseware combines several interrelated teaching approaches, ranging from a functional/notional approach used in LSP (Languages for Specific Purposes), through a more traditional language form approach which primarily focuses on structures, to a more contextual approach. In determining the course design and structure, the functional/notional approach allowed us to specify the desired learning outcomes in terms of language functions (e.g. making a request, advising a colleague on how to proceed), general as well as specific notions (e.g. duration, location), and rhetorical skills (e.g. extracting information from a dialogue). The language form approach helped shape the structures present in the language functions in order to achieve learner awareness of the linguistic forms being used, and the contextual approach enabled us to determine the situations in which the functions, notions and structures were embedded.

2.3.1.2 Learner Autonomy in *Intermediate Online English*[11]

Intermediate Online English was developed according to a number of different design principles such as system reliability, interoperability, scalability, accessibility, didactic efficiency, etc. (Colpaert 2004, p. 40) in an attempt to offer the EFL community a useful and efficient educational tool. Since the requirements in designing online self-access materials are substantially different to those in designing face-to-face supplementary materials, great effort was put into providing learners with all the necessary resources to support the autonomous learning process. These include provision of self-explanatory reference materials, additional explanations to support theoretical concepts, links to external sources, and student assessment principles. Provision of effective feedback is especially important when designing online self-access materials; additionally, attempting to predict learners' behaviour and reactions when completing exercises of this sort is fundamental.

Intermediate Online English includes a variety of features to aid learners in becoming independent learners, based on the assumption that one of the possible scenarios in which independent learning takes place is the following: "when students learn from open learning materials, they are essentially learning at their own pace and in their own ways from materials specially prepared to activate their want to learn, giving them the chance to learn by doing, and providing them with feedback on their efforts." (Race 2005). Among these features are:

(a) Self-explanatory reference materials
    (i) Grammar notes
    (ii) Glossary
(b) Hints to aid exercise completion
(c) Feedback
    (i) Automatically generated random immediate feedback
    (ii) Exercise-specific feedback
(d) Performance/progress reports
(e) Help files
(f) Audio enhancement of written text
(g) Self-assessment exercises with limitation in number of attempts and time control

These are briefly described below:

Self-Explanatory Reference Materials

Provision of appropriate reference materials for the language level and objectives of the course being designed is, needless to say, of vital importance in autonomous

[11] For further reference see Gimeno Sanz et al. (2011).

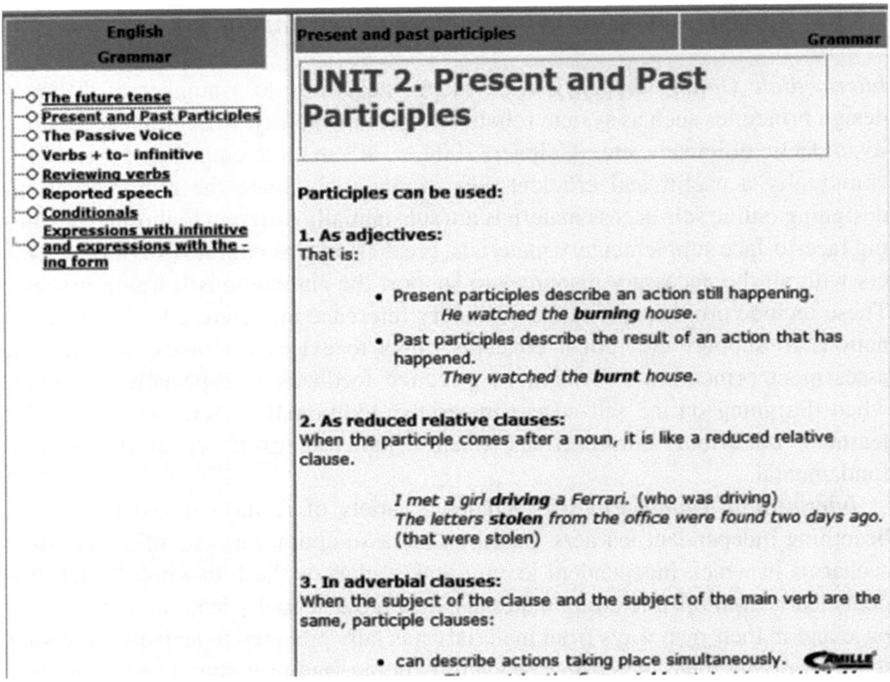

Fig. 2.2 Preview of the grammar notes in *Intermediate Online English*

language learning. When designing *Intermediate Online English* we therefore tried to ensure that the target language would provide all the necessary elements to support the process of the learner's acquisition of language. To this end, *InGenio* offers a number of templates which enable materials writers to create reference materials that can be associated individually with single exercises or called up as independent tools during the student's course of study (see Fig. 2.2).

The *InGenio* authoring tool also enables authors to create monolingual or multilingual glossaries and dictionaries. Each exercise template includes an option whereby any of the words can become a hypertext link which displays the glossed item or dictionary entry in student mode. The entries appear as pop-up windows (see Fig. 2.3). If a highlighted word is not found in the courseware glossary, the author may specify a default online dictionary from which to retrieve the word entry in response to a student's query. All entries may, optionally, be enhanced with an audio file or an illustration.

Figure 2.3 above shows a screen capture taken from *Intermediate Online English* illustrating an entry from the glossary. Since the course is aimed at learners with an intermediate level of English, it was decided to include only monolingual entries, each word being accompanied by its phonetic transcription.

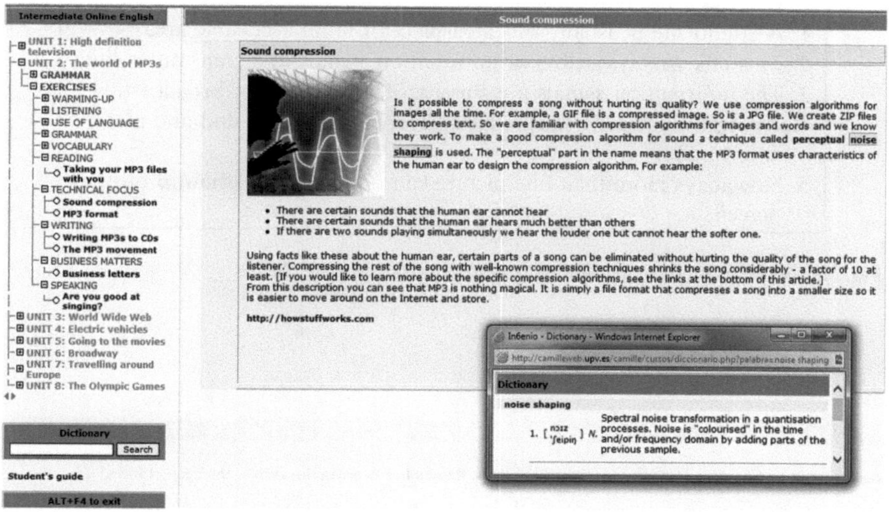

Fig. 2.3 Pop-up window displaying entry in dictionary

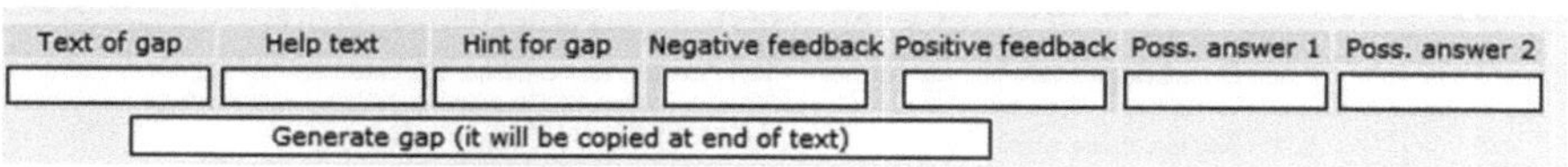

Fig. 2.4 Segment of the *InGenio* gap-filling exercise template

Hints to Aid Exercise Completion

Because we are dealing with a language level where learners are expected to have "a broad active reading vocabulary" (CEFRL, p. 69), *Intermediate Online English* makes use of one of the features common to most *InGenio* templates, i.e. allowing materials writers to design exercises where more than one correct answer may be possible. As we can see in Fig. 2.4, two possible correct answers can be specified for each blank space in the text of a gap-filling exercise. Additionally, many of the exercise templates allow writers to provide extra help and hints to support the learner on completing an exercise. To give an example, the template for designing gap-filling exercises, as well as generating gaps in texts automatically, allows us to supply a short text to help complete a gap correctly and/or insert a text to provide the learner with an appropriate hint.

Figure 2.5 below illustrates part of the script used to create the exercise shown in Fig. 2.6 below, where the learner is given a synonym in order to complete the sentence.

This feature enables us to create exercises at different levels of difficulty within the courseware, in addition to fostering autonomy by anticipating the type of help that the learner will need in order to successfully complete an activity. Figure 2.7 illustrates the Hint and Help utility described above.

1. A studio site is usually **#located||placed#** in an accessible area.
2. This link **#relays||delivers#** information signals to a transmitter site.
3. The information signals are **#prepared||arranged#** for broadcast.
4. The transducers are **#reproducing||recreating#** the sound and picture information.
5. Nowadays more than one picture can be **#displayed||shown#** on the screen.

Fig. 2.5 Script taken from gap-filling exercise illustrated in Fig. 2.6

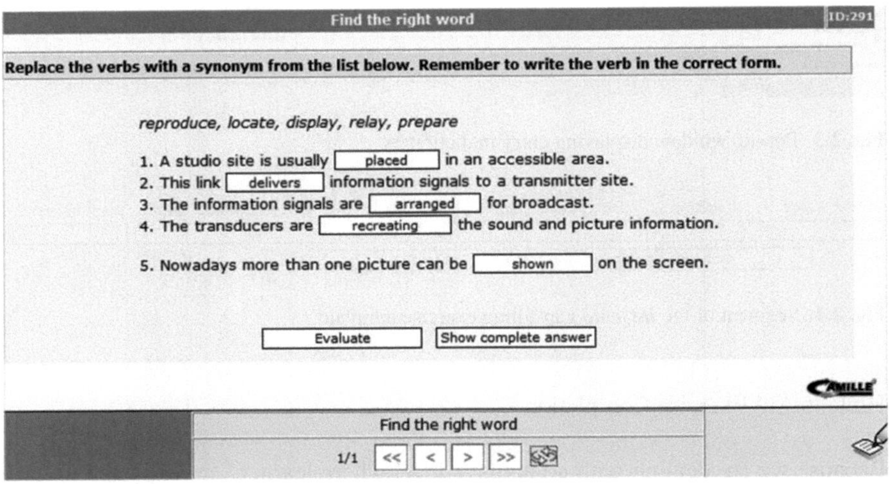

Fig. 2.6 Gap-filling exercise with hint in blank space

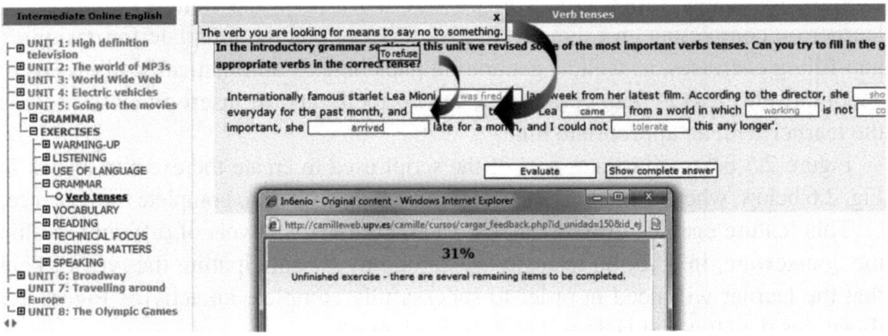

Fig. 2.7 Sample Hint and Help text in a gap-filling exercise

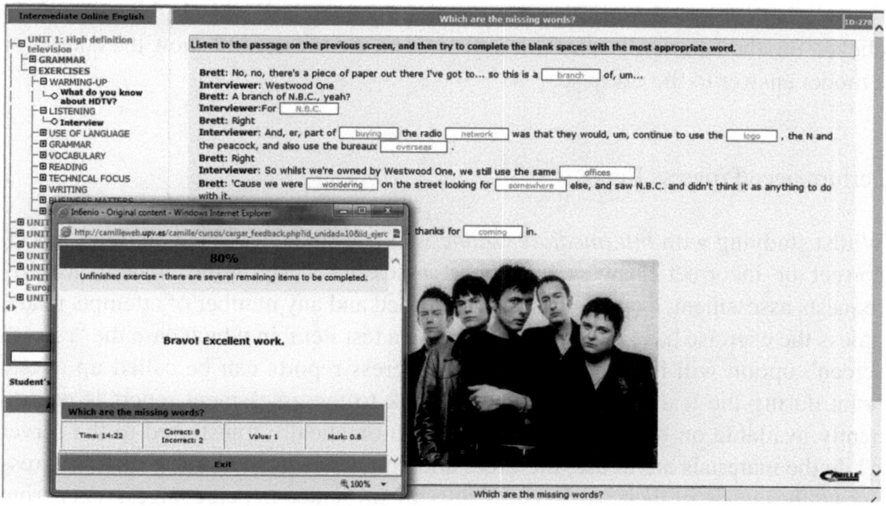

Fig. 2.8 Sample immediate feedback

Feedback

Providing autonomous learners with adequate assessment tools (scores, individualised comments, etc.) and appropriate feedback, whether this is immediate or delayed (Pujolà 2001), is essential to avoid unnecessary frustration which can arise by a perceived lack of support.

Feedback in *InGenio* can be delivered according to various modalities. The exercise templates include a default feedback mode providing learners with immediate feedback after completing an exercise and once the data has been transferred to the server. This default feedback opens up as a separate pop-up window with a random comment and/or recommendation from a list that has been programmed into the system following a number of parameters describing learner performance. Scores themselves are also given, in addition to an indication of the time that has been spent on a given exercise (Fig. 2.8).

The default feedback can be altered by the materials writer at any time and specific feedback can be added for any given exercise, although individualised corrective feedback may only be provided by the tutor when supervising the learner's input through the *InGenio* tutor interface. In a gap-filling exercise, for instance, both positive and negative feedback can be provided for each blank space which has to be completed by the learner, alongside the hint and contextual help to aid comprehension and exercise completion – as mentioned above – and overall feedback after completing the entire exercise. One of the advantages of multimedia technology is the possibility of providing a student with an immediate response at the mere touch of a key or mouse click. This is especially useful when dealing with positive or negative feedback in reaction to the learner's performance in completing an activity or exercise. To cater for the independent learner, each exercise in *Intermediate*

Online English has two utilities, i.e. "assess my exercise" and "I give up". When clicked on, the latter will transfer a null score to the server, and show the correct or a model answer to the exercise.

Performance/Progress Reports

Whilst studying with *Intermediate Online English,* students, can at all times, check correct or incorrect answers or request assessment. Until the student actually requests assessment, exercises may be refreshed and any number of attempts made, unless the exercise has been marked as being a test item, in which case the "refresh screen" option will have been disabled. Progress reports can be called up at any point during the learning process since a link to the assessment report is permanently available on the screen. The data is automatically transferred to the server while the materials are in use, therefore allowing students to monitor their progress during the course of their work. The results are presented in percentages, registering date and time, number of completed exercises, scores, etc., as shown in Fig. 2.9.

Because the system automatically keeps track of student performance, tutors using *Intermediate Online English* with registered users can access progress reports, and also monitor students' written production based on open input activities, so that it can be corrected, assessed and appropriate feedback provided. Marks are automatically averaged by the system in order to give students a final score. When specified in an activity, learners may also upload any type of file (spread sheets, audio, etc.) onto the server for their tutors to evaluate and assess together with all the other course work.

Help Files

A number of help files describing how the online system works are available at all times for learners to consult. These have been designed to quickly provide a clear overview of the system's functionalities, as well as including a brief description of the exercise typologies and reference materials. Navigational guidance has also been included although the courseware has been described by its users (Gimeno Sanz 2010) as being intuitive and user-friendly.

Audio Enhancement of Written Text

Because two of the skills that *Intermediate Online English* sets out to encourage practice for are listening comprehension and speaking production, a large number of the activities include audio files either as part of the exercise proper or to reinforce contact with the target language. In addition, some of the activities rely on audio to provide positive feedback; i.e. the audio file of a particular exercise automatically plays when the learner provides a correct answer.

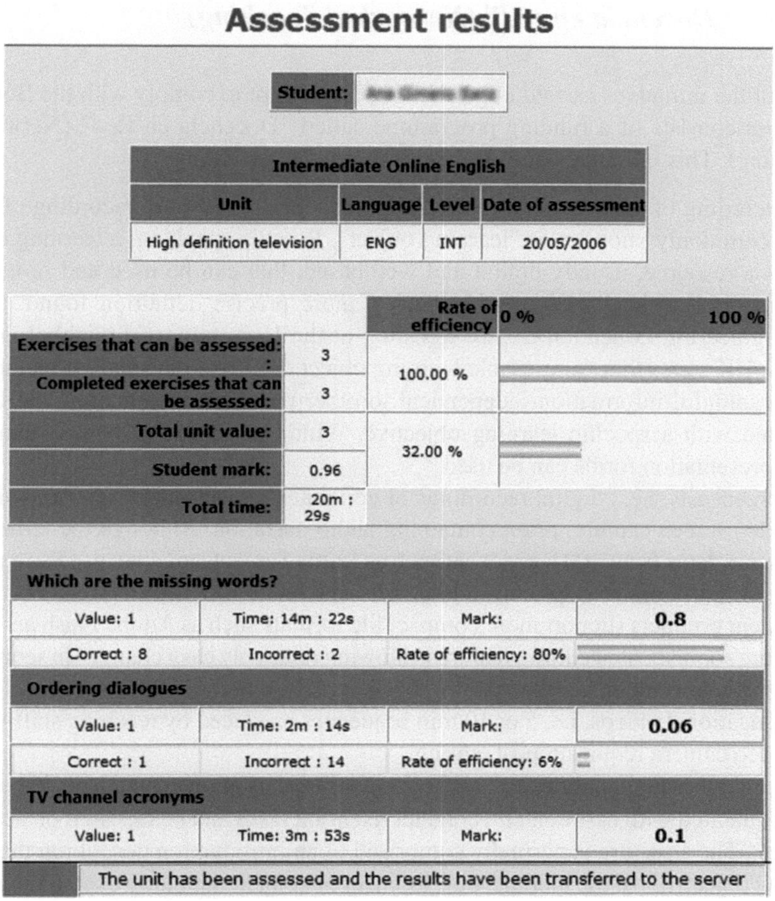

Fig. 2.9 *InGenio* sample student assessment report

Self-Assessment Exercises with Limitation in Number of Attempts and Time Control

As mentioned in section d) above, the *InGenio* authoring tool templates can be adjusted, on the one hand, to limit the number of attempts a learner is allowed in order to complete an exercise, and on the other, the time given for its completion. Both of these utilities were designed to include self-assessment activities in the courseware in order to provide learners with the possibility of being able to monitor their progress individually by taking the test items. These activities have proven to be very successful among learners, who have reported that they find them challenging and indicative of the progress they are making in the course of their work.

2.3.2 *"Docencia en red" (Networked Teaching)*

One of the initiatives carried out at UPV in an attempt to comply with the Bologna Process consists of a funding programme called "Docencia en Red" (Networked teaching). This initiative comprises several options, including:

- Recording of what are known as "Polimedia", i.e. 5–10 min' recording of what is commonly known as a "learning object". Broadly speaking, a learning object "is a resource, usually digital and web-based, that can be used and re-used to support learning." However, perhaps a more precise definition found on the Engineering Education Centre website[12] at the University of Loughborough in the UK states that "a re-usable learning object (RLO) is the smallest element of meaningful information independent to other pieces of information and correlated with a specific learning objective. Within a single RLO more than one representation forms can be used."
- Screencasts, i.e. "digital recordings of computer screen output, also known as a video screen capture, often containing audio narration. Although the term screencast dates from 2004, products such as Lotus ScreenCam were used as early as 1994. Early products produced large files and had limited editing features. More recent products support more compact file formats such as Adobe Flash and have more sophisticated editing features, allowing relatively easy changes in sequence, mouse movement, audio, etc."[13]
- Educational videos, i.e. 5 or 10 min sequences produced by teaching staff with a video camera requiring post editing.
- Digital learning modules, i.e. self-contained lessons allowing students to become acquainted with new content, conduct retention tasks and be assessed on acquisition. The structure is normally comprised of an introduction describing the aims and objectives of the module, development of content including explanations and raising awareness, a practical application of the module, a summary of the entire module including learning outcomes and, lastly, a form of learner assessment.
- Open courseware, by publishing through *Universia,* one of the Open CourseWare Consortium sustaining members, of which UPV is a member. Universia is a Latin American, Spanish and Portuguese network that promotes and facilitates the integration and development of university members in the knowledge and information society, as well as in the telecommunications sector. Universia's mission is to offer the Latin American, Spanish and Portuguese university community the optimum mix of content and services so as to facilitate the creation of a common forum for higher education through training, culture, research, and collaboration with the business world. Universia's membership includes 1,056 universities and institutions of higher education, which represents approximately ten million students.[14]

---

[12] For further information go to http://eec.lboro.ac.uk/learningtech/jtor.htm

[13] For further reference go to http://en.wikipedia.org/wiki/Screencast

[14] For further information go to http://www.ocwconsortium.org/component/ocwc/memberprofile/123

The repository of UPV's teaching materials is known as *RiuNet* and is freely available from http://dspace.upv.es/manakin. All of the above options to create learning materials are integrated in the University's Learning Management System (LMS) – PoliformaT – which is based on the "open source suite of learning" developed by the Massachusetts Institute of Technology in the USA, known as Sakai.[15]

Learning Management Systems (LMS),[16] such as Moodle, Blackboard/WebCT, Sakai, etc., which enable the management and delivery of learning content and resources to students, commonly integrate a great number of synchronous and asynchronous communication tools in addition to content-based materials such as coursework, exercises and revision materials. LMSs are delivery platforms, usually with a great deal of versatility, where online courses are normally embedded and are linked to other teacher-student and student-student communication tools thus allowing online tutoring and supervision of student work, as well as peer reviewing. To this end, discussion forums, file-sharing and chat are commonly used to support co-operative learning. While these virtual group spaces provide a platform for co-operative activities, it is important to provide a meaningful layout to both the assignment and the use of the space for the online environment to be used effectively. A well-established virtual space has several advantages when used with co-operative learning exercises. The space provides an archive of student work that can be accessed by both the students and the tutor. This archive provides both a means to assess student comprehension and achievement as well as a way to reinforce student learning.

2.4 Learning Objects

The initiatives described above all have a common feature, that of creating learning objects – be they micro lessons, self-contained modules or ready-made exercises as in the *InGenio* system – to generate institutional repositories. Although there is no general consensus on the definition, the following features may be of help to narrow down what is commonly understood by learning object:

(a) Reusability (Davies and Riley 2009): Information and Communications Technology for Language Teachers (ICT4LT), http://www.ict4lt.org/en/en_glossary.htm: learning objects should be usable and reusable in different contexts and educational circumstances.
(b) Transportability (Longmire 2000): this feature is closely linked to reusability, and can be regarded as its technical counterpart, because for learning objects to be reusable they should work well on different platforms and systems and it should be easy (or at least possible) to move them around distant locations.

[15] For further information go to http://sakaiproject.org/

[16] Edu Tools http://www.edutools.info/item_list.jsp?pj=8 features comparative reviews of current Learning Management Systems.

The evolution of the Web, in this respect, shows a clear trend towards shared and movable resources.

(c) Modularity (Polsani 2003): learning objects that are reusable and transportable must be modular, i.e. resemble modules or building blocks which are somehow self-contained, able to be grouped or to stand alone. This also implies that they are small enough to be embedded in a learning activity, lesson, unit or course. Such a characteristic is very much in line with the reticular and interconnected quality of the Web.

(d) Granularity (Polsani 2003; Wiley 2000a, b): this concept has to do with the size of a learning object and the components or building blocks of a given learning resource. The question of *how big should a learning object be?* is still a big issue for educational designers which is far from resolved. This concept is also linked to that of modularity and reusability, since normally the larger and more complex the learning object is, the less reusable it is.

(e) Meta-information, metadata (Wiley 2000b): language learning objects in our context are digital objects and therefore contain data, information and certain features that conform what is known as *linguistic input*. In order to be (re)used appropriately, the information and data that clearly describes learning objects must be incorporated separately (e.g. in labels) within the resources in form of metadata and meta-information. Therefore, the problem is what information should be included and how such information should be presented. As Negroponte would put it, there should be *bits describing other bits* (Negroponte 1995).

(f) Searchability (Liber 2005): another important characteristic that a learning object should possess in order to be (re)usable is its ability to be available, i.e. easily and readily stored, searched and retrieved. Clear meta-information labels can help learning objects to become highly searchable and consequently reusable.

(g) Flexibility and adaptive capability (Gibbons et al. 2000): in our view, these requirements that learning objects should meet to be fully reusable involve both technical and pedagogical features which are not always easy to evaluate, but are fundamental from the point of view of the end-user.

These general features are the ones that are going to allow us to maximise the increasing efforts to provide learners with consistent repositories comprised of learning materials to enhance autonomous or independent learning. An example of some such repository is being created in England, at the Open University. It is known by the acronym LORO and is a collection of resources to support language teaching and learning. Some of the materials in LORO have been specifically designed to support Open University Language courses and are deposited in LORO as Open Educational Resources to be adapted and re-used freely in any context.[17]

[17] For further reference go to http://loro.open.ac.uk/

2.5 Conclusion

Technology in education is best exploited when an environment favouring student participation is developed. The approach that takes into account a student's prior knowledge in order to build upon it when new knowledge acquisition takes place is the constructivist approach to learning, i.e. students construct learning from several combined modes of input, including prior knowledge, and learn by doing, by applying things that have been learnt through experimenting. Foreign language learning, as opposed to second language acquisition -where the learner lives in a society where that second language is spoken- can rarely depend on real-life situations in which students can experiment in a cause and effect-type learning mode, since learning mostly takes place within a traditional classroom or lab setting. This is where computers have already proven to be extremely useful aids. Computers are an open window to the world without. They are the window that opens to a wealth of authentic materials, multimedia or otherwise, and to a wealth of resources and tools which can transport our learners to a situation where it no longer matters whether the foreign language they are learning is spoken or not outside the actual classroom.

The use in a classroom of the ICT naturally opens up a myriad of opportunities for designing creative learning environments. Our classroom can become a *library* where our students can find and retrieve information from various online or standalone multimedia sources; a *pressroom* where they enquire about and publish their views and opinions on the web via blogs and wikis; a *delivery platform* where they can publish their project work on the web and have it peer-reviewed or commented; an *auditorium* where live presentations on specific – individual or group – project-work takes place; a *communications parlour* where live video and audio broadcasts and instant chatting is possible; to sum up, a *workshop* where innumerable tools to support learning are interconnected and at the student's disposal.

The modern classroom should therefore be seen as an environment where the learner gathers information from different inputs (both technological and human), processes this information, integrates it with previously acquired knowledge and expands existing knowledge (Gimeno Sanz 2009b). Learning should be seen as a constant, interactive and dynamic process that combines observational, exploratory and productive skills. This learning theory, which is built upon Vygotsky's investigations,[18] is better known as "scaffolding". The metaphor refers to the teaching process where learners are seen as individuals immersed in the process of constructing a building, the building blocks of their cognitive abilities. The construction relies on the foundations of what is already known and the new is built upon the known. According to Hartman (2002), in the educational setting, scaffolds may include models, cues, prompts, hints, partial solutions, think-aloud modelling and direct instruction. To this end, information technologies can play a major role.

---

[18] Vygotsky, L. (1934/1986). **Thought and Language**, trans. A. Kozulin. Cambridge, MA: Harvard University Press.

References

Blin, F. 2005. *CALL and the development of learner autonomy – An activity theoretical study*. Unpublished doctoral thesis, Institute of Educational Technology, The Open University. http://webpages.dcu.ie/~blinf/BlinThesis.pdf. Accessed 10 June 2007.

Colpaert, J. 2004. *Design of online interactive language courseware: Conceptualization, specification and prototyping*. Antwerp: University of Antwerp.

Davies, G., and F. Riley. 2009. Glossary of ICT terminology. In *Information and Communications Technology for Language Teachers (ICT4LT)*, ed. G. Davies. Slough: Thames Valley University [Online]. http://www.ict4lt.org/en/en_glossary.htm. Accessed 17 Nov 2009.

Gibbons, A.S., J. Nelson, and R. Richards. 2000. The nature and origin of instructional objects. In *The instructional use of learning objects*, ed. D.A. Wiley. http://reusability.org/read/chapters/gibbons.doc. Accessed 17 Nov 2009.

Gimeno Sanz, A. 2009a. Online courseware design and delivery: The InGenio authoring system. In *Teaching academic and professional English online*, 83–105. Bern: Peter Lang.

Gimeno Sanz, A. 2009b. How can CLIL benefit from the integration of information and communications technologies? In *Content and language integrated learning: Cultural diversity*, 77–102. Bern: Peter Lang.

Gimeno Sanz, A. 2010. Intermediate online English: An attempt to increase learner autonomy. *Teaching English with Technology – Developing Online Teaching Skills* Special Issue 10(3): 31–44. http://www.tewtjournal.org/VOL%2010/ISSUE%202/volume_10_issue_02-05_article_3.pdf. Accessed 23 Oct 2011.

Gimeno Sanz, A., A. Martínez Sáez, A. Sevilla Pavón, and J.M. de Siqueira Rocha. 2011. Fostering autonomy in a pedagogically sound e-learning environment for learners of English for specific purposes. In *Multiple voices in academic and professional discourse: Current issues in a specialised language research, teaching and new technologies*, 547–560. Newcastle upon Tyne: Cambridge Scholars Publishing.

Hartman, H. 2002. *Scaffolding & cooperative learning, in human learning and instruction*, 23–69. New York: City College of City University of New York.

Liber, O. 2005. Learning objects: Conditions for viability. *Institute of Educational Cybernetics: Journal Articles*. University of Bolton. http://digitalcommons.bolton.ac.uk/cgi/viewcontent.cgi?article=1001&context=iec_journalsp. Accessed 10 Oct 2009.

Littlewood, W. 1997. Self-access: Why do we want it and what can it do? In *Autonomy and independence in language learning*, 79–91. Essex: Longman – Applied Linguistic and Language Study.

Longmire, W. 2000. A primer on learning objects. Learning circuits, American Society for Training and Development. http://www.astd.org/LC/2000/0300_longmire.htm. Accessed 23 Oct 2011.

Negroponte, N. 1995. *Being digital*. London: Hodder and Stoughton.

Polsani, P.R. 2003. Use and abuse of reusable learning objects. *Journal of Digital Information* 3/4. http://journals.tdl.org/jodi/article/view/89/88. Accessed 17 Nov 2009.

Pujolà, J.T. 2001. Did CALL feedback feed back? *ReCALL* 13(1): 79–98.

Race, P. 2005. Effective learning. In *Deliberations*. London: Metropolitan University. http://www.londonmet.ac.uk/deliberations/effective-learning/independent.cfm. Accessed 18 Sept 2010.

Seiz Ortiz, R., A. Gimeno Sanz, and B. Serra Cámara. 2010. Applying learning objects metadata theory for pedagogical evaluation of web-based CALL. In *New trends in CALL: Working together*, 187–194. London: Macmillan.

Trinder, R. 2006. *Language learning with computers: The student's perspective*. Frankfurt: Peter Lang.

Wiley, D.A. 2000a. Learning object design and sequencing theory. Unpublished doctoral dissertation, Brigham Young University. http://www.opencontent.org/docs/dissertation.pdf. Accessed 23 Oct 2011.

Wiley, D.A. 2000b. Connecting learning objects to instructional design theory: A definition, a metaphor, and a taxonomy. In *The instructional use of learning* objects, ed. D.A. Wiley. http://reusability.org/read/chapters/wiley.doc. Accessed 17 Nov 2009.

Chapter 3
The I-AGENT Project: Blended Learning Proposal for Professional English Integrating an AI Extended Version of Moodle with Classroom Work for the Practice of Oral Skills

Elena Martín-Monje and Noa Talaván

3.1 Introduction

The ATLAS (Artificial inTelligence for Linguistic ApplicationS)[1] research group[2] is currently at the final stage of developing I-AGENT (Intelligent Adaptative Generic English Tutor), a project that has attempted to merge Intelligent Computer Assisted Language Learning (ICALL) with face-to-face (F2F) education in an innovative way. Clearly sequencing the various stages for the student to be guided at all times – be it online or in class – I-AGENT has come to prove particularly efficient in the enhancement of the often methodologically undervalued oral skills.

The present paper deals with blended learning in general, as well as with how the online extended Moodle can be used following that methodology, so as to focus on the use I-AGENT has made of such system. The second section of the paper delves into the stand taken by the ATLAS group as far as foreign language learning methodologies are concerned; here, the main emphasis is on the enhancement of oral skills, since they are the main concern of the face-to-face (F2F) sessions, apart from reinforcing the online work students perform. The paper ends with a description of the F2F sessions per se, so as to finish drawing the whole blended sequence.

[1] http://atlas.uned.es/inter/

[2] The I-Agent Project is funded by the Spanish Ministry of Education (grant number FFI2008-06030).

E. Martín-Monje (✉) • N. Talaván
Departamento de Filologías Extranjeras y sus Lingüísticas, Universidad Nacional de Educación a Distancia (UNED), Madrid, Spain
e-mail: emartin@flog.uned.es; ntalavan@flog.uned.es

E. Bárcena et al. (eds.), *Languages for Specific Purposes in the Digital Era*, Educational Linguistics 19, DOI 10.1007/978-3-319-02222-2_3,

3.2 Blended Learning: State of the Art

The term "blended learning" (BL henceforth) has been in use for a long time, mainly in the context of business, referred to an employee who is working full time and at the same time following some training programme (Barrett and Sharma 2007). Such training courses are normally hosted in an online platform and have been much favoured by business companies, since they tend to reduce costs: employees who enrol in BL training programmes do not need time off work to attend a training session, since all that can be done out of working hours, at a time and place which is convenient for them.

Many of the benefits described above can be applied to the context of foreign language learning. In that field, BL indicates various forms of teaching and learning, but it generally refers to a course in which students attend classes and also have some support through a virtual learning environment.

Sharma (2010), however, opens up the scope of BL and offers some more options in the definition of this concept:

- The combination of a number of technologies, such as e-mail, chat or internet telephone, all of them in an e-learning environment. In this model there are no F2F language classes.
- The combination of different methodologies, from "transmission" to "constructivist" pedagogic approaches, including task-based learning.
- The combination of F2F and online teaching. This is probably the most extended definition of the term. F2F language lessons would be identified with "traditional learning" and the online part would be delivered through a Virtual Learning Environment (VLE) such as Blackboard, LAMS or Moodle.

This last model is the most relevant one for the ATLAS research group, which the authors of this article belong to, since it coincides with the current project this research group has undertaken. Along these lines Claypole (2010: 26) offers a more conclusive definition of BL than those of Sharma. According to him, BL is "the integrated use of human and electronic delivery platforms and communication techniques, tailored or adapted to suit the needs of the learner and the capabilities of the teacher."

Both Claypole (2010) and Sharma (2010) have thus conceptualised BL as a methodology in which a teacher delivers a F2F lesson and then organizes some follow-up activities or tasks in the VLE to reinforce and extend the learning that has taken place in the class. However, the ATLAS research group has taken an innovative approach and put forward I-AGENT, a Computer Assisted Language Learning system incorporating Artificial Intelligence techniques (ICALL) which encourages exactly the opposite process: learning takes place firstly in the VLE and is reinforced and expanded afterwards, in the subsequent F2F session. This means a novel approach to BL in language teaching and learning in the context of English for Specific Purposes (ESP).

The combination of F2F sessions and distance learning is not new in ESP or foreign languages in general. It has been used since the beginning of Computer

Assisted Language Learning (CALL) in the 1960s (Barrett and Sharma 2007; Claypole 2010; Hubbard 2009; Levy 1997; Neumeier 2005), when teachers started to combine e-learning and traditional classes. Universities specialized in distance learning, such as the Spanish National University for Distance Learning (UNED) have had this methodology as a trademark for decades.

Distance learning or, more specifically, e-learning and F2F learning have their own distinctive features, as it is shown in Table 3.1 below.

Foreign language instructors and researchers need to be aware of all this and aim in their practice towards what Bax calls "normalisation":

> [T]he stage when a technology is invisible, hardly even recognised as a technology, taken for granted in everyday life. [...] [O]ne criterion of CALL's successful integration into language learning will be that it ceases to exist as a separate concept and field for discussion. CALL practitioners should be aiming at their own extinction (2003: 23).

As Bax (2003, 2011), Chambers and Bax (2006) rightly points out, CALL has not reached that stage yet, but is making steady progress in that direction and a significant contributing factor has been the use of BL in language teaching and learning.

One of the main advances in CALL in the turn of the century has been the appearance of Adaptive CALL (Chapelle 2007). Adaptive CALL systems are based on the application of Artificial Intelligence (AI) with the purpose of modifying the content of these VLEs according to the students' needs (Chapelle 2007; Felix 2008; Levy and Stockwell 2006). A substantial part of the research done in this field is aimed at solving problems normally associated with distance learning, making it more interactive and attempting to control the progress of each and every student individually (Pancorbo et al. 2005). This is the framework within which the ATLAS research group is currently working, taking a multi-disciplinary approach based on Applied Linguistics,

Table 3.1 Differences between e-learning and F2F learning

E-learning	Face-to-face learning
It allows students to learn at their own pace	It has a fixed starting point in the learning process and the student must adjust to it
Is based on the concept of "just-in-time training"	The student receives knowledge passively. This should trigger innovative, critical attitudes in him/her
One online application can be enough to cater for a larger number of students in a course	It relies mostly on printed materials and the teacher as main source of information
It allows for collaborative learning among students	The learning process and communication are mainly between teacher and student
The contents are interactive, and so is the communication between teacher and students and among students themselves	It is not necessarily interactive
It allows for both individual and group teaching and learning	There is mainly group teaching and learning
There is flexibility in the time and place allocated for learning	It takes place in a fixed time and place

Based on López Meneses (2008: 170)

Pedagogy and Computer Science in order to develop an intelligent, adaptive, generic English tutor, I-AGENT with a BL methodology which combines F2F learning and the use of Moodle as Learning Management System (LMS) (see Godwin-Jones 2012 for an insightful study on LMS and expanding pedagogy in online learning).

3.3 Moodle as a Learning Management System

When analysing BL and the use of LMS for teaching and learning, it is important to pay attention to technical features, but it is even more relevant to reflect on the underlying theoretical framework and the pedagogy that is behind them. There are three core learning theories that have influenced the development of e-learning in general and have led to the creation of LMS such as Moodle: Behaviourism, Cognitivism and Constructivism (Martín-Monje 2010). The first two were the main learning theories for most of the past century, but in the last decades of the 1900s constructivist theories took over: "The first significant steps in modelling instructional design were based upon behaviourist psychology. This was followed in the 1960s and 1970s by cognitive psychology culminating with the third and fourth edition of "The conditions of learning" (Gagné 1985) [...] The current "rage" is constructivism" (Kirschner 2001: 2–3).

Behaviourism is based on the principle of stimulus and response and deals mainly with behaviours that can be observed. It does not fully consider thinking processes that take place in the learner's mind. Relevant behaviourists are Pavlov, Watson, Thorndike, Skinner, and Gagné (Richards et al. 1992). Skinner's *Verbal Behavior* (1957) deals directly with language learning, seen as a sequence of stimuli, responses and reinforcements: "We have no reason to assume [...] that verbal behavior differs in any fundamental respect from non-verbal behavior, or that any new principles must be invoked to account for it" (1957: 10).

Cognitivism, on the contrary, does not consider humans mere animals which respond to environmental stimuli. According to this approach, people are rational beings, who require active participation in order to learn, and much of human behaviour can be understood precisely in terms of how people acquire, structure, store and use knowledge (Neisser 1967). Following the cognitive approach, language learning is regarded as an active practice in which the student builds meaning out of what is perceived by the senses (Suharno 2010). Relevant cognitive authors are Dewey, Piaget, Vygotsky or Gagné, and this theory has played an important role in the development of instructional design.

Constructivism is the learning theory on which Moodle is based. It is founded on the premise that students acquire knowledge through their personal interpretation of the learning process and their own previous knowledge and beliefs. Last century Piaget established its founding principles (1980: 377):

> Fifty years of experience have taught us that knowledge does not result from a mere recording of observations without a structuring activity on the part of the subject. Nor do any a priori or innate cognitive structures exist in man; the functioning of intelligence alone

> is hereditary and creates structures only through an organization of successive actions performed on objects. Consequently, an epistemology conforming to the data of psychogenesis could be neither empiricist nor preformationist, but could consist only of a constructivism, with a continual elaboration of new operations and structures.

Papert, one of the pioneers of AI, who worked with Piaget in the 1950s and 1960s, developed a variant which he called Constructionism (1991: 1):

> Constructionism – the N word as opposed to the V word – shares Constructivism's connotation of learning as 'building knowledge structures' irrespective of the circumstances of the learning. It then adds the idea that this happens especially felicitously in a context where the learner is consciously engaged in constructing a public entity, whether it's a sand castle on the beach or a theory of the universe.

Dougiamas, creator and main developer of Moodle, has extensively researched on the principles of Constructivism and Constructionism, as can be seen in *A Journey into Constructivism* (1998). The author looks at the distinctive features of both and also differentiates several types of Constructivism (trivial, radical, social, cultural and critical). It is Social Constructivism that is more relevant for LMS such as Moodle, since it states that learning takes place through interaction with others, it should never be an individual process. It is in this context of social constructivism that VLEs or LMS such as Moodle started gradually to be developed (Kim 2001; Prefume 2007; Rice 2006).

3.3.1 Main Characteristics

The definition and classification of VLEs differ from author to author. The most common one is the distinction between Content Management Systems (CMS) and Learning Management Systems (LMS). However, in the United Kingdom and some other European countries it is more common to use the term VLE referred to CMS and Managed Learning Environment (MLE) as a synonym for LMS (BECTA 2004; Bent 2001). In this paper the authors have opted for the dichotomy CMS/LMS.

A CMS is an online management system created to facilitate the publication of content on a website. It allows an unlimited number of users, subject to authorization by the administrator, without any previous technical experience. The main features of a CMS include: web publishing, indexing, review, search and retrieval of information (De la Torre 2005).

An LMS, however, goes beyond the features of any CMS, since it also manages all learning activities: it registers users, helps organise courses, stores data about participants, allows tracking of results, etc. Some of the most popular LMS are WebCT and Blackboard, but Moodle has taken over in the past decade, because of its low cost. It is open source software (http://www.opensource.org/), which means that it allows users to copy, modify or distribute the content under certain rules (Cobo and Pardo 2007; Zapata 2008).

The name "Moodle" is an acronym for "Modular Object-Oriented Dynamic Learning Environment". As LMS, its main characteristics can be classified into four different categories (curriculum design, discussion and communication, performance assessment and course administration), as described in Fig. 3.1 (Tsang et al. 2007: 221).

Moodle appeared in the 1990s, when Dougiamas worked for the commercial LMS WebCT. He released Moodle 1.0 some years later, in 2002, only for some small groups at university level (www.moodle.org). Successive versions swiftly followed, with the latest one, Moodle 2.0, released at the end of 2010. This is the version that has been extended for I-AGENT, the project on which the ATLAS research group is currently working.

3.3.2 Moodle and Computer-Assisted Language Learning

It is a well known fact that Moodle is not designed specifically for language learning, but it has certain features that make it completely adequate for CALL, especially for collaborative work (Brandl 2005; Martín-Monje 2010; Mougalian and Salazar 2005).

CALL-specific software has been often criticised for its behaviourist approach, being mostly based on drilling activities that do not differ much from Skinner's stimulus – response experiments. This is why the trend is now to have a constructivist approach when creating virtual learning environments for language learning.

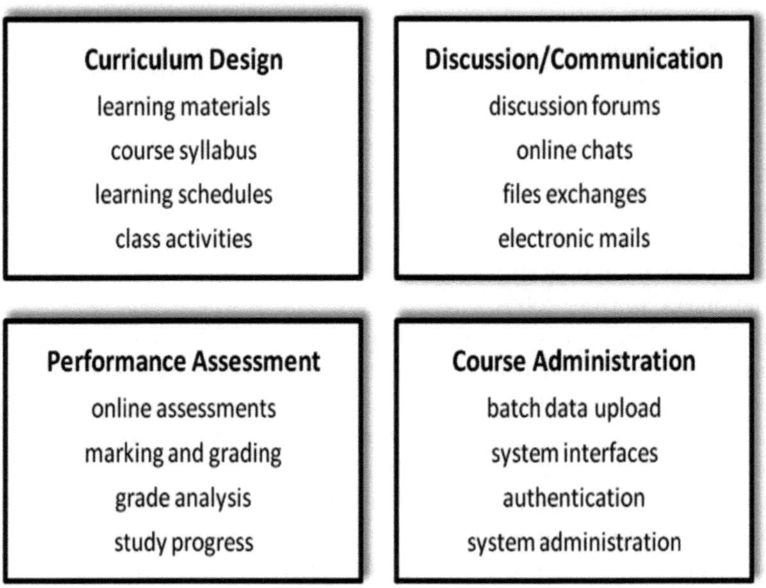

Fig. 3.1 Main characteristics of LMS

According to Chapelle (2001), the main objective of the implementation of CALL in language teaching is to add a communicative context and encourage social interaction among students. Furthermore, technology should contribute to teaching and learning, but not substitute the role of the teacher. These premises fit perfectly well with BL methodology and the use of Moodle as LMS, as this software allows for the creation of a virtual learning environment with a wide range of tools that favour interaction (forums, chat, wikis, instant messaging, workshops, surveys, etc.) (Campos 2007; Gisbert et al. 2007; Lara and Duart 2005; Scagnoli 2001). It also supports the use of the target language in different ways:

- The language of the virtual environment can be specified and set up accordingly.
- Computer-mediated communication (CMC) is made easy and accessible, both in a synchronous and asynchronous way through chat and forums, for example.
- There are different opportunities for collaborative work: wikis, workshops, language negotiation, and peer-marking.

Numerous organisations have chosen Moodle as their LMS, even for language courses (Molist 2008). One of the largest ones is The Open University, from United Kingdom, which started using Moodle in 2006 (www.open.ac.uk). However, up to now, there have been few initiatives focusing on language learning exclusively (Robb 2004). One of the most interesting ones is the COVCELL (Cohort-Oriented Virtual Campus for Effective Language Learning) project, coordinated by the University of Iceland, Humboldt University in Berlin (Germany), Ca' Foscari University in Venice (Italy) and the University of the Basque Country (Spain).

COVCELL (www.covcell.org) is a Socrates-Minerva European project that was developed from 2005 until 2007, with the aim of setting up a virtual environment in which students could interact in a foreign language and practise all skills (listening, reading, speaking, writing). It also intended to analyse the use of BL methodology and the flaws and/or needs of Moodle in such a context, in order to develop its features specifically for CALL. Their grant finished 4 years ago, but the project has continued in www.moodle.org under the heading "Moodle for Language Teaching". The authors developed several tools for language teaching with Moodle, some explicitly for the improvement of oral skills: "Videochat" to enhance synchronic oral interaction, or "Recording of Audio for Evaluation", which enables oral online recording and marking of students' work. Probably one of the most original tools developed by COVCELL is "Whiteboard", which makes it possible to give visual explanations to students as if they were in a F2F context.

3.4 Set-Up of a Business English Course with Moodle: I-AGENT

At the beginning of the current project developed by the ATLAS research group, I-AGENT, the decision was made to use a platform that is well known in the e-learning community and students may already be familiar with (Read et al. 2011). The LMS selected initially was LAMS (Learning Activity Management System), which features several distinctive elements that made it appropriate for I-AGENT (Dalziel 2003; Read et al. 2011):

1. Its design and collaborative learning activities: it provides teachers with a visual authoring environment for creating sequences.
2. Simplicity of use: it allows teachers to reflect on their own teaching activities.
3. Greater degree of integration of students: students are more willing to participate and discuss ideas through LAMS than in an open classroom.
4. Appropriateness for the students' profile the current research at the ATLAS group is aimed at: adults who work or will work in a business environment and with interest in learning Business English.
5. LAMS can be integrated with other Virtual Learning environments: Moodle, Sakai, WebCT, etc.

As the ATLAS research group made progress in the I-AGENT system, it became evident that LAMS would better fit as a module within a different LMS. Moodle 2.0 had just been released and it seemed to be "an ideal e-Learning platform for this project since access to the overall student progress and results is a lot more feasible than from LAMS" (Read et al. 2011: 136).

3.4.1 Comparative Analysis with Other LMS for the Purpose of a Specialized English Course

Cole (2005) has investigated and compared the main features of the three main open source/commercial LMS, which are Blackboard, WebCT (both commercial) and Moodle, as specified in Table 3.2:

Table 3.2 LMS feature comparison

Feature	Blackboard	WebCT	Moodle
Upload and share documents	Yes	Yes	Yes
Create content online in HTML	No	Yes	Yes
Online discussions	Yes	Yes	Yes
Grade discussions/participation	No	Yes	Yes
Online chat	Yes	Yes	Yes
Student peer review	No	No	Yes
Online quizzes/survey	Yes	Yes	Yes
Online gradebook	Yes	Yes	Yes
Student submission of documents	Yes	Yes	Yes
Self-assessment of submission	No	No	Yes
Student workgroups	Yes	Yes	Yes
Lessons with paths	Yes	Yes	Yes
Student journals	No	No	Yes
Embedded glossary	No	No	Yes

Adapted from Cole (2005: 6)

Therefore, Moodle is much more versatile than Blackboard and WebCT. It allows student peer review, self-assessment, student journals and embedded glossaries, which is something that neither Blackboard nor WebCT permit. Furthermore, Dougiamas, the creator of Moodle, puts much emphasis on collaborative work with Moodle, which is keystone for a constructivist approach to teaching and learning. All this has been taken even further with the release of Moodle 2.0 in November 2010 (www.moodle.org).

3.4.2 I-AGENT Business English Online

One of the strengths of I-AGENT is what lays at the core of the present paper: the way it integrates collaborative work via Moodle with F2F classes. This BL is a keystone in the project, since students benefit from the flexibility provided by the LMS but also get the support of their instructor, who reinforces their online learning and gives them feedback on their open activities, such as written and oral production. This is precisely one of its main innovations, as it has been previously stated, since students access materials in the VLE first and then have their F2F class (whereas in other BL courses the sequence is usually the opposite: F2F class first and VLE materials after, as support material).

I-AGENT has been used for an ESP course (Business English) for A2 students (according to the Common European Framework for Languages, Council of Europe 2001). It is intended to last a semester, covering 125 teaching hours, that is, five ECTS (European Credit Transfer System) credits. There are a total of nine units that follow a structure which builds on the practice of the different skills from a sequenced task-based viewpoint.

The sequence in every unit is defined by the course teacher and represented as part of a Web Ontology Language (OWL) network in the I-AGENT AI module. Hence, as a student finishes an activity, the results are transferred to the AI module which selects the next activity, adapting the material selection to the student's progress. This flexibility provides each student with the additional support they arguably require to overcome individual weaknesses. Such an approach is said to "scaffold" the learning process (Bárcena and Read 2003).

Figure 3.2 shows an example of one of the multiple-choice online quizzes included in the units at the listening comprehension section:

After this Moodle stage comes the first F2F class, to be followed by the grammar content practised online, which is organised in three stages, with the possibility of extended grammatical input. An example of this phase can be seen in Fig. 3.3.

The grammar section follows a systemic functional approach and comprises practical theory and functional tasks. The student's work here is reinforced in the second F2F class through examples, questions and answers, games, role-plays, etc. Then, the following part of the online unit covers the cultural, socio-linguistic aspects, looking at intercultural communication related to Business English and

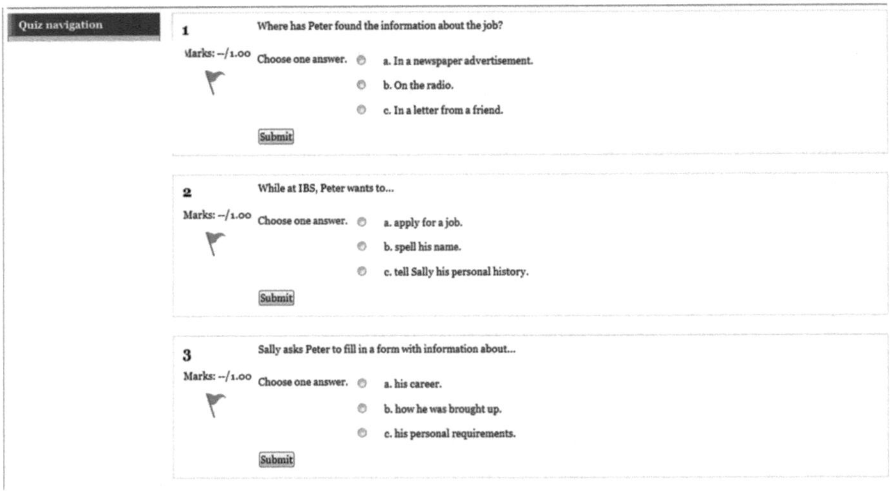

Fig. 3.2 Example of online activity

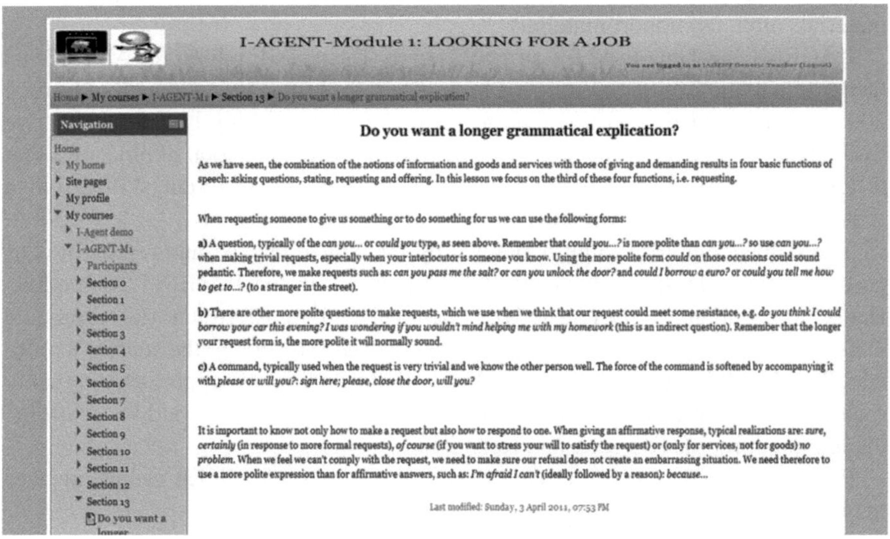

Fig. 3.3 Example of online grammar content

through multimedia material, as shown in Fig. 3.4. Once the third F2F class (based on cultural items and general review) is taken, students face the end of the online unit, with some activities on written production and interaction, all of which is to be completed and rounded up in the final F2F session.

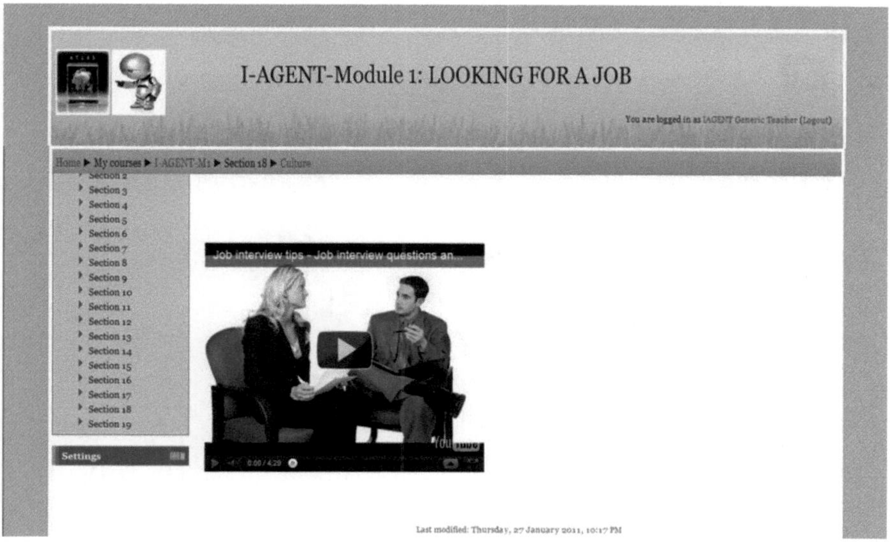

Fig. 3.4 Example of online culture content

I-AGENT is, therefore, a true example of BL, since it carefully combines F2F and online work. It should be mentioned, though, that this fixed sequencing of activities does not mean that all students have to follow it in the same way or exactly at the same time. Another of the strengths of this project is its adaptive nature (Read et al. 2011: 137):

> [E]ach student will be presented the resources and activities in an order depending on the way in which s/he has undertaken the work to date. As errors are committed then a cognitive scaffolding mechanism adapts the presentation of the materials to include additional work as required.

A special effort has been made to create an attractive interface for students when accessing their I-AGENT course (see Fig. 3.5). It has all the common elements and features of a Moodle course: a central block with the course contents, thematically organised, a navigation block on the left, in order to be able to find the various sections in the units in an easy, intuitive way, and a calendar that highlights important dates (deadlines for tasks, calendar for the different units, etc.), plus an online English dictionary, where students can easily check the meaning of unknown words. It also allows to see which participants are online and if they have received any message from the teacher or the other course-mates, making it easier to keep in touch in this online, distance learning environment.

Now the online part has been described, it cannot be forgotten that the system included in I-AGENT is an integration of online and F2F work, where the sequence becomes more intricate yet extremely thorough and practical. The following Fig. 3.6 shows such blended sequence; the F2F part is to be explained in the paragraphs to come.

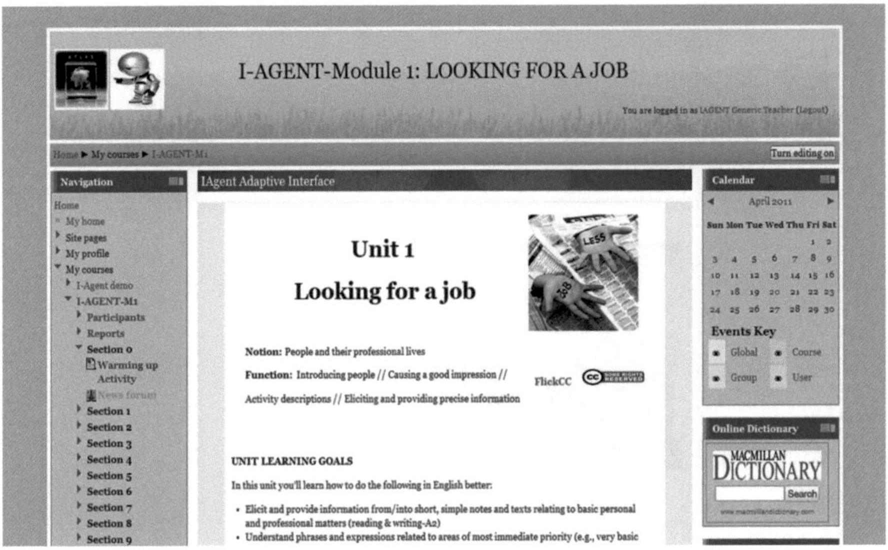

Fig. 3.5 I-AGENT interface in Moodle

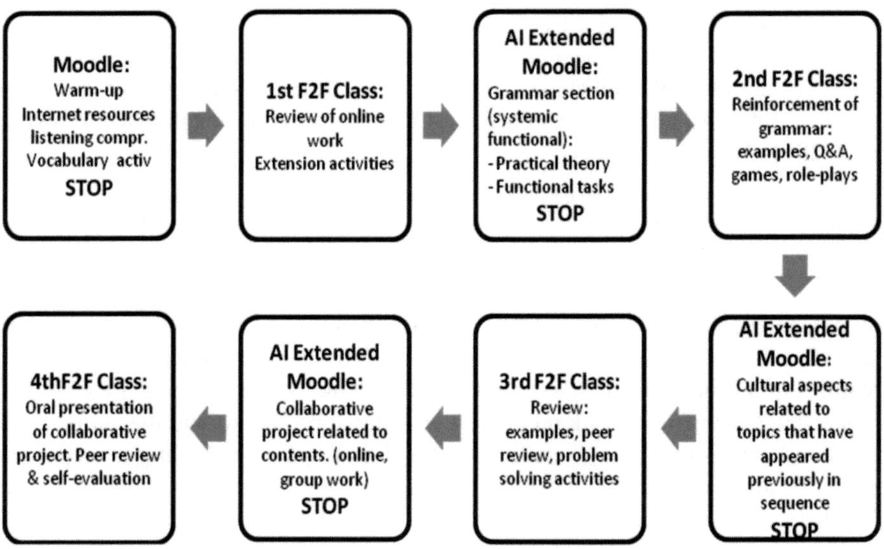

Fig. 3.6 An example sequence of I-AGENT Business English course

3.5 Foreign Language Methodology Applied to I-AGENT

The value of second language (L2 henceforth) instruction has not often been so obvious as it is in other educational contexts (Sharwood 1994). In fact, after centuries of systematic research on foreign language education, the 'golden method' that may guarantee an efficient acquisition for every single student is still to arise. Fortunately, however, every method has something valuable to profit from (Steinberg 2001: 216):

> No method is a total failure because in all methods, students are exposed to the data of a second language and are given the opportunity to learn the language. However, to the disappointment of all, there is no magic method [...] Still, teachers can do much to make the experience for the learner rewarding and enjoyable whatever method is employed [...] A teacher who can afford the luxury of selecting a method might well consider putting together a personal method of second-language teaching [...] Most methods will have some features which can be of benefit to the language learner.

In this sense, at the end of the twentieth century, language teaching was no longer conceptualized in terms of a single undifferentiated methodological prescription (Carter and Nunan 2007; Stern 1997). In order to adapt foreign language education to the great variety of situations in which it can take place, the multiple types of students, contexts and motivations, it is necessary to go beyond the idea of method and create broader and more flexible approaches, which may provide a greater degree of adaptability. Thus, while nowadays some authors opt for a particular method (such as the communicative approach or the action-based approach[3]), others adapt to the modern eclectic or integrative tendencies (Brown 2007).

Hence, it can be said that the twenty-first century takes an integrative viewpoint on foreign language learning, once it has become evident that a single method or approach cannot be applied to every single educational context. A clear instance of this type of attitudes is the so-called Post-method, a theory based on the idea that methodology is a creative, exploratory and dynamic process that restarts every time the teacher interacts with a new group of students (Richards 2001). The Post-method aims at studying the effective and functional nature of the L2 learning-teaching process. One of the main advocators of this stance is Kumaravadivelu (2005), an author who defines this condition as a set of strategies to advance a context-sensitive, location-specific pedagogy based on a true understanding of local linguistic, socio-cultural, and political particularities. The idea is to give the situational context (i.e. the corresponding educational situation in each case) the appropriate relevance it deserves. This change will determine, accordingly, the strategies to be used on each occasion. Within this framework, Kumaravadivelu (ibid.: 173) suggests in three levels of pedagogical division within the Post-method: particularity, practicality and possibility:

> The first deals with teaching context sensitivity such as people, local knowledge, physical settings, course and institution nature, time, and teaching resources. The second encourages language teachers to "theorize what they practice and practice what they theorize". The last criterion pertains to macro-social factors such as institutional, social, economic, cultural, and political environments which shape identity formation and social transformation.

On the whole, all these ideas encourage teachers to go beyond methods and admit the inexistence of the perfect one. A weakness of this trend, though, is that it provides pedagogical concepts that are merely theoretical or philosophical. In this

[3] See Nunan (2000), Richards and Rodgers (2001), or Rosen and Varela (2009).

sense, readers and L2 teachers in particular have to make a great effort to put such ideas into practice. In this line of thought, De Bot et al. (2005: 86) point towards the emergence of a new sort of mixed teaching:

> Whereas the Grammar-Translation method consisted of mostly explicit focus on forms and the Audio-Lingual method on implicit focus on forms, the Communicative Language Teaching approach focused especially on meaningful communication. But over the last decades it has become clear that providing a mixture of meaningful input and some implicit or explicit instruction on form may be the most effective in teaching an L2.

No matter what name this integrative and eclectic form of instruction receives, it is becoming increasingly extended in L2 didactics and is the one adopted for I-AGENT. First of all, I-AGENT makes use of BL, as it has been pointed out throughout this article, so a unique approach would have hardly suited. Secondly, it is not the type of BL that has traditionally been used, where CALL lessons support and/or accompany F2F instruction, but the other way round: F2F lessons support and accompany the work performed in Moodle. Therefore, no predefined method can really apply. Furthermore, one of the main reasons behind the choice of this new type of BL is the need to cover a traditionally criticized drawback in the field of CALL: the shortage of tools and opportunities to practice oral skills. These skills involve a very important element of negotiation that is still quite impossible to integrate in CALL systems in a realistic way. Consequently, what we find here is a totally new situational context in L2 educational terms, so the approach needs to be adapted to this new setting accordingly.

3.5.1 The Development of Oral Skills

As it has been mentioned above, a major element of concern in the design of the F2F lessons that accompany I-AGENT has been the practice of oral skills, both in terms of Listening Comprehension (LC) and Oral Production (OP). It could be said that these two skills present a series of aspects that hinder research, given the fact that they are both rather subjective, highly context-dependent and difficult to analyze, study, understand, and be efficiently taught. However, they are the most necessary ones when it comes to perform real communicative exchanges with other speakers in the *real world*; they are the pillars of real life communication, as well as one of the aspects students usually find most difficult to develop.

LC is a very relevant skill in L2, since no less than 45 % of our communication time is devoted to listening (Buck 2001). Besides, it is a very complex skill, where different processes (neurological, linguistic, pragmatic and psycholinguistic) take place in the individual when he/she faces the understanding of an oral text. Defining LC is not easy because it is an intangible mental action. Besides, it is a very subjective process: when a particular person builds the global meaning of an oral text, this is influenced by multiple factors relative to the person building the message, the moment when it is produced, the type of text used, and the situation where it is inserted.

It should be noted that LC has been neglected in foreign language education for many years, given this intrinsic complexity that makes it a very difficult skill to teach and research. Likewise, many educators have avoided devoting too much time to it in class; firstly, because resources and information on how to enhance LC are scarce, and secondly, because most of the materials available for LC just test it instead of teaching it. Fortunately, this situation has improved in the last decades thanks to the work of several authors (Brown 1995; Buck 2001; Rost 2002), who have claimed its relevance, analyzed its components thoroughly, and suggested different types of strategies for its proper acquisition.

In terms of CALL, LC is usually practiced in a similar way: in an assessment-based mode. Audio texts or video clips are usually provided online accompanied by multiple choice questions that merely assess comprehension. The teaching of specific skills that may allow the learner to enhance the global skill of LC per se (such as summarizing, repetition, humor, transfer, personal rewarding, etc.) is difficult to perform automatically, given the degree of individual subjectivity involved in all of them; thus, CALL does not seem the most suitable niche for their practice.

Turning now to OP, traditional CALL speaking practice often takes the form of drills in which the system asks a question and the student gives an answer. The question and the answer are structured and predictable, and often there is only one correct, predetermined answer. In contrast, the purpose of real communication is to accomplish an actual task, where participants must manage uncertainty about what the other person will say. Authentic communication involves, then, an information gap in which each participant has information that the other does not have. In addition, in order to achieve their purpose, participants may have to clarify their meaning or ask for confirmation of their own understanding and there is no machine capable of achieving this yet.

Moreover, one of the main differences between speech and writing is that we do not usually speak using sentences but the so-called "idea units" (Luoma 2004: 12). That is to say, we speak with short phrases or clauses, joined or not by conjunctions, structured around a much simpler grammar than that of the written language. When we speak, we need to communicate ideas that the listeners need to understand in real time; thus, the parameters of the listeners' working memory need to be born in mind, and that is why idea units do not usually last longer than 7 s and are marked by little pauses and/or hesitation markers. This is the structure of unplanned speech, which is the one teachers should be more concerned about when practicing speaking skills with their students. The problem is that, being so context-dependent (and listener-dependent), CALL systems still have a long way to go in terms of both AI and Natural Language Processing, in order to have ready available systems where real OP practice can be produced.

Unfortunately, OP could be said to be the least studied Foreign Language Learning (henceforth, FLL) skill (even less researched than LC), so many times teachers and materials developers feel somewhat at a loss when attempting to prepare lessons where speaking is to be enhanced. According to Hughes (2002: 6), "[o] ne of the central difficulties inherent in the study of speaking is that it overlaps with a considerable number of other areas and activities".

Cultural factors, discourse elements, intelligibility issues, grammar structures, and many other areas play a role in the realm of speaking. In the last decade, several attempts have been made so as to provide OP in FLL with a niche of its own right (Nation and Newton 2008; Folse 2006; Luoma 2004; Hughes 2002, among others), so this can offer a more consistent point of departure for teachers and materials developers, who should, in turn, actually focus on finding their own way within a series of general guidelines provided by researchers; that is very much in line with the Post-method ideas:

> We should be less concerned with stipulating what methods to follow and much more concerned with discovering what effective teachers actually do. Resisting the *deprofessionalizing* effect of some slavish adherence to methods frees us and teachers more generally to examine what the practices of effective language teaching might be
> (Candlin and Mercer 2001: 5).

Hence, within the Post-method, oral skills are supposed to receive the interest they deserve, since teachers can apply their own strategies and educational choices to the needs and goals of their corresponding group of students. Although a real communicative context is nearly impossible to reproduce in the class, one can attempt to get as close as possible to reality through communicative activities, content-based, task-based and similar tasks; but it is still hard to reproduce such framework in CALL. This is why the authors have aimed at covering that drawback through this new type of BL, where the class supports the online work, especially in terms of oral skills, as will be described in the following section.

3.6 Face-to-Face Tasks: The Other Half of I-AGENT

Each I-AGENT lesson is made up of four F2F sessions, just as it was described in Fig. 3.6. Each class is directly related to the previous Moodle session in different ways; depending on the point of the lesson it is situated. Be it as it may, the four classes are mainly focused on the improvement of both LC and OP, basically because of the previously mentioned difficulty in the development of such skills within the realm of CALL.

All F2F sessions follow a similar general structure, starting with a warm-up, following with the main topic to review from the online session (be it listening exercises, vocabulary, grammar, culture, or collaborative work), and finishing up with a role-play (this last item is not included in the fourth lesson, as it will be explained below) and optional teacher's feedback and/or students' discussion.

It should be noted that there is a difference between teaching OP or LC and using LC and OP to teach; "[w]hereas a teacher or materials writers may feel some confidence with stable written forms and genres […], the notion of how spoken genres are structured and what forms are most typical of them is difficult to establish" (Hughes 2002: 7). In these F2F classes that accompany and support the work performed by students in Moodle, both things have been used: teaching oral skills and using oral skills to teach. In this section, every class (the four of them) will be dealt with individually, based on the information included in the teacher's handouts that have been created ad hoc for each and single class of every unit. Hence, every aspect can be clearly understood and identified.

The warm-up section of the first class of every unit starts connecting the class to the contents studied online. Then, there is an oral comprehension task (20 min) that complements the oral comprehension practice performed online, since it deals with the same oral text. However, there are elements here that cannot be mirrored online in any way whatsoever. Rost (2002: 109) affirms that "participation in verbal interactions following a listening experience offers the learner the opportunity to follow-up on new words and structures" more easily, and that is something that could only be done online if a videoconference followed a listening experience; this is not usually the case and it is rather hard to organize in distant contexts. In this sense, it should be noted that oral reception skills do not only include listening, but interaction, a key element in language acquisition in general and a primary means of oral reception skills development, given the negotiation element involved in communication, especially in terms of oral exchanges. Once again, interaction in these terms within CALL is hardly ever possible.

This first class continues with a vocabulary section (20 min) that reinforces both the previous listening task and the vocabulary learned online, and is always connected with a particular area of ESP. After this, the class proposes a role-play exercise (30 min) based on the contents practiced throughout the session; it is not "speech in isolation", but "speech in context" (Hughes 2002: 57), the one that has been the focus of the whole class. The teacher's handout gives a series of directions in that regard, as can be read in Table 3.3.

The class finishes with a 10 min section of optional teacher's feedback and/students' discussion where a written homework is suggested; for example, 'make a list of foreign dishes and explain what they contain and how they are cooked', in unit 5.

The second class of every unit starts, once again, with a warm-up. There, teachers and students exchange questions and answers related to the grammar section that has been the focus of the previous online work undertaken at home. After that, there is a 20-min review and explanation under demand of the grammar points studied, where the teacher is prompted to look for examples of the different structures learned and to ask for possible problems that students may have encountered when trying to understand the corresponding grammar section. This is followed by another 20-min grammar practice in pairs with two pre-established exercises that are supposed to confirm and reinforce the previous learning process and review, as can be seen in Table 3.4.

The last section of the second class contains a 35-min role play (15 min for preparation and 20 for performance), where grammar items are used in functional contexts; it should be noted that grammatical competence is not regarded in the traditional sense anymore in recent FLL studies, but as: "the ability to understand and express meaning by producing and recognizing well-formed phrases and sentences in accordance with these principles (as opposed to memorizing and reproducing them as fixed formulae)" (Council of Europe 2001: 113). As a final optional point, and when time allows for it, the class may contain a small section (10 min top) of optional teacher's feedback and/or students' discussion.

Table 3.3 Role-play example (first class) from unit 2

Role Play
Preparation (15 min) *In groups of 4. Take the following picture; they are some of Peter's new mates. Choose one of the characters and that will be you. You are in a meeting where you have to introduce yourselves, and talk about your pluses and minuses, both physically and psychologically. The rest can ask you questions or discuss whatever you say. It is a group discussion combined with monologues*
 Role-play performance (15 min) Everybody should equally collaborate in the conversation. The situation should last 5 min approximately. This is a speaking exercise so you won't be allowed to read any notes. Improvisation is encouraged. Mind your pronunciation and your intonation and…HAVE A GOOD TIME!! ☺

Table 3.4 Grammar practice example (second class) from unit 1

Grammar exercises (20 min)

In pairs

Choose the most appropriate answer for expressing the idea specified in parentheses

1. __________ I speak to Mr. Smith, please? (Formal polite request)

(a) Can	(b) May	(c) Would	(d) Would you mind if

2. __________ you open the window, please? It's hot in here. (Polite request)

(a) Could	(b) Couldn't	(c) Won't	(d) Wouldn't

3. __________ closing the window, please? It's cold in here. (Polite request)

(a) Could you	(b) Will you	(c) Would you	(d) Would you mind

[…]

Answers

1-b	2-a	3-d	4-a	5-a	6-b	7-d	8-a	9-a	10-b

Say sentences to your classmate using the first part of the second conditional structure (If + past simple). Your classmate must end the sentences.

Ex.

- If you got a good job…

- If you had some problems with your computer…

- If you became a Chairperson in your company…

Table 3.5 Warm-up example (third class) from unit 5

Warm up (15 min.)
Questions and answers:
- Have you ever attended a business meal in English?
If so, how did you feel? (confident, at ease, embarrassed, uncomfortable, etc.)
- Did you learn any new words or expressions?
- What nationality were the people you were with?
Have you got any particular (cultural) anecdote to share? (foreign eating habits or tools, rare food...)

Table 3.6 Group work example (third class) from unit 5

Group work (20 min)
In two groups, prepare two menus that contain:
3 starters
6 main courses (include 2 vegetarian options)
3 deserts
Drinks
Group work presentation (20 min)
Each group presents their menu (writing it on the board and explaining choices)
Teacher's feedback

The third class, on the other hand, deals with the main cultural aspects that are practiced in Moodle in the corresponding third section. Table 3.5 shows an example of how the class starts, as usual, with a warm-up (15 min) made up of questions and answers related to the contents practiced online.

The next part of the third class contains a brainstorming exercise/game where grammar and vocabulary are practiced together. This activity takes up around 15 min and it prepares students for the group work that comes right after in the class. An example of this type of work is presented in Table 3.6.

FLL students need to learn how to cooperate effectively both in pairs and in group (Council of Europe 2001) and this type of task cannot still be performed online in any way whatsoever; videoconference would be the only way to achieve this through Moodle but the development of such a communication tool is not powerful enough yet, so as to cope with more than three or four students working well and understanding each other synchronically.

The third class finishes, as usual, with a role-play (20 min), where the main goal is the practice of oral skills (both listening and speaking), and this time contextualized with the help of cultural elements. The existence of this class focused on culture is of great importance, given its high relevance in the realm of communication. If FLL is not contextualized in cultural terms, real language learning does not really take place and a great number of misunderstandings may occur when using the foreign language (Peterson and Coltrane 2003). This type of cultural-based role-play is also hard to be performed online without the support of a real teacher who can monitor, advice and reinforce such a practice. At the end of this F2F class, there is, again, an optional time (10 min top) for teacher and/or students' feedback and/or questions.

Finally, the last class of each unit (the fourth class) is totally focused both on presenting the collaborative work performed online and on self-assessment. It starts with a small warm-up regarding self-assessment (10 min). It continues with the presentation of the groups' collaborative work (15 min per group; 30–60 min total); the groups were previously formed online, and their work was orientated and monitored before this final class. In the end, there is a final peer assessment section (20–30 min).

From a collaborative point of view, it can be noted that the principle of negotiation that is fundamental in the development of oral skills in general (Rost 2002) is taken into consideration at all times in the course of the F2F lessons in I-AGENT, increasingly from the first to the last class, as it has been clearly shown in the previous description.

3.7 Conclusions

All in all, I-AGENT is a complete system that real instructors can use to integrate collaborative online work via Moodle and F2F classroom lessons, where oral skills can be practiced in a natural communicative environment. It could be said to be a real materialization of that "integrated CALL" era that Bax (2003: 23) envisaged and longed for almost a decade ago, where technology could be a tool for learning: normalised, integrated into syllabus and adapted to learners' requirements, where analysis of needs and context would precede decisions about technology.

The introduction and sequencing of activities via the AI module, the careful selection of tasks to be performed and the meditated combination of online and F2F teaching and learning make I-AGENT a unique VLE that takes a step forward in the progress of adaptive CALL and ICALL in general. I-AGENT has been carefully designed so as to fit each and every learner's needs and adapt the course materials to individual progress. The constructivist pedagogical framework ensures students make sound progress while they interact with the teacher and their peers, connecting new learning material to their previous knowledge. The use of Moodle allows a thorough tracking of learners' progress in a flexible way. This avoids one of the main drawbacks of online learning, which may make learners feel they are being left to their own devices. With I-AGENT students are guided through their learning in a non-prescriptive way, giving them the opportunity to make the most of their own, unique path of meaningful language learning.

Apart from giving learners the chance of developing productive and receptive oral skills, the lessons complement, reinforce and help the teacher check the students' work performed online. Furthermore, the instructor, in this context, can also correct the results of open production exercises undertaken by the students, something that would be beyond what can be currently corrected by an ICALL program. Such a BL approach allows students to really profit from the individual and collaborative possibilities offered by Moodle, and it provides them with the support of a real teacher who can help them monitor, supplement and safeguard the benefits of the tasks undertaken on the e-learning platform.

I-AGENT is currently undergoing an evaluation process where students from a Business English group are following the sequence and methodology described in the present paper. The following step, thus, will be the analysis of the data obtained after the evaluation process. Once assessed, the system will probably undergo an expansion in terms of levels (so that it can be applied to advanced, intermediate and beginner students alike) and an adaptation of the software in order to be easily used with handheld devices, looking into the possibilities of mobile learning.

References

Bárcena, E., and T. Read. 2003. Los sistemas de enseñanza de inglés para fines específicos basados en el aprendiente. *Revista Iberoamericana de Educación a Distancia* 6(2): 41–54.

Barrett, B., and P. Sharma. 2007. *Blended learning*. Oxford: Macmillan.

Bax, S. 2003. CALL – Past, present and future. *System* 31: 13–28.

Bax, S. 2011. Normalisation revisited: The effective use of technology in language education. *International Journal of Computer-Assisted Language Learning and Teaching (IJCALLT)* 1(2): 1–15.

Bent, M. 2001. MLE or VLE – Is that the question? http://www.leeds.ac.uk/. Accessed 22 Feb 2013.

Brandl, K. 2005. Are you ready to "Moodle"? *Language Learning & Technology* 9(2): 16–23. http://llt.msu.edu/vol9num2/review1/default.html. Accessed 25 Feb 2013.

British Educational Communications and Technology Agency (BECTA). 2004. What the research says about Virtual Learning Environments in teaching and learning. http://partners.becta.org.uk/upload-dir/downloads/page_ documents/research/wtrs_vles.pdf. Accessed 25 Feb 2011.

Brown, G. 1995. *Speakers, listeners and communication*. New York: Cambridge University Press.

Brown, H. 2007. *Teaching by principles: An interactive approach to language pedagogy*. White Plains: Pearson Education.

Buck, G. 2001. *Assessing listening*. Cambridge: Cambridge University Press.

Campos, V. 2007. Moodle-Quaderns digitals, una herramienta colaborativa. Bits 7. http://espiral.xtec.net/web/index.php?option=com_content&task= view&id=130&Itemid=100. Accessed 25 Feb 2013.

Candlin, C., and N. Mercer. 2001. *English language teaching in its social context: A reader*. New York: Routledge.

Carter, R., and D. Nunan (eds.). 2007. *The Cambridge guide to teaching English to speakers of other languages*. Cambridge: Cambridge University Press.

Chambers, A., and S. Bax. 2006. Making CALL work: Towards normalisation. *System* 34: 465–479.

Chapelle, C. 2001. *Computer applications in second language acquisition*. Cambridge: Cambridge University Press.

Chapelle, C. 2007. Towards adaptive CALL. http://www.public.iastate.edu/~apling/TSLL/5th_2007/proceedings2007/contents.html. Accessed 27 Feb 2013.

Claypole, M. 2010. *Controversies in ELT*. Norderstedt: LinguaBooks.

Cobo, C., and H. Pardo. 2007. Planeta Web 2.0. (Electronic book). http://www.planetaweb2.net/. Accessed 22 Feb 2013.

Cole, J. 2005. *Using Moodle: Teaching with the popular open source course management system*. Sebastopol: O'Reilly Community Press.

Council of Europe. 2001. *Common European framework of reference for languages*. Cambridge: Cambridge University Press.
Dalziel, J. 2003. Implementing learning design: The learning activity management system. In *Interact, integrate, impact: Proceedings of the 20th annual conference of the Australasian Society for Computers in Learning in Tertiary Education (ASCILITE)*, ed. G. Crisp, D. Thiele, I. Scholten, et al., 593–596. Adelaide: ASCILITE.
De Bot, K., W. Lowie, and M. Verspoor. 2005. *Second language acquisition: An advanced resource book*. New York: Routledge.
De la Torre, A. 2005. CMS y LMS. http://www.adelat.org/media/docum/nuke_publico/cms_y_lms.html. Accessed 25 Feb 2013.
Dougiamas, M. 1998. A journey into constructivism. http://dougiamas.com/writing/constructivism.html. Accessed 22 Feb 2013.
Dougiamas, M. 2002. Interpretive analysis of an Internet-based course constructed using a new courseware tool called Moodle. http://dougiamas.com/writing/herdsa2002/. Accessed 25 Feb 2013.
Felix, U. 2008. The unreasonable effectiveness of CALL: What have we learned in two decades of research? *ReCALL* 20(2): 141–161.
Folse, K. 2006. *The art of teaching speaking. Research and pedagogy for the ESL/EFL classroom*. Michigan: University of Michigan Press/ESL.
Gagné, R.M. 1985. *The conditions of learning and theory of instruction*. New York: Holt, Rinehart and Winston.
Gisbert, M., J. Adell, L. Anaya, and R. Rallo. 2007. Entornos de formación presencial virtual y a distancia. http://www.rediris.es/difusion/publicaciones/boletin/40/enfoque1.html. Accessed 25 Feb 2013.
Godwin-Jones, R. 2012. Emerging technologies. Challenging hegemonies in online learning. *Language Learning & Technology* 16(2): 4–13.
Hubbard, P. (ed.). 2009. *Computer-assisted language learning*, vols. I–IV. London/New York: Routledge.
Hughes, R. 2002. *Teaching and researching speaking*. Harlow: Pearson Education.
Kim, B. 2001. Social constructivism. In *Emerging perspectives on learning, teaching, and technology*, ed. M. Orey. http://projects.coe.uga.edu/epltt/. Accessed 13 May 2013.
Kirschner, P. 2001. Using integrated electronic environments for collaborative teaching/learning. *Research dialogue in learning and instruction* 2(1): 1–9. http://www.ou.nl/Docs/Expertise/NELLL/publicaties/Using%20integrated%20electronic%20environments%20for%20collaborative%20teaching%20learning.pdf. Accessed 20 Feb 2013.
Kumaravadivelu, B. 2005. *Understanding language teaching: From method to post-method*. New York: Routledge.
Lara, P., and J.M. Duart. 2005. Gestión de contenidos en el e-learning: acceso y uso de objetos de información como recurso estratégico. *Revista de Universidad y Sociedad del Conocimiento (RUSC)* 2(2). http://www.uoc.edu/rusc/2/2/dt/esp/lara.pdf. Accessed 25 Feb 2013.
Levy, M. 1997. *Computer-assisted language learning: Context and conceptualization*. Oxford: Oxford University Press.
Levy, M., and G. Stockwell. 2006. *CALL dimensions: Options and issues in computer-assisted language learning*. Mahwah: Lawrence Erlbaum.
López Meneses, E. 2008. *Análisis de los modelos didácticos y estrategias de enseñanza en Teleformación: Diseño y experimentación de un instrumento de evaluación de las estrategias de enseñanza de cursos telemáticos de formación universitaria*. PhD dissertation, Universidad de Sevilla.
Luoma, S. 2004. *Assessing speaking*. Cambridge: Cambridge University Press.
Martín-Monje, E. 2010. *Preparación de la PAU de inglés como lengua extranjera con el apoyo del aula virtual de Moodle*. Dissertation, Univeridad nacional de Educación a Distancia (UNED).
Molist, M. 2008. Moodle llena la geografía española de campus virtuales. El País. http://www.elpais.com/articulo/portada/Moodle/llena/geografia/educativa/espanola/campus/virtuales/elpepisupcib/20081204elpcibpor_1/Tes. Accessed 25 Feb 2011. December 4.

Mougalian, C., and A. Salazar. 2005. Moodle, the electronic syllabus, lends itself to PrOCALL. http://faculty.miis.edu/~bcole/CALLme/page2/page9/files/page9_3.pdf]. Accessed 25 Feb 2013.

Nation, I.S.P., and J. Newton. 2008. *Teaching ESL/EFL listening and speaking*. New York: Routledge.

Neisser, U. 1967. *Cognitive psychology*. New York: Appleton-Century-Crofts.

Neumeier, P. 2005. A closer look at blended learning – parameters for designing a blended learning environment for language teaching and learning. *ReCALL: The Journal of EUROCALL* 17(2): 163–178.

Nunan, D. 2000. *Language teaching methodology*. Harlow: Longman.

Pancorbo, J., T. Read, E. Bárcena, and R. Varela. 2005. Diagnosis de los estados de conocimiento en un sistema tutor inteligente. *Revista Iberoamericana de Sistemas, Cibernética e Informática* 2(2). http://www.iiisci.org/Journal/CV$/risci/pdfs/P479745.pdf. Accessed 20 Feb 2013.

Papert, S. 1991. Situating constructionism. In *Constructionism: Research reports and essays, 1985–1990*, ed. I. Harel and P. Seymour, 1–11. Cambridge, MA: Massachusetts Institute of Technology.

Peterson, E., and B. Coltrane. 2003. Culture in second language teaching. *CAL Digest*, EDO-FL-03-09. http://www.cal.org/resources/digest/0309peterson.html. Accessed 21 Sept 2007.

Piaget, J. 1980. The psychogenesis of knowledge and its epistemological significance. In *Language and learning*, ed. M. Piattelli-Palmarini, 377–384. Cambridge, MA: Harvard University Press.

Prefume, Y. 2007. Constructivism in foreign language learning. The Free Library. http://www.thefreelibrary.com/Constructivism+in+foreign+language+learning.-a0165912633. Accessed 12 May 2013.

Read, T., N. Talaván, L. Pomposo, and J. Arús. 2011. Have computers ever assisted language learning? Problems and prospects. In *Technological innovation in the teaching and processing of LSPs: Proceedings of TISLID'10*, ed. N. Talaván, E. Martín-Monje, and F. Palazón, 132–139. Madrid: UNED.

Rice, W. 2006. *Moodle*. Birmingham: Packt Publishing.

Richards, J.C. 2001. Beyond methods. In *English language teaching in its social context*, ed. C.N. Candlin and N. Mercer. London/New York: Routledge.

Richards, J.C., and T.S. Rodgers. 2001. *Approaches and methods in language teaching*. New York: Cambridge University Press.

Richards, J.C., J. Platt, and H. Platt. 1992. *Longman dictionary of language teaching and applied linguistics*. Harlow: Longman.

Robb, T. 2004. Building your own course management system. http://moodle.org/file.php/31/MoodleforESL.doc. Accessed 25 Feb 2013.

Rosen, E., and R. Varela. 2009. *Claves para comprender el Marco común europeo de referencia para las lenguas*. Madrid: Enclave-ELE/CLE International.

Rost, M. 2002. *Teaching and researching listening*. London: Longman.

Scagnoli, N. 2001. El aula virtual: Usos y elementos que la componen. http://students.ed.uiuc.edu/scagnoli/pubs/AulaVirtual.pdf. Accessed 25 Feb 2013.

Sharma, P. 2010. Blended learning. *ELT Journal* 64(4): 456–458.

Sharwood, M. 1994. *Second language learning: Theoretical foundations*. London: Longman.

Skinner, B.F. 1957. *Verbal behavior*. Englewood Cliffs: Prentice-Hall.

Steinberg, D.D. 2001. *Psycholinguistics: Language, mind, and world*. London: Longman.

Stern, H. 1997. *Fundamental concepts of language teaching*. New York: Oxford University Press.

Suharno, S. 2010. Cognitivism and its implication in the second language learning. *Parole* 1: 48–63. http://ejournal.undip.ac.id/index.php/parole/article/view/811/697. Accessed 25 Feb 2013.

Tsang, P., R. Kwan, and R. Fox. 2007. *Enhancing learning through technology*. London: World Scientific Co.

Zapata, M. 2008. Un cuarto de siglo de ayuda pedagógica en ordenadores y en redes. *Quaderns Digitals* 51: 13–32. http://www.quadernsdigitals.net/index.php?accionMenu=hemeroteca. Accessed 25 Feb 2013.

Chapter 4
Student Assessment in the Online Language Learning Materials Developed and Delivered Through the InGenio System

Ana Sevilla-Pavón, Antonio Martínez-Sáez, and José Macario De Siqueira Rocha

4.1 Introduction

Assessment, the "dynamic developmental process which develops and changes as the needs arise and as understanding of the process improves" (Brown and Glasner 2003, preface), is considered as one of the key aspects in education. The importance of assessment derives from both its influence in the way teachers and students address language teaching and learning and the changes it might introduce as far as methodologies, approaches and behaviour of all participants in the language learning process are concerned. The assessment process has a very important and remarkable effect on the way educators and learners face the whole teaching process. Therefore, specific adaptations and also general changes are made and are introduced into the classroom context as well as into the teaching methodologies with a view to facing the final evaluation process in a more efficient manner.

This article focuses on assessment, a specific phase within the whole language learning experience: the assessment process, which is sometimes mistakenly considered as a separate process – e.g. independent from the learning experience – in spite of the fact that assessment is indeed an essential component of language learning which should not be left behind or seen as an independent process. The authors of this paper explore the assessment process of the basic skills tested by the *Cambridge ESOL First Certificate in English Examination* (FCE) and the ways in which the *InGenio* online preparatory materials contribute to the effectiveness and

A. Sevilla-Pavón (✉) • A. Martínez-Sáez
Departamento de Lingüística Aplicada, Universidad Politécnica de Valencia, Valencia, Spain
e-mail: ansepa@upvnet.upv.es; anmarsae@upvnet.upv.es

J.M. De Siqueira Rocha
Departamento de Informática, Universidad Carlos III, Colmenarejo (Madrid), Spain
e-mail: jsiqueir@inf.uc3m.es

E. Bárcena et al. (eds.), *Languages for Specific Purposes in the Digital Era*, Educational Linguistics 19, DOI 10.1007/978-3-319-02222-2_4,

efficiency of this assessment in both student self-assessment and tutor assessment, the two modalities of assessment offered by the most recently developed learning materials within the CAMILLE Research Group (Department of Applied Linguistics) at the Universidad Politécnica de Valencia (UPV): *FCE Online Course* and *FCE Online Tester*. These materials are being published and implemented through the *InGenio* platform, almost a decade after this "web-delivered language-independent authoring tool capable of managing databases on a remote server which allows language specialists to design and publish materials to suit their students' particular needs" (Gimeno Sanz 2010) was developed. The fact that *InGenio* is constantly evolving and integrating improvements proves its maturity and reliability. Indeed, its authoring tool and delivery platform were completed as early as in 2002 and since then a number of online courses and materials have successfully been designed, published and used. One of the main improvements is the development of an online tutoring system and a translation tool to adapt the different *InGenio* courses into any number of source languages. The implementation of the *FCE Online Course* and *Tester*, as it happens with most *InGenio* materials, has been based on the template approach to software authoring (Gimeno Sanz 2002). This approach enables developers and content providers to create different types of exercises and activities by means of the use of predefined templates that integrate video, graphics, audio and text. The system also includes "a content manager which allows subject specialists to create a database from which to share and select materials by organising the multimedia components (learning objects) according to a number of specifications (e.g. language, level, skill, target group, etc.), thus creating a pool of multimedia exercises and resources" (Gimeno Sanz 2010). The authoring tool "automatically converts the contents into learner-ready materials in the form of an online course, delivered via the *InGenio* web-based Learning Environment" (Gimeno Sanz 2010), as in the case of the *InGenio FCE Online Course* and *Tester*.

4.2 General Context and the InGenio Tool

The preparatory materials known as *FCE Online Course* and *Tester* have been designed in an attempt to provide UPV students with all the necessary resources that would enable them not only to practise but also to evaluate and to critically assess the way in which their learning process is taking place. Following that, the students will have to find the most suitable way for each of them to acknowledge their linguistic competence. To this end, the UPV Students are provided with five different options among which they can choose one which would allow them to acknowledge their language level. The first possibility consists of sitting a B2 level exam (according to the levels determined by the Common European Framework of Reference for Languages – CEFRL) co-ordinated by the University's Department of Applied Linguistics. This possibility points out the need to create and develop a course and a tester capable of providing preparation for a general B2 level exam which could either have a similar structure to the *Cambridge First Certificate in English*

Examination (FCE) or a different one. In an attempt to provide the students who decide to choose this option with the necessary resources and materials, the CAMILLE Research Group are already conducting research in order to design and develop an expanded base of B2 level extra resources. The second option would be to validate a language official certificate that the learner either has held previously or will hold in the near future. In any case, this certificate has to be the equivalent to a Vantage level. The third available option is that a number of the subjects which the students are taking as part of their degree are delivered in a foreign language. As for the fourth option, it gives students the possibility to attain and to acknowledge the B2 level of English by means of a stay abroad of at least 3 months, as part of an official exchange or mobility programme in order to finally submit their final year project in a foreign language. Finally, the UPV students can choose to attend a 90-h language course in order to achieve the required level of English (or of another foreign language). It is important to bear in mind that English is the most common foreign language taken at Spanish universities. Since the *First Certificate in English* is one of the certificates that UPV students would be able to use as a means to validate the established linguistic requirements, a group of specialists from the CAMILLE Research Group have set about to design and develop the abovementioned preparatory materials which are going to be eventually delivered through the *InGenio* online authoring tool and content manager.

The authors have also born in mind the general context of the UPV, which presents a technical and non-specifically linguistic learning scenario. This has made language specialists analyse and investigate for years on new ways and techniques that could help to create, promote and implement learning systems aimed at contributing towards making the whole language learning process more dynamic and efficient. It is thought that today's very tighten and intense timetables could encourage students to make use of this kind of online language learning environments as they cannot devote a large amount of time to learning a foreign language in a level equivalent to B2 from the CEFRL (2001), even though this is a compulsory requirement that UPV students need to fulfil in order to be awarded with their grade diploma. These kinds of online language learning environments, which are currently seen as a very useful and attractive channel to foster language practice, learning, and assessment, are aimed not only at providing learners with a means to "access information and course content", but also at offering tools and devices that enable them "to interact and collaborate with other online participants" within a particular course (White 2003, p. 27) or when using other kinds of materials. This contributes towards the enrichment of the whole learning and assessment process.

InGenio, an online authoring tool and content manager funded by the UPV and developed by the CAMILLE Research Group, is the platform being used to create and finally deliver the abovementioned B2 level (CEFRL 2001) materials, on which the authors of this paper are currently working to offer a definitive, though extendable, version of those resources. These materials are now being trialled and will soon be ready to be used by UPV students either autonomously or implemented within the syllabuses of several English courses at the UPV. One of the main advantages offered by the materials provided via *InGenio* is their flexibility, an advantage which allows students to have access to two different modalities of assessment and also to two different learning options, thus enabling a wider range of students with different characteristics and needs to choose and to organise their learning processes in the most convenient way for each of them to obtain better results.

The *InGenio* System is the main tangible result from the *InGenio* Project[1] funded by the UPV. It emerged in the late 1990s when education in general and language learning in particular turned their back to multimedia courseware development on CD-ROM due to the rapid development of the Internet and the emergence of a considerable number of applications intended for pedagogical purposes. The main goal was to create an online tool which could be able to exploit the most recent technological developments in order to deliver flexible, student-centred, electronic language learning environments to support the acquisition of a foreign language (Gimeno Sanz 2009a). As described by Gimeno-Sanz (2008, pp. 93–94):

> The *InGenio* System comprises a web-delivered language-independent authoring tool capable of managing databases on a remote server and allowing teachers from around the world to design and publish materials to suit their students' particular needs. The implementation of the materials is based on the template approach to software authoring, with predefined templates that integrate video, graphics, audio and text. The system includes a "content manager" enabling subject specialists to create a database from which to share and select materials by organising the multimedia components and materials according to a number of specifications (e.g. language, level, skill, target group, etc.), thus creating a pool of multimedia exercises and resources. The authoring tool automatically converts the contents into learner-ready materials in the form of an online course, delivered via the *InGenio* web-based Learning Environment. Lastly, the system incorporates a student assessment utility that allows tutors to supervise student scores, written input and general progress.

The features described above made *InGenio* not only the most appropriate tool for implementing new pedagogically-sound learning materials such as the ones intended to be part of the online preparatory *FCE Course* and *Tester* but also an adequate and efficient tutor-assessment and self-assessment tool. This is possible thanks to the fact that it offers an extremely valuable and dynamic asset in terms of distance education, and it comprises a completely online assessment utility. This utility enables autonomous students to receive feedback and to know their results right after having completed each of the sections within the materials provided. As for the tutor-assessment modality, this tool also allows language teachers or tutors to supervise a learner's performance and provide adequate personalised feedback, especially for those sections which do not comprise exercises or tasks able to be corrected automatically. This learner assessment system has been used for the past seven years at the University to evaluate learners enrolled on an elective subject called Computer-Assisted English (Gimeno-Sanz et al. 2010). The learners enrolled on this subject follow a B1 level (CEFRL 2001) course entitled *Intermediate Online English*.

InGenio is a free tool only requiring user registration. Perhaps more importantly, though, is the fact that the system allows teachers, from any given point in

[1] Several articles have been published extensively describing the system and its functionalities. For a full description see Gimeno Sanz 2008.

the world, to create, adapt and publish materials to suit their students' particular needs (Gimeno Sanz 2009a). In addition, the system also includes a "translation utility" enabling existing courseware to be adapted into any number of source languages and a utility to translate the graphical user interface into any number of languages.

As for the edition and creation of new materials, the *InGenio* authoring tool comprises 15 exercise templates and also two additional templates which allow authors to create or introduce reference materials and glossaries (Gimeno Sanz 2009a). These templates have been designed bearing in mind that they must ensure variety, coherence and consistency when an author is engaged in the process of creating multimedia activities. The main principle followed when designing the templates was that they should be as complete, open and flexible as possible in order to encourage authors to design creative tasks rather than restricting and confining their pedagogical input. The templates that are available allow courseware writers to design exercises ranging from learner observation to learner production in order to practice all four language skills (reading and listening comprehension, and writing and speaking production). These templates include traditional e-learning activities such as multiple choice exercises, gap-filling exercises, reordering exercises, open input exercises, association exercises and vocabulary building. The templates can be used to design exercises and activities deriving from a number of teaching and assessment methodologies. Some templates also permit learners to upload a number of file types (spreadsheets, audio files, etc.) onto the server for their tutors to evaluate and assess together with any other course work. Moreover, authors can use a number of templates which enable them to create reference materials that can be associated individually to exercises or accessed as independent tools. These materials or utilities can be shared and associated to any of the courses delivered via *InGenio*, as well as being able to link the newly created pages to existing exercises or included as an introductory section to the exercises within a learning unit. Furthermore, the authoring platform enables authors to add or create monolingual or multilingual glossaries and dictionaries. In each of the exercise templates, there is an additional option whereby any of the words can become a hypertext link that displays the glossed item or dictionary entry in student mode. In the event that a highlighted word should not be found in the courseware glossary, the author may specify a default online dictionary and include external links that could contribute to make users' work easier and more effective.

InGenio can thus be described as a flexible and versatile tool that allows authors to include constant updates and improvements as well as small adjustments to exercises and course contents in real time, and enables them to adapt the contents and the levels to the users' specific requirements and needs. This premise was one of the fundamental issues which determined the *InGenio* assessment methodology. The fact that the system distinguishes between two very distinct assessment modalities is especially relevant in the case of the aforementioned materials, in which user performance and the exercises can be corrected automatically so that a score would be provided; or it can require the intervention of a tutor, in the case of exercises, activities and tasks which require human correction (Fig. 4.1).

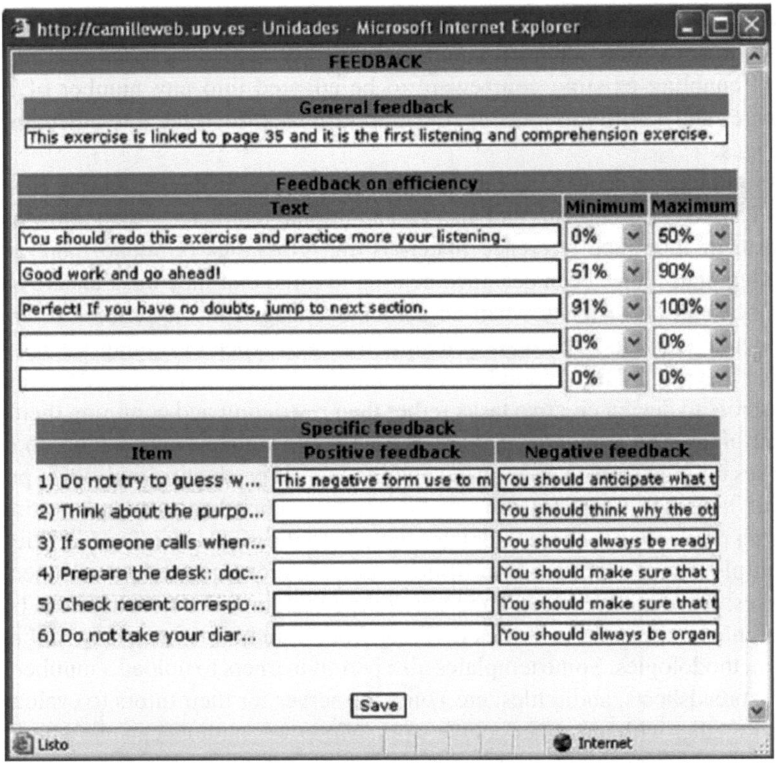

Fig. 4.1 Author feedback form in *InGenio*

4.3 Student Assessment as Part of the Language Learning Process

The importance of assessment mainly derives from the fact that it is capable of influencing the way language teaching and learning are addressed, in such a way that two of the main participants in the learning process – teachers and learners – are likely to introduce changes in their methodologies, approaches, behaviour and learning strategies based on the particular kind of knowledge or ability that a test is designed to measure (Read 2000), that is, the construct. According to Buck (2001), the essential condition for any test to be acceptable is that it measures the appropriate construct, this being the only possible way to ensure validity and usefulness of that assessment. In order to design the right construct to measure the four main skills tested by a B2 level exam such as the FCE, it is important to know the micro-skills and strategies that the candidates need to put into practice in order to ascertain that they have the appropriate level; as well as the best way to assess those skills. Moreover, the *washback* effect is another of the main factors to be taken into account when it comes to assessment processes.

The abovementioned effect aligns testing with instruction and is very notable in those processes specifically aimed at coaching students to pass a high-stakes, competitive test or official examination, as it is the case of the FCE exam candidates. Teachers adapt the learning materials which are developed, the methodologies which are followed and the contents which are taught in an attempt to get focused on the demands set out by a specific test, exam or evaluation process so that the final results can be as satisfactory as possible. These positive results could indicate if learners have acquired the required level with regard to those skills tested and measured through the exam's construct. The concept of construct is closely linked to the one of test validity, defined by Fulcher and Davidson (2007, p. 6) as 'any attempt to show that the content of a test is a representative sample from the domain that is to be tested'. Djuric (2008) conducted research on the difference which exists between the variables of positive and negative feedback and reflected on how important it is that testers "minimize construct under-representation and construct-irrelevance in the assessment" as the effect of the assessment on the whole learning process is a crucial and remarkable factor.

The *washback* effect is usually found in the language classroom in the form of innovations and new ways of teaching aimed at fostering students' motivation and the emergence of a greater variety of learning strategies. Teachers usually make an effort to adapt the contents and materials that they develop to the individual needs, goals, interests and expectations of their students, but also to the requirements that may emerge from the conditions of an evaluation process in general or from the parameters of a specific exam in particular. On the other hand, the abovementioned effect could be seen as something negative when approached from the opposite point of view, i.e. when the whole learning process is too focused just on the need to pass a specific exam or test while some other important linguistic or communicative contents, skills or competences, which are not measured or are not part of the exam construct, are left unattended. This fact would have a very negative impact, as pointed out by Bern Rüschoff (2009), who quotes Ellis (1985, p. 10) reflection that any kind of successful language learning should be based on the principle of "language in use", which seems to be very far off the idea of studying a language just to pass an official examination. Therefore, all those existing language exams that are currently devoted to assessing written skills could be seen as a negative sample of the *washback* effect, as the rest of necessary or required skills and competences would not be tested during the evaluation phase and thus would not be practised and fostered enough during the teaching and learning process. Therefore, when designing and developing new language learning materials to be delivered online, authors and future teachers and tutors should always bear in mind that "the overall aim of learning a language needs to be regarded in terms of an integrated set of skills and competencies which, coupled with a degree of language awareness enable learners to become competent agents in a foreign language" (Rüschoff 2009). Students should also take into consideration the previous idea, as they should adopt an active role within the so-called "Web 2.0 enhanced learning scenarios" as they should acquire the "meta-skills needed to become autonomous learners, capable of controlling and self-directing their learning experiences" (Rüschoff 2009).

The modalities of self-assessment and tutor-assessment would be associated with two different learning environments. The former would be integrated into a context based on distance learning whereas the latter would be part of a blended learning environment. Regarding distance learning, learners' independence, autonomy, training and involvement are usually seen as key issues in relation with the learning experiences, especially when considering that "learning a language in the distance mode presents learners with what may be new demands and new opportunities for self-direction" and in both "self- and environment- management (students) are faced with numerous decisions that may previously have been made by the teacher" (White 2003, pp. 149–150). In such a context, students need to be able to "assume more responsibility and control in identifying learning goals, in developing awareness of the learning process and directing their learning experiences", even though the distance mode *per se* does not give "rise to learner autonomy" (White 2003, p. 150). Moreover, the learners, in order to "exercise control", must have "freedom to explore and make choices" as they must also have "a sufficient level of proficiency to carry out learning activities" as well as "appropriate support" (White 2003, p. 150).

As for the blended learning environment, Ruth Trinder (2009) defines it as a combination of "face-to-face (f2f) and computer-assisted language learning (CALL)" and highlights the fact that "blended learning programmes should not consist of a traditional face-to-face syllabus on to which self-access CALL elements are added later", as "the proper distribution of learning content and objectives should be planned in advance". There are many possible varieties and representations of how blended learning programmes could be introduced into contexts in which the traditional teaching methodologies have a dominant role. These kinds of blended programmes offer the option to "exploit learning opportunities in accordance with individual needs" and students can be aware of "their own needs as language learners" when organising "not only their learning, but also their self-evaluation" (Trinder 2009). An example of blended-learning could be found in the modality of tutor-assessment provided by the materials published and delivered via the *InGenio* platform. In this case, students face the conditions of a CALL learning environment while they are also tutorised and monitored by teachers who have a different role if compared with their traditional role. Trinder emphasises the importance of the "rethinking/redefinition of the roles of the teacher, student, and the entire learning environment" (2009b). According to Gimeno Sanz (2009b), "the use of Information and Communications Technologies (ICT) in the language curriculum has, to some extent, been responsible for the shift from focusing on the teacher to focusing on the learner when designing web-enhanced materials". This fact has led courseware designers to "adopt a constructivist approach to learning", i.e. the student is "encouraged to construct knowledge actively" whereas the teacher becomes "a guide to support learners through the process of learning" (Gimeno Sanz 2009b).

The *InGenio* system has been designed to provide responses to both learning options and allows users to assess the skills and competences which are developed throughout the process. Productive and receptive skills are considered to be old and simplistic concepts unable to show in an accurate way the true dimension of the language learning process. The idea that the student adopts a passive role when training or assessing their reading or listening skills could not be considered as appropriate anymore since today's learner is immersed in an active process of learning. Renewed learning processes should be able to combine the practice of each and every skill through varied and sophisticated tasks which would leave behind the closed and archaic clusters developed under the theory that each skill should be trained in and individual and independent way. The new European context also presents a new situation in which the practice of skills is combined with the development of competences by students during the learning process. All skills, competences and the contents learnt and constructed by students are not just based on linguistic issues but also on a varied range of everyday life factors and other necessary conditions. The implementation of curricula suiting all these requirements would eventually offer more enriching and efficient results at the end of the process as well as at the moment when students finally determine their professional careers and face the real world. Although the classification which follows might be too rigid and does not reflect the interconnectedness and the complexity of the different skills and competences, the different skills have been organised around the categories of "reading, writing, listening and speaking" for the sake of clarity and also because this is the way in which the linguistic knowledge is usually dealt with in official language examinations.

The effectiveness of the *InGenio* system as well as the levels of satisfaction of its users have been proven through different procedures since 2004. In that year, a subject known as *Computer Assisted English*, in which the *InGenio* system was used on a regular basis, was offered to the students of different scientific and technical degrees at the Universitat Politècnica de València (UPV). At the end of every semester, the students who took this subject were asked to complete a questionnaire and their answers, together with the students' overall results, were thoroughly analysed. A full description and a discussion of these data can be found in *Linguistic tools for teachers of English: towards a bilingual education*.[2] As for the FCE materials dealt with in this paper, these are currently undergoing a 1 year-long validation process. It is hoped that the results obtained will be equally or even more satisfactory than the ones obtained in previous years, as significant improvements have been introduced into the system since it was first used with students.

4.3.1 Assessing Reading

When it comes to assessing reading, it is important to follow several guidelines for teaching and curriculum planning mentioned by authors such as Grabe (1991): reading should be integrated together with other skills within content; the texts

[2] Book chapter entitled "Student Assessment in the InGenio Online Authoring System: Results taken from *Intermediate Online English*", published in *Linguistic tools for teachers of English – towards a bilingual education* (2010) (Eds. Sonsoles Sánchez-Reyes Peñamaría and Ramiro Durán Martínez), Aquilafuente: Salamanca (51–78).

should be interesting and related to the candidates' education, hobbies and interests; the different reading sub-skills should be measured; silent reading should be fostered, and so should be reading comprehension; and the person in charge of the assessment should be able to accept different interpretations of the texts, previously organising skills and strategies systematically, taking into account the characteristics and objectives of each group. To these guidelines, Alderson (2000) adds that it is important to find a way to measure reading accurately, considering to what extent the tests reflect and are based on previous research and literature referred not only to the process but also to the product.

There are, at least, two reading comprehension levels to be evaluated: the first level is that of the literal comprehension of a text, and the second level is related to the comprehension of meanings that are not explicitly included in the text, that is, the information that the text conveys in an implicit way (Alderson 2000, p. 7). This is what is known as "reading lines" Gray, 1960, quoted Alderson 2000, p. 7), that is, understanding the literal meaning of a text; while "reading between the lines" has to do with the inference of meanings; a third level could be "reading beyond the lines", understood as the ability to read and judge a text critically. This third level is very important in the case of B2-level materials development, since in the descriptors of the reading ability of this level within the CEFRL it is stated that the student should be able to "read articles concerned with contemporary problems in which the writers adopt particular attitudes or viewpoints" (CEFRL 2001), which requires critical reading skills.

Another important element to be assessed is whether the reading process is fluid enough. This, according to Grabe (1991) can be measured by looking at the following aspects: automatic recognition skills, knowledge about vocabulary and structure, knowledge about the formal discourse structure, summarising and evaluating skills and strategies, and metacognitive knowledge. Grabe (1991) also provides guidelines for teaching and curriculum planning, which Alderson (2000) relates with the way in which the assessment of reading should be carried out. First, reading should be included in a curriculum of skills which should be integrated within content, as content can very much influence motivation; and the integration of skills fosters learning. In the same way, in order to increase motivation reading should be assessed within a battery based on content, and the texts used should be related to the students' education and training, their hobbies, their interests, etc. Bearing this in mind, the authors of *FCE Online Course* and *Tester* have developed contents adapted to the specific needs and characteristics of the UPV students, who are doing scientific and technical degrees.

Another aspect to consider is whether reading is going to be taught individually in a reading lab where the different reading sub-skills and strategies are examined. Doing this would be very helpful, as the construct would only test reading skills and the results could then be presented in a diagnostic format adapted to every student's profile. Also, silent reading should be fostered, since it leads to automaticity, confidence and pleasure for reading. In our materials, an effort has been made in order to foster the students' silent reading and in order to achieve our goal the students are provided with longer texts and with tasks concerning those texts, bearing in mind their level, the average time they can devote to language learning and topics that are likely to be of interest to them. Moreover, it is important to try to detect the students' previous knowledge and skills and try to connect them with the knowledge to be acquired and the skills to be developed. The previous knowledge and experience can also be useful to facilitate comprehension. As for specific skills and strategies, these should be practised in an organised and systematic way, while bearing in mind the characteristics and objectives of the group and of each individual within the group. Another advisable thing to do is to foster team and cooperative work in the form of debates about the texts and about the different ways to interpret the texts and to solve the different tasks. In the case of the *InGenio* FCE materials, collaborative work among students is fostered by the use of Web 2.0 features which are being introduced into the *InGenio* platform. These include a forum, a chat, a blog and other social networks which help students work in teams, to exchange ideas and even materials and to develop a sense of belonging to a community. Finally, students should be encouraged to read extensively, and the reading assessment process should not be detrimental for extensive reading.

Not only can Information and Communications Technologies (ICT) be beneficial in collaborative working, but their use can also be positive in many other ways. ICT provide students and teachers with access to a wide variety of authentic and communicative materials through the Web or through Learning Management Systems (LMS) such as *InGenio* without special-temporal constraints, and gives users the opportunity to use and add hyperlinks to vocabulary and grammar explanations, as well as multimedia files as a complement for texts. Furthermore, ICT enable teachers and students to monitor reading speed as well as other learning aspects, as pointed out by Levy and Stockwell (2006). Also, the web and databases such as *InGenio*'s are rich sources of written materials which can contribute towards the improvement of both the reading skills and the levels of intercultural competence (Taylor and Gitsaki 2004). Nevertheless, some disadvantages related to the use of computers for reading were pointed out, such as the fact that it is sometimes difficult to find and detect appropriate texts out of the huge amount of available information and materials, as well as out of the wide range of levels regarding both linguistic and social aspects that could make a text be appropriate or not for some particular purposes. In spite of that, a teacher who is aware of these limitations would be able to face them in an attempt to take advantage of the variety of resources and thus introduce and adapt them as part of their teaching practice (Dudeney 2000).

Another advantage which is related to computer based reading is the possibility to introduce links to other websites that allow teachers to include additional information, translations, extra multimedia resources (Gettys, Imhof y Kautz 2001, in Levy and Stockwell 2006, p. 183), etc., thus helping students guess and check the meaning of new words with no need to look up them in a dictionary or asking them to their teacher. According to Morin (1991, in Levy and Stockwell 2006, p. 183), CMC in general and other asynchronous options such as the email or online forums in particular contribute towards the improvement of reading skills. Nevertheless several interactions could just be based on an exchange of monologues between participants, being this a fact which has already been proved as students are not used to replying and dealing with all the topics which they could have been asked for in previous emails (Stockwell 2003, in Levy and Stockwell 2006, p. 183).

4.3.2 Assessing Writing

As for writing, it is worth noting that in the past, it was considered as an indicator of someone's belonging to the elite of the well-educated, but it is now an essential tool of communication in the global community we are living in. The role of writing has therefore shifted from conveying information to transforming knowledge in order to create new knowledge while helping to predict future professional and academic success, which explains the great demand of valid and reliable ways to test the writing ability (Weigle 2009).

There are two main ways to assess writing: direct and indirect. According to Hamp-Lyons (1991, in Weigle 2009), the five main characteristics of a 'direct' test are that candidates must write at least one piece of continuous text, they are given a set of instructions or 'prompts', but have some freedom in their responses to it, each test is usually read by more than one trained rater, judgments are tied to a set of sample responses or rating scales, and these judgments are expressed as numbers. In addition, there are other important characteristics such as the limited time frame, generally between 30 min and 2 h; and the fact that the topic is unknown to test takers in advance (Weigle 2009). As for the 'indirect' tests of writing or 'timed impromptu writing tests', they most often consist of multiple-choice tests of grammar and usage. As far as the process of test development is concerned, it occurs in three main stages: design, operationalisation and administration (Bachman and Palmer 1996, in Weigle 2009). These stages are followed by a very important procedure: scoring, which is used in making decisions and inferences about the performance by the exam takers and therefore must be accurate and derive from appropriate, theoretically-grounded and consistent rating scales and scoring rubrics (Weigle 2009). Writing assessment has overcome dramatic changes due to the impact of technology and the increased global communication. In fact, the nature of writing itself has been affected by ICT in terms of process, norms and standards (Weigle 2009) and the emergence of scoring of writing by computer is picturing the future of computers as supplements of human raters, especially in the case of large-scale writing assessments such as FCE.

The design and assessment of writing tasks has to be carefully planned in order to ensure that both the tasks and the construct do only involve writing and that therefore no other skills are interfering. This is not an easy thing to do, since quite often writing skills overlap with other skills, which is especially true and relevant in the case of online writing. Even though, there are still differences between skills and it should be born in mind that, in spite of these differences, no skill is intrinsically superior to the other. Although reading and writing are usually considered as the most interconnected of all skills, several differences between both skills have been pointed out by authors such as Brown (1994). The first difference has to do with the different degrees of permanence of reading and writing; this means that whereas the oral language is transitory and speakers process it in real time, the written language is not permanent and can be read and reread as many times as the reader wants. Another difference is that production time is longer in the case of written texts, because the writer has time to plan and to review, unlike the speakers, who need to plan, formulate and pronounce their words in a short period of time so as to be able to keep a fluid conversation. Also, the special-temporal distance is bigger in the case of written texts and, unlike spoken interaction, orthography plays a role in it as a limitation which is not such when it comes to speaking, since speakers have a wider variety of resources relating to context which help them put their messages across with less effort. Finally, there is usually a difference in the complexity level, which is higher in the case of writing, since longer sentences and subordination tend to be used, the degree of formality tends to be higher, and the vocabulary is most often richer than that of spoken interaction.

4.3.3 Assessing Listening

As far as listening is concerned, this is considered as the least understood of all skills (Alderson and Bachman, in Buck 2001), despite being the most important one due to its potential influence over teaching methodologies. It is also the most difficult skill to measure at a technical level, and it is time-consuming too, which may cause some teachers to be reluctant to test listening. Even though, it is essential to give listening assessment the importance it deserves, given that the consequent *washback* could influence teachers and make them aware of the fact that developing listening abilities is crucial for students to be able to communicate in the target language.

Buck (2001) distinguishes between two types of knowledge within the linguistic comprehension system: linguistic knowledge and non-linguistic knowledge. The linguistic knowledge includes phonology, lexis, syntax, semantics and discourse structure; whereas the non linguistic knowledge has to do with the knowledge about the topic and about the context, as well as the general knowledge about the world and about the way it works. Drawing on previous research carried out by different authors, Buck (2001) acknowledges that there is a great overlapping between the reading ability and the listening ability, even though some characteristics are not shared between both. According to Buck (2001) material developers should take the similarities into account, but they should focus even more on the differences: phonetic modification, in the form of assimilation, elision or intrusion; accent; prosodic elements; stress in words and sentences, intonation and speech speed; hesitation; and discourse structure. To these elements we could add the non verbal elements involved in oral communication.

When the teaching and practice of Listening is assisted by computers, e.g. in Computer-Assisted Language Learning (CALL) settings, technology should be used in such a way that it provides something which would not be available in more traditional settings in such a way that it contributes to enriching and improving the whole learning experience (Levy and Stockwell 2006). This is also true as far as the other linguistic skills are concerned.

4.3.4 Assessing Speaking

Finally, in relation to the assessment of speaking skills, numerous studies point out that this is one of the most complex and controversial aspects within second language teaching (O'Sullivan et al. 2006). This is due to the difficulties encountered when trying to join the targets of the assessment and the appropriate tasks or instruments that assessment requires (Luoma 2009). Moreover, speaking is considered as the hardest skill to be taught and tested through computers, which might explain the lack of representativeness of the studies focusing on speaking (Levy and Stockwell 2006). This makes the integration of the assessment of communicative speaking into CALL materials a true challenge.

Luoma (2009) conceives speaking assessment as a cycle in which the participants involved are the examinees, interlocutors, examiners, and the rating/marking criteria. The cycle starts when a necessity of speaking assessment is perceived; and planning and development stages follow, resulting in the definition of the construct. Next, the criteria are determined and so is the way in which the exam is to be administered; following that, assessment takes place by means of two interaction processes: first, exam administration and candidates' performance in interactions (among the candidates and/or the examiner) in which they show their oral production skills; and second, a rating process in which the examiners apply the assessment criteria to the candidates' performance in order to obtain a grade for each of the candidates.

Prior to assessing speaking, the type of speech to be assessed has to be determined: planned or not, formal or informal, etc., because there might be substantial changes in the vocabulary choices, grammar constructions or pronunciation depending on the type of discourse (Luoma 2009). Another factor that is likely to influence the type of speech acts is the social/situational context, which can be determined by using Hymes' SPEAKING model (1974) when planning and describing the construct (Table 4.1):

4.4 Modalities of Assessment in InGenio and in the *FCE Online Course* and *Tester*: Self-Assessment and Tutor-Assessment

The modalities of assessment offered by the materials delivered by the *InGenio* Learning Management System developed by the CAMILLE Research Group at the Universidad Politécnica de Valencia, *FCE Online Course* and *Tester,* are self-assessment and tutor assessment.

Table 4.1 SPEAKING Model

Setting/Scene	"Setting refers to the time and place of a speech act and, in general, to the physical circumstances" (Hymes 1974, p. 55) Scene is the "psychological setting" or "cultural definition" of a scene, including characteristics such as range of formality and sense of play or seriousness (Hymes 1974, p. 55–56)
Participants	Speaker and audience. Linguists will make distinctions within these categories; for example, the audience can be distinguished as addressees and other hearers (Hymes 1974, p. 54 & 56)
Ends	Purposes, goals, and outcomes (Hymes 1974, p. 56–57)
Act sequence	Form and order of the event
Key	Cues that establish the "tone, manner, or spirit" of the speech act (Hymes 1974, p. 57)
Instrumentalities	Forms and styles of speech (Hymes 1974, p. 58–60)
Norms	Social rules governing the event and the participants' actions and reaction
Genre	The kind of speech act or event

Adapted from Hymes (1974)

CALL materials corresponding to the self-assessment modality aim to present a greater variety of resources and activities so as to allow learners with different learning styles and preferences to use them in the most convenient ways. They include a greater number of reference materials, additional explanations, extra readings and extra self-assessment activities in order to help those students who are mainly learning with less or no help from a human tutor. Their main advantage is that they enable students to conduct their own process of learning and to evaluate their own learning achievements in an independent, autonomous and individual way (Fig. 4.2).

As for the materials designed within the tutor assessment modality, they provide more support materials to be used in the classroom context. These resources are specifically designed to provide support from the tutor, such as a teachers' guide, as well as the possibility of getting detailed reports about the students' performance and other tracking devices (Gimeno Sanz 2008). One of the positive things about this modality is the fact that it leads to the development of the students' autonomy and sense of responsibility in the learning process while enabling them to get help, guidance and support from a human tutor.

FCE Online Course and *Tester* also give students access to test simulations which are similar to the actual FCE in terms of level, structure, exercise typology and even administration mode, given that since January 2010 a computer-based version of FCE – CBFCE – is available. The current development work carried out by the CAMILLE Research Group is now focusing on relating and adapting the content of these materials to the scientific and technical context of the Universidad Politécnica de Valencia with a view to enriching the students' specific knowledge (e.g. their technical and scientific vocabulary) so as to prepare them better for their future; while enabling the students to certify their B2 level of English, a new requirement to earn their degree at UPV, according to the guidelines established by the UPV in order to fulfil in order to comply with the Bologna Process.

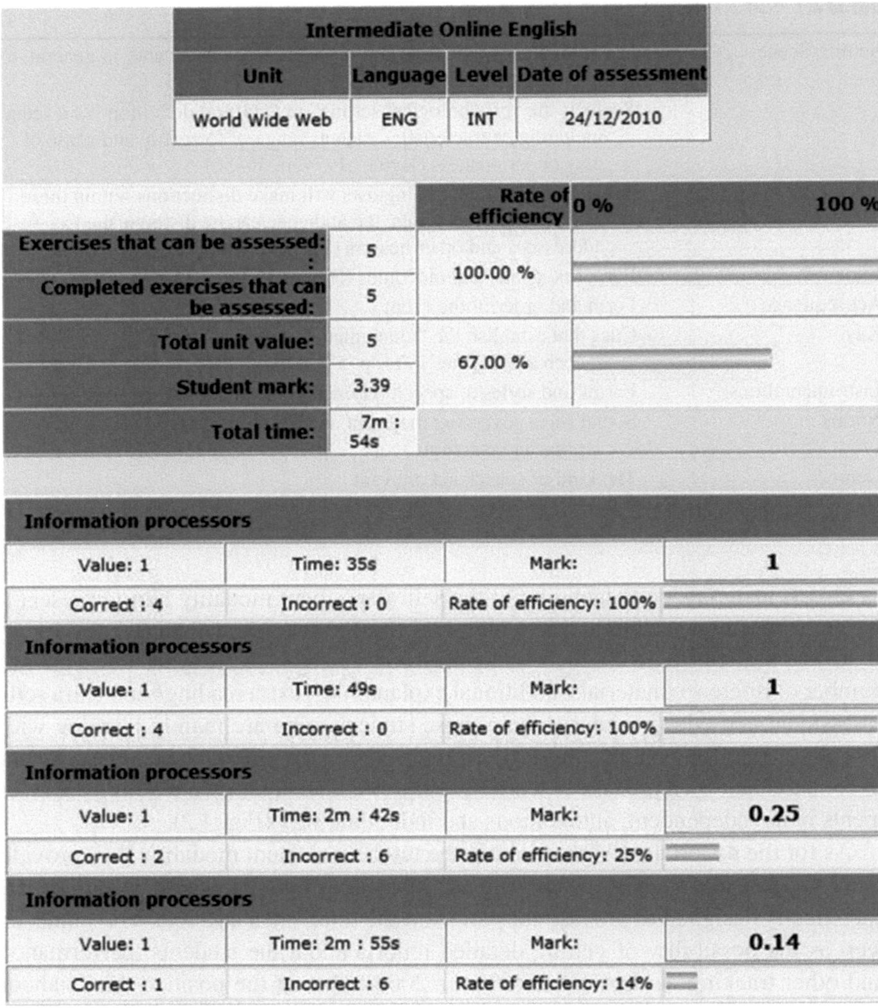

Fig. 4.2 *InGenio* learner's assessment module: automatically corrected exercises

The self-assessment exercises and simulations included in *FCE Online Course* and *Tester* benefit from recent advances in the field of CALL in such a way that they put students in a similar situation to that of the FCE, helping them to be aware of their strengths and weaknesses at a point in which they can still work hard on those particular aspects they need to improve before facing the actual test. This is likely to lead to better results not only linguistically but also in affective terms, as being able to improve and even to predict their results before taking the test can foster the students' self-confidence and motivation while reducing their anxiety levels. These materials also allow designers to generate online assessment elements that provide valuable information about the students, available for teachers at any point so that they can observe and assess adequately the progress of every student. This is particularly useful in those cases in which these materials are used not only when getting prepared for the FCE, but also as learning and assessment tools specifically oriented to technical and scientific language learning.

FCE Online Course and *Tester* develop their full potential when used in combination, the first of these materials being an online course with different kinds of exercises – similar to the ones included in the FCE papers – to be completed first; and an assessment program including self-assessment exercises and simulations of the actual online examination, to be completed once the online course is finished and the students feel ready to face an examination situation. Prior to the design of simulations, a great number of exercises had to be compiled in a corpus of B2 exercises accessible through an online database including different typologies, either independent or based on texts, the text-based typology being more abundant, just as it is very frequent in the FCE papers. The simulations can be generated upon the users' request, the great number of texts and exercises included in the database allowing for numerous and randomised combinations.

4.5 Conclusions

The *Online FCE Course* and *Tester* comprise a varied range of resources aimed at allowing students not only to be familiarised with the typologies of exercises and tasks included in the FCE official examination and evaluation criteria, but also to facilitate social and cultural-specific contexts so that other channels of practice and communication can be opened up in order for students to establish relationships with other candidates preparing for the Cambridge FCE at the same time or to be in contact with authentic English accents or different national cultures. To achieve this and leave behind the rigid and traditional classification and distinction between competences, these materials have been developed in an attempt to favour the expansion of communicative skills by introducing tasks and scenarios aimed at fostering real practice.

The design of the *InGenio FCE Online Course* and *Tester* is a good example of the way in which the use of technologies in language learning can contribute to the effectiveness and efficiency of the assessment process of basic skills such as reading, writing, listening and even speaking in two main modalities: student self-assessment and tutor assessment. The students are allowed to choose between these two different modalities of assessment thanks to the flexibility of the materials provided, and their choice depends on their needs, preferences, learning styles and individual characteristics.

The self-assessment modality enables students to conduct their own learning process and to assess their own learning achievements in an independent, autonomous and individual way; while tutor assessment leads to the development of the students' autonomy and sense of responsibility in the learning process while enabling them to get as much help and support from a human tutor as they need.

Both modalities have the common goal of making students think critically about their L2 development while enabling them to make decisions and judgements about their own progress, what may be done in different ways depending on the assessment modality they choose.

References

Alderson, J. 2000. *Assessing reading*. Cambridge: Cambridge University Press.

Brown, H.D. 1994. *Teaching by principles: An interactive approach to language pedagogy*. Englewood Cliffs: Prentice Hall Regents.

Brown, S., and A. Glasner (eds.). 2003. *Assessment matters in higher education: Choosing and using diverse approaches*, 3rd ed. Buckingham and Philadelphia: The Society of Research into Higher Education and Open University Press.

Buck, G. 2001. *Assessing listening*. Cambridge: Cambridge University Press.

Council of Europe. 2001. *Common European framework of reference for languages: Learning, teaching, assessment*. Cambridge: Cambridge University Press.

Djuric, M. 2008. Dealing with situations of positive and negative washback. *Scripta Manent: Testing and Assessment of Languages for Specific Purposes* 4(1), In M. Djuric (ed). Retrieved from http://www.sdutsj.edus.si/ScriptaManent/2008_4_1/djuric.html. Last accessed 31 Mar 2011.

Dudeney, G. 2000. *The internet and the language classroom*. Cambridge: Cambridge University Press.

Ellis, R. 1985. *Understanding second language acquisition*. Oxford: Oxford University Press.

Fulcher, G., and F. Davidson. 2007. *Language testing and assessment: An advanced resource book*. London: Routledge.

Gimeno Sanz, A. 2002. *Call software design and implementation: The template approach*. Valencia: Servicio de Publicaciones de la Universidad Politécnica de Valencia.

Gimeno Sanz, A. 2008. *Aprendizaje de Lenguas Asistido por Ordenador: Herramientas de Autor para el desarrollo de cursos a través de la web*. Valencia: Servicio de Publicaciones de la Universidad Politécnica de Valencia.

Gimeno Sanz, A. 2009a. How can CLIL benefit from the integration of information and communications technologies? In *Content and language integrated learning cultural diversity*, ed. M. Carrió, 77–102. Bern: Peter Lang.

Gimeno Sanz, A. 2009b. Online courseware design and delivery: The InGenio authoring system. In *Teaching academic and professional English online*, ed. M.C. Foz Gil, M. Jaime Siso, and M.J. Luzón Marco, 83–106. Bern: Peter Lang.

Gimeno Sanz, A. 2010. Intermediate online English: An attempt to increase learner autonomy. *Teaching English with Technology – Developing Online Teaching Skills* Special Issue 10(2): 35–49.

Gimeno-Sanz, A., A. Martínez-Sáez, A. Sevilla-Pavón, and J.M. de Siqueria-Rocha. 2010. Student assessment in the InGenio online authoring system: Results taken from intermediate online English. In *Linguistic tools for teachers of English: Towards a bilingual education*, ed. R. Durán Martínez and S. Sánchez-Reyes Peñamaría, 51–78. Salamanca: Ediciones Universidad de Salamanca.

Grabe, W. 1991. Current developments in second language reading research. *TESOL Quarterly* 25(3): 375–406.

Hymes, D. 1974. *Foundations in sociolinguistics: An ethnographic approach*. Philadelphia: University of Pennsylvania Press.

Levy, M., and G. Stockwell. 2006. *CALL dimensions: Options and issues in computer-assisted language learning*. Mahwah: Erlbaum Associates.

Luoma, S. 2009. *Assessing speaking*, 5th ed. Cambridge: Cambridge University Press.
O'Sullivan, B., C. Weir, and T. Horai. 2006. Exploring difficulty in speaking tasks: An intra-task perspective. *The British Council: IELTS Research Reports* 7: 119–160.
Read, J. 2000. *Assessing vocabulary*. Cambridge: Cambridge University Press.
Rüschoff, B. 2009. Output-oriented language learning with digital media. In *Handbook of research on Web 2.0 and second language learning*, ed. M. Thomas, 42–59. Hershey: Information Science Reference.
Taylor, R., and C. Gitsaki. 2004. Teaching WELL and loving IT. In *New perspectives on CALL for the second/foreign language classroom*, ed. S. Fotos and C. Browne, 129–145. Seattle: Lawrence Erlbaum Associates.
Trinder, R. 2009. The potential of blended learning environments in terms of beneficial language learning conditions. In *Teaching academic and professional English online*, ed. M.C. Foz Gil, M. Jaime Siso, and M.J. Luzón Marco, 35–56. Bern: Peter Lang.
Weigle, S. 2009. *Assessing writing*, 6th ed. Cambridge: Cambridge University Press.
White, C. 2003. *Language learning in distance education*. Cambridge: Cambridge University Press.

Part II
Computer-Assisted Experiences for the Development of Language Competences and Skills

Chapter 5
Internet Dictionaries for Teaching and Learning Business English in Spanish Universities

Pedro A. Fuertes-Olivera

5.1 The Function Theory of Lexicography

Over the course of a number of years, scholars such as Scerba (1995), Hausmann (1977), Kromann et al. (1992), and Wiegand (1977a, b, 1987), among others, have proposed different theoretical frameworks for explaining the concept of lexicography. Wiegand, for example, defends a contemplative view of lexicography by describing lexicography as an independent academic discipline concerned with producing and analysing dictionaries, especially their production and use, with the aim of discovering if dictionaries and other possible lexicographical products satisfy the users' needs in *actual* usage situations.

More recently, Nordic scholars at the Centre for Lexicography, Aarhus School of Business, disagree with some of the above theoretical proposals. Bergenholtz and Tarp (2002, 2003, 2004, 2005) for example, defend a transformative view of lexicography, and present lexicography as an area of social practice and independent science concerned with analysing and building dictionaries which can satisfy the needs of a specific type of user with specific types of problems related to a specific type of user situation (see Tarp 2008, for a review). This functional approach to lexicography, called the *function theory of lexicography* or the *theory of lexicographical functions*, "shifts the focus from actual dictionary users and dictionary usage situations to potential users and the social situation in which they participate." (Tarp 2008: 40) Consequently, understanding extra-lexicographical social situations, such as the teaching and learning of specialised languages in Spanish universities, is also a metalexicographical exercise necessary for both constructing pedagogically-oriented dictionaries and understanding their lexicographical characteristics.

P.A. Fuertes-Olivera (✉)
Departamento de Filología Inglesa, University of Valladolid, Valladolid, Spain
e-mail: pedro@tita.emp.uva.es

E. Bárcena et al. (eds.), *Languages for Specific Purposes in the Digital Era*, Educational Linguistics 19, DOI 10.1007/978-3-319-02222-2_5,

Within the tenets of the function theory this paper presents an extra-lexicographical social situation (Sect. 5.2), comments on some basic requirements of pedagogical specialised lexicography, here illustrated with examples taken from business dictionaries (Sect. 5.3), defends that free Internet specialised dictionaries can be used for pedagogical purposes providing that they satisfy three basic requirements of pedagogical specialised lexicography (Sect. 5.4), and illustrates the view taken focusing on vocabulary support for independent online reading (Sect. 5.5). The paper concludes by summarising the main ideas discussed, and envisaging future trends for e-lexicography.

5.2 An Extra-Lexicographical Social Situation: The Teaching and Learning of Business English in Spanish Universities

Recent research, e.g. Fuertes-Olivera and Arribas-Baño (2008), has refined the category of 'semi-expert' initially described in Bergenholtz and Kaufmann (1997), and have defended that there are three subtypes of semi-experts in the teaching and learning environment associated with *English for Specific Purposes* (ESP) taught and learnt in Spanish universities: (a) semi-experts from other related fields; (b) students from unrelated disciplines; (c) translators and interpreters. For instance, Business English courses in Spanish universities are usually open to students from different degrees, and therefore some of them have a broader knowledge of business/economics discourse than other students.

There are a number of issues that merit the attention of researchers concerned with the teaching and learning of Business English in Spanish universities. Some of them are outside the scope of this paper: the role of instructors inside and outside the classroom (for example, if team teaching is possible or even desirable); whether or not instructors must have a working knowledge of the conceptual domain; when and how needs analysis should be carried out; and which type of material should be used.

On the other hand, the influence of external and internal learning factors as well as which type of words present more difficulties for students have also been the object of interest of researchers and are relevant for this paper. Fuertes-Olivera and Gómez-Martínez (2004), for example, have found that *thinking in L1* and *reading* are correlated. This means that the more students read in English, the less they think in Spanish. They have also found that although factors such as *attendance* and *homework* are judged positively by students, they tend to pay them little or no attention at all. These results are consistent with the Spanish university framework, where students do not regularly attend lectures and/or tutorials, and English instructors have to struggle with inappropriate conception of L2 within Spanish society. Finally, they have also found that the principles and practices associated with *communicative methods* are sometimes absent from Spanish schools. For example, in some nurseries children are taught written words and numbers (for instance, irregular verbs) instead of spoken functional expressions and formulae. Hence, instructors of Business English may have to devote some time to be sure that their students correctly understand and accept the daily routines of communicative methodologies, among which the use of pedagogically-oriented specialised dictionaries and the promotion of extensive and intensive reading are highlighted in this article, which assumes that Business English students have no special lexicographical training nor have been explained which dictionary (type) is more adequate for solving their specific needs.

Finally, this paper connects the above findings with the advent of web-based systems, which has led researchers to ask new questions on the teaching and learning process. Mackey and Ho (2010: 387) cite research by Baruque and Melo (2004), Deubel (2003), and Mayer (2001) on the influence of behaviourist, constructionist, and cognitive approaches that aim to understand the impact of multimedia on learning. Behaviourism explains that learning is a change in behaviour due to experience and the function of building associations between the stimulus event and the response event. Constructivism argues that learning "is constructed by the complex interaction among students' existing knowledge, the social context, and the problem to be solved" (Baruque and Melo 2004: 346). Finally, cognitivism asserts that learners gain a deeper level of understanding through the associations made between words and images in an integrated environment (Mayer 2001).

To sum up, the teaching and learning of Business English in Spanish universities can be analysed from different perspectives. Two of them are of interest in this paper. The first one focuses on the pedagogical characteristics of specialized dictionaries, especially the dictionaries that can be used by Spanish students of Business English. The second aspect is concerned with evaluating whether web-based systems can be adapted and used in a teaching and learning environment that is characterized by rapid changes, and lack of focus. Gasparetti et al. (2009: 287), for example, have explained that the principal advantages of web-based systems are to be seen in the opportunity to overcome restrictions such as few teaching resources, organise complex and tailored courses for single learners, and evaluate their acquired knowledge levels more or less easily.

5.3 Basic Requirements of Pedagogical Specialized Lexicography

Empirical studies on printed dictionary use have found discrepancies on which dictionary type students really use and which type they would like to use. On the one hand, students report that they use bilingual dictionaries much more frequently than monolingual ones, regardless of the language level and the specific task. On the other hand, they also show that they are more satisfied with the information found in monolingual learners' dictionaries, considering that their entries provide more detailed and precise information (Atkins and Varantola 1998; Cowie 1999; Laufer and Melamed 1994). Although these findings seem contradictory, they are easily understandable assuming that most LSP students lack lexicographical training and therefore take for granted that the access route to the unknown lexical items is more familiar in a bilingual dictionary than in a monolingual one, and that equivalents are more meaningful than definitions.

From a pedagogical perspective, the practice of relying on bilingual lexicography should be taken with some caution, as it has some weaknesses in the teaching-learning environment here commented. The dissatisfaction with current bilingual dictionaries may be based on three main claims. Firstly, the bilingual dictionary encourages the study of L2 via L1. Secondly, the bilingual dictionary is influential in promoting the illusion of isomorphism between languages through inter-linguistic lexical equivalents. Thirdly, many specialised bilingual dictionaries do not offer adequate ways of disambiguating meaning and, even more, they cannot be used in most cognitive and communicative situations (see Fuertes-Olivera and Arribas-Baño 2008 for a review). A case in point is the *Pirámide Economía y Empresa* (Lozano Irueste 2005), which is the most widely used business English-Spanish/Spanish-English dictionary, thanks to its distribution by *Expansión* (a respected financial newspaper), a Chilean publishing house, and its several editions from the year 1989 onwards. Since its introduction in the year 1989, this dictionary has been updated regularly but without paying much attention to its lemma selection and pedagogical orientation. For example, in its 2005 edition it has not even included the lemma **euro** as a currency; rather, it still refers to it as a prefix in the English-Spanish wordlist or an adjective in the Spanish-English one. More importantly, it continues attaching equivalents without using meaning discriminator devices or resorting to prototypes for limiting the excessive use of equivalents. Examples (1) and (2) illustrate this lexicographical practice which must be discarded from a pedagogical point of view:

(1) Article in the English-Spanish side of *Pirámide Economía y Empresa*:

delinquent (adj. y n.). Delincuente, moroso.
d. (overdue, past-due) account. Crédito vencido hace tiempo, cuenta morosa.
d. list. Lista de morosos, listado de morosos [Hisp.].
d. payments. Morosidad en el pago.
d. return. Declaración morosa.
d. tax. Impuesto atrasado, pendiente de liquidación. Impuesto en mora.
d. taxpayer. Contribuyente moroso.

(2) Article in the Spanish-English side of *Pirámide Economía y Empresa*

delincuente (p.a. y s.). Deinquent. Criminal. Culprit. Offender. Defaulter. Guilty. Defaulter (soldier).

moroso, sa (adj.) Slow. Delinquent (in payment). Tardy. Heavy. Laggard. Morose. Debtor in arrears. Defaulter. Slow pay. *Contribuyente moroso*: Delinquent taxpayer. *Cuenta morose*: Delinquent account. *Declaración morosa:* Delinquent return. *Deudor moroso*: Bad (tardy) debt. Defaulting debtor. Unsafe debtor. *Lista de morosos:* Delinquent list.

The above articles are of little help for Spanish students of Business English for several reasons (Fuertes-Olivera and Arribas-Baño 2008; Andersen and Fuertes-Olivera 2009; Fuertes-Olivera 2010). First, the grammar terminology is confusing and obsolete. For example, we have the symbols 'n' and 's' for the same word class. Second, the grammatical differences between the adjectival and nominal uses of **delinquent** are neither shown explicitly nor implicitly. Third, the access structure in the Spanish-English side is confusing and does not favour the process of consultation. For example, *lista de morosos* is given as a run-on and not as a sub-lemma. Four, the list of equivalents given equates common words (e.g., *delinquente*) and terms (e.g. *moroso*). They are not synonyms in Spanish, nor *delinquent*, *criminal*, *culprit*, *offender*, *defaulter*, and *guilty* are synonyms in English. Five, it does not use examples. Six, the conceptual information is absent. In sum, examples (1) and (2) show entry dictionaries whose pedagogical orientation is very poor and consequently should not be used by Spanish students of Business English.

In my view, pedagogically-oriented dictionaries for Spanish students of Business English must satisfy three basic requirements. Firstly, they must pay attention to the lexicographical implications associated with a better understanding of the related concepts *business* and *economics*. Some of them are the following:

- The analysis of the social (i.e., pragmatics) dimension of business discourse, especially Business English, indicates that this specialised language is a hybrid characterised by having a large number of users and would-be users with a previous working knowledge of business, as we all carry out typical business activities on a daily basis: we all sell and buy something; we all make presentations; we all take part in meetings; we all negotiate. Consequently, the concept of the *business dictionary* is mostly regarded as a commercial label without scientific backing, and may be preferable recommending our students consulting specific subdomains dictionaries instead of general business dictionaries, i.e., consulting dictionaries of accounting, dictionaries of marketing, etc., instead of a multi-field dictionary of business.
- There is no agreed scientific limitation to the lemma selection of business dictionaries. On the one hand, the vocabulary of most business texts consists of a large proportion of non-terms, some of which acquire business/economic meanings in days, or even hours. On the other hand, the process of de-terminologisation is very active in business. For example the word *inflación* [Eng: inflation] is so frequently used in every day discourse that we no longer consider it a term, although this word refers to key concepts in Business and Economics. On the other hand, the English formal word *repossess* has acquired a very specific meaning in connection with the 2007 slump of the American house market. We all understand that the term *reposses* should be explained in connection with *subprime mortgage,* and *credit crunch*. In sum, terms and non-terms are core words in business texts and are part and parcel of their word list.
- The process of lemma selection and description must also make room for coping with two opposing forces: cultural traditions and globalisation. On the one hand, lexicographers have to deal with culture-bound traditions and legislation while on the other hand they need to respond to the process of internationalisation and globalisation which is increasingly affecting most spheres of life, especially those connected with business/economics, science and technology, and the status of English as *lingua franca*. Regarding the Spanish lemma list, lexicographers are expected to overcome the problems posed by the frequent coinage of English terms (Fuertes-Olivera 2011; Fuertes-Olivera and Nielsen 2011, 2012). In some occasions they have to face strong criticism as calques and loan words are regarded as inadequate by prescriptive grammars. The criticism aroused tends to sink into obscurity in time, perhaps because prescriptive grammars do not deal

with real language as communication but with language as a social weapon. For example, the English term *marketing* is typically used in Spanish although the Spanish *mercadotecnia* was regarded the only "correct equivalent" some time ago. In sum, lexicographers must not shy away from coining calques and loan words when no better solution exists. Moreover, the process of calquing is a characteristic of specialised discourse (Montero-Martínez et al. 2001).

Secondly, they must be all inclusive and therefore satisfy both cognitive and communicative needs. In this respect, learners can be subdivided into those *learning skills* and those *acquiring knowledge* although the modern educational methods, in most cases, combine the learning of skills with a certain acquisition of related knowledge, and vice versa. This distinction between skills and knowledge is important for modern lexicography because it helps to focus on the different roles dictionaries may play in the learning process. In the lexicographically perceived language learning process, i.e. the learning of language skills, dictionaries may provide assistance on two levels: *indirectly* by transmitting *knowledge* about the native, foreign or special-purpose language's vocabulary and grammar in connection with the systematic study of the language in question; and *directly* by providing *information* that can be used to solve specific problems in the actual process of communication – in connection with text reception, text production, and translation (Fuertes-Olivera and Tarp 2011). Example (3) illustrates this requirement:

(3) Article in the *New Oxford Business English* (Parkinson 2005):

The, Boston 'Matrix/'bostən; *AmE* 'bo:s-/(*also*, **growth-share 'matrix**) *noun* [C, usually sing] (*Marketing*) a way of analysing how successful a range of company's products or services are by looking at the percentage of sales it has in the market and how fast the sales are growing

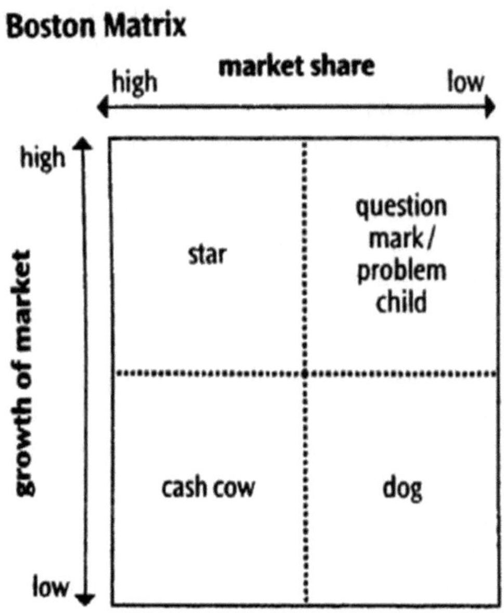

This entry offers adequate cognitive information, together with language data which can be very useful for communicative purposes. Especially relevant from a pedagogical point of view are the following characteristics: (i) the definitional style and the drawing in the *New Oxford Business English* are very illustrative offering both simple and clear conceptual data; (ii) there are implicit and explicit data (for example, pronunciation, intonation, grammar, and synonyms), adequate for performing communicative tasks; (iii) using it will help our potential Spanish users use English and eliminate L1 transfers.

This requirement also focuses on the treatment of function words, common words that are also necessary for understanding education systems in different countries, and the access structure and arrangement of related words. Function words must be included as headwords when they have specific semantic, functional, or discoursal meaning. For instance, **Further to** is used in commercial correspondence to signal previous business contacts, i.e., it signals politeness, and has to be included in the dictionary lemma list as the notion of politeness is crucial in this sub-domain (Fuertes-Olivera and Nielsen 2008). Similarly, the emergence of students' mobility, e.g. the Erasmus project, makes a case for including common words that are necessary for understanding different education systems (for example, the concept of *tertiary education* is different in England and Spain), and the coming of age of e-lexicography eliminates most of the restrictions suffered by printed dictionaries (Fuertes-Olivera and Bergenholtz 2011a).

Thirdly, pedagogically-oriented specialised dictionaries should reconcile what students do (they usually consult bilingual dictionaries) with what they should do for upgrading their language skills (they should work with L2 texts). This can be achieved by working with *proxy bilingualised dictionaries*.

A bilingualised dictionary maintains the identity facets of the monolingual pedagogical work, together with an equivalent in L1. The bilingualised dictionary functions on the principle that an entry that is supposed to be unfamiliar to the user is better explained in terms that are familiar to the latter. Empirical tests seem to indicate the effectiveness of such a dictionary. Laufer and Melamed (1994), for example, conducted a study comparing the effectiveness of bilingualised, bilingual and monolingual dictionaries. Learners, who were segmented into unskilled, average and good dictionary users, were tested on their comprehension of unknown words and production of original sentences with these unknown words in different conditions. They found that the highest scores were obtained when the bilingualised dictionary was used. This was true in the case of comprehension with all groups of students and in the case of production with good and average dictionary users. On the basis of these results, they concluded that the combination of the monolingual information which contains a definition and examples with a translation of the new word into the learner's tongue tended to produce the best results.

The above results can be easily adapted to the Spanish university environment by broadening the concept of *bilingualised dictionary* with the aim of using technological improvements such as the widespread use of the Internet for teaching and learning purposes. The process of lexicographical bilingualisation consists in adapting a monolingual reference work "to a bilingual purpose by means of TRANSLATION."

(Hartmann and James 1998: 14). Consequently a bilingualised dictionary is based on a monolingual dictionary "whose entries have been translated in full or in part into another language." (Hartmann and James 1998: 14) Thanks to the Internet, we do not need creating business bilingualised dictionaries for learners, but using the thousands of free Internet dictionaries for solving both cognitive and communicative needs. In other words, my claim is that free Internet dictionaries can work as *proxy bilingualised dictionaries* for two reasons.

First, there are hundreds or thousands of dictionaries accessible either by clicking on them or by performing a general search in the main search engine of the dictionary system. Second, the widespread use of multiple-language dictionaries – for example Wikipedia and Wiktionary – which tend to contain similar entries in many languages facilitate the process of consulting parallel and/or comparable texts, thus favouring the process of working with real texts in the L2. For example, a Spanish user can access an English and/or a Spanish entry in the *Wikipedia* or the *Wiktionary* containing similar data in similarly constructed entries which for the purpose of teaching and learning an L2 work as proxy bilingualised entries, assuming that in most occasions these different entries tend to be translations of the entry produced in the "main" or "dominant" language (usually English) of the multiple-language dictionary (Fuertes-Olivera 2009a).

5.4 Evaluating Free Internet Dictionaries for Teaching and Learning Business English

The evaluation of the pedagogical orientation of free online specialised dictionaries can be achieved by paying attention to the three basic requirements previously commented on. The first requirement is concerned with whether or not the free Internet specialised dictionary has paid attention to recent developments regarding the concept *business* and *economics*. The analysis of lemma selection and the lexicographical treatment of both terms and non-terms, for example, will shed light on whether this requirement is fulfilled or not. For example, by browsing in the free Internet dictionary BusinessDictionary.com, I have found out that this requirement is fulfilled, as demonstrated by the following:

- The dictionary contains 20,000 words belonging to typical business/economics domains, arranged in forty odd sub-fields (for example, *accounting and audit*, *agreements and contracts*, *currency trading*, etc). Very useful is the fact that users can access them either by clicking in the sub-field required or by using the general search engine.
- The dictionary contains interactivity facilities that allow email editors or users in order to make claims, queries, suggestions, etc.
- All the terms can be retrieved by clicking in each letter of the alphabet. An analysis of the entries found under the letter **a**, for example, shows that the dictionary lemmatises terms (**A shares**), non-terms (**ability**), loans (**á la carte**), acronyms (**ACCA**), and multiword terms (**alternative dispute resolutions, ADR**).

- It sends users to related texts where the term is used, usually in adequate informative contexts.

The second requirement is concerned with whether or not the free Internet specialised dictionary is all-inclusive or not, i.e., whether it offers a general knowledge of the LSP in question, together with linguistic data for text production, reception and translation. Regarding conceptual information, pedagogically-oriented free Internet specialised dictionaries must contain encyclopaedic notes, labels, and, if possible, *systematic introductions* or *subject-field components* (Bergenholtz and Nielsen 2006; Fuertes-Olivera 2009b; Svensén 2009).

Systematic introductions are outside matter components that provide an overview of those parts of the subject field the lexicographers believe to be particularly relevant to the learner (Bergenholtz and Nielsen 2006). Considering that *business* can be very diverse and cover many different sub-domains, the systematic introduction envisaged are expected to be either general or specific. The former focuses on *business/economics* whereas the latter deals with a single and specific sub-domain. An analysis of the free Internet dictionaries available in dictionary aggregators (Lew 2011) such as YourDictionary.com (there are around more than 870 English dictionaries on the day accessed, November 10, 2011) reveals that free Internet dictionaries do not usually include systematic introductions. This lacuna, however, can be partly overcome by consulting *Wikipedia* or other free Internet reference materials, as that they contain encyclopaedic notes, labels, and references to external texts explaining the concept dealt with in the entry. For example, in *Wikipedia*, the entry for **growth-share matrix i**ncludes more conceptual information than the one previously commented on in example (3). In *Wikipedia*, users learn that a **growth-share matrix**:

- helps a company allocate resources (i.e., it informs on the purpose of the matrix);
- is used as an analytical tool in brand marketing, product management, strategic management, and portfolio analysis (i.e., it places the term in different conceptual realms);
- describes the exact meaning of the colloquial terms *cash cows*, *dogs*, *question mark/problem child*, and *stars*, which are used to categorise business units on the basis of their relative market share and growth rates;
- is extensively used, sometimes with some slight modifications. For example, McKinsey and General Electric have developed a three-cell by three-cell matrix;
- is related with specific norms, pieces of legislation, or traditions. To that end, *Wikipedia* includes the date of inclusion of the term, the date of its possible modification, and texts where the term is contextualised and explained in more detail.

Regarding linguistic information, I have found mixed results. On the one hand, some free Internet dictionaries only contain very scarce linguistic data. An analysis of the free Internet specialised dictionaries grouped in the section Specialty Dictionaries of *YourDictionary.com* shows that the 14 dictionaries included as 'business dictionaries' only offer very scarce linguistic information. For example, the New York Times Glossary of Financial and Business Terms includes a list of

2,500 alphabetically arranged terms. The dictionary uses an analytical macrostructure, which favours reception, and includes synonyms and/or related words in some entries. For example, in (4), users are informed that **default risk**, and **insolvency risk** are synonyms of **bankruptcy risk**, and that the term **bankruptcy** is in attributive position in some compounds and phrases:

(4) Articles in the New York Times Glossary of Financial and Business Terms

Bankruptcy
State of being unable to pay debts. Thus, the ownership of the firm's assets is transferred from the stockholders to the bondholders.

Bankruptcy cost view
The argument that expected indirect and direct bankruptcy costs offset the other benefits from leverage so that the optimal amount of leverage is less than 100 % debt financing [sic].

Bankruptcy risk
The risk that a firm will be unable to meet its debt obligations. Also referred to as default or insolvency risk.

Bankruptcy view
The argument that expected bankruptcy costs preclude firms from being financed entirely with debt.

In the above entries users cannot come across phonetical, morphological, syntactic, semantic, and pragmatic data. But if they are properly instructed on what to search in the Internet, they will come across the requested data by performing a general search in the search engine located in the homepage of the free dictionary aggregator *YourDictionary.com*. For example, a search of the entry **bankruptcy** retrieves both adequate cognitive and communicative information:

- pronunciation (we can hear how this term is pronounced);
- phonetic symbols showing its pronunciation;
- spelling (**bank-ruptcy**);
- singular and plural forms;
- word class;
- two general definitions;
- a list of synonyms with hyperlinks cross-referencing users to some of these synonyms: insolvency, failure, financial loss or ruin, nonpayment, defaulting, repudiation, overdraft, defalcation, liquidation, chapter 11, economic death, pauperism, destitution, indigence, privation, distress, straitened circumstances, beggary, impecuniosity, ruin, ruination, going to the wall*
- a list of antonyms with hyperlinks cross-referencing users to some of these antonyms: (solvency, prosperity*, soundness;
- two specific definitions, one for finance and one for law; Example (5, below) shows a specific definition, with encyclopaedic notes, and implicit language data;
- definitions of specific types of **bankruptcy**, all of which are lemmatised as sub-lemmas (i.e., it uses an analytical macrostructure which favours reception): *Chapter 7 bankruptcy; Chapter 11 bankruptcy; Chapter 12 bankruptcy; Chapter 13 bankruptcy; involuntary bankruptcy; voluntary bankruptcy;*
- usage examples where **bankruptcy** is an object of the verbs *declare, avoid, face, suffer, consider*), or forms collocations with adjectives (*impending, utter, moral,*

spiritual, subsequent, personal), or nouns (*petition, proceeding, restriction, order, attorney, filling*).
- A quote ("Capitalism without **bankruptcy** is like Christianity without hell").

The third requirement refers to whether or not free Internet specialised dictionaries favour working with L2 texts. The above entry for **bankruptcy** agrees with this requirement, and favours solving users' communicative needs by offering most of the language data students may need when facing text production, reception, and translation. For example, the texts used for explaining the concept of **bankruptcy finance** (example 5) illustrate formal language, typically used for producing formal documents, such as letters and reports.

(5) Definition of **bankruptcy** retrieved from *YourDictionary.com*:

A legal proceeding initiated by an individual or company that is unable to pay its debts. A bankruptcy can either liquidate the debts or attempt to develop a reorganization plan under which the debt, or some of it, will be paid. The most common type of bankruptcy filing is Chapter 11, in which a business is allowed to continue running while it reorganizes its debts. Creditors are prevented from attempting to collect debts from a company that is in a Chapter 11 bankruptcy proceeding. In a Chapter 11, the debtor and creditors meet to draw up an agreement for repaying some of the debt.

Some companies close down through a Chapter 7 bankruptcy (also called a liquidation), instead of attempting to reorganize. In a Chapter 7 bankruptcy, a court-appointed interim trustee is given discretion to make management changes, arrange unsecured financing, and wind down the business. Individuals who want to get rid of their debt and not attempt to pay anything back file for Chapter 7 bankruptcy.

Individuals who want to reorganize their debts and pay back a portion file for a Chapter 13 bankruptcy. Typically, people who make this type of filing pay something each month for several years to the bankruptcy court, which distributes the funds to the creditors. When the payments are completed, the debtor's debts are discharged. Chapter 13 bankruptcies allow individuals to hold onto more assets than Chapter 7 bankruptcies do.

Bankruptcies fall into two categories. A voluntary bankruptcy occurs when the debtor petitions the court to begin a bankruptcy proceeding. An involuntary bankruptcy occurs when the creditors petition the court to put the debtor into bankruptcy. The term chapter refers to the chapter of the bankruptcy law where the provisions are outlined.

5.5 Moving Ahead: Free Independent Dictionaries for Independent Online Reading

Munby (1979), Knutson (1997), Carrell and Wise (1998), and Gilmore (2007), among others, have shown that frequent reading practice is one of the best ways to develop vocabulary and improve reading comprehension. In addition, they have shown that both *extensive reading*, i.e., reading large amounts of texts without looking up all unknown vocabulary, and *intensive reading*, i.e., reading small amounts of texts and closely examining and consulting each unknown word, are highly productive vocabulary builders. Researchers have also shown that the dictionary is the most common type of reading aid, and that web-based systems allow instructors to develop English courses that are based on dynamic learning materials that favour adaptive learning for individual students (Liu and Lin 2011; Wang and Liao 2011).

Wang and Liao (2011: 6480) describe an adaptive learning system as a "system developed to accommodate a variety of individual needs and differences", and review the possibilities offered by online systems that rest on modified item response theory (Chen et al. 2006), modular frameworks that segment and transform teaching materials into modular learning objects (Tseng et al. 2008), and data mining techniques (Wang and Liao 2011). In general, these works conclude that the future of education is in the generation of online systems that set different levels of teaching content for vocabulary, grammar, and reading for students with different profiles, i.e., in systems that are based on the concept of adaptive learning.

Regarding the process of reading comprehension and vocabulary learning, recent research focuses on the combination of online reading and the use of computer-mediated aids, especially Internet dictionaries, with the aim of discovering how changes in technology affect learning. LeLoup and Ponterio (2005: 3) comment that students can learn "to browse online news and magazine articles that interest them personally", and thus "become more highly motivated to continue to use their language skills long term because this is a real, day-to-day use of those skills, not just a classroom exercise." Following suit researchers are currently investigating aspects such as the possibility of Internet dictionaries for changing the long-standing pedagogical practice of printed dictionary usage (Liu and Lin 2011), the usability of Internet dictionaries (Heid 2011), as well as creating online tools that can be used for favouring reading comprehension and vocabulary learning (LeLoup and Ponterio 2005).

Liu and Lin (2011: 374), for example, hypothesise that Internet dictionaries may be more convenient than their paper counterparts as online dictionaries "could potentially free up more cognitive resources for comprehension." This hypothesis, which is subdivided into nine more specific hypotheses, is analysed in the context of a Taiwanese university by identifying the learning process associated with using printed dictionaries, type-in dictionaries, pop-up dictionaries and no dictionaries. They evaluate how the above systems affect the processes of understanding written English texts and favouring the acquisition of incidental vocabulary, i.e., the words students "pick up" as a result of a comprehension input (Laufer and Hulstijn 2001; Krashen 1989), indicate that the pop-up dictionary appears to reveal "advantages in terms of frequency of use and learning efficiency" (p. 382), and conclude that the vocabulary search process may be more related to extraneous cognitive loading, i.e., this occurs when irrelevant information occupies and reduces working memory for simultaneous processes, than to germane cognitive loading, i.e., efforts exerted by the learner that "facilitate learning performance rather than impair it." (375).

The above conclusions lead me to assume that the process of teaching and learning Business English in Spanish universities can be upgraded by providing students access to online ways of understanding the meaning of unfamiliar words, as well as encouraging them to browse online news and magazine sites for articles that interest them. LeLoup and Ponterio (2005) present two online web-based systems that contain access to written texts and pop-up dictionaries: Ultralingua.Net and WordChamp. These two systems can be used for offering vocabulary support for independent online reading, and filtering articles through each of them "will give students

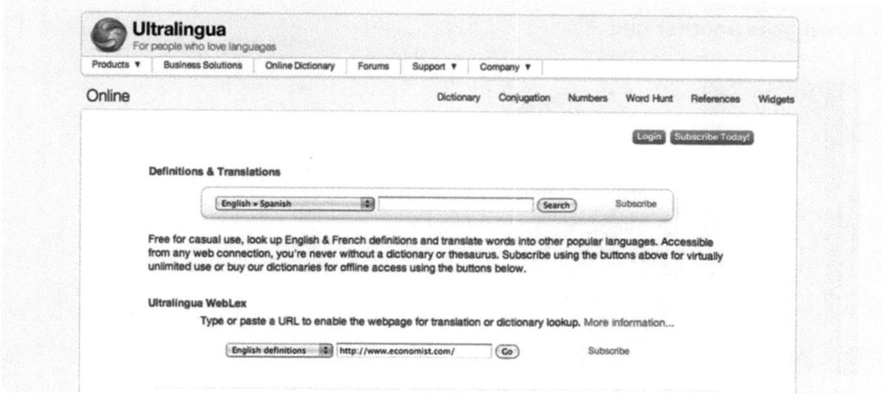

Fig. 5.1 Screenshot for *Ultralingua*

interactive vocabulary help by turning every word into a link that opens a pop-up dictionary entry for that word." (LeLoup and Ponterio 2005: 3).

For example, a Business English student reading *The Economist* can insert its URL for a magazine article and choose several options, e.g. 'English definitions', English to Spanish', etc., for the pop-up dictionary selection (Fig. 5.1).

Ultralingua displays a copy of the article from *The Economist.* All the words are now hypertext links and clicking on a word will open a pop-up window with vocabulary support in several forms: an English definition, a translation equivalent in several languages (French, Spanish, German, Italian and Portuguese), videos, related articles, etc. For example when clicking on **eurozone debt crisis** Spanish students of Business English access a definition from *Wikipedia,* a Spanish translation equivalent, four related articles, grammar data, and a video lasting more than 7 min that explain why the Eurozone has a debt crisis. equivalent, etc. (Fig. 5.2) In a word, these web-based systems can be used for teaching and learning Business English in Spanish universities and have several advantages: they offer data that can be used in both communicative and cognitive use situations; they follow the basic tenets of communicative methodologies; and they allow students to work with authentic materials.

5.6 Conclusions: Free Internet Specialised Dictionaries for Teaching and Learning Purposes

This chapter has illustrated that today's Internet dictionaries and Internet pedagogical dictionaries are much more than electronic versions of printed dictionaries. They are no longer a dream, especially because they can be turned into powerful language learning and teaching (and research) tools (Verlinde and Binon 2009) (See Fuertes-Olivera and Tarp, 2014 for a review of specialised online dictionaries). For example, in the dictionary aggregator *YourDictionary.*

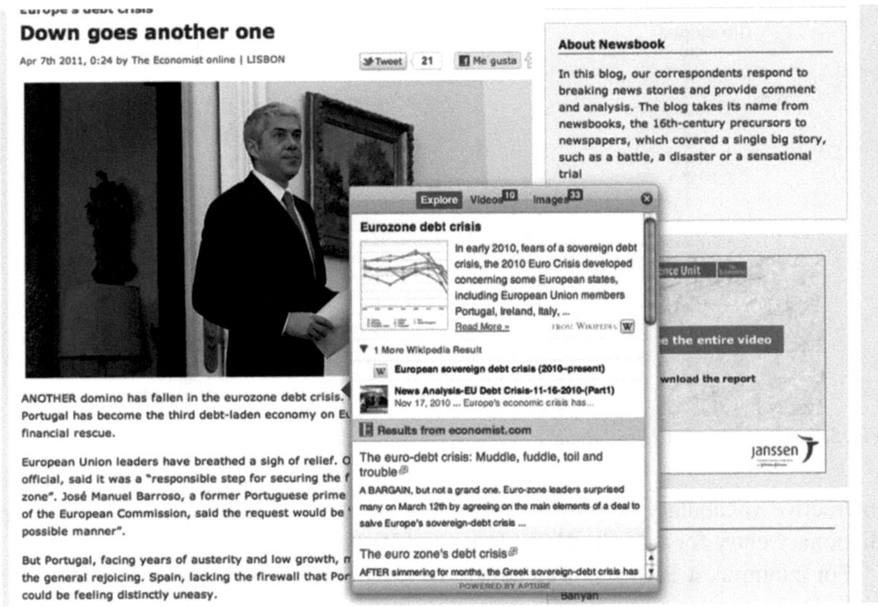

Fig. 5.2 Screenshot for **eurozone debt crisis** taken from *Ultralingua* (Excerpts)

com, users also can access blogs, grammar books, language articles, texts, etc. where users can upgrade their lexicographical needs with grammar and usage information.

Also important is the fact that a new generation of online dictionaries are being compiled which are taking into consideration the tenets of adaptive learning and the characteristics of the Internet. Fuertes-Olivera and Bergenholtz (2011b), for instance, maintain that old typologies of electronic dictionaries (De Schryver 2003) are being substituted by more informed ones, which take into consideration the difference between an information database and an information tool, the access process used, and their integration within pedagogical environments. They add that these new online dictionaries, both pop-up and type-in online dictionaries, are exploring the introduction of Boolean searches, maximising and minimising searches, and using data banks from which different types of dictionaries, and even different dictionaries of the same type can be extracted. A typical example is the so-called *accounting dictionaries* (Fuertes-Olivera and Nielsen 2011, 2012), a set of specialized dictionaries that comprise one database and 23 dictionaries (Bergenholtz 2012), each focused on a specific function:

Danish

1. Meaning of Danish accounting terms
2. Use of Danish accounting terms, search with a known term
3. Use of Danish accounting terms, search based on a known meaning
4. Knowledge of Danish accounting terms, search with a known term

English

5. Meaning of English accounting terms
6. Use of English accounting terms, search with a known term
7. Use of English accounting terms, search based on a known meaning
8. Knowledge of English accounting terms, search with a known term

English-Danish

9. Reception of English terms in English accounting texts
10. Translation of English accounting texts into Danish
11. Knowledge of English and Danish accounting terms

Danish-English

12. Translation of Danish accounting texts into English
13. Knowledge of English and Danish accounting terms

  - no reception dictionary with English explanations and equivalent because non-English user is reading Danish accounting texts

Spanish

14. Meaning of Spanish accounting terms
15. Use of Spanish accounting terms, search with a known term
16. Use of Spanish accounting terms, search based on a known meaning
17. Knowledge of Spanish accounting terms, search with a known term

Spanish-English

18. Reception of English terms in English accounting texts
19. Translation of Spanish accounting texts into English
20. Knowledge of Spanish and English accounting terms

English-Spanish

21. Reception of English terms in English accounting texts
22. Translation of English accounting texts into Spanish
23. Knowledge of English and Spanish accounting terms

In sum, Internet offers a lot of possibilities for teaching and learning Business English, and we must make use of it. In this paper, I have presented my claim for using free Internet specialised dictionaries when teaching and learning Business English in Spanish universities for two main reasons. First, they can be used for solving our students' both cognitive and communicative needs. Second, they favour interconnectivity through different procedures (blogs, e-mails; related searches, etc.) thus encouraging the use of language, which is the basic principle that underlies communicative methodologies.

Finally, a caveat has also been mentioned and discussed: the amount of data retrieved from the Internet is so vast that potential users may need some guidance. For example, our students will benefit if they are instructed on what characteristics pedagogically-oriented dictionaries must have. This paper has presented and discussed three basic requirements, also illustrated with examples taken from free Internet dictionaries, and has presented Internet systems that can offer vocabulary support for independent online reading. These systems can be very helpful provided that instructors of Business English teach their students to discriminate among the vast amount of data that can be retrieved from the Internet. In a word, free Internet dictionaries may be adequate teaching and learning materials if their potential users are not suffocated by the Google effect, but contribute to adaptive learning thus serving the purpose of Gasparetti et al. (2009) who envisaged that the principal advantages of web-based systems are to be seen in the opportunity to overcome restrictions such as few teaching resources, organise complex and tailored courses for single learners, and evaluate their acquired knowledge levels more or less easily.

References

Andersen, Birger, and Pedro A. Fuertes-Olivera. 2009. The application of function theory to the classification of English monolingual business dictionaries. *Lexicographica. International Annual for Lexicography* 25: 213–240.

Atkins, B.T.S., and K. Varantola. 1998. Language learners using dictionaries: The final report on the EURALEX/AILA project on dictionary use. In *Using dictionaries. Studies of dictionary use by language learners and translators*, Lexicographica series maior 88, ed. B.T.S. Atkins, 21–81. Tübingen: Max Niemeyer.

Baruque, Lucia B., and Rubens N. Melo. 2004. Learning theory and instructional design using learning objects. *Journal of Educational Multimedia and Hypermedia* 13(4): 343–370.

Bergenholtz, H. 2012. Concepts for monofunctional accounting dictionaries. *Terminology* 18(2): 243–263.

Bergenholtz, Henning, and U. Kaufmann. 1997. Terminography and lexicography. A critical survey of dictionaries from a single specialised field. *Hermes. Journal of Linguistics* 18: 91–125.

Bergenholtz, H., and S. Nielsen. 2006. Subject-field components as integrated parts of LSP dictionaries. *Terminology* 12(2): 281–303.

Bergenholtz, H., and Sven Tarp. 2002. Die moderne lexikographische Funktionslehre. Diskussionsbeitrag zu neuen und alten Paradigmen, die Wörterbücher als Gebrauchsgegenstände verstehen. *Lexicographica. International Annual for Lexicography* 18: 253–263.

Bergenholtz, H., and Sven Tarp. 2003. Two opposing theories: On H.E. Wiegand's recent discovery of lexicographic functions. *Hermes Journal of Linguistics* 31: 171–196.

Bergenholtz, H., and Sven Tarp. 2004. The concept of dictionary usage. *Nordic Journal of English Studies* 3: 23–36.

Bergenholtz, H., and Sven Tarp. 2005. Wörterbuchfunktionen. In *Schreiben, Verstehen, Übersetzen, Lernen. Zu ein- und zweisprachigen Wörterbüchern mit Deutsch*, ed. I. Barz, H. Bergenholtz, and J. Korhonen, 119–126. Frankfurt a.M./Bern/New York/Paris: Peter Lang.

BusinessDictionary.com. http://www.businessdictionary.com/. Last accessed 6 Apr 2011.

Carrell, P.L., and T.E. Wise. 1998. The relationship between prior knowledge and topic interest in second language reading. *Studies in Second Language Acquisition* 20: 285–309.

Chen, C.M., C.Y. Liu, and M.H. Chang. 2006. Personalized curriculum sequencing utilizing modified item response theory for web-based instruction. *Expert Systems with Applications* 30: 378–396.

Cowie, A. 1999. *English dictionaries for foreign learners: A history*. Oxford: OUP/Clarendon Press.

De Schryver, G.-M. 2003. Lexicographers' dreams in the electronic-dictionary age. *International Journal of Lexicography* 16(2): 143–199.

Deubel, P. 2003. An investigation of behaviorist and cognitive approaches to instructional design. *Journal of Education Multimedia and Hypermedia* 12(1): 63–90.

Fuertes-Olivera, Pedro A. 2009a. The function theory of lexicography and electronic dictionaries: Wiktionary as a prototype of collective free multiple-language internet dictionary. In *Lexicography at a crossroads dictionaries and encyclopedias today, lexicographical tools tomorrow*, Studies in language and communication, 90, ed. H. Bergenholtz, S. Tarp, and S. Nielsen, 99–134. Bern: Peter Lang.

Fuertes-Olivera, Pedro A. 2009b. Systematic introductions in specialised dictionaries. In *Lexicography in the 21st century. In honour of Henning Bergenholtz*, Terminology and lexicography research and practice, 12, ed. S. Nielsen and S. Tarp, 161–178. Amsterdam/Philadelphia: John Benjamins.

Fuertes-Olivera, Pedro A. (ed.). 2010. *Specialised dictionaries for learners*. Berlin/New York: De Gruyter.

Fuertes-Olivera, Pedro A. 2011. Equivalent selection in specialized e-lexicography: A case study with Spanish accounting terms. *Lexikos* 21: 95–119.

Fuertes-Olivera, Pedro A., and A. Arribas-Baño. 2008. *Pedagogical specialised lexicography. The representation of meaning in business English and Spanish dictionaries*, Terminology and lexicography research and practice, 11. Amsterdam/Philadelphia: John Benjamins.

Fuertes-Olivera, Pedro A., and H. Bergenholtz (eds.). 2011. *E-lexicography. The internet, digital initiatives and lexicography*. London/New York: Continuum.

Fuertes-Olivera, Pedro A., and H. Bergenholtz. 2011b. Introduction. The construction of internet dictionaries. In eds. Pedro A. Fuertes-Olivera and H. Bergenholtz, 1–16.

Fuertes-Olivera, Pedro A., and S. Gómez-Martínez. 2004. Empirical assessment of some learning factors affecting Spanish students of business English. *English for Specific Purposes* 23: 163–180.

Fuertes-Olivera, Pedro A., and S. Nielsen. 2008. Translating politeness in bilingual English-Spanish business correspondence. *Meta* 53(3): 667–678.

Fuertes-Olivera, Pedro A., and S. Nielsen. 2011. The dynamics of terms in accounting: What the construction of the *accounting dictionaries* reveals about metaphorical terms in culture-bound subject fields. In *The dynamics of terms in specialized communication. An interdisciplinary perspective*, eds. Rita Temmerman, and M. Van Campenhoudt, Special Issue of *Terminology. International Journal of Applied Issues in Specialized Communication* 17(1): 157–180.

Fuertes-Olivera, Pedro A., and Sandro Nielsen. 2012. Online dictionaries for assisting translators of LSP texts: The *accounting dictionaries*. *International Journal of Lexicography* 25(2): 191–215.

Fuertes-Olivera, Pedro A., and S. Tarp. 2011. Lexicography for the third millennium: Cognitive-oriented specialised dictionaries for learners. *Ibérica* 21: 141–162.

Fuertes-Olivera, Pedro A., and S. Tarp. 2011. *Theory and practice of specialised online dictionaries. Lexicography versus terminography*, Lexicographica Series Maior. Berlin/New York: De Gruyter.

Gasparetti, F., A. Micarelli, and F. Sciarrone. 2009. A Web-based training system for business letter writing. *Knowledge-Based Systems* 22: 287–291.

Gilmore, A. 2007. Authentic materials and authenticity in foreign language learning. *Language Teaching* 40: 97–118.

Hartmann, R.K.K., and G. James. 1998. *Dictionary of lexicography*. New York: Routledge.

Hausmann, F.J. 1977. *Einführung in die Benutzung der neufranzösischen Wörterbücher*. Tübingen: Niemeyer.

Heid, U. 2011. Electronic dictionaries as tools: Towards an assessment of usability. In: eds. Pedro A. Fuertes-Olivera and H. Bergenholtz, 287–304.

Knutson, E.M. 1997. Reading with a purpose: Communicative reading tasks for the foreign language classroom. *Foreign Language Annals* 30(1): 49–57.

Krashen, S. 1989. We acquire vocabulary and spelling by reading: Additional evidence for input hypothesis. *Modern Language Journal* 73: 440–463.

Kromann, H.P., T. Riiber, and P. Rosbach. 1992. Principles of bilingual lexicography. In *Wörterbücher, dictionaries, dictionnaires. An international encyclopedia of lexicography*, vol. 3, ed. Franz Josef Hausmann, Oskar Reichmann, Herbert Ernst Wiegand, and Ladislav Zgusta, 2711–2728. Berlin/New York: Walter de Gruyter.

Laufer, B., and J. Hulstijn. 2001. Incidental vocabulary acquisition in a second language: The construction of task-induced involvement. *Applied Linguistics* 22(1): 1–26.

Laufer, B., L. Melamed, et al. 1994. Monolingual, bilingual and 'Bilingualised' dictionaries: Which are more effective, for what and for whom? In *Euralex'94 proceedings*, ed. W. Martin, 565–576. Amsterdam: VU.

LeLoup, Jean W., and Robert Ponterio. 2005. Vocabulary support for independent online reading. *Language Learning & Technology* 9(2): 3–7.

Lew, Robert. 2011. Online dictionaries of English. In eds. Pedro A. Fuertes-Olivera and H. Bergenholtz, 230–250.

Liu, T.-C., and P.-H. Lin. 2011. What comes with technological convenience? Exploring the behaviors and performance of learning with computer-mediated dictionaries. *Computers in Human Behavior* 27: 373–383.

Lozano Irueste, J.M. 2005. *Diccionario bilingüe de Economía y Empresa (inglés-español/español-inglés)*, 7th ed. Madrid: Ediciones Pirámide.

Mackey, Thomas P., and Jinwon Ho. 2010. Exploring the relationships between Web usability and students' perceived learning in Web-based Multimedia (WBMM) tutorials. *Computers and Education* 50: 386–409.

Mayer, Richard E. 2001. *Multimedia learning*. Santa Barbara: Cambridge University Press.

Montero-Martínez, S., Pedro A. Fuertes-Olivera, and M. García de Quesada. 2001. The translator as 'language planner': Syntactic calquing in an English-Spanish technical translation of chemical engineering. *Meta* 46(4): 687–698.

Munby, J. 1979. Teaching intensive reading skills. In *Reading in a second language: Hypotheses, organization, and practice*, ed. R. Mackay, B. Barkman, and R.R. Jordan, 142–158. Rowley: Newbury House.

New York Times Glossary of Financial and Business Terms. http://www.nytimes.com/library/financial/glossary/bfglosa.htm. Last accessed 5 Jan 2011.

Parkinson, D., assisted by J. Noble. 2005. *Oxford business English dictionary for learners of English*. Oxford: Oxford University Press.

Scerba, L.V. 1995. Towards a general theory of lexicography. *International Journal of Lexicography* 8(4): 315–350.

Svensén, B. 2009. Subject-field classification for metalexicography revisited. In *Lexicography in the 21st century. In honour of Henning Bergenholtz*, Terminology and lexicography research and practice, 12, ed. S. Nielsen and S. Tarp, 147–159. Amsterdam/Philadelphia: John Benjamins.

Tarp, S. 2008. *Lexicography in the borderland between knowledge and non-knowledge*, Lexicographica series maior, 134. Tübingen: Niemeyer.

Tseng, S.S., J.M. Su, G.J. Hwang, C.C. Tsai, and C.J. Tsai. 2008. An object-oriented course framework for developing adaptive learning systems. *Educational Technology & Society* 11(2): 171–191.

Ultralingua.Net. http://www.ultralingua.com/onlinedictionary/index.html. Last accessed 6 Apr 2011.

Verlinde, S., and J. Binon. 2009. Pedagogical lexicography revisited. In *Lexicography at a crossroads dictionaries and encyclopedias today, lexicographical tools tomorrow*, Studies in language and communication, 90, ed. H. Bergenholtz, S. Tarp, and S. Nielsen, 69–89. Bern: Peter Lang.

Wang, Y-h, and H.-C. Liao. 2011. Data mining for adaptive learning in a TESL-based e-learning system. *Expert Systems with Applications* 38: 6480–6485.

Wiegand, H.E. 1977a. Nachdenken über Wörterbücher. Aktuelle Probleme. In *Nachdenken über Wörterbücher*, ed. Günther Drosdowski, Helmut Henne, and Herber E. Wiegand, 51–102. Mannheim/Vienna/Zürich: Bibliographisches Institut.

Wiegand, H.E. 1977b. Einige grundlegende semantisch-pragmatische Aspekte von Wörterbucheinträgen. Ein Beitrag zur praktischen Lexikologie. *Kopenhagener Beiträge zur Germanistischen Linguistik* 12: 59–149.
Wiegand, H.E. 1987. Zur handlungstheoretischen Grundlegung der Wörterbenutzungsforschung. *Lexicographica. International Annual for Lexicography* 3: 178–227.
Wikipedia. http://www.wikipedia.org/. Last accessed 6 Apr 2011.
Wiktionary. http://www.wiktionary.org/. Last accessed 6 Apr 2011.
WordChamp. http://www.wordchamp.com/lingua2/Home.do. Last accessed 6 Apr 2011.
YourDictionary.com. http://www.yourdictionary.com/. Last accessed 6 Apr 2011.

Chapter 6
Moodle Glossary Tasks for Teaching Legal English

Ruth Breeze

6.1 Background

The introduction of e-learning platforms for distance and blended learning has opened up a wide range of possibilities for collaborative learning projects across the educational spectrum. Within this field, web-based collaborative tasks have recently been explored in various areas of higher education. Their educational potential is considerable, particularly in courses offered by blended or distance learning (Bruns and Humphreys 2005), but also as a complement to traditional classroom-based instruction. On the one hand, such tasks can be used to exploit the potential offered by the Internet as a resource for learning about course contents. On the other, they provide a wide range of opportunities for helping the students to acquire different competences, such as research, organisation and communication skills. Moreover, the advent of platforms such as Moodle has made it easy for students to publish and share their work in an attractive format. The creation of collaborative online material enriches students' learning experiences, adding a dimension that is new in pedagogical terms, but which matches well with the learning style and habits of the Facebook generation.

In general terms, the challenge facing the use of groupware tools in academic programmes is to find ways of activating rich learning experiences, encouraging active involvement by students and promoting learner autonomy (Argüelles Álvarez 2009), while maintaining the rigorous learning methods required in academic contexts, which should include some form of corrective feedback. It is important that the online activities should be appropriately integrated into the course programme, however, because dual delivery in the form of classroom teaching plus learning through web-based platforms may lead to redundancy or duplication, and might

R. Breeze (✉)
Institute of Modern Languages, University of Navarra, Pamplona, Spain
e-mail: rbreeze@unav.es

E. Bárcena et al. (eds.), *Languages for Specific Purposes in the Digital Era*, Educational Linguistics 19, DOI 10.1007/978-3-319-02222-2_6,

possibly result in an increased workload for students and/or teachers. It is therefore important that teachers should create educational activities that integrate both learning contexts in a positive way, and ensure that the two learning media are mutually complementary (Dabbagh 2002). The creation of online collaborative glossaries or encyclopaedias designed to complement and enrich students' learning on a particular course undoubtedly offers possibilities in this area. Online writing projects of this kind may serve as a useful complement to the traditional English language class, since they provide a stimulus for learners to interact and share their knowledge in an online space, while allowing the teacher to maintain a controlled environment (Breeze 2005). In general, it is motivating for students to know that they are writing for a real audience of peers, rather than only for the teacher. Moreover, the degree of interest is heightened if peer feedback options are permitted, since other students' comments may help students develop their writing skills and encourage them to improve their language and content knowledge (Davoli et al. 2009). On the other hand, it is also necessary for the teacher to make it clear to the students how much guidance and correction he or she intends to provide, and at what point in the task he or she is going to provide it, since students often feel insecure about making their work public, and about using the work done by their classmates. Students tend to accept the idea of publication more readily once they are sure that the teacher will provide suggestions and corrections that guarantee that their work meets a certain standard.

In the context of language courses for specific purposes, the use of groupware applications such as wikis and glossaries has enabled teachers to design learning activities that allow students to interact asynchronously in collaborative tasks, sharing or jointly constructing their knowledge of specialised lexis or relevant content areas. Such collaboration may take the form of compiling joint glossaries, dictionaries or encyclopedias, to which students contribute entries either individually or in groups (Área 2009; Lázaro et al. 2009; Bocanegra and Perea 2011). Since specialised terminology and the integration of language and content are two key issues in the teaching of languages for specific purposes, tasks related to creating a glossary or encyclopaedia appear to offer considerable promise in this field.

This chapter describes the design and implementation of two collaborative legal glossary writing tasks over two successive years as part of a university legal English course, and provides an analysis of the procedure and outcomes. In the first year, 2009–2010, the project consisted of compiling an online legal English glossary, with definitions of key terms and examples. The scale was relatively small, with each student contributing only three entries. The outcome was a glossary that could be used by the whole class for study purposes. In the second year, 2010–2011, a more ambitious plan was carried out: students were each given a country with a common law or mixed legal system, and asked to research a series of topics in order to write an encyclopaedia entry for that country. To round off this project, students were given worksheets which required them to read the other participants' entries in order to answer different types of question.

First, the two cycles of the project are described and the results assessed. Then the principles underlying the two glossary activities are discussed, and some key points regarding the pedagogical structuring and management of the tasks are discussed. Finally, conclusions are drawn as to ways in which the present study could be extended with similar groups of students, or broadened to other contexts.

6.2 First Cycle: Legal English Glossary

The task for the first cycle of practitioner research (the legal English glossary) was designed on the basis of two previous projects carried out by researchers with similar groups of students at other Spanish universities. These studies are reviewed, and then the design of the present task is outlined.

6.2.1 Review of Previous Studies

Several previous reports are available concerning the collaborative creation of glossaries, encyclopaedias and class reference tools, using a variety of platforms. To take one example, Área (2009) used a Moodle Wiki as the basis for collaborative work on a "virtual encyclopaedia" containing the key concepts for the course. His students worked in groups of 4–6, to write entries for 15–25 concepts. One student wrote an entry, and the other students read it and added any modifications they thought appropriate. At the end of the project, the students presented their encyclopaedias to other groups during the class. Área emphasises the versatility of the Moodle tool, and the records which enable the teacher to track what the students are doing. In his project, the students modified each others' work and edited the final version, but the teacher did not intervene. The final group products were then evaluated. The project was successful as a whole, but one difficulty that arose as a consequence of the design was that the task could only be undertaken towards the end of the course, because only then would the student have acquired enough knowledge of the subject to render the task feasible. This type of activity should therefore be viewed as a consolidation or review exercise, rather than as an opportunity for research or autonomous learning.

In another case study, Lázaro et al. (2009) used Wikispaces with groups of students to create glossaries containing the new vocabulary they encountered when reading legal texts in English. This was intended to encourage learner independence and use of reference works, and to provide a tool for further study. Although these authors emphasise the benefits of collaborative work, and stress the importance of involving students in the creation of material that is useful for their own learning process, they note that in their legal glossary project, students appeared to lose motivation quickly. Moreover, they found that their students were unwilling to correct or comment on each other's work, and that students expressed insecurity because they felt that the teachers were not correcting their contributions. These authors found it difficult to evaluate the different levels of participation, and they recommend that a clear set of assessment criteria should be established before students embark on the Wiki task.

6.2.2 Design of Legal Glossary Task

The present case study builds on the findings of these previous studies in order to design and implement the collaborative construction of a legal English glossary by 28 undergraduate students as part of the 6-credit course "Inglés jurídico", taught in the academic year 2009–2010. Legal English presents many difficulties for Spanish law students, because the world of common law is quite different from the civil law system that the students have studied during their degree course. For students to understand texts, cases and procedures from a common law background, it is necessary for them to have a working knowledge of many of the key concepts in common law. One example is sufficient to illustrate this problem: in civil law, the theory of contract focuses on the consent between the parties, the object and the "causa", that is, the motive which justifies entering into the contract. In common law, however, the classic definition of a contract is as an offer, which is accepted, for which "consideration" is given. The definition of concepts such as "consideration" is extremely important for students to understand how contracts work in the English-speaking world, and to gain an insight into the nature of the disputes that may arise.

The basic idea underlying the legal English glossary project was that writing entries would help the students to revise their knowledge of legal terminology and concepts for the final exam, and that it would enable them to practise giving explanations of key concepts in English. The creation of this online glossary was also intended to be useful for the whole class as a reference and study tool.

The procedure for creating the glossary was as follows. Each student was assigned three key concepts, and shown how to contribute entries (100–150 words per entry) to the Moodle legal English glossary. Students worked in small groups during class time to compile three model entries, which were then discussed in terms of contents and language. This preparatory stage served to "scaffold" the task, by helping students to see what was required and how they could achieve this themselves. The final group versions of these were then inserted by the teacher during the class, in order to demonstrate how the platform worked. Various reference works were recommended, and students were also encouraged to draw on the course notes in compiling their entries. The students were required to upload their entries before an initial deadline, and incorporate the changes proposed by the teacher before a second deadline. Before both deadlines, reminders were sent out to students using the Moodle messages function. In terms of assessment, students were given a maximum of five points (5 % of the final course grade), for entries that were submitted before the first deadline, fulfilled all the requirements and incorporated the teacher's suggestions before the second deadline. Students who failed to comply with these requirements were given lower scores. The main practical purpose underlying this task structure was to ensure that the class had a functional glossary of key terms to use for self-study before the final exam. However, the use of strict deadlines for new entries and for editing proved beneficial in general terms, because it meant that the students knew exactly what they had to do to obtain the five points, and that there was no loss of momentum.

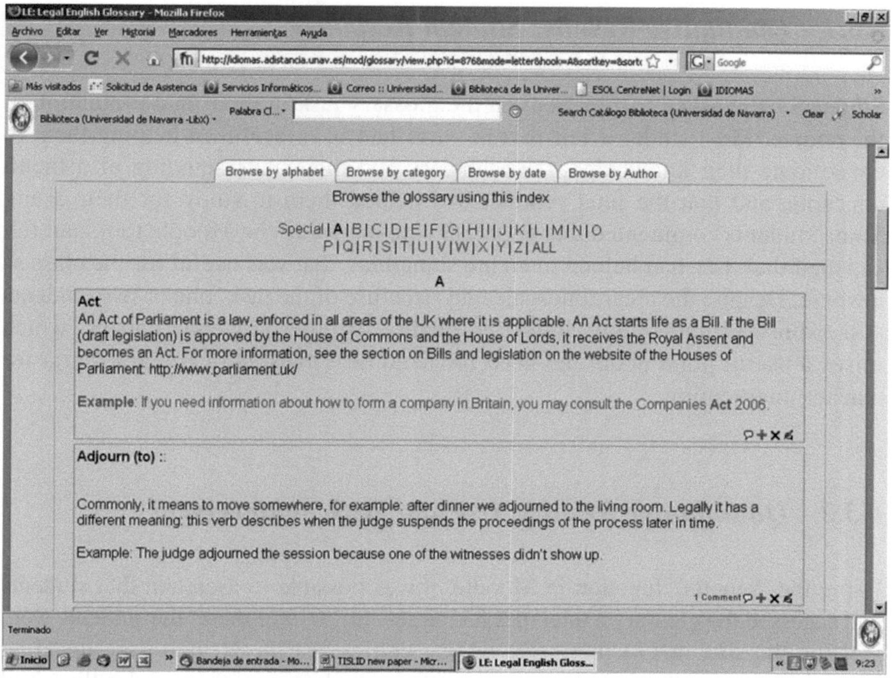

Example 6.1 Screenshot of legal English glossary

Regarding the platform, the decision was made to use the Moodle glossary tool for three reasons. First, this tool offers security rather than openness, so that each student could contribute the entries that had been assigned to him or her, and the teacher could make comments and corrections individually, to which the student could then respond. Secondly, the tracking facilities in Moodle allow the teacher to establish easily how much work has been contributed, when, and by whom. Finally, as in other Wiki and glossary platforms, the entries and comments were visible to all the students throughout the process, so that the glossary could serve its ultimate purpose as a class reference work. It is also useful to note that the Moodle glossary is attractively presented, and can be searched in various different ways by the students, as well as by the teacher using the "reports" function. An example of the finished product is provided in Example 6.1.

6.3 Legal English Glossary: Results and Evaluation

The procedure and product were evaluated using several different methods in order to obtain an all-round vision of what had been achieved during the task.

6.3.1 Qualitative Results: Student Response

Students were asked to comment on the glossary task in their final evaluation of the course. Most students felt that the task had been useful in helping them to consolidate their knowledge of vocabulary and their understanding of difficult concepts, and that the final product had helped them to study for their exam. Some students commented that they had enjoyed using the Moodle tool, and felt satisfied that they had helped to create something that was useful for the class as a whole. Despite the clear timescale and structure of the task, one or two students still expressed uncertainty about the quality of other students' entries, which raises a useful point about the need for fixed deadlines and explicit criteria for teacher intervention.

6.3.2 Quantitative Results: Use and Task Achievement

Using the "reports" function in Moodle, it was possible to ascertain that students had accessed the glossary a total of 2,352 times. In 2,019 of these, the students were viewing the site, in 174 they were adding entries, and in 81 they were updating entries. Regarding the timing of the task, all the students met the first deadline, and all but two of them met the second deadline.

6.3.3 Quantitative Results: Editing and Comments

The types of action that needed to be undertaken by the teacher and, subsequently, by the students, were classified using a taxonomy developed for this purpose. Previous taxonomies such as those of Meishar-Tal and Gorsky (2010) and Pfeil et al. (2006) identified various types of action or change, and several areas of revision, focusing particularly on changes at sentence level and below. In the present case, it was decided to start from further back and make a broad initial classification concerning whether the changes related to content or language. Once this had been determined, the comments on content were classified according to whether they were intended to correct content, add content or request examples, while the comments on language were classified as referring to spelling, vocabulary or structure (grammar and syntax).

The number of comments requesting change of each kind is shown below in Table 6.1.

As far as students' responses to comments were concerned, at the deadline for correction, only five entries were left uncorrected (two students). It was necessary for the teacher to perform these corrections herself, to guarantee the students' trust in the glossary as a study tool.

Table 6.1 Type of changes that were requested: Glossary

Type of change requested	Number of entries in which changes were requested
Content	
Correction	9
Addition of new content	11
Request for example	7
Language	
Spelling	13
Vocabulary	15
Structure	20

6.3.4 *Quantitative Results: Exam Performance*

Both the mid-term and final exam for "Inglés jurídico" include a section in which students are required to define key terminology. These students made a considerable improvement from the mid-term to the final exam in this section (means: 37 and 69.7 % respectively). The difference was found to be highly significant ($p<0.0001$) using Student's paired t-test. The results for this section of the final exam for this year's course (2010) were also compared with those from the previous year (2009), when no equivalent glossary task had been performed. The mean score in the terminology section of the exam was 68 % in 2009 and 69.5 % in 2010. Student's t-test was again applied, but the differences between the results for the 2 years in question were found not to be significant, although the standard deviation was higher for the 2009 group (4.51 as opposed to 3.94), which suggested that the 2010 group had a more homogeneous level of attainment. The median score in both 2009 and 2010 was 68.2. However, the very small improvement noted in the exam score did not fully reflect the students' achievement. It was noticeable that the students who had participated in the glossary task (2010) on average gave fuller and more detailed answers in this section of the exam than the students who had not (2009); if this had been reflected in their examination mark, the students in 2010 would have obtained much higher scores.

6.4 Second Cycle: Encyclopaedia of Common Law Countries

Since the first Moodle glossary project was judged to be successful, a second project was designed which built on the experiences gleaned from the first. This project was carried out by the 22 students enrolled on the six-credit course "Inglés jurídico" in the academic year 2010–2011, that is, 1 year after the glossary project. Since students had been found to have little difficulty accessing the Moodle site and writing and editing their entries, it was decided that a more demanding writing task could be set, requiring students to compose and edit longer texts of greater complexity. Moreover, this task could include a wider range of creative options, such as the choice of including images or maps, and changing background or font colours, since the students in the previous year had found Moodle easy to use in this respect. Against this background, the task chosen for the second year of the project was to write an encyclopaedia of the legal systems of common law countries, consisting of entries about the different countries across the world that have common law or mixed systems. Since many of these countries are former British colonies in which other legal systems, such as Muslim law, also have official status, it is interesting for students to be able to acquire an overview of the very different contexts in which common law operates.

6.4.1 Review of Previous Studies

Class encyclopaedias resemble the type of glossary task outlined above, in that they require online reading and research about a specific field. However, in comparison to the glossary, they incorporate a larger amount of information, including multimodal material, and therefore require a more sophisticated approach to seeking, compiling and reorganising information. In educational terms, this type of activity can be seen to draw on some of the principles underlying the "webquest". The invention of webquests is attributed to Dodge and March (see Dodge 1995), who devised inquiry-oriented activities involving use of the Internet, which were structured to encourage students to develop skills of analysis, synthesis and evaluation. In their original design, the information search is open-ended, and students are supposed to work in groups to achieve the objectives that have been defined for the quest. Most authors agree that the quest should involve more than simply answering questions (Starr 2000; Adell 2004): ideally, the activity should be structured so that students have to obtain information from more than one source, summarise or rework it, and then use it to create something new (see Dodge 2001a, and The WebQuest Page for a wide range of examples).

However, it is also now clear that for a webquest to be successful, complete open-endedness is not necessarily useful: Dodge (2001b) highlights the need for scaffolding, which should be provided at three key stages during the webquest process, namely when evaluating sources and looking for information, when transforming the information in order to fit with the task that has been set, and when producing the new information according to a particular scheme or format. Moreover, as in the case of many forms of task-based learning, webquests are most successful when the finished product can be shared and used. Thus many webquests end with a powerpoint presentation in which one group of students explain their results to another, and the class vote for the presentation which met the initial requirements best. Others may culminate in a writing task, or in a video production. The main underlying principle is that the students' work should lead up to a meaningful outcome which can be shared with other students and evaluated by the teacher and/or other members of the learning community.

Many benefits have been attributed to the use of webquests at different levels in the educational system. Some qualitative studies have shown that webquests help to involve students more in the topics that they are studying, generating a greater degree of interest in the subject matter and helping them to develop their own perspective on the issues at hand (Angeli and Valanides 2004; Hung 2004). Webquest-type activities are particularly useful in encouraging students to take responsibility for their own learning, and helping them to develop specific strategies, particularly in the areas of finding and selecting information, summarising and synthesising data from different sources, and working in collaboration with other learners (Lara and Repáraz 2007). Quantitative research has also suggested that students' learning can be enhanced and reinforced through webquest-type activities (Gaskill et al. 2006).

In the present case, the main benefits sought from the use of a webquest-type activity were those of helping students practise their research skills and gain a better working knowledge of both language and content by performing a task that could be shared with the rest of the group. The online activity was designed to be motivating for the students, allowing them a certain degree of creativity, and enabling them to explore aspects of common law countries that were not discussed on the course. It was also intended to promote a sense of community among the class members, who were from different years of the degree programme and were also enrolled in a variety of different learning itineraries within the Law School.

6.4.2 *Design of Encyclopaedia of Common Law Task*

The situation described in this case study differs from most of the previous studies on webquest activities in that undergraduate students can already be expected to have effective Internet research skills, and so less scaffolding was required regarding the information search stage than would have been the case with younger students. On the other hand, the cognitive challenge of performing the task in a second language, in a specialised area for which information is not widely available in the Internet, made this webquest-type task suitable for use at university level.

In accordance with the principles outlined above, a task was designed to meet the following objectives: to make students read widely about the legal systems of different common law countries, in order to gain practice at reading within a specialised domain, and to become more conversant with technical and semi-technical vocabulary; to encourage students to take an interest in the legal systems of other countries, and in comparative law in general; and to provide a stimulus for students to write about legal issues for a specialised audience. Since the idea was not just to write, but to write and be read, the design also incorporated a final quiz activity which students would complete by reading each others' work.

The task was structured in three principal stages. During the first stage of the task, students were all given a worksheet with a set of topics related to common law legal systems, and each student was assigned a different country which would form the object of his/her research. Thus students all had the same topics (development of the legal system, sources of law, constitution, important differences between the law of your country and other neighbouring legal systems, courts and procedures, human rights, legal training, and so on), but were required to research these topics with respect to different countries (Bangladesh, Ireland, Uganda, Malaysia, Singapore, and so on). The students were given a list of websites that they could use for their research, and were recommended to start with the NYU Global Law and the Jurist World Law pages; they were informed that they should only rely on secondary sources such as Wikipedia for supplementary information.

For the first deadline, students had to research the topics on the worksheet and bring the information to the class. At this stage, the paper worksheet served as a tool for the teacher to correct or guide students as to how to complete the task, and as a means of correcting students' language. It also provided the basis of a spoken information exchange activity which was carried out in pairs in the classroom. Once students had exchanged facts about their countries, they were asked to think of any other questions they would like to know about concerning the law in their partner's country, and to note down any questions that their partner asked. At this stage, students consulted their teacher individually, to check that their research included the right type and quantity of information, and to clear up any difficulties with language and contents.

For the second deadline, students had to create an entry for their country in the Moodle Encyclopaedia of Common Law Countries, and write in the information they had gathered on their worksheets. It proved useful for the students to start this part of the task in class time, so that they could obtain "hands-on" experience and help each other to resolve any difficulties with the tool. They then completed the entries as homework. Since the Moodle glossary application also allows users to add images, the students were encouraged to find at least one map and a representative image for their country. Once the entries had been made, the teacher reviewed the language and contents of the encyclopaedia, and added some comments to each entry using the box provided for this purpose. A third deadline was imposed to ensure that all the entries would be edited by a specific date. An example of the finished product is provided in Example 6.2.

The last stage of the Encyclopaedia task consisted of an information gap activity. In this, students were given a worksheet based on the contents of the encyclopaedia, and had to read each others' entries in order to complete it. Although it would have been possible for students to copy each others' answers, the fact that the teacher was able to check whether students had used Moodle through the "records" application meant that they were likely to do the work individually. The worksheet consisted of a blend of questions with different purposes. Some were straightforward questions ("What is the age of legal capacity in Scotland?" or "How long can someone be president of South Africa?") which were simply intended to encourage students to scan the entries for specific information. Other questions were designed to elicit a longer explanation ("Is family law the same for all citizens of India?" or "What does the principle of 'one country – two systems' mean in Hong Kong?"); in this case, students were supposed to read and rephrase information provided in the entries. Finally, there were also some questions intended to encourage students to read

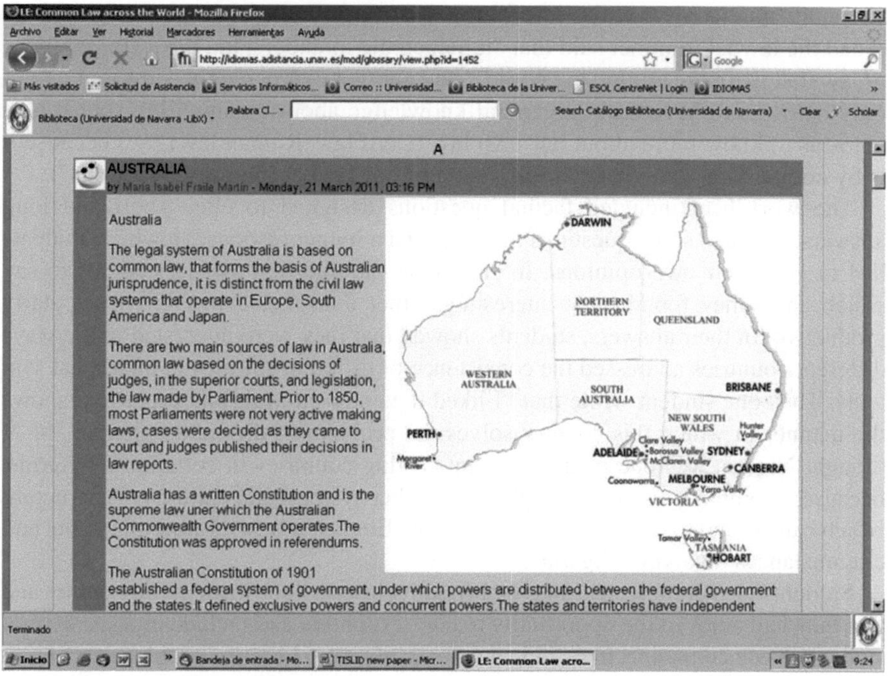

Example 6.2 Screenshot of encyclopaedia of common law countries

across different parts of the encyclopaedia and contrast information obtained from different entries ("In which common law countries does Islamic law have official status, and how does its status vary?"). The worksheet ended with an evaluative question requiring a longer answer ("Explain which entry you found most interesting, and why").

As in the case of the Legal English Glossary, students were aware that they would earn 5 % of their final mark for the course by completing the task properly, which acted as an incentive for them to contribute to the encyclopaedia.

6.4.3 Qualitative Results: Student Response

The students responded positively to the task, and all of them completed the entry for their country, and the final worksheet. Several of the students, particularly those enrolled on the Anglo-American law programme, expressed the opinion that this task enabled them to put together knowledge that they had gained in different areas of their law degree. Others said that it was interesting because it helped them to understand more about legal systems that were very different from their own, or even to understand their own system more fully. One student commented that

"I found (the activity) really interesting and useful in order to get to know how broad the law is", another said that "it helped me to understand the different types of law that there are around the world", and another expressed the view that "it not only helps us to have a more general knowledge about common law, but it also helps us to know more about our own law (Civil law, Roman law) (…) because it is by comparison that we get a full vision of our background and traditions".

The worksheet included factual questions designed to elicit short and long answers, and also some questions that required a longer response in which students had to give their own opinions. In particular, the question asking students to say which entry they found most interesting (other than their own) was particularly productive. In their answers, students showed that they were interested in the ways different countries addressed the coexistence of different cultures in their legal systems. Thus one student wrote that "I liked the entry on Malaysia because it shows the manner in which this country solves the problem of different cultures", or "I thought Nigeria was one of the most interesting countries in common law terms, because it combines lots of principles from other systems and cultures in a structure which can be said to be solid (…) adapting the English law to the special factors and circumstances involving Nigeria".

Students also commented that the Moodle glossary tool was easy to handle, and that they had enjoyed the opportunity to edit text online and include images: several students made comments like "I liked making my entry because it looks nice", or "it did not take very long to write and the result was satisfying".

6.4.4 Quantitative Results: Use and Task Achievement

Using the "reports" function in Moodle, we established that students had accessed the glossary a total of 2,047 times. In 1,785 of these, the students were viewing the site, in 43 they were adding entries, and in 219 they were updating entries. Regarding the timing of the task, all the students met the first deadline, and all but four of them met the editing deadline. Twenty-one students completed the final worksheet on time. Although the overall numbers were smaller than those for the previous year, it should be remembered that there were fewer students, and that the nature of the task meant that fewer entries (and therefore fewer editing and viewing records) were generated in Moodle.

6.4.5 Quantitative Results: Editing and Comments

The taxonomy used for the Legal English Glossary was adjusted for the purposes of evaluating the type of changes requested in the case of the encyclopaedia. In this case, rather than requesting an example, the teacher occasionally had to request that an image should be added to the text. The other items on the taxonomy remained the

Table 6.2 Type of changes that were requested: Encyclopaedia

Type of change requested	Number of entries in which changes were requested
Content	
Correction	3
Addition of new content	4
Request for image	3
Language	
Spelling	18
Vocabulary	4
Structure	13

same as before. The number of comments requesting changes of each kind is shown below in Table 6.2.

Since the students had to write a much larger quantity of text in this task, it is not surprising that more attention had to be devoted to checking spellings. On the other hand, relatively few of the entries required comments relating to terminology. This could have been due to the fact that the students were writing from a previous text in English, so the terminology was mainly provided for them, and they only needed to rephrase the information so that it would fit into the structure of their entry. Finally, more attention had to be dedicated to grammatical problems, because the students wrote a larger quantity of text. As can be seen from Table 6.2, the teachers made comments on structure in over half the entries (13 out of 22), which is a much higher proportion than in the previous year's glossary task (20 out of 84 entries).

All the students used the encyclopaedia to complete the worksheet, and it was noticeable that this task sparked a considerable amount of class discussion and consultation. The activity as a whole added a further dimension to the course, helping to bond together a fairly heterogeneous group of students from different years of the degree course, and proved fruitful in terms of student motivation and satisfaction. Above all, it helped to raise students' awareness of the world's legal systems and the importance of gaining an understanding of common law concepts and terminology. In the end-of-course questionnaire, several students commented that they had found the encyclopaedia useful as a way of consolidating their knowledge of vocabulary and their understanding of key concepts in common law.

6.5 Discussion

Although new technologies in themselves do not necessarily drive pedagogy, it has often been observed that material changes in the way courses are delivered are accompanied by broader changes in the underlying paradigms of teaching and learning (Brown 2005). The move to using ICT in language teaching may involve various types of change, such as a more learner-centred focus, or a more open constructivist vision of learning whereby students are encouraged to construct their own knowledge, and teachers, rather than imparting knowledge, act as guide and support for the student's learning process (Gimeno 2008). However, not all pedagogical activities involving ICT reflect all these changes to the same extent. It is therefore interesting to analyse in more detail how far the present task bore evidence of a shift in teaching-learning paradigms.

In the case of the present projects, several observations should be made:

First, in both cases use of the online platform helped to build a bridge between the teacher and the students outside the classroom, opening up a new channel of communication. By looking at the initial entries posted by the students, the teacher was able to gain insights into their understanding of the course contents (in the case of the legal English glossary) and of legal concepts and language in general (in the case of the encyclopaedia of common law countries). Where necessary, the teacher asked students to change content, add new information, or add examples of the word in use, and was able to track whether or not the student acted on these comments. In this, there is no doubt that the projects contributed to making the course more learner-centred, provided opportunities for the teacher to give individual feedback, resolve conceptual problems, and provide encouragement where necessary (Gimeno 2008; Brown 2005). In a sense, by supporting the learning process in this way, the teacher could be said to have acted as a facilitator, aiding students as they transformed information (course contents, reference material) into knowledge (entries expressed in their own words), and thereby optimising the learning process in an individualised way. As Kershaw and Safford (1998) state, such changes are typical of the way in which computer technology has transformed teaching practices: "instructional staff no longer are the fountainhead of information since the technology can provide students with access to an infinite amount of and array of data and information. The role of the instructor, therefore, changes to one of learning facilitator. The instructor assists students to access information, to synthesize and interpret it and to place it in a context – in short to transform information into knowledge."

Secondly, regarding the nature of the learning that was taking place, it should be noted that the two projects represented stages along a path that was moving progressively away from tightly controlled contents and learning objectives to greater open-endedness and freedom. It has been noted that the development of technology means that increasing amounts of information are accessible daily for many people in all parts of the world (Brown 2005). Knowledge and information are no longer limited to libraries, books and experts, and there is a growing need for graduates to learn how to manage information from different sources, discriminate between what is reliable or useful and what is not, and ultimately reshape it in order to apply it to changing circumstances. In other words, knowledge production or reproduction are making room for so-called knowledge configuration. In the words of Gibbons (1998: i): "Universities have been far more adept at producing knowledge than at drawing creatively (re-configuring) knowledge that is being produced in the distributed knowledge production system." In the context of European post-Bologna university courses, it is imperative that students should be encouraged to develop the resources needed to conduct and manage knowledge configuration effectively. In the present case, the first project (the legal English glossary) made a small step in this direction, by asking students to contribute their own definitions and examples, and share them in a class platform. The second project (the encyclopaedia of common law countries) represented a much greater move towards this objective, by asking students to read from different sources and write their own entries, which they knew would be published for others to use. It is worth noting, however, that the stage of the project that involved researching and writing was carefully structured, so that students could not simply download whole sections of the material they had found. The first worksheet consisted of a set of topics on which students had to write notes while reading the source texts, which they then used in the classroom in an oral information-exchange activity. This material then had to be reworked to make a coherent written encyclopaedia entry. This stage was added in order to make the task more challenging, but it also functioned to scaffold the learning process. Students had to find information, explain it to another person with the presence of the teacher if help was needed with concepts or language, and then write it up. They thus obtained the benefit of peer and teacher feedback, and had an opportunity to "digest" the information before they produced their encyclopaedia entry.

Thirdly, although preparation of the entries undoubtedly helped students to construct their own knowledge of key concepts, it was essential for the teacher to be able to correct the final versions that the students produced, not only in order to give individual feedback, but so that the entries could be used by the rest of the class. In other words, the teacher not only had to guide and sometimes redirect the construction of knowledge, but also had to intervene to ensure that uncorrected entries were not allowed to stay on the site. The first task (the legal English glossary) was fundamentally content-based, and lacked the type of open-endedness that has sometimes been regarded as characteristic of the new learning paradigms associated with ICT (Brown 2005). It is likely that the highly structured nature of the task, with clear definitions of what was required, two clear deadlines, and teacher corrections, meant that the project was able to avoid some of the problems that previous authors had encountered, such as lack of momentum or insecurity about corrections (Lázaro et al. 2009) and peer-corrections (Meishar-Tal and Gorsky 2010). However, it could be criticised on the grounds that it allowed little scope for creativity and did not contribute greatly towards wider objectives such as fomenting reading and writing skills or promoting learner autonomy. The second task (the encyclopaedia of common law countries) was somewhat more open-ended, allowing for a greater degree of creativity and self-directed enquiry. To complete the main part of this task satisfactorily, students had to read from at least two different specialist sources and reorganise the information to fit into a particular format. The final worksheet proved extremely fruitful as a way of encouraging students to read each others' entries, thereby fostering a sense of community within the group, and as a way of rounding off the project. It is important to note, however, that the students themselves expressed anxiety about the quality of their entries, specifically because they knew that their classmates were going to read them. They felt more secure about this when they were told that the teacher would use the "comment" function to help them correct both the language and content of the encyclopaedia. Their understanding of the correction process also made them feel that the final product was a reliable source of information and language. Moreover, in both tasks, the application of strict deadlines was a crucial factor: the use of a definite timescale for student and teacher corrections, and (in the second project) for the completion of the final worksheet, meant that there was no loss of momentum, and the participants' interest was maintained until the end.

Finally, it is significant that the students expressed satisfaction after participating in the projects. Importantly, they felt that the end-products were a useful study tool, either directly, in the case of the legal English glossary which helped them to review terminology and ideas, or indirectly, in the case of the encyclopaedia of common law countries, which provided a way of reviewing vocabulary and consolidating key concepts. Furthermore, in both cases, the fact that the Moodle glossary project was available to all the students, and all the students had taken part in its construction, helped to reinforce the sense of community in the classroom. It has often been stated that the use of technology has led to a shift from a constructivist to a social constructivist paradigm: learning takes place in a community, and knowledge is constructed by learners in active cooperation with each other and with the teacher (Brown 2005). The projects described in this chapter helped to promote the notion of the class as an active learning community, as well as providing useful and attractive resources for all the students to use.

6.6 Conclusions

This chapter describes two cycles of practitioner research using Moodle glossary as part of a course teaching legal English at university level. It documents the experiences obtained in the first year, and describes the more ambitious project carried out in the second year. Key principles of the task design are emphasised, such as modelling the writing activity in the classroom, imposing strict but realistic deadlines, providing individual feedback, creating reasons for students to read each others' entries, and including the task in the assessment scheme for the course. At this level, such tasks must balance creativity with control, so that students have freedom to experiment, but know the parameters within which they are supposed to operate. In future versions of the legal English course, the Moodle glossary activity could be adapted to cover other aspects of Common Law, such as leading cases, courts, or famous jurists. In addition to requiring basic research using material published in English, these tasks should also be structured so that students have to re-work the information they find, perhaps by writing answers to questions or following a standard structure for the text that cannot be copied from their source material. Activities of this kind would also be a useful complement to courses in other areas of English for Specific Purposes: for example, students could compile biographical or technical encyclopaedias related to their degree course, for which they would have to carry out research and write in the target language, using the appropriate register and terminology. This more active approach to learning fits well with the type of project work envisaged in the Bologna framework for undergraduate degrees.

Bibliography and Webliography

Adell, J. 2004. Internet en el aula: las WebQuest. *Edutec Revista de Tecnología Educativa* 17. http://www.cyta.com.ar/presentacion/mejora_archivos/edutec.htm. Accessed 24 Mar 2011.

Angeli, C., and N. Valanides. 2004. The effect of electronic scaffolding for technology integration on perceived task effort and confidence of primary school teachers. *Journal of Research on Technology in Education* 37(1): 29–43.

Área Moreira M. 2009. Las wikis en mi experiencia docente. Del diccionario de la asignatura al diario de clase. *Red U Revista de Docencia Universitaria* V. http://www.um.es/ead/Red_U/m5/. Accessed 16 June 2010.

Argüelles Álvarez, I. 2009. About the integration of b-learning in EPP to reinforce learner autonomy. *Revista de Lingüística y Lenguas Aplicadas* 4: 11–23.

Bocanegra, A., and M. Perea. 2011. ICT-based instruction for specialised vocabulary development. In *Technological innovation in the teaching and processing of LSPs: Proceedings of TISLID'10*, ed. N. Talaván, E. Martín Monje, and F. Palazón, 55–68. Madrid: Universidad Nacional de Educación a Distancia.

Breeze, R. 2005. The sight and sound project: Developing an online film magazine as part of a university-level ESP course. In *Language @t work: Language learning, discourse and translation studies in internet*, ed. S. Posteguillo, 57–70. Castellón: Universitat Jaume I.

Brown, T. 2005. Beyond constructivism: Exploring future learning paradigms. *Education Today* 2: 1–11. http://www.bucks.edu/IDlab/Beyond_constructivism.pdf

Bruns, A., and S. Humphreys. 2005. Wikis in teaching and assessment – The M/Cyclopedia Project. In *Proceedings of the 2005 International Symposium on Wikis*, ed. D. Riehle, 25–32. http://www.wikisym.org/ws2005/proceedings/. Accessed 16 June 2010.

Dabbagh, N. 2002. Using a web-based course management tool to support face-to-face instruction. The Technology Source. http://ts.mivu.org/default.asp?show=article&id=1034. Accessed 16 June 2010.

Davoli, P., M. Monari, and K. Eklundh. 2009. Peer activities on web-learning platforms – Impact on collaborative writing and usability issues. *Educational Information Technology* 14: 229–254. http://www.springerlink.com/content/b342334u2134427v/fulltext.pdf. Accessed 4 May 2010.

Dodge, B. 1995. Some thoughts about webQuest. http://edweb.sdsu.edu/courses/edtec596/about_webquests.html. Accessed 20 Mar 2011.

Dodge, B. 2001a. The WebQuest Page: Matrix. http://webquest.org/matrix3.php. Accessed 20 Mar 2011.

Dodge, B. 2001b. A rubric for evaluating WebQuest. http://webquest.sdsu.edu/webquestrubric.html. Accessed 20 Mar 2011.

Gaskill, M., A. McNulty, and D. Brooks. 2006. Learning from WebQuests. *Journal of Science Education and Technology* 15(2): 133–136.

Gibbons, M. 1998. *Higher education relevance in the 21st century*. Paper presented at the UNESCO World Conference, Paris, i–ii and 1–60.

Gimeno, A. 2008. Intermediate online English: An example of self-access courseware development. In: *Proceedings of the WorldCALL 2008 conference*, ed. T. Koyama, 54–56. Fukuoka: The Japan Association for Language Education and Technology. http://www.j-let.org/~wcf/proceedings/proceedings.pdf. Accessed 16 June 2010.

Hung, C. 2004. *The use of webquest as a constructivist learning tool in secondary school geography in Singapore*. National Educational Computing Conference 2004. http://center.uoregon.edu/conferences/ISTE/NECC2004/about_NECC/default.php. Accessed 12 Apr 2009.

Kershaw, A., and S. Safford. 1998. From order to chaos: The impact of educational telecommunications on post-secondary education. *Higher Education* 35: 285–298.
Lara, S., and C. Repáraz. 2007. Effectiveness of cooperative learning fostered by working with WebQuest. *Electronic Journal of Research in Educational Psychology* 13(15,3): 731–756.
Lázaro Gutiérrez, R., Díaz C. Pena, and B. Vitalaru. 2009. Wikis en lenguas para fines específicos y su traducción. *Red U Revista de Docencia Universitaria V*: 1–22. http://www.um.es/ead/Red_U/m5/. Accessed 16 June 2010.
Meishar-Tal, H., and P. Gorsky. 2010. Wikis: What students do and do not do when writing collaboratively. *Open Learning: The Journal of Open and Distance Learning* 25(1): 25–35.
Oliveira, C. 2003. Towards a knowledge society. Keynote address delivered at the IEEE international conference on advanced learning technologies (ICALT). July 2003, Athens.
Pfeil, U., P. Zaphiris, and C.S. Ang. 2006. Cultural differences in collaborative authoring of Wikipedia. *Journal of Computer Mediated Communication* 12(1). http://jcmc.indiana.edu/vol12/issue1/pfeil.html. Accessed 16 June 2010.
Starr, L. 2000. Creating a WebQuest: It's easier than you think! *Education World*. http://www.education-world.com/a_tech/tech011.shtml. Accessed 20 May 2011.

Web Resources

Jurist World Law. http://jurist.law.pitt.edu/world/
NYU Global Law. http://www.nyulawglobal.org/globalex/
The WebQuest Page. http://edweb.sdsu.edu/webquest/matrix.html

Chapter 7
Promoting Specialised Vocabulary Learning Through Computer-Assisted Instruction

Mª Dolores Perea-Barberá and Ana Bocanegra-Valle

7.1 Introduction

The European Space of Higher Education (ESHE) is gradually changing the roles of teachers and learners and promoting the view of learning as a process in the long run that extends beyond the more immediate educational stages in life and comprises "all phases and forms of learning from pre-school to post-retirement" (Commission of the European Communities 2001: 9). On a first instance, teachers are urged to adopt new roles within the teaching/learning process as facilitators, counsellors, material creators, self-direction managers, lifelong encouragers, etc. and embed Information and Communication Technologies (ICTs) in classroom work or to complement to face-to-face sessions – as Brett and González-Lloret (2009: 351) put it "technology has indeed permeated the [teaching] profession deeply". Likewise, learners are required to change their attitudes towards traditional teaching/learning in formal settings, becoming aware of the need to become self-directed learners, accepting an active role in their own learning processes and tackling potential ICT illiteracies.

This paper focuses on the teaching and learning of specialised vocabulary through ICTs in general and, more precisely, on computer-supported teaching and learning of Maritime English (ME) vocabulary. After a long period of relative neglect, today it is widely recognized that vocabulary has always been an essential component of language teaching (Schmitt 2010). Applied linguist's lack of interest in vocabulary prior to the 1990s favoured research on other aspects of language (grammar teaching, for instance) as it seemed to be a general consent that "in due time learners would 'acquire' the vocabulary necessary to deal with specific communicative situations through their exposure to the target language"

M.D. Perea-Barberá (✉) • A. Bocanegra-Valle
Departamento de Filología Francesa e Inglesa, Universidad de Cádiz, Cádiz, Spain
e-mail: mariadolores.perea@uca.es; ana.bocanegra@uca.es

E. Bárcena et al. (eds.), *Languages for Specific Purposes in the Digital Era*, Educational Linguistics 19, DOI 10.1007/978-3-319-02222-2_7,

(Chacón-Beltrán et al. 2010: 1). Today, however, the situation is different: vocabulary learning and teaching attracts researchers' attention and studies on this issue appear regularly in book collections and reputed international journals. In fact, in his review of the studies published in four major English-language journals in the field of CALL from 2001 to 2005, Stockwell (2007) found out that "grammar was the most commonly investigated, followed by vocabulary" (Stockwell 2007: 110), that there was a tendency to focus on these two language areas (vocabulary remaining relatively constant with a peak in 2004) and, moreover, that research on computer-assisted vocabulary learning had undergone "an evolution in methods, moving from simpler client-side interactive (…) to more complex AI-based systems" (Stockwell 2007: 116).

In language learning/teaching, ICTs is an umbrella term widely used when referring to the implementation of technology in language courses, and embraces:

> … the use of the Internet (multimedia sources, online dictionaries); communication tools such as MOOs, email, chat rooms, and audio/videoconferencing; software and applications designed specifically for language learning, the authoring and publication of web, digital audio and video materials, etc., all of which seek to enhance and promote language learning. (Brett and González-Lloret 2009: 350)

In this paper we will use the term ICTs "to cover all the technological advances that are being applied in the field [of language learning]" (Ruiz-Madrid and Sanz-Gil 2007: 65), and also when taking into account the possibilities afforded by technology in general for language teaching and lifelong learning; however, the classroom project presented in this paper is particularly focused on the implementation of "computer and network hardware and software" and, thus, expressions such as "computer-based", "computer-assisted", "computer-enhanced", "computer-mediated" or "computer-supported" will be used when referring to the particular way ICTs have been integrated into the ME course.

In the following sections we address the challenges of ICT-based pedagogy to the English for Specific Purposes (ESP) classroom in general, and the ME classroom in particular. First, some key issues on ICT-based pedagogy and vocabulary instruction are analysed: the different ways vocabulary is learnt and taught, the definitions of specialised vocabulary in general and of ME vocabulary in particular, the meaning and implications of digital literacy, the role of computers in enhancing vocabulary learning, and the construct of lifelong learning as a particular ESHE requirement. Secondly, some relevant publications are reviewed with particular reference to recurrent topics in this paper – i.e. computer-based vocabulary teaching/learning, ICTs and specialised languages, and learning autonomy. Then, we examine the Moodle glossary tool, a specific computer-based academic platform at the University virtual campus, and how it can be implemented in view of strategic ME vocabulary development. We provide a detailed account of the creation of the *Maritime Glossary* (a project aimed to complement classroom work) and, finally, discuss learners' opinions based on a questionnaire administered upon the completion of the glossary and interviews held at the end of the course.

7.2 Key Issues on ICT-Based Pedagogy and Vocabulary Instruction

7.2.1 Vocabulary Learning and Instruction

Oxford and Crookall (1990) classify vocabulary teaching techniques into four groups. Each of these comprising other techniques which, in some cases, are not totally independent and may overlap in different degrees (dictionary use, for example, may become a semi-contextualizing technique if a particular activity includes context of use). Such four groups of techniques may be summarised as follows:

1. "Decontextualizing techniques": these refer to those techniques that remove the word from any communicative context. They include word lists, flashcards, and conventional dictionary use.
2. "Semi-contextualizing techniques": these refer to those techniques that "allow some degree of context but fall short of full contextuality" (Oxford and Crookall 1990: 10). They include word grouping, word or concept association, visual imagery, aural imagery, keyword, physical response, physical sensation, and semantic mapping.
3. "Fully contextualizing techniques": these techniques embed new words in communicative contexts. They include reading and listening practice on the one hand, and speaking and writing practice on the other.
4. "Adaptable techniques": these reinforce any one of the previous techniques, which include structured reviewing.

As far as vocabulary learning is concerned, Ellis (1994) focuses on the ways new vocabulary is processed and, hence, distinguishes between the unconscious and conscious acquisition of new words and new meanings ("implicit" and "explicit" vocabulary learning hypothesis, respectively).

Following a rather different approach, Nation and Chung (2009) reflect on the ways vocabulary should be taught and learned and contend that for a well-balanced course four strands of activities should be implemented with the same time length. These four strands, discussed and detailed by Nation in an earlier work (Nation 1990), include:

1. "Meaning-focused input": this means learning via comprehensible input through listening and reading activities (listening to stories, providing glosses from reading, etc.)
2. "Meaning-focused output": this means learning through speaking and writing activities (retelling, role plays, etc.).
3. "Language-focused learning": this means the direct and deliberate study of vocabulary and the implementation of vocabulary-learning strategies.
4. "Fluency development": this means making use of listening, speaking, reading and writing activities that allow for the learning of new language items and their fluent access and use.

Taking into consideration the three classifications above, we can conclude that the vocabulary instruction detailed in this paper may be considered as:

- "explicit learning", since students focus on a number of words and apply conscious and planned strategies (noticing, selection, repetition, etc.) with the final aim of learning them by heart;
- "semi-contextualizing", since some degree of contextuality is not only permitted but even encouraged (definitions, pictures, etc.); and,
- "language-focused", since vocabulary-learning strategies are fostered and a glossary *per se* implies direct and deliberate practice.

Moreover, our vocabulary instruction option (the development of the *Maritime Glossary* project) is consistent, on the one hand, with Nation's (1990) argument that when teaching time is short, devoting some classroom time to the implementation and practice of vocabulary learning strategies is deemed necessary; and, on the other, with Paribakht and Wesche's (1998) suggestion that when the learning period is limited and specific vocabulary outcomes are sought, more (language-) focused instruction is desirable.

7.2.2 Specialised Vocabulary

Broadly speaking, there are several types of vocabulary. According to Graves (2006), a first classification comprises the vocabulary we understand ("receptive vocabulary") and the vocabulary we use ("productive vocabulary"). A second classification concerns the written and oral modes; hence, four vocabularies apply and overlap: "receptive-oral, words we understand when we hear them; receptive-written, words we can read; productive-oral, words we use in our speech; and productive-written, words we use in our writing" (Graves 2006: 11). But vocabulary can also be classified according to not only the mode of delivery, but also the degree of specialist use individuals make of it.

The vocabulary contained in academic and professional language (i.e. specialised vocabulary) may be classified into technical, sub-technical or semi-technical, and general. Technical vocabulary is defined as "words that are very closely associated with a specialist area" (Nation and Chung 2009: 545); or, more precisely, "content words whose meaning is restricted to the specific subject, characterizes the specific language as an individual area of the global language and constitutes the terminology of the domain" (Rea 2009: 162). Sub-technical or semi-technical vocabulary is defined as "general content words whose meaning becomes specialized in a domain but it is understandable from its meaning in a general context" (Rea Rizzo 2009: 162). Finally, general vocabulary refers to those words that are known to the general speaker and coexist with technical and sub-technical vocabulary in a specialised text. Regardless of any of these levels, words may display a high frequency or a low frequency in language use depending on the target piece of discourse – i.e. subject-matter, topic, register, mode, tenor, etc.

As far as the specialised vocabulary in maritime settings is concerned, Pritchard (2003: 157) classifies what he calls "Maritime English lexis" into five distinctive groups, of which 1, 2, 4 and 5 are the focus of this paper:

1. "a very limited number (up to 7 %) of strictly technical/nautical terms, whose central lexical meaning (...) is restricted to maritime use only and thus 'unambiguous' by nature". Examples of these are: "starboard", "hull", "buoy" or "bow";
2. "numerous semi-specific general vocabulary items, often highly polysemous, which are disambiguated in the maritime context only". Examples of these are: "haul", "overtake", "position" or "fairway";
3. "function words", such as auxiliary verbs or prepositions, and "semi-lexical items", such as verbs like "let" or "make";
4. "an unlimited number of very productive multi-word lexical units consisting of the words of general vocabulary having specific meaning in the maritime context and setting". These may be compound nouns such as "vessel traffic service" or "shipping forecast", or prepositional/adverbial phrases of the type "heave in", "heave on", "heave up", "heave to" or "heave away";
5. "linguistic expressions of speech acts in maritime communication, discourse connectors and markers in maritime texts". Examples of these are: "mayday" or "stand by".

7.2.3 The Concept of Literacy

"Literacy" may be defined as the ability to read and write in a language but, with the advent of ICTs, simple literacy becomes "digital literacy" to refer to the ability to read and write in a language through the use of ICTs. Individuals possessing such ability are regarded as "digitally literate" (or "digitally illiterate" if they show a lack of it). Lewis (2009: 16–17) classifies "digital literacy" into three types as follows:

1. Computer literacy. Individuals are computer literate when they are able to handle computers for everyday tasks (leisure or work) and include basic skills for computer handling such as formatting and printing a document or playing audio on a computer.
2. Information literacy. Individuals are information literate when they are able to use ICTs, and particular computers, selectively; that is, when they "look critically at what they are accessing" (Lewis 2009: 17), explore and reflect critically so as to be selective given the tremendous amount information close at hand.
3. Multimedia literacy. Individuals are multimedia literate when they are able to handle simultaneously all the constituent multimedia elements which dress a text (video, sound, hyperlinks, etc.)

Given the generation gap that characterizes teachers and learners and the relatively recent implementation of ICTs in educational programmes, are today's teachers digitally literate? Are today's tertiary learners digitally literate? Individuals who have grown up in an ITC-governed world are said to be "digital natives". In contrast, today's teachers, as individuals who have grown up in a computer-free childhood, are said to be "digital immigrants" because they have become acquainted with ICTs and have embraced digital literacy in adulthood. The e-Learning initiative promoted by the European Commission (Commission of the European Communities 2003) sets targets and defines priority areas in view of digitally literate students at different education levels. But, are our university students digital natives? Would it be appropriate to talk about a "digital divide" – that is, an ITC-motivated generation clash – between today's teachers and learners? We dare say that today's university students are, in general, used to the use of ICT in their daily lives, but not digital natives yet. Some may feel comfortable with technology but some others may need some training, or even still feel intimidated by computers; hence, there is a need on the teacher's part to face the "digital divide" and overcome learners' potential digital illiteracies so as to make the most of computer-mediated courses.

7.2.4 Computer-Assisted Vocabulary Learning

Nation and Chung (2009: 552) contend that "computer-assisted vocabulary learning can be an effective way of getting help with vocabulary". As research in the field of computer-based vocabulary learning reveals, this has proved to be true; however, learners are also required to become both active learners (i.e. invest time and effort so as to increase their involvement load) and strategic learners (i.e. apply how-to-learn skills or vocabulary learning strategies) if they want to be successful vocabulary learners.

Based on published literature, Nation and Chung (2009) stress the contribution of computers for language-focused learning and suggest five ways of implementing computers in vocabulary learning:

1. to include computer-based analysis of vocabulary and procedures for determining technical vocabulary;
2. to analyse texts for research and assessment purposes;
3. to include programs for the deliberate learning of vocabulary;
4. to use text-linked aids (e.g. concordances or electronic dictionaries) which support reading; and
5. to use word-processing tools for feedback on electronically submitted written work.

The computer-based instruction detailed in this paper falls within the scope of the third way as it is explicitly focused on vocabulary learning through the implementation of vocabulary-learning strategies for deliberate and active learning.

7.2.5 Lifelong Learning and Learning Autonomy

The European Space for Higher Education (ESHE) framework addresses action on lifelong learning through six key messages (Commission of the European

Communities 2000), number three being "Innovation in teaching and learning". With the objective of developing effective teaching/learning methods and contexts in view of lifelong and lifewide learning, this key message highlights that ICT-based learning technologies have a prominent role in achieving innovation in teaching and learning methods as well as in enabling individuals to become active learners. More precisely, educational systems are encouraged to "adapt to the changing ways in which people live and learn their lives today" as well as "generate productive self-directed learning" (Commission of the European Communities 2000: 14). In so doing, teachers are urged to adapt to the rapidly changing educational contexts and promote active learners in view of lifelong learning:

> Teaching as a professional role faces decisive change in the coming decades: **teachers and trainers become guides, mentors and mediators**. Their role – and it is a crucially important one – is to help and support learners who, as far as possible, take charge of their own learning. The capacity and the confidence to develop and practise open and participatory teaching and learning methods should therefore become an essential professional skill for educators and trainers, in both formal and non-formal settings. Active learning presupposes the motivation to learn, the capacity to exercise critical judgement and the skill of knowing how to learn. The irreplaceable heart of the teaching role lies in nurturing precisely these human capacities to create and use knowledge. (Commission of the European Communities 2000: 14)

As an educational construct, "lifelong learning" may also be labelled as "self-directed learning" or "autonomous learning"; however, lifelong learning implies a goal in the much longer term – i.e. a continuum of learning throughout life, according to the Commission. More precisely, the Commission defines lifelong learning as "all learning activity undertaken throughout life, with the aim of improving knowledge, skills and competences within a personal, civic, social and/or employment-related perspective" (Commission of the European Communities 2001: 9).

At the level of European education plans, the lifelong learning issue spreads through different initiatives with a view to the realisation of a European area of lifelong learning. One such initiative is the "eLearning initiative" (a part of the "eEurope Action Plan") that seeks to encourage a digital culture, promote a wider use of ICTs in education and training, and raise levels of digital literacy among students of all kinds (Commission of the European Communities 2001, 2003). Moreover, the Commission underlines that "the effective use of ICT will make a significant contribution to implementing lifelong learning by widening access and introducing more varied ways to learn" (Commission of the European Communities 2000: 21), and at the same time contends that e-learning is a useful tool for achieving better access to lifelong learning, a facilitator to lifelong learning not only at school but also at the workplace: "e-learning offers real possibilities for improved lifelong learning opportunities, as the boundaries between education, training and adult learning become blurred" (Commission of the European Communities 2003: 12). It may therefore be argued that ICTs is one of the means available to the particular end of implementing lifelong learning and nurturing self-directed individuals.

7.3 Literature Review

Researchers have examined how ICT-based technologies benefit vocabulary learning and instruction from different points of view – see Son (2001) and Stockwell (2007) for general reviews – and emphasise the contribution of computers in vocabulary retention and recognition (Groot 2000; Coll 2002; Tozcu and Coady 2004; Ma and Kelly 2006).

One of the most popular research aspects to date has perhaps been the relationship between vocabulary and context or, more precisely, the development of vocabulary through computer-enhanced reading skills programmes and the contribution of computer-assisted reading instruction to vocabulary development (Ellis 1995; Goodfellow 1995; Tozcu and Coady 2004; LeLoup and Ponterio 2005; Cobb 2007). Based on the belief that context contributes to vocabulary learning, and that using context is the most widely recommended strategy (Graves 2006), the use of multimedia environments and the implementation of context-embedded approaches for explicit and implicit vocabulary development through extensive on-line reading activities or the implementation of hypermedia tools – i.e. hypermedia-enhanced learning environments – have attracted a great deal of attention (Kang 1995; Coll 2002; Nikolova 2002; Jones 2004; Yoshii 2006; Sydorenko 2010).

Another relevant aspect of research is the acquisition of vocabulary thanks to the use of electronic dictionaries/glossaries. The use of conventional (or paper) dictionaries and glossaries for the learning of new words has long been regarded as a positive learning strategy for vocabulary growth and development and the advent of electronic dictionaries has contributed to further the research on this issue. Electronic features may be found in the literature on vocabulary learning as portable electronic dictionaries, software-based dictionaries or online dictionary websites (Stockwell 2007). Several studies agree on the crucial role electronic dictionaries/glossaries play for vocabulary retention and understanding, presented either in isolation or through reading comprehension activities. Works such as those by Leffa (1992), Knight (1994), Chun and Plass (1996), Colazzo and Costantino (1998), Laufer (2000) or Louky (2002) help to demonstrate, as a whole, the effectiveness and positive effects of electronic dictionaries/glossaries as opposed to conventional dictionaries/glossaries, based on the fact that in the experimental studies carried out the groups of learners using electronic dictionaries/glossaries benefited in general from computer-assisted activities and scored higher rates of vocabulary learning – i.e. vocabulary retention and understanding.

As regards ICTs, learning autonomy, and specialised language learning, there has been an upward trend of studies that explore the relationship between these three constructs, and both theoretical and quasi-experimental studies have been recently conducted to illustrate how learners in specialised language settings can benefit from the implementation of ICTs for autonomy and self-direction. A review of the latest literature shows three main groups of studies: those which investigate the usefulness of computer-assisted ESP learning from a broad perspective; those which focus on web-based resources for ESP course implementation; and those which provide a detailed account of the pros and cons of using particular platforms or courseware in ESP courses.

1. Some studies are of a more general nature. Deavux et al. (2006), for instance, explore how to use technology to facilitate effective learning and engender lifelong learners among a group of Asian students engaged in three different courses for specific (ESP) and academic (EAP) purposes; Fernández Toledo (2006) advocates the implementation of computer-supported collaborative learning in an English for Library and Information Science course; Ruiz-Madrid and Sanz-Gil (2007) theorise over the integration of ICTs in language learning in view of achieving "autonomising competence"; and Mungra (2009) describes an online writing course to promote blended learning among English for Medicine students.
2. Dealing with Internet and web-based environments, works are abundant and varied. Besides reviewing how networked self-accesses EAP materials have been developed at her university, Nesi (1998) explores teachers' and learners' resistance and unwillingness to the implementation of the Internet in an educational context. Canapero's (2004) work pays attention to the potential of *Web Enhanced Language Learning* (WELL) in encouraging collaborative and constructive learning among English for Science and Technology students; Luzón and González (2006: 178) analyse the potential of the Internet for ESP teaching so that teachers can exploit Internet-based materials "to design activities that can be used by ESP students to develop their capacity for autonomous learning"; and Trinder (2006) analyses the benefits of implementing the "autonomy perspective" among English for Economics students through the *Online English Mentor*, a web-delivered course. She concludes that electronic resources do not assure learner autonomy but, instead, learner autonomy is a product of "nature and nurture" that needs awareness and training on the learners' part as well as help from teachers to cope with self-directed e-learning.
3. As regards self-directed learning in specialised language contexts and the use of particular courseware, Gimeno-Sanz (2002) discusses some of the findings of a courseware for the Airline Industry to be developed in English, German and Spanish under the Leonardo da Vinci project framework and pays particular attention to learner needs and autonomy. Ruiz-Madrid (2006) investigates the contribution of forums available at *Moodle* as "autonomising tools" for a group of English for Computer Science students. Argüelles Álvarez (2009) explores the possibilities of applying *Moodle* to a learner-centred English for Professional Communication context and highlights its benefits for a blended learning approach; Bueno Alastuey (2009) examines the possibilities of *WebCT* for English for Agriculture students and the effect of this platform on students and teachers alike.

Finally, the studies dealing with ICTs, learner autonomy and specialised vocabulary development specifically are much fewer in number, but their clear experimental nature provides insights on the validity of computer-assisted vocabulary development and the teaching/learning options afforded by technological courses.

Coll (2002), for instance, investigates how low-proficiency English for Chemistry students benefit from a hypermedia-enhanced learning environment, particularly as regards the incidental acquisition of Chemistry terms. The implementation of the courseware set up suggests that such hypermedia-based instruction contributes to vocabulary retention and provides a favourable environment for vocabulary development. A very illuminating work supporting computer-assisted vocabulary development is that of Kilickaya and Krajka (2010) who compared the usefulness of online vocabulary teaching and the traditional methods with a group of Academic English students. In their study, Kilickaya and Krajka (2010) used a dictionary look-up system called *WordChamp* Web Reader, a vocabulary hypertext programme that provides support to selected words appearing in a reading text, and found that: (i) the *WordChamp* group of learners performed significantly better while studying vocabulary items than the group engaged in traditional vocabulary learning activities; (ii) the computer-based teaching contributed to individualising the language learning experience and also to raising awareness on learning strategies for autonomy and self-direction. Last, the creation of an online legal English glossary at *Moodle* is the focus of Breeze (2011: 397), who, as she puts it, "describes the design and implementation of a collaborative legal glossary writing task as part of a university legal English course, and provides and analysis of the procedure and outcomes" with the purpose of assisting students when revising for the final exam, helping them to practise when giving explanations of key concepts in legal English, and providing them with a reference and study tool.

From the review above it may be inferred that the combinations ICTs/autonomy/specialised language on the one hand, and ICTs/autonomy/specialised vocabulary development on the other, arouse high expectations of promising research within the ESP arena; nonetheless, despite the late proliferation of publications on this triple issue, there is still a dearth of real experimental research on the role and contribution of ICTs for self-directed learning in specialised language settings that helps to quantify and assess how much and to what extent ESP learners can benefit from technological classrooms.

7.4 The Maritime Glossary

7.4.1 Context and Participants

The project discussed in this paper took place in the Spring Semester of the 2009–2010 academic year. The target students were enrolled in the course *Nautical English*, the first compulsory English for Professional Purposes course in the second year of their university degree in navigation. In general, the students' level of proficiency in English varied from B1 to B2 levels of the Common European Framework of Reference for Languages (CEFR).

Of the 32 students who made up the group, our study focuses on the 20 students who regularly attended class and followed all the outside class activities. Their average age is 29, the mean average age of students at the University of Cadiz

(Universidad de Cádiz 2010) being 17–21 years old (40 %). A possible explanation for this difference in age might be that many of our students (70 %) have had some kind of working experience before and, thus, entered university later than the average student. Sixteen were from different places in Spain, mainly from Andalusia, two were from Morocco and two from South-America, specifically, from Bolivia and Venezuela. Their English backgrounds were quite diverse, but most of them had spent some time in an English-speaking country (63 %), mainly to learn English or for professional reasons, and had studied English for an average of 7.5 years before taking the *Nautical English* course.

The virtual instruction carried out through the whole course consisted in the use of MarEng, a web-based maritime English language learning program, and of Moodle, a virtual learning environment. Moodle is the course management system for the University's Virtual Campus. It is based on a socio-constructionist framework of education and provided as open source software. The glossary is one of the many activity modules offered by Moodle. There are many interesting options to choose from the glossary setup. However, the most attractive aspect is that it has a number of features that make it easy for students to develop a shared list of terms with definitions.

7.4.2 Objectives

Based on our previous experience in the use of learning strategies in the ESP context (Bocanegra Valle 2004; Bocanegra Valle and Perea Barberá 2011; Bocanegra Valle et al. 2013; Perea Barberá 2007, 2009), the chief aim of the *Maritime Glossary* project was to investigate if the use of the glossary tool worked as an efficient learning strategy and increased specialised vocabulary retention among students of ME. There were also other general objectives, namely, promoting learning autonomy awareness, enhancing cooperative learning among participants, and providing a resource tool (the glossary itself) for further reference and use. In the first place, students participated in the creation of the glossary by adding their own terms; we tried to promote their autonomy by letting them choose the terms and where to look for the information they needed, though some guidance was provided. In the second place, all the students worked together to create a final glossary of almost 400 specialised terms from the maritime field; this became a group work experience which was expected to boost cooperative learning.

The specific competency-based learning objectives were twofold. Regarding the terms introduced in the *Maritime Glossary*, students should be able to:

- provide the Spanish translation of the terms;
- identify the terms and their meaning in a specific context;
- recall the English terms when looking at pictures, drawings of the concept or at the "object" itself.
- know where to locate and how to use different sources of information, mainly online specialised glossaries and specialised dictionaries, to find out the meaning of unknown terms in their future career.

– succeed in finding pictures or images to help them understand an English term.

Concerning the use of the *Maritime Glossary* to look up and study the course terminology, students should be able to:

– appreciate collaborative work and the resulting product of all students' efforts.
– recognize the value of the glossary as a study tool.

7.4.3 Description of the Project

We believe that intentional/explicit and incidental/implicit vocabulary learning are two complementary approaches and, as such, necessary to maximize the number of words learnt. This activity falls within the scope of intentional or explicit learning and some of its advantages are that it "generally leads to more robust and faster learning; generally involves deeper engagement leading to better retention; focuses on important vocabulary selected by the teacher (e.g. high frequency, technical, targeted)" (Schmitt 2010: 40).

Given the difficulties of ME specialised vocabulary, we decided to explicitly work with it in our class and outside class activities. Thus, students would not be left alone to "pick up" the technical terms while practising the four language skills, but would be encouraged to use vocabulary learning techniques. Oxford and Crookall (1990: 26–27) observe eight steps in any training sequence related to explicit vocabulary learning:

(1) determine learners' needs by exploring expectations and current vocabulary learning techniques;
(2) choose relevant techniques to teach;
(3) find ways to integrate these techniques into everyday language instruction;
(4) consider issues of student motivation toward and anxieties concerning learning L2 vocabulary;
(5) prepare materials and activities;
(6) conduct completely informed training, in which learners are explicitly told how to use a particular technique to learn a given word, how to evaluate the success of the technique, and how to transfer it to a new word or set of words;
(7) evaluate the training in terms of improvement in vocabulary learning, attitudes, and self-confidence;
(8) revise the training as needed.

Steps 1–5 were developed before the implementation of the activity. We had previously drawn up our own Vocabulary Learning Strategies (VLS) questionnaire (Perea Barberá 2007), which was distributed among the students at the beginning of the academic year. The results helped us to find information about our students' strategic behaviour and choose which VLS should be promoted in our instruction. Then, we decided to integrate VLS with ICTs and designed the glossary project, adapting the Moodle glossary tool to our needs. In the following paragraphs we will describe step 6, which outlines the main phases of the *Maritime Glossary* project. These are creation, training and implementation.

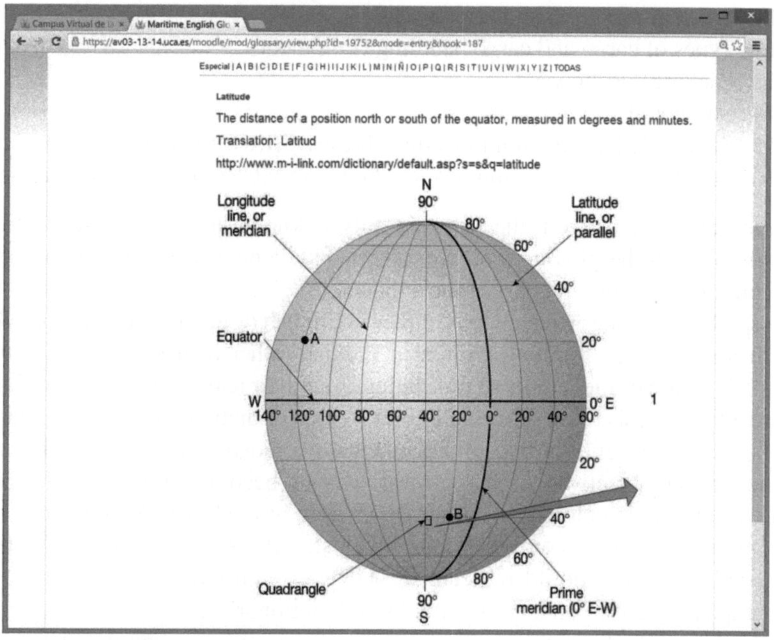

Fig. 7.1 Example of glossary entry

Phase 1. Creation of the *Maritime Glossary*. We inserted the glossary activity in our Virtual Campus course and placed it on the site front page. We gave it the descriptive name *Maritime Glossary*, indicated its purpose and provided instructions in the "Description" area. From the different display formats, we chose the "dictionary style", which looks like an ordinary dictionary and entries can be ordered alphabetically or by the author's name or surname, so easing the teacher's follow-up. The teacher, as administrator of the glossary, could edit or delete any entry at any time. Users could also edit their glossary entry at any moment and resort to the help icons.

Phase 2. Student training. First of all, the teacher provided a detailed explanation of the project and its specific learning goals. Then, students were shown an example entry that we, as teachers, had previously uploaded (see Fig. 7.1) and given clear instructions on how to use the glossary tool.

Only specialised terms from the maritime field were accepted. The final glossary was considered course material and, as such, was subject to examination. We specified that archaic, outdated and infrequently used terms should be avoided. We recommended that the terms be taken from the texts they worked with in the course units or in the suggested web sites on the various topics. The lexical content falls within the scope of the terminology in the units studied in the second semester. An example for the second-semester content-based units is as follows:

Unit 8. An introduction to navigation
Unit 9. Buoyage systems
Unit 10. Ship handling

Unit 11. Weather reporting and forecasting
Unit 12. Types of cargo and cargo handling equipment
Unit 13. Packing and stowage
Unit 14. Shipboard communications
Unit 15. Standard Marine Communication Phrases (SMCP): External Communication
Unit 16. Standard Marine Communication Phrases (SMCP): On board Communication

This restriction stems from the fact that only unknown terms were susceptible to being inserted in the glossary and we assumed students had become familiar with the terminology in the first part of the syllabus.

No spelling mistakes were allowed either in English or Spanish. Definitions should come from a source originally written in English rather than translations; students were made aware of the pitfalls of translating from their native language into English.

Students were asked to use specialised glossaries or dictionaries from the maritime field, be they on paper or online. Wikipedia was excluded as a source of information for one of the objectives of the project was to become familiar with specific resources, and lessons learnt from our experience have shown Wikipedia to be the most, and sometimes the only, consulted web site. All sources should be correctly referenced; students should indicate the URL of web pages and use the course bibliography style for conventional books and dictionaries.

Students could edit their entries on spotting a mistake or when instructed by the teacher in the revision stage. They were strongly encouraged to communicate with the teacher through the virtual campus e-mail or during her office hours.

Finally, we carried out a hands-on session in which students were asked to introduce an example term in the glossary.

Phase 3. Implementing the project. Each glossary entry consisted of the maritime term, a definition in English, the translation into Spanish and a picture (see Fig. 7.1 again). Students were required to add, at different times during the whole semester, a total number of 15 terms. They expressed their difficulties to keep up with the activity, so deadlines were somewhat flexible. Likewise, we were overwhelmed with the correction and edition of the glossary entries. Providing feedback to the students through the glossary editing tool or the e-mail, as intended, was found to be a time-consuming task and we, occasionally, chose to print some entries, make corrections on paper and talk to the students at the end of the class. Invested time exceeded the teacher's allotted time for the project. We can verify how teacher-student communication increased by comparing Figs. 7.2 and 7.3 showing the graphs of the number of exchanged messages in the Virtual Campus e-mail during the academic years 2008–2009 and 2009–2010. The top (green) line indicates the total number of messages, the middle (red) line the incoming messages and the bottom (yellow) line the sent messages. The total number of messages rises from 500 in 2008–2009 to above 800 in 2009–2010 – the year when the project was developed.

The last stage entailed the completion of the glossary, which happened to be made up of almost 400 terms in all. At that time, a printer-friendly version was made available for personal use, though the glossary could also be consulted online or downloaded. Finally, students filled in a questionnaire on the activity (see

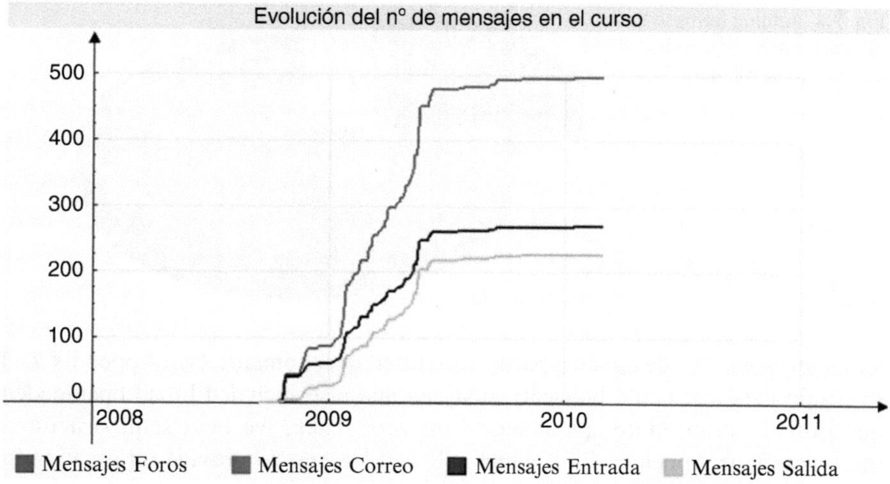

Fig. 7.2 2008/2009 Virtual Campus e-mail messages

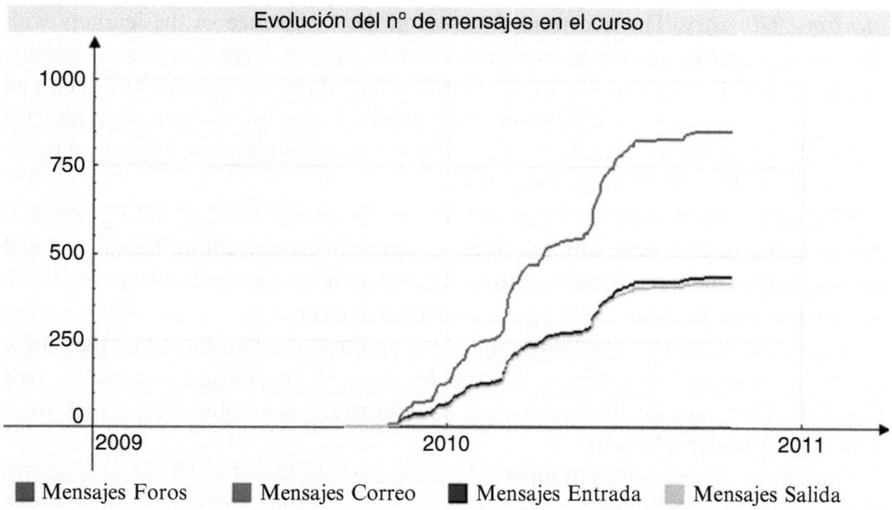

Fig. 7.3 2009/2010 Virtual Campus e-mail messages

Appendix 7.1), and vocabulary retention was tested in the final exam. These two actions correspond to step 7 of the Oxford and Crookall (1990) training sequence.

7.4.4 Students' Opinions and Perceptions of the Glossary

At the end of the semester, after the final exam but prior to course grades, students were invited to assess the *Maritime Glossary* project by means of questionnaires

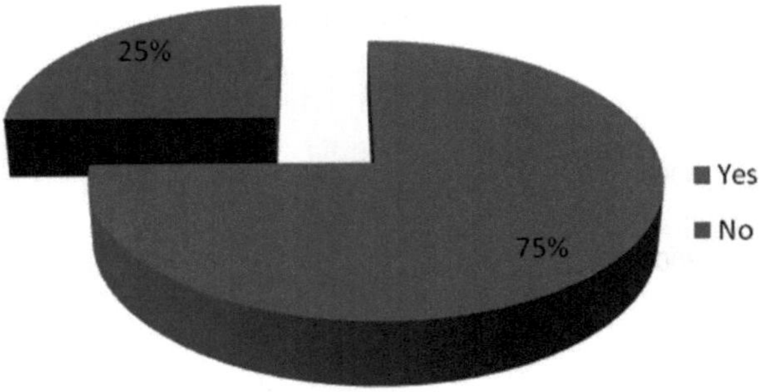

Fig. 7.4 Adding terms to the glossary was helpful to learn specialised vocabulary

and interviews. We designed a partly structured questionnaire (see Appendix 7.1) to obtain data that could be easily analysed and also included broad open-ended questions to draw more spontaneous answers. Then, we held semi-structured interviews (see Appendix 7.2), which allowed learners to provide information in their own words and generated thought-provoking ideas. Later on, recordings were transcribed and analysed. Both activities were conducted in Spanish.

The questionnaire was handed out to the 20 students who had participated in the *Maritime Glossary*. The questions focused on the experience of the learners with the glossary and its perceived usefulness. Questions 1–9 were closed and students had to choose from a number of answers; the last three questions were open and students could express their opinions more freely. In the following paragraphs, we will highlight some relevant data collected in the questionnaires and then turn to the information obtained from the interviews.

Question 3 addressed the issue of how the individual task of adding terms to the glossary, that is, choosing the term, looking for its definition, translation and picture, helped them retain the maritime vocabulary more successfully (see Fig. 7.4). The majority of students (75 %) gave a positive answer.

We also observed that the vast majority of students (85 %) stated that they drew on the final *Maritime Glossary* for the learning of specialised vocabulary (see Fig. 7.5). This indicates that creating a class glossary is a collaborative task from which most students benefit.

Concerning the perceived usefulness (1 being the least useful and 3 the most useful) of the different sections within each entry, the translation of the term into Spanish seems clearly to be the students' favourite, followed by the picture and the definition (see Fig. 7.6).

As to what extent the *Maritime Glossary* contributed to the learning of specialised vocabulary; most learners (65 %) thought that the contribution was useful (see Fig. 7.7), and were also positive about the activity itself (see Fig. 7.8); however, some were not so sure about its value as an outside class activity (see Fig. 7.9).

From the main difficulties they encountered when adding entries to the glossary (see Fig. 7.10) "choosing a term" (since duplicated entries were not allowed) and "finding reliable sources of information" stand out. Providing a list of potential terms for the glossary and increasing the number of links to online specialised dictionaries and maritime glossaries could help them devote their time to more

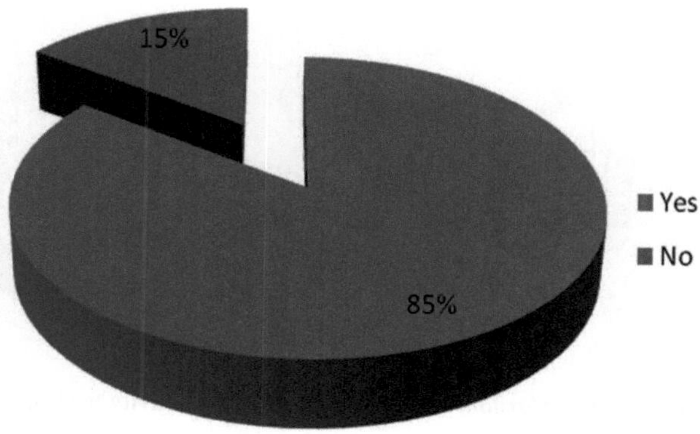

Fig. 7.5 The *Maritime Glossary* makes a good study tool

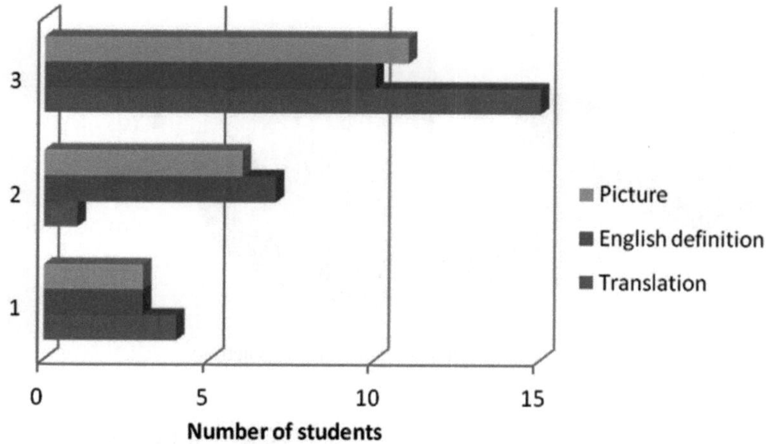

Fig. 7.6 Usefulness of the different sections in each glossary entry

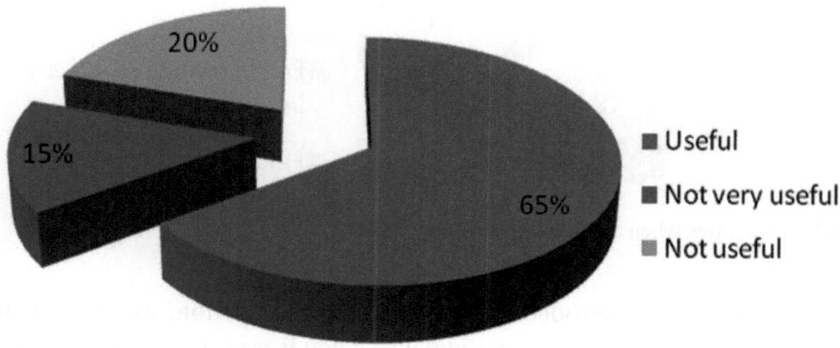

Fig. 7.7 Contribution of the *Maritime Glossary* to the learning of specialised vocabulary

interesting parts of this or other activities. Surprisingly enough, some students (10 %) lacked the necessary basic computer skills to carry out the tasks efficiently; this shows that, at least at this stage, we cannot take students' ICTs literacy for granted.

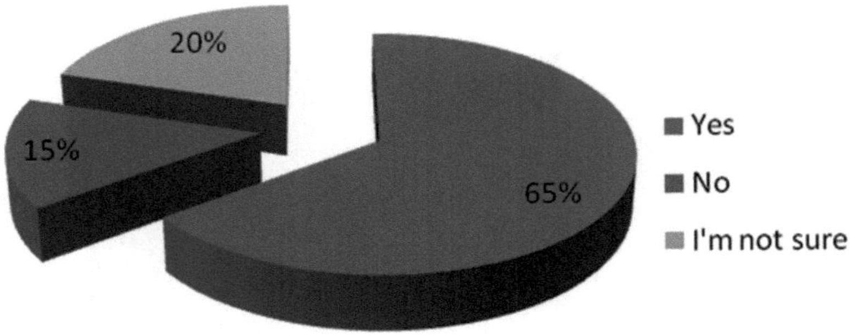

Fig. 7.8 The *Maritime Glossary* is an effective activity for learning vocabulary

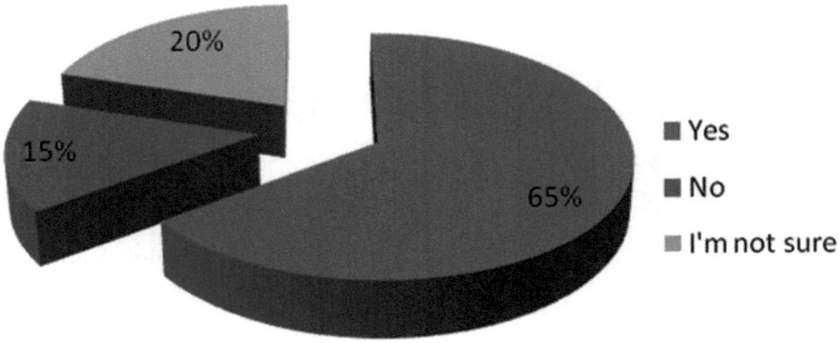

Fig. 7.9 The *Maritime Glossary* has been a good outside class activity

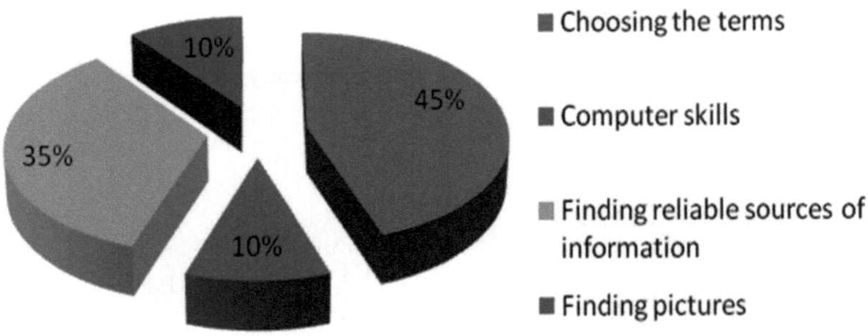

Fig. 7.10 Difficulties when adding entries to the glossary

As mentioned in the introductory paragraph to this section, we also conducted individual interviews with all the participants. They were asked to reflect on all the outside class activities – not only those related to the compilation of the glossary – and to provide feedback on the course to the teacher. Some of the most outstanding and recurrent observations about the glossary activity can be seen in the excerpts taken from questions 10 and 11 in the questionnaire, where students could give their opinions about the most and the least interesting and/or useful aspect of the project, and from the recorded interviews. The students' answers are originally in Spanish and have been translated into English for the purposes of this paper. The code following each excerpt indicates student identification (e.g. St.1) and whether it comes from the questionnaire (Q) or the interview (I).

In general, visual imagery is viewed positively. This strengthens our belief that establishing meaningful pictorial-verbal combinations is particularly efficient to learn ME terminology and needs to be further exploited.

- "The minute I see the picture, the term stays in my head". (I-St.4)
- "The most useful aspect was associating a picture with a term" (Q-St.5)
- "As soon as I see the picture, I understand the word. I would give this activity 10 out of 10". (I-St.7)
- "A picture paints a thousand words" (I-St.13)

On the process of creating the glossary, students point out they learnt "their terms" and, in some cases, as a consequence of extensive reading, incidental learning of associated terms also did take place.

- "I'd say a categorical yes. It helped me a lot with vocabulary." (I-St.3)
- "Adding entries to the glossary helped me learn not just the terms I had chosen but related words. I surfed the web. I went from one document to another, a very dynamic activity, and I ended up reading more than I needed for the definition..." (I-St.20)

Computer literacy is a transversal skill a few students had to be trained on so as to do the glossary activity. The English teachers acted as counsellors and guides to help students overcome their difficulties to carry out the project.

- "For me, the best thing is that I improved my computer skills a lot. At the beginning it took me a very long time to add an entry. I didn't know how to do it. I had never used the Virtual Campus before and knew very little about computers in general. Little by little I learnt. But I believe I would learn more vocabulary just by writing down the words, in my own way." (I-St.8)

Many students also claim to have acquired a better knowledge of the specialised materials, especially online sources of information.

- "It really helped me discover new resources in the Internet where I can find maritime information in English. If you take it seriously, you learn a lot." (I-St.15)

Concerning the glossary as a final product for study use, we find encouraging opinions.

- "All of us together... yes, we have made a good maritime glossary. I can download it and have it in my own computer, or print it. Picture, definition, translation... yes, I'll definitely use it in my professional career."(I-St.13)
- "I liked looking at all the glossary terms, especially the pictures and the translations into Spanish". (I-St.11)
- "When studying for the exam, I really used it a lot." (I-St.12)

– "Helping build the glossary made me feel good. I like to know that other people can use my work… that we work together for everyone's benefit." (I-St.15)

Students mention they encountered serious problems to select what they thought to be "interesting terms" (see Fig. 7.10 again).

– "I think a negative point is that everyone rushes to choose the most interesting terms first" (Q-St.2)
– "The problem I personally found was that the minute the activity was available in Virtual Campus, everyone rushed to upload the most interesting terms… so many times I selected a term which had already been uploaded. Then I had to choose another term, maybe not so interesting. And it was time consuming." (I-St.10)
– "Sometimes, I must confess, I chose a term because it wasn't already in the glossary, but I already knew it." (I-St.15)

Consequently, when asked on how to improve the project (question 12), students suggested organizing the search for the term in a different fashion.

– "Finding terms should be made easier" (Q-St.2)
– "A list of terms should be made so as to see which have already been selected and, above all, every term should be relevant in our field." (Q-St.3)
– "I would accept duplicated entries. Then, we would select the best definition, the best picture, etc." (Q-St.17)

The most serious criticism refers to the excessive time devoted to the project, which, at times, became a painstaking activity.

– "It takes a long time to find a proper definition… yes, and sometimes I had to spend too much time looking for the picture. I like the activity but I don't think it's worthwhile, too much effort. I learn more terms in the same time with my own method. (…) Well, my method consists of matching a word in English with its Spanish translation and copying them over and over until I learn the English word by heart. I test myself now and then." (I-St.4)
– "It was too much effort. It isn't worth my while to spend so much time to learn only a few words." (I-St.14)
– "The terms I prepared for the glossary… yes, those terms are in my head. But I didn't use the whole glossary. Some definitions were too long and difficult to understand." (I-St.9)

If the *Maritime Glossary* is believed to be a helpful activity to learn specialised vocabulary by 75 % of the students, as shown in question 3, we wonder why this figure changes to 65 % when evaluating the activity in questions 6, 7 and 8. We deem the explanation to these numbers may be found in the open questions and, above all, in the interviews, which give us interesting and thought-provoking insights. The complaint about the time spent in doing the activity is the key answer. We have already seen how we could help overcome this problem; however, we cannot forget that becoming active learners requires investing more time and effort than playing the role of passive learners students are used to. It must also be stated that the challenging task of acquiring new roles is also time-consuming for the lecturer, who must act as counsellor and guide through the whole process. Our responsibility, however, is to give the students "a fighting chance to learn the vocabulary they need to function in their second language" (Schmitt 2010: 40) and, more specifically, to participate in their future domain-specific community.

7.5 Conclusions

This paper has sought to show how computer-based instruction can be implemented in an ESP course in view of specialised vocabulary learning. It has suggested that enhancing ESP courses with computer-based technology fosters learners' collaborative work and raises awareness of self-direction. Together with this, other issues of particular concern have been addressed; namely, vocabulary learning instruction, Maritime English lexis as a subset of specialised vocabulary, the challenges of digital literacy and the so-called digital divide, the implementation of computers for vocabulary learning, or the lifelong learning dimension and the roles of teachers and learners under the ESHE framework. It has also discussed the main lines of research within the field of vocabulary learning with particular attention to the relation between computer-assisted reading instruction and vocabulary retention, the contribution of electronic dictionaries/glossaries as opposed to paper dictionaries/glossaries, and computer-enhanced ESP courses with particular reference to specialised vocabulary development.

Following all this, this paper has offered the details of a project aiming at the compilation of a glossary of Maritime English terms through the Moodle platform involving the collaborative participation of students and in an effort to encourage active self-directed learners. The project has been discussed with reference to context, participants, objectives and the three-phased procedure for implementation. Finally, learners' answers to a questionnaire and an interview have been analysed to gather opinions and insights for the improvement of later courses and refinement of similar projects. It stands out that the project could be improved in a variety of ways by exploiting more features of glossary module. To name but a few examples, enabling the autolinking would make it possible for any instance of a glossary term anywhere in Moodle to have a link to its entry; allowing all students to grade or add comments to all entries could make the glossary a more collaborative activity; even inserting pronunciation links or attaching audio files to each entry would enhance the quality of the final glossary.

As discussed in an earlier section of this paper, current works have reported on the relationship between the use of electronic dictionaries/glossaries and vocabulary instruction/learning, and also on the positive contribution of computer-based technologies for general vocabulary development. As far as we see it, and current literature shows, this particular aspect still remains underresearched for the case of specialised vocabulary; hence, a closer exploration and detailed discussion on to what extent ESP learners may benefit from ICT-based vocabulary instruction would help to further the research on the actual contribution of ICTs to specialised vocabulary development.

We agree with Brett and González-Lloret (2009: 351) that "technology is (…) no more or no less that the use practitioners and learners make of it". ICTs *per se* do not involve more effective, more motivating teaching/learning unless ways are found to enrich the learning experience through technology. The *Maritime Glossary* is just an example of how ESP learners in general, and Maritime English learners in particular, may benefit from one of the many possibilities afforded by today's technology.

Appendices

Appendix 7.1

Course: Nautical English 2009–2010

The *Maritime Glossary* Project

Questionnaire

If you have participated in the *Maritime Glossary* project, please fill in this questionnaire.

1. Had you ever used this tool to learn vocabulary?

   □ Yes
   □ No

2. Have you added all the required terms (15) during this semester?

   □ Yes
   □ No

3. Do you think introducing the terms you selected in the *Maritime Glossary* has helped you to learn them?

   □ Yes
   □ No

4. Have you consulted the terms introduced by your classmates in the Mar*itime Glossary*?

   □ Yes
   □ No

5. You can find below the different sections of each glossary entry in the *Maritime Glossary*. Please, indicate how useful they were for you (1 being the least useful, 3 the most useful).

□ Translation	1	2	3
□ Definition in English	1	2	3
□ Picture	1	2	3

6. How would you assess the contribution of the *Maritime Glossary* in the learning of English maritime/nautical vocabulary? Tick the statement you feel most identified with.

□ Very useful
□ Not very useful
□ Not useful at all

7. In your opinion, is the *Maritime Glossary* an efficient tool for the learning of English maritime/nautical vocabulary? Tick the statement you feel most identified with.

□ Yes
□ No
□ I am not sure

8. In your opinion, is the *Maritime Glossary* a good outside class activity? Tick the statement you feel most identified with.

□ Yes
□ No
□ I am not sure

9. What difficulties, if any, have you found when adding your terms to the *Maritime Glossary*?

□ Choosing the terms
□ Computer skills
□ Finding reliable sources of information
□ Finding pictures
□ Others (specify):

10. Describe the least interesting aspect of the *Maritime Glossary* and explain why.
11. Describe the most interesting aspect of the *Maritime Glossary* and explain why.
12. Can you give any suggestions on how to improve this project?

Appendix 7.2

Course: Nautical English 2009–2010

The *Maritime Glossary* Project

Interviews

The Maritime Glossary

Initial questions aiming at eliciting students' opinions.

- What are the main advantages you see in creating a *Maritime Glossary*?
- What are the main disadvantages?
- Do you think participating in the creation of the glossary has helped you to learn specialised vocabulary?
- What do you think of the glossary as a collaborative project?
- Have you had any problems when using your computer, Internet and the Virtual Campus to do this project?
- What is your overall opinion of the project?
- Please, feel free to make any comments on this outside class project.

References

Argüelles Álvarez, I. 2009. About the integration of b-learning in EPP to reinforce learner autonomy. *Revista de Lingüística y Lenguas Aplicadas* 4: 11–23.

Bocanegra Valle, A. 2004. La competencia estratégica en el contexto de aprendizaje de las lenguas con fines específicos. In *Las nuevas tendencias de las lenguas de especialidad en un contexto internacional y multicultural*, ed. I. Sanz and A. Felices, 555–563. Granada: Universidad de Granada.

Bocanegra Valle, A., and M.D. Perea Barberá. 2011. ICT-based instruction for specialised vocabulary development. In *Technological innovation in the teaching and processing of LSPs: Proceedings of TISLID´10*, ed. N. Talaván Zanón, E. Martín Monje, and F. Palazón Romero, 41–53. Madrid: Editorial UNED.

Bocanegra Valle, A., M.D. Perea Barberá, and L.E. Romero Zúñiga. 2013. CLIL methodology in higher education: Integrating the English language across the Chemical Engineering curriculum. In *La Lingüística Aplicada en la era de la globalización/Applied Linguistics in the age of globalization*, ed. A. Llanes Baró, L.A. Ciro, L. Gallego Balsá, and R.M. Mateu Serra, 260–265. Lleida: Edicions de la Universitat de Lleida.

Breeze, R. 2011. Creating a collaborative online legal English glossary in Moodle: Process and product. In *Technological innovation in the teaching and processing of LSPs. Proceedings of TISLID'10*, ed. N. Talaván Zanón, E. Martín Monje, and F. Palazón Romero, 397–404. Madrid: Editorial UNED.

Brett, D., and M. González-Lloret. 2009. Technology-enhanced materials. In *The handbook of language teaching*, ed. M.H. Long and C.J. Doughty, 351–369. West Sussex: Wiley-Blackwell.

Bueno Alastuey, M.C. 2009. Using WEbCT in a course of English for academic/specific purposes: The case of english for agriculture. In *Teaching academic and professional English online*, ed. I. González-Pueyo, C. Foz Gil, C. Jaime Siso, and M.J. Luzón Marco, 127–152. Berlin: Peter Lang.

Canapero, M. 2004. Connecting, motivating and raising awareness via WELL: Developing e-learning environments for science students. *ReCALL* 16: 330–344.

Chacón-Beltrán, R., C. Abelló-Contesse, and M.M. Torreblanca-López. 2010. Vocabulary teaching and learning: Introduction and overview. In *Insights into non-native vocabulary teaching and learning*, ed. R. Chacón-Beltrán, C. Abelló-Contesse, and M.M. Torreblanca-López, 1–12. Bristol: Multilingual Matters.

Chun, D.M., and J.J. Plass. 1996. Effects of multimedia annotations on vocabulary acquisition. *Modern Language Journal* 80: 183–198.

Cobb, T. 2007. Computing the vocabulary demands of L2 reading. *Language Learning & Technology* 11: 38–64.

Colazzo, L., and M. Costantino. 1998. Multi-user hypertextual didactic glossaries. *International Journal of Artificial Intelligence in Education* 9: 111–127.

Coll, J.F. 2002. Richness of semantic encoding in a hypermedia-assisted instructional environment for ESP: Effects on incidental vocabulary retention among learners with low ability in the target language. *ReCALL* 14: 263–284.

Commission of the European Communities. 2000. A memorandum on lifelong learning. http://www.bologna-berlin2003.de/pdf/MemorandumEng.pdf. Accessed 25 June 2010.

Commission of the European Communities. 2001. Making a European area of lifelong learning a reality. http://www.bologna-berlin2003.de/pdf/MitteilungEng.pdf. Accessed 14 Mar 2011.

Commission of the European Communities. 2003. eLearning: Designing tomorrow's education. http://www.elearningeuropa.info/extras/pdf/mid_term_en.pdf. Accessed 14 Mar 2011.

Deavux, C., R. Otterbach, and Y.Y. Cheng. 2006. Technology for trust, collaboration, and autonomy among Asian students at the University level. In *Information technology in languages for specific purposes: Issues and prospects*, ed. E. Arnó Maciá, A. Soler Cervera, and C. Rueda Ramos, 123–138. New York: Springer.

Ellis, N.C. 1994. Vocabulary acquisition: The implicit ins and outs of explicit cognitive mediation. In *Implicit and explicit learning of languages*, ed. N.C. Ellis, 211–282. London: Academic.

Ellis, N.C. 1995. The psychology of foreign language vocabulary acquisition: Implications for CALL. *Computer Assisted Language Learning* 8: 103–128.

Fernández Toledo, P. 2006. Computer, information and academic literacies in LSP pedagogy: Implication for curriculum design. *Anglogermanica Online* 2006: 44–56.

Gimeno-Sanz, A. 2002. E-language learning for the airline industry. *ReCALL* 14: 47–57.

Goodfellow, R. 1995. A review of the types of CALL programs for vocabulary instruction. *Computer Assisted Language Learning* 8: 205–226.

Graves, M.F. 2006. *The vocabulary book. Learning & instruction*. New York: Teachers College Press.

Groot, P.J.M. 2000. Computer-assisted second language vocabulary acquisition. *Language Learning & Technology* 4: 60–81.

Jones, L. 2004. Testing L2 vocabulary recognition and recall using pictorial and written test items. *Language Learning & Technology* 8: 122–143.

Kang, S.-H. 1995. The effects of a context-embedded approach to second-language vocabulary learning. *System* 23: 43–55.

Kilickaya, F., and J. Krajka. 2010. Comparative usefulness of online and traditional vocabulary learning. *TOJET: The Turkish Online Journal of Educational Technology* 9: 55–63.

Knight, S. 1994. Dictionary use while reading: The effects on comprehension and vocabulary acquisition for students of different verbal abilities. *Modern Language Journal* 78: 285–299.

Laufer, B. 2000. Electronic dictionaries and incidental vocabulary acquisition: Does technology make a difference? In *Proceedings of EURALEX 2000*, ed. U. Heid, S. Evert, E. Lehmann, and C. Rohrer, 849–854. Stuttgart: Universität Stuttgart.

Leffa, V.J. 1992. Reading with an electronic glossary. *Computers & Education* 19: 285–290.

LeLoup, J.W., and R. Ponterio. 2005. Vocabulary support for independent online reading. *Language Learning & Technology* 9: 3–7.

Lewis, G. 2009. *Bridging technology into the classroom*. Oxford: Oxford University Press.

Louky, J.P. 2002. Improving access to target vocabulary using computerized bilingual dictionaries. *ReCALL* 14: 295–314.

Luzón, M.J., and I. González. 2006. Using the Internet to promote autonomous learning in ESP. In *Information technology in languages for specific purposes: Issues and prospects*, ed. E. Arnó Maciá, A. Soler Cervera, and C. Rueda Ramos, 177–190. New York: Springer.

Ma, Q., and P. Kelly. 2006. Computer assisted vocabulary learning: Design and evaluation. *Computer Assisted Language Learning* 19: 15–45.

Mungra, P. 2009. Online delivery of a writing course: Description of a blended language course integrated into medicine. In *Teaching academic and professional English online*, ed. I. González-Pueyo, C. Foz Gil, C. Jaime Siso, and M.J. Luzón Marco, 181–208. Berlin: Peter Lang.

Nation, P. 1990. *Teaching and learning vocabulary*. Boston: Heinle & Heinle.

Nation, P., and T. Chung. 2009. Teaching and testing vocabulary. In *The handbook of language teaching*, ed. M.H. Long and C.J. Doughty, 543–559. West Sussex: Wiley-Blackwell.

Nesi, H. 1998. Using the internet to teach English for academic purposes. *ReCALL* 10: 109–117.

Nikolova, O.R. 2002. Effects of students' participation in authoring of multimedia materials on student acquisition of vocabulary. *Language Learning & Technology* 6: 100–122.

Oxford, R., and D. Crookall. 1990. Vocabulary learning: A critical analysis of techniques. *TESL Canada Journal/Revue TESL du Canada* 7: 9–30.

Paribakht, T.S., and M. Wesche. 1998. 'Incidental' and instructed L2 vocabulary acquisition: Different contexts, common processes. In *Perspectives on foreign and second language pedagogy*, ed. D. Albrechtsen, B. Henriksen, I.M. Mees, and E. Poulsen, 203–220. Odense: Odense University Press.

Perea Barberá, M.D. 2007. Classification of vocabulary learning strategies in the context of ESP. In *English for specific purposes: Studies for classroom development and implementation*, ed. A. Bocanegra, M.C. Lario, and E. López, 53–72. Cádiz: Servicio de Publicaciones de la Universidad de Cádiz.

Perea Barberá, M.D. 2009. Promoting vocabulary learning strategies through the use of word maps. In *VIII Congreso Internacional AELFE. Las lenguas para Fines Específicos ante el reto de la Convergencia Europea*, ed. E. Caridad de Otto and A.F. López de Vergara Méndez, 281–293. La Laguna: Servicio de Publicaciones de la ULL.

Pritchard, B. 2003. Maritime English syllabus for the modern seafarer: Safety-related or comprehensive courses. *WMU Journal of Maritime Affairs* 2: 149–166.

Rea Rizzo, C. 2009. A first approach to the lexical profile of telecommunication English: frequency, distribution, restriction and keyness. *Revista de Lingüística y Lenguas Aplicadas* 4: 161–173.

Ruiz-Madrid, M.N. 2006. The role of forums in the construction and development of the teaching-learning discourse in the ESP classroom. A new autonomising tool within the language teaching-learning context? *Anglogermanica Online* 2006: 27–43.

Ruiz-Madrid, N., and M. Sanz-Gil. 2007. Integration of the ICT in language learning. In *Pedagogical reflections on learning languages in instructed settings*, ed. E. Usó-Juan and N. Ruiz-Madrid, 62–77. Newcastle: Cambridge Scholars Publishing.

Schmitt, N. 2010. Key issues in teaching and learning vocabulary. In *Insights into non-native vocabulary teaching and learning*, ed. R. Chacón-Beltrán, C. Abelló-Contesse, and M.M. Torreblanca-López, 28–40. Bristol: Multilingual Matters.

Son, J.-B. 2001. CALL and vocabulary learning: A review. *English Linguistic Science* 7: 27–35.

Stockwell, G. 2007. A review of technology choice for teaching language skills and areas in the CALL literature. *ReCALL* 19: 105–120.

Sydorenko, T. 2010. Modality of input and vocabulary acquisition. *Language Learning & Technology* 14: 50–73.

Tozcu, A., and J. Coady. 2004. Successful learning of frequent vocabulary through CALL also benefits reading comprehension and speed. *Computer-Assisted Language Learning* 17: 473–495.

Trinder, R. 2006. Integration of e-learning into a tertiary educational context. In *Information technology in languages for specific purposes: Issues and prospects*, ed. E. Arnó Maciá, A. Soler Cervera, and C. Rueda Ramos, 191–210. New York: Springer.

Universidad de Cádiz. 2010. *Memoria Universidad de Cádiz 2009/2010*. Cádiz: Servicio de Publicaciones de la Universidad de Cádiz.

Yoshii, M. 2006. L1 and L2 glosses: Their effects on incidental vocabulary learning. *Language Learning & Technology* 10: 85–101.

Chapter 8
A Practical Application of Wikis for Learning Business English as a Second Language

Pilar Rodríguez-Arancón and Cristina Calle-Martínez

8.1 Introducción

In this day and age, it is impossible to think of teachers limiting themselves to oral explanations in their classes and doing so without any kind of didactic aid. In fact, according to Reiser and Gagné (1983) "even the teacher's voice is a didactic resource". However, beyond the voice of the teacher and more traditional didactic methods such as books and blackboards and chalk, English teachers have been using technological tools since the beginning of the twentieth century such as record players, tape recorders, slide projectors, etc. Business English teachers nowadays have a wide range of resources available to them to use in their classes such as DVDs, videos, multimedia (*PowerPoint*, hypertexts), blogs, virtual platforms, applets and wikis (Bohigas et al. 2003), to name but a few.

The advance of technology has enabled it to become an important asset in the development of the teaching-learning process. There is no doubt that the Internet, especially the World Wide Web originated in 1989, has made an important impact in people's lives (Davies 2002). The web has provided the tools to encourage interaction and cooperative learning. The programs and applications are easy to use and do not require great prior expertise in technology. On the one hand the functions of Information and Communication Technology (ICT, henceforth) in education are many and varied, ranging from the development of a simple text by a single student to the use and development of websites as information resources. On the other hand,

P. Rodríguez-Arancón (✉)
Departamento de Filologías Extranjeras y sus Lingüísticas,
Universidad Nacional de Educación a Distancia, Madrid, Spain
e-mail: prodriguez@flog.uned.es

C. Calle-Martínez (✉)
Departamento de Filología Inglesa I, Universidad Complutense de Madrid, Madrid, Spain
e-mail: cristinacalle@ucm.es

E. Bárcena et al. (eds.), *Languages for Specific Purposes in the Digital Era*,
Educational Linguistics 19, DOI 10.1007/978-3-319-02222-2_8,

ICT allows teachers to maintain a broad vision of their discipline, incorporating new work methodologies and updating their knowledge of the subject matter, as well as improving communication with the students and even amongst them.

Teachers as well as students, who know and manage ICTs, acquire skills which help them to adapt to the use of new technology. For example, they are able to browse the Internet, perform data estimates, use email, etc. It is this that authors such as Salomon et al. (1991) refer to as "cognitive residue". The computer is a machine which provides the user with an extra intellectual tool to interpret the world. However, despite all these advantages, some teachers nowadays still fail to understand how much benefit they can gain from the use of ICTs in the planning and managing of their classes, even if they make use of them to some extent. New technologies have been instrumental in the development of digital literacy and although researchers focussed on web 1.0 asynchronous communication a few years ago, more recent efforts have also started to analyse the use of blogs (Jones and Nuhfer-Halten 2006), or wikis (Laursson and Alterman 2009).

Technology can help students to acquire knowledge at a faster pace and in a deeper manner. However, this is not enough for students to learn as they are not always aware of how to apply this new knowledge to practical purposes. Thus, the teacher plays a key role in the understanding and use of these new technologies given the didactic importance they can have if they are put to good use. As Forte and Bruckman (2007) explain, the use of technology can contribute to the strengthening of what has been previously been learned through "hands-on" experience. Thus, it can facilitate the combination of abstract and experimental learning.

This particular study has focused on the use of wikis as they provide the teacher with information about the development process of the task performed by the students. Students can write and rewrite information about a topic whilst the wiki keeps a record of all interventions (Del Moral 2007). Thus, it allows for the evaluation of the whole process of knowledge construction. A wiki is an online tool for collective writing, it is a text processor open and accessible to all those who are granted permission of access. The responsibility for the creation of materials is shared (Wheeler et al. 2008). Wikis are closely associated with project-based and task-based language learning practices where students and teachers contribute to the creation of knowledge and share their findings. This tool became popular a few years ago with the creation in 1994 of the virtual encyclopaedia known as Wikipedia (http://en.wikipedia.org) by Ward Cunningham; but now wikis are extensively used in many sectors for people to work in collaboration in a single project via the Internet.

8.2 Diagnosis

In this study we present a proposal for innovation, attending to the needs of students aiming to improve the processes for mastering their English in the business sphere. We studied 100 first year students of the new Degree in Economics (*Bachelor's*

Degree in Business Administration) offered by the Faculty of Economics and Business at the Universidad Complutense de Madrid. The number of places offered annually for new students in this degree is a total of 387, which reveals the large extent of proportional participation obtained in the study, nearly 26 %. The subject that these students were taking was "*Idioma Moderno: Inglés*" which is compulsory, or part of the Basic Subjects as it is categorised in the *Degree Study Plan*, and it offers 6 ECTS credits in the first semester of the academic year. It is taught through 3 h of teacher-led weekly seminars and another 3 extra hours in the multimedia classroom. The description of the course specifies that it is "an English course within the framework of Languages for Specific Purposes, in this case, part of the Bachelor in Economics, with academic and professional vocation leading to a B2 (Vantage) English level in the *European Frame of Reference*".

The study started with two information collecting methods: a test with specific Business English questions, and a personal interview. Both methods aimed at gathering information from the students in relation to their level of English in the first place, and secondly the needs and expectations that the students had with respect to the English pedagogical proposal in their academic and professional development. The research would also help identify the specific situations in which the students consider it likely that they would need to use the English language in their future professional occupations.

The results showed that 76 out of 100 students (76 %) were at a beginner level, in other words, the students were unable to show "basic skills in communicating and exchanging information in English". It could be regarded as an A2 (Waystage or elementary) level according to the *Common European Framework of Reference for Languages: Learning, Teaching, Assessment* (Council of Europe 2001) which defines the competence of students at this stage with the following explanation:

> Uses some simple structures correctly, but still systematically makes basic mistakes.
>
> Can make him/herself understood in very short utterances, even though pauses, false starts and reformulation are very evident. (p. 29)

These results coincide with the observations made in the personal interview, given that the majority displayed a low listening comprehension level, producing isolated words and making frequent mistakes in cohesion, coherence, meaning and syntax combined with nervous and anxious behaviour during the conversation. The recommended level at the beginning of the degree is a B1 (Breakthrough) and the objectives of the course are to achieve a "participative methodology aimed at motivating and stimulating students to learn English, taking into account their needs and interests whilst encouraging self-learning and self-evaluation".

In the needs analysis the results obtained pointed out some of the problems that the students considered had hindered their learning progress in the past. It is obvious that something had not gone well, considering firstly that the level of English reached by 76 % of them was still an A2 after a minimum of 6 years of tuition through Secondary Education, and secondly that the objective of the syllabus drawn by the Ministry of Education (http://www.educacion.es) for all students at the end of such level is to reach a B1, and a B2 from next academic year 2011–2012.

The students considered that their experience of learning English in Primary and Secondary education had been deficient. Among the problems mentioned were: monotonous classes, irrelevant tasks, textbooks with only "*drill*" type exercises, little or no communicative activities and displaying content out of context.

Even though their experience had not been very positive they still valued learning the English language as an indispensable tool for their training in the field of business and wanted to be able to communicate in meetings in the future, attend conferences, introduce companies or products and read documents related to their area in English. From a more personal point of view they wanted to be able to understand the news, to travel without the problems of communication with people from other countries, and to search the Internet.

The students thought that for these objectives to be possible they needed a less monotonous experience of English learning with less rigid pedagogical practices, more personalized attention from the teacher, a variety of activities, and the use of different and more modern resources such as computers in general, or the Internet in particular.

After collecting the data from the survey and the following interview, our priority was to minimize these disconcerting results. In turn, since the main concern was to improve the management of their English learning in general and specifically Business English, and having many tools and technologies available to us throughout the web which are widely used by students already, the use of wikis as an educational tool was the choice made. These students belong to what Tapscott (2009) calls the "net generation" adults who have used computers since they were children in the 1990s and now use them routinely for communication. Wikis allow students to devote more time to study and carry out appropriate tasks in Business English in collaboration with their classmates via a process that is monitored by the teacher and developer. The use of this tool can help students develop oral and listening skills that would meet their future requirements highlighted in the needs' analysis previously carried out. Among their objectives were: negotiating contracts, managing meetings, giving presentations and interacting during business trips, for example.

Wikis are useful because students can learn outside the classroom as they work in collaboration (Baggetun et al. 2003). They learn by doing and they learn from each other. They feel responsible for the results and interaction within the project, "it is through the talk that learning occurs" (Gerlach 1994). The teacher monitors the progress and ensures the cognitive learning process is taking place at the same time as the three stages of the work develop, that is, input, output and feedback. Thus, wikis are a perfect complement for the new challenges faced by teachers and students alike (de Paula et al. 2001) in the new European Space for Higher Education. They are a step forward from the old teacher-centered setup to allowing the students to play an active role in their own learning process (Mindel and Verma 2006): a necessary methodological change in order to adapt to the Bologna Process.

8.3 Theoretical Framework

8.3.1 Wikis

"*Wiki*" is a Hawaiian word meaning "*fast*". A WikiWikiWeb or simply a Wiki is a collection of interlinked web pages, each of which can be accessed and edited by a group of people. Therefore, a wiki is a web site which allows the users to create, edit, delete or modify the contents of a web page, in an interactive, quick and easy way. Such features make a wiki an effective tool to generate web pages collaboratively creating news content on the Internet quite easily. This has many uses: from developing the contents of an encyclopaedia on the Internet, to making a collaborative tool for internal information management in an enterprise through to a personal tool such as a content organizer or a personal agenda.

It is considered a content management system because most wikis have a way of creating templates and other features along the entire site, and help manage user permissions at site and page level. To enjoy highly dynamic web sites, or for those who need a strong feedback from users, a wiki may be the most appropriate platform to work in. The main use of a wiki is to create and enhance the pages instantly, giving great freedom to the user, through a simple interface. This means that more people can participate in the editing process, unlike traditional systems, where it is more difficult for users of the site to improve it. The major disadvantage of wikis is that their emphasis is on the editing of content and not on the interface, so it is not usually the most appropriate system if you want to provide an individual user appearance.

The origins of the wikis are in the design patterns community, who used to write about and discuss their patterns. The first WikiWikiWeb was created by Ward Cunningham, a programmer in Oregon, who invented and named the wiki concept, and produced the first implementation of a WikiWiki server for the *Portland Pattern Repository* in 1995. In Ward's own words a wiki is "the simplest online database that could possibly work". Ward's wiki is still one of the most visited sites on the Internet wiki.

In January 2001, the founders of Nupedia encyclopaedia project, Jimbo Wales and Larry Sanger, decided to use a wiki as a basis for the *Wikipedia* encyclopaedia project. Originally, *UseMod* software was used, but they decided to create their own software, *MediaWiki*, later adopted by many other wikis.

Currently, the largest existing wiki is the English version of *Wikipedia*, followed by several other versions of the project. The non-Wikipedia wikis are much smaller, usually due to the fact of being much more specialized. For example, the creation of wikis to provide software documentation is very frequent.

According to Lamb (2004) the most salient features of wikis are:

(a) Anyone can change anything. Wikis are quick because the processes of reading and editing are similar. A link to the page you are reading allows you to edit, add, delete or modify any content. The typical wiki is open to contributions and assistance from anyone you want, although this is not a prerequisite. *Wikipedia* is a successful example of such projects: an encyclopaedia written by hundreds of thousands of volunteers from the Internet, in which anyone can include their ideas and knowledge or modify the ideas expressed by others previously, however, it maintains a good level of quality in its articles. *Wikipedia* exceeds the flagship of traditional encyclopaedia, the *Encyclopaedia Britannica* (http://www.britannica.com) in size and daily visits and, in many cases, also in accuracy and timeliness (Giles 2005).

(b) The second feature is technical and is essential to make collaboration possible: wikis use a simplified hypertext marking system. It is not necessary to know *HTML (HyperText Markup Language)*, the language in which web pages are written, or use a web editor to collaborate on a wiki. The language of wikis eliminates nonessential elements of *HTML* and reduces them to a minimum. The system also eliminates the opening and closing tags, simplifying the creation of texts, links, lists, formats, etc. For example, to create a list of items it is enough to type each one in a line and precede them with an asterisk or a hyphen. To make a link it is enough to simply type the *URL* (*uniform resource locator*) and the wiki software handles everything else. Simplified editing eliminates the technical barriers to participation: anyone can contribute, if desired, and the text has a uniform appearance (some critics say that all texts look the same, but now it is possible to use style sheets (CSS) in some systems so that the appearance can be customized to a certain extent), maintaining a consistent visual style across all the wiki. The language of wikis is not standardized and different systems use different markers. Thus, a star is used to define an item in some lists and in others a hyphen. In recent times, some wikis have started to incorporate embedded visual editors, in *Javascript* (http://www.javascript.com) or *ActiveX* (http://www.active-x.com), to further facilitate editing by novice users.

A characteristic feature, and strongly criticized by some people, is the "wiki writing" of *Wikiwords* or "*CamelCase*", with two or more capital letters (which are figuratively the humps of the camel). Its use is explained below in the context of the structure of wikis.

(c) The third feature is the flexibility: a wiki does not have a predefined structure to which the users have to accommodate. Anyone can create new pages in a wiki, and link them to any other existing pages. In most of them, to create a new page, it is enough to just type the title in *CamelCase* in an existing page (or bracketed, depending on the wiki software used). When you move to the reading mode, the software will have created a page with that title and a link to it in the text written in *CamelCase*. Clicking on the link (usually a question mark) will take you to the new blank page which can also then be edited.

A wiki is so extremely flexible in its structure that without some editing and rules it can become chaos very quickly, although, at the same time, its flexibility allows the collaborative and progressive construction of complex hypertext information spaces.

(d) The fourth key feature that Lamb (2004) highlights is that traditionally, the pages of wikis are "free from ego" and temporal and unfinished references ("ego-less, time-less, and never finished"). The anonymity of the contributions is not a technical imperative but a tradition of the "wiki spirit". The concept of "author" is blurred in wikis to the extent that any site has been made by several people who add, delete, amend, comment, etc. what has been written by those who were there before.

Wikis are always in a state of flux. A page is never considered as final or complete. They are like our ideas and knowledge: constantly changing. They are timeless to the extent that the topics covered evolve, change and progress. *Wikipedia* is an excellent example: it will never be finished, always requiring new contributions as the pace that it is updated greatly exceeds that of traditional printed encyclopaedias.

Although the four principles above describe the "wiki spirit" and the most prominent features of the software, the reality is that the Internet is full of exceptions. You can find a continuum in which both computing deployment and the original idea of the wiki as a collaborative space lie, as much as the practices of specific communities using wikis on the Internet. At one extreme is the maximum simplicity and freedom represented by Ward Cunningham's original wiki. Since then many wiki engines have been developed, usually open source, in many programming languages, with different architectures (a relational database to store the pages or using flat text files) and with variations in the marking language. Different sensitivities and needs have led to different types of wiki. There are now some wikis that request pre-authentication from the authors, editing system permissions and management tools, and that can export their content in different formats, etc. The opposite extreme to the most purist view, which tries to keep wikis simple and open, are the companies that develop commercial wikis as a tool for knowledge management in the business world – the easy editing of the web page using the browser being the only remaining feature of Cunningham's original idea.

Following the success of *Wikipedia*, wikis are attracting considerable attention from various fields, such as the theory of mass media. Ebersbach and Glaser (2004), for example, have examined whether wikis and wiki philosophy meet the seven criteria Enzensberger (1970) imposed to the emancipatory use of media: (1) decentralization; (2) each receiver a potential transmitter; (3) mass mobilization; (4) collective production; (5) participant interaction (feedback); (6) social control through self-organization; and (7) political learning processes.

Ebersbach and Glaser conclude that it is extraordinary that Enzensberger had written such text in 1970 as it gives the impression of having anticipated the development of the Internet and, in particular, that of the wikis, which amply fulfil all those conditions. All media must be analyzed not only from its technical capabilities (technological determinism), but also from the objectives and purposes of those who use it. It is no coincidence, they say, that many non-governmental organizations and political and social movements use wikis to inform and organize their members around the world. Therefore participating in an initiative such as *Wikipedia* would be a political act, and even the project of an open collective encyclopaedia a paradigmatic example of the emancipatory use of a mass medium.

8.3.2 *Wikis in Education*

The use of wikis in education is not overly extended when compared to other types of applications and environments designed from the dominant educational discourse (such as "*Virtual Campus*"), which defines in advance *how* the teaching/learning process should be structured, *which* should be the roles of the participants and *how* to regulate their activity. Wikis can be viewed as a "breakthrough" technology when compared to the one way structure of most web applications as they give symmetrical or equal rights to all participants, and base their success on the collective activity of reflection and communication and the self-organization of the community. However, wikis play a more prominent role in traditional educational environments every day. Thus many systems have incorporated them as a tool for didactic activities which require some of their technical characteristics. An example of this integration is Moodle (http://moodle.org), a socio-constructivist teaching / learning, open source environment, which offers a wiki among other tools such as forums, chat rooms, learning objects, lessons, glossaries, assignments, etc. for online learning activities.

Lott (2005) drew a list of the typical uses of wikis in education. Here are some of them:

(a) **Space of classroom communication**
A wiki can serve as a primary communication space in the classroom or in conjunction with a traditional virtual teaching and learning method as an integrated communication tool. The freedom and ease with which content can be created and edited on a wiki contrasts with the hierarchical and structured communication manner of tools such as forums, bulletin boards, objective tests, all of which are learning objects pre-designed by experts. The choice made by the teacher or institution can be seen as representing opposing educational orientations. However, they could also be accepted as complementary resources – there are times to study and learn what the experts have written about a given topic and times for students to create their own content, alone or in collaboration with their peers. This brings us to the next use of wikis: a space for collaborative development of artefacts.

(b) **Area of class collaboration/knowledge base**
A wiki can be used as a focal point in a community around a specific topic related to a subject. A general area can be created on a given subject or a more focused one on a particular aspect, which could contain resources or the products of student research.

(c) **Space to make and present work/online portfolio**
Academic tasks or artefacts that the students develop to learn, either alone or in groups, can be placed in a wiki for further review, for evaluation by teachers and/or their own peers, for review by outside experts, etc. Wikis can also serve as support for forms of portfolio assessment. When used as a portfolio a certain degree of structure is needed: aimed objectives; selection of artefacts produced during the training process; reflection on how these artefacts demonstrate the

achievement of the developed competencies or previous learning objectives; other skills developed or made, feedback from the tutor or tutors, etc.

Portfolios or the results of projects undertaken by students can be open to the Internet in general or have limited access to course participants or tutors. Publishing the production of the students on the Internet involves considerations beyond the scope of this text, but learning is crucial to move from the current training of users and consumers to information producers or, as some authors have suggested, "from users to producers" (Lim 2005). New technologies have dramatically lowered the technological, economic and political relationship division between users / consumers and producers/distributors of information.

(d) **Texts file in preparation**
A wiki, for its flexibility and ease of creation and editing, is a natural space to house texts and other materials during the writing process. Wikis maintain internally a searchable history of changes and it is easy to go back to a previous version, make side comments, use a debating format, etc. A wiki can be the ideal place to create texts collaboratively regardless of distance and time barriers.

(e) **Class manual/Collaborative authoring**
Another type of activity for which a wiki lends itself particularly well is the collaborative creation of textbooks, manuals or monographs, collections of problems or cases, by a group of teachers from a more traditional perspective, or from a more social constructivist perspective by the students themselves. In this sense, "taking" a course would be to collectively rewrite its "textbook", giving personal and collective sense to it, placing it in context and "appropriating" the ideas that form the core of the learning of the subject (as is the case of part of this study).

(f) **Space for group projects**
Finally, a wiki may be the ideal tool to house and/or publish the final drafts of student groups working projects. Self-assessment and peer assessment activities can be designed, cross-links between projects can be promoted, peer reviews can be performed, etc. to promote the analysis and study of the other groups' projects (also evident in this study).

In addition to the uses mentioned above, which only consider the use of a wiki by a single unit or classroom group within the educational institution, there are other inter-institutional uses which are open to cooperation in a broader context. Let's imagine a group of teachers of a particular subject who belong to various institutions and are collectively interested in creating learning resources for students. They could use a wiki to prepare and share their activities and suggested reading materials. A wiki could house a community of students from several universities to share news, resources, or materials on their future profession. Even more interestingly, it could house the activities of a community of practice in which experienced professionals relate with apprentices in training, a space for "legitimate peripheral participation" (Lave and Wenger 1991) and building shared practices portfolios.

Wikis used either as a replacement for teaching and learning platforms or as virtual environments within them; as spaces for specific activities that require collaboration and easy editing of web pages; or as open spaces in the Internet in general for the publication of student work; or as electronic portfolios for assessment or support of collaborative work, etc. should be designed taking into account the rules and dynamics of institutionalized education and the roles and expectations of the participants. In other words, a revolutionary educational use of a wiki depends not so much on the functionality of the software, which can only help or hinder the activities, as on our ability to change the traditional relations, norms and expectations of formal education. For example, if at the end of the collaborative process it is necessary to assess students basing our decision on their performance on a test of knowledge (an imposition of the institution or tradition), the behaviour of the students during the activity on the wiki will be aimed at acquiring the skills necessary to overcome such a test. Very little unselfish collaboration can be expected from them because we are not actually encouraging it with our evaluation system. On the contrary, another example would be if a wiki that does not track individual contributions is used, we can hardly encourage student participation in a collective process of knowledge construction through the development of artefacts if you cannot discriminate between those who participated and those who limited their contributions to building on the work of their peers ("lamers" – those who only care about learning the bare minimum necessary to operate the device in the way originally intended). In short, the "revolutionary" aspect of wikis is not as much on the technology as in the educational process we are able to orchestrate around it. The technology only facilitates or hinders the process, but does not guarantee the result. Using a wiki in our subject does not make the group / classroom an open community of knowledge construction, or a miniature *Wikipedia.*

The basic elements of a wiki are:

- **Edit**. Allows the edition of a page. Images, files, videos, charts, etc. can be uploaded.
- **Edit browser**. Allows the edition of the navigation bar.
- **Page**. Every wiki can have multiple pages. Each page is a website which can have content and links to other pages.
- **Discussion**. Each page has its own area or forum.
- **History**. The changes made to the pages can be seen. It allows you to go back to a previous version in case you want to correct errors.
- **Notification**. Changes in the wiki pages are notified.
- **New page**. It allows the creation of new pages. For example, a link page for each student.
- **Recent changes**. Recent changes made to the wiki can be checked.
- **Manage wiki**. Allows the management of the members of the wiki pages, files, changing the logo, permissions, subscriptions, discussion or forum, reports and statistics of the wiki.

The curriculum of the Business English course aimed at first year students of the Degree in Economics and reported on in this paper was developed with a wiki.

8.4 Methodology

8.4.1 Subject Development

Within the theoretical framework that has been outlined, the teaching innovation intended to be developed with this piece of research was to foster collaborative work within the classroom and with other groups where the same subject was taught. We used wikis for this purpose.

Activities using four different skills were undertaken, namely *listening, speaking, reading* and *writing*. Pair and group work were promoted as well as role-play in the field of Economics with which students will be faced in the future. In the six units on the course program each of the three course groups (groups A1, A2 and F2), would develop written theoretical concepts (related to Vocabulary), activities about the texts provided (Reading) and oral skills (Role-plays), on a rotating basis according to the following schedule:

	Group A1 does:	Group A2 does:	Group F2 does:
Unit 1	Vocabulary/writing	Reading	Role-play/speaking
Unit 2	Reading	Role-play/speaking	Vocabulary/writing
Unit 3	Role-play/speaking	Vocabulary/writing	Reading
Unit 4	Vocabulary/writing	Reading	Role-play/speaking
Unit 5	Reading	Role-play/speaking	Vocabulary/writing
Unit 6	Role-play/speaking	Vocabulary/writing	Reading

Once the work in the wiki had ended, it could be checked by all students, each of them having to issue a report that would serve as evaluation of this collaborative work for each of the groups. Groups A1, A2 and F2 had their own representative who was responsible for writing the vocabulary tasks on the wiki.

We believe that this desire to encourage students to plan specific tasks, write properly, edit and revise each other in a simultaneous manner can be considered as an important educational innovation that is the focus of this project.

The planning of the course, which was available to students from the first day, contained a schedule indicating the dates of opening, closing and evaluation for each item of work planned to be carried out in the wikis within each of the six units. Wikis, at the time of their construction had to be defined as separate entities so that each group of students could work without "being seen" by the others. Once the wiki "was closed", it became "visible" to all the participants so that the evaluation process could take place.

The teachers made a series of recommendations at the time according to the nature of the work to be carried out:

- **Vocabulary (Writing)**
  Students were asked to be the "teachers" of the unit so, therefore, they were responsible for searching on the web and making the effort to explain the contents to their peers.

  At the same time, they were building a glossary or "Personal Dictionary of Economics": that is, writing in their own words the meanings of the terms and expressions related to the Economic field found in each unit. These new terms had to show the translation into their mother tongue, the appropriate definition and synonyms. As the course progressed, these definitions could be completed with the new concepts that were studied, or changed where the learning process was making the students gain in maturity and, therefore, it was the pupil who needed to define more precisely the different concepts, a fact that is characteristic of the language of Economics.

  Among other activities, the student had to practice this skill by:

  1. Developing a CV, a cover letter, a memo, a fax and several reports on the conclusion of a meeting held previously under the guidelines specified by the teacher for their preparation.
  2. Producing a written report on a number of companies, obtaining the information from the Internet.

- **Reading**
  This skill was implemented with 12 selected texts that students had to work on throughout the course. These texts would be placed in the wiki with enough time for students to read and prepare at home. The teacher informed them about the point from which they were available in the wiki. The activities related to these texts versed, among other things, about synonyms, "True/False" questions to check the degree of their reading comprehension ability and questions about the general understanding of the text content.
- **Speaking (Role-play)**
  Students had to practice this skill in each unit using videos that included sound. This work was carried out in groups or pairs depending on the activity requirements. Students had to record their conversations and their staging of the role-plays and place their videos on the wiki. Throughout the course they did the following:

  1. The presentation of a product in small groups of 3 students. In this activity they had to use the knowledge acquired in the subjects related to the introduction of a product in a market, its description and use, sale points, etc.
  2. A role-play of a job interview in groups of 5 students (1 student was interviewed and the other 4 were the interviewers).
  3. The staging of negotiations, meetings and phone calls carried out to reach agreements, to make appointments or to sell a product.

4. Oral answers to questions that the teacher made with respect to the topic of the particular unit of the textbook being studied at the time and that the students followed in the conventional classroom. At the beginning of each unit the teacher introduced the relevant topic and made questions orally to gather the prior knowledge that the students had about it (warm-up).

For the work on these oral activities, students had to use:

- Voice recording tools such as:

  Audacity (http://audacity.sourceforge.net),
  Callburner (http://www.callburner.com),
  PowerGramo (http://www.powergramo.com)
  Audiopal (http://www.audiopal.com), or
  Viewpoint (http://clear.msu.edu/viewpoint/index.php),
  among others.

- Tools to make videos such as:

  PhotoPeach (http://photopeach.com),
  Screen-o-matic (http://www.screencast-o-matic.com), or
  Movie Maker (http://www.softonic.com/s/movie-maker).

The manual for using these tools could be found within the *Virtual Campus* as they had been placed there by the teacher at the beginning of the course.
Before the development of these activities which required an acceptable oral competence, the teacher provided the students with a series of useful tools for students to check their pronunciation:

- *Text-to-Speech* (http://text-to-speech.imtranslator.net).
- *Merriam Webster Online Dictionary* (http://www.merriam-webster.com).
- *Wordweb* (a free downloadable application, very useful to have to hand when writing or preparing an oral presentation) (http://wordweb.info/free).
- *How J Say* (a free online Talking Dictionary of English Pronunciation) (http://www.howjsay.com).
- *Forvo* (pronunciation of words by people from different places, for example: US, UK, Australia) (http://www.forvo.com).

- **Listening**
  The students were shown many sites in the wiki where they were able to assess their listening comprehension through different activities. One of the most widely used was *Randall's ESL Cyber Listening Lab* (http://www.esl-lab.com). On this site they could find different listening comprehension activities in order to check their level of skill. These extra tasks helped them to practice progress and improve this skill.

  The teacher placed the audios related to the unit in the wiki and students had to listen and answer several questions. To this end, they had to use voice recording tools such as those described in the previous section (Speaking).

8.4.2 *Objectives and Phases*

The learning objectives of the course through the use of wikis were:

- To encourage the student in the process of learning the English language using a collaborative methodology.
- Initiation of the skills related to communication: listening and speaking competence.
- Reading and understanding texts related to the area of knowledge of Economics in the English language.
- Make oral presentations using video.
- Familiarize the student with the use of ICTs.
- Encourage self-learning and self-evaluation. The student exchanged exercises with their peers and corrected and evaluated them at the same time.
- Encourage participation and interaction in the wiki working in small groups on case studies and negotiations to reach agreements or make decisions.
- Acquire the specialized terminology which would allow them to understand texts in the field of Economics and Business.
- Learn how to submit a CV, a letter of presentation, write memos or follow a schedule and also make phone calls or write business letters.

In order to achieve these goals the teaching methodology was based on the following three phases:

- **Teaching**
  Theory: The teacher explained and developed the previous knowledge that the students had. Therefore, to get student involvement from the outset, before the beginning of each lesson a Pdf file was available to them. This Pdf file contained all the theoretical points and development of the ideas of the classroom textbook. The students had to read and work on these points before going to class where the teacher would elaborate on that explanation.

  Activities: The teacher defined the learning objectives that complemented the lectures, tutoring and guiding the work carried out by the students on a set of activities. To this end, the students had a file of the subject "*Idioma Moderno: Inglés*" program with the activities, which had to be done in class.
- **Learning**
  The teacher provided the students with a series of learning activities:

  Wiki: In order to learn the content of each of the units the students used a wiki, through which they developed "their own textbook". Each of the groups worked on the assigned material within each of the units and then incorporated their own teamwork effort in order to build the so called "their own textbook". At a certain time the teacher considered the work finished and closed the wikis (at the same time for all groups), thus each teacher proceeded to place the work done by the students in their group in the *Moodle* platform. The evaluation of this work is explained below.

Glossary: In order to develop the theory of "their own textbook ", students had to gather all the new words within each unit and add them in alphabetical order. In addition, the references used were taken into account and highly valued, either those obtained through Internet searches or those found in the Recommended Books List.

Tasks: The teacher could set up an activity in class at any time and it would be evaluated within the chapter of "classroom marks", as explained below.

Virtual Campus: The subject was virtualized in a *Moodle* platform from the beginning of the course so that the students had access from that point to all the information they may have needed. In the section devoted to this subject, students had:

- The official program of the course.
- A calendar with the dates for the beginning of each unit and the deadline for the delivery of the work.
- 12 selected articles from journals in Economics.
- A model of Curriculum Vitae, a memo, a fax and a letter.
- Instructions about how to make a presentation.
- An audio made by the teacher on the presentation of a company.
- An introduction to each unit of the textbook which was the basis for the work carried out in the conventional classroom.
- A forum where students could exchange views and make suggestions.

Seminars or tutoring: In this space students had the assistance of the teacher to solve any problems they might have had about how to approach the work they had to perform, especially in the development of activities in the wiki. The students had tutorials to show the teacher the progress of the work placed on the wiki and get support in its preparation or correct any mistakes they might have made.

- **Evaluation**
  The students evaluate the work of others in the wikis. The students had to evaluate the outcome of the work and effort of their peers in "their own textbook". In order to do this, when the teacher decided to "close" the wiki for the unit, each student had to evaluate the work performed by students from other groups, give it a grade which would be within the range indicated in a table previously drawn up and send it to their teacher. These marks could be up to 32 points, that is, 32 % of the overall grades for the subject. The marks that students proposed had to be reasoned and could be "qualified" (corrected or weighted) by their teachers.

  The teacher evaluated the questionnaires and tasks: 18 % of the global rating (that is, up to 18 points) consisted of "classroom marks" (participation in class and the "tasks" proposed by the teacher, as explained above) and the 50 % left (50 points) was obtained by performing two tests in "Questionnaire" (another tool in the *Moodle* platform).

8.5 Results

The aim of this section is to present the most significant results of the evaluation of all the pupils who took the course.

The following table shows the final grades of 57 of the students:

	Group A1		Group A2		Group F2		Group A1 A2 F2	
Mark	Nº	%	Nº	%	Nº	%	Nº	%
Fail	1	0,00	0	5,00	1	5,56	2	3,51
Pass	18	94,74	14	70,00	16	88,89	48	84,21
Grade B	1	5,26	5	25,00	1	5,56	7	12,28
Totals	19	100,0	20	100,00	18	100,00	57	100,00

From the previous table it is worth noting that only two students failed, namely 1 in group A1 and one in group F2, which represents 3.51 % of those enrolled. Therefore, 55 students passed, this is 96.49 %. It must also be noted that there were no grade As for any honours awarded. We must also bear in mind that the evaluation was conducted in four major items: assignments, wikis and two *Moodle* questionnaires, with a rating of 18, 32, 25 and 25 % respectively, as previously mentioned. The following table shows the most significant of these items:

Values	Classroom mark	Wiki	Questionnaire 1	Questionnaire II	Final mark
Minimum	6,0	14,0	0,0	0,0	14,0
Maximum	18,0	30,0	18,5	21,5	74,5
Average	12,9	25,6	5,3	9,5	53,1
Standard deviation	3,2	2,7	5,4	5,3	10,0

As is clear from the table above, the maximum values are the class marks (there is one student who obtained the highest possible rating), followed by the work in the wikis, questionnaire II and finally, questionnaire I. However, if we consider the average rating, the wikis has been the highest of all of them, namely 25.6 of the possible 32 points.

What follows is a more in depth analysis of the test scores obtained in the wikis. The topics of the units in the program for the subject that were evaluated in the wikis were:

- Unit 1: Organisations. Company structure
- Unit 2: Advertising
- Unit 3: Human Resources
- Unit 4: Money. Financial terms
- Unit 5: Leadership
- Unit 6: International Markets

The set of tables below shows, in the first three rows, the average score obtained for each of the units by each of the three groups. In the last three rows there is information about each wiki: the maximum score, the average, the standard deviation and the percentage obtained on the maximum score assigned to each of them respectively.

Group	Wiki-Unit 1	Wiki-Unit 2	Wiki-Unit 3	Wiki-Unit 4	Wiki-Unit 5	Wiki-Unit 6
A1	2.41	3.29	3.91	4.93	5,64	6,26
A2	2,41	2,97	4,13	5,21	5,70	6,10
F2	2,26	3,18	4,21	5,09	5,84	6,07
Maximum score	3,00	4,00	5,00	6,00	7,00	7,00
Average	2,36	3,15	4,08	5,08	5,73	6,14
Standard deviation	0,09	0,16	0,16	0,14	0,10	0,10
Mark %	78,67	78,67	81,67	84,61	81,81	87,76

According to the chart above, it must be noted that all the wikis exceed 78.50 % as a maximum score. Moreover, the best scores have been those allocated for units four and six, respectively, that is, the lessons dedicated to *Money, Financial Terms* and *International Markets*. Also, the marks in the three groups were very homogeneous, as the values of standard deviation indicate.

8.6 Conclusions

This project needs continued monitoring to ensure that the objective of the course (teaching and learning of a specific subject: "*Idioma Moderno: Inglés*" of the Economics Degree) is not blurred by striving to achieve the goal of collaborative work among students, nor by developing good reports on the evaluation of students by other students, nor through online bibliographic searches, etc. All of these aspects should only help to contribute to the acquisition of the skills and competences necessary to reach the level of the course, and also to develop knowledge about the free resources available on the Internet which can become part of the students' lifelong learning culture (Field 2006). This aspect could help them to consolidate their knowledge of the English language and help them in the future professional lives.

There are some aspects that can be improved in new projects in future years. Firstly, the number of wikis seemed excessive in the opinion of the students, so we have considered structuring the work in larger blocks by skill (Reading, Writing and Speaking), grouping the six units in three blocks, or perhaps by unit, grouping the three skills within them. That will also probably entail a change in the evaluation procedure which will necessarily have to adapt to a more "visible" system for all the students involved.

Secondly, it is very important to insist on the fact that the students have to read and study the theoretical content of each unit (from the Pdf files provided) before the actual class takes place to make it more active and participative, with the objective of resolving doubts and not having to explain all the concepts from the beginning. It is obvious that there is no learning without effort, so we have to encourage our students to perform the tasks set up for them, assessing their performance in a constructive manner.

On a more positive note it is clear that the objectives set for the course were fulfilled as the active participation of the students was evident and they proved to be very motivated. Self-learning and self-evaluation stimulated them into feeling in control of their learning progress, and this learner-centered process, which took into account their interests and needs (McCombs and Whisler 1997), encouraged them to achieve an above-average rate of success in the course.

References

Baggetun, R., B. Wasson, and K.H. Andersen. 2003. *Collogatories: Collaborative learning communities on the web*. Pre-project final report, ITU Learning Arenas. InterMedia, Bergen University.

Bohigas, X., X. Jaén, and M. Novell. 2003. Applets en la enseñanza de la física. *Enseñanza de las Ciencias* 21(3): 463–472.

Council of Europe. 2001. Common European framework of reference for languages: Learning, teaching, assessment. Available at: http://www.coe.int/t/dg4/linguistic/Source/Framework_EN.pdf

Davies, G. 2002. ICT and modern foreign languages: Learning opportunities and training needs. In *International Journal of English Studies* 2: 1: Monograph issue, *New trends in computer assisted language learning*, eds. P. Pérez Paredes and P. Cantos Gómez. Murcia: Servicio de Publicaciones de la Universidad de Murcia.

De Paula, R., G. Fischer, and J. Ostwald. 2001. *Courses as seeds: Expectations and realities*. Paper presented at the European CSCL 2001, Maastricht.

Del Moral, M. 2007. *Una herramienta emergente de la Web 2.0: la wiki. Reflexión sobre sus usos educativos*, 73–82. Unión: Revista Iberoamericana de Educación Matemática, 9. Available at: http://www.fisem.org/paginas

Ebersbach, A, and M. Glaser. 2004. Towards emancipatory use of a medium: The Wiki. *International Journal of Information Ethics* 2. Available at: http://container.zkm.de/ijie/ijie/no002/ijie_002_09_ebersbach.pdf

Enzensberger, H.M. 1970. Constituents of a theory of the media. *New Left Review* 64: 13–36. Available at: http://www.calarts.edu/˜bookchin/mediatheory/essays/18-enzensberger-03.pdf

Field, J. 2006. *Lifelong learning and the new educational order*. Stoke on Trent: Trentham Books.

Forte, A., and A. Bruckman. 2007. Constructing text: Wiki as a toolkit for (collaborative?) learning. *Wikisym*, 31–42. Montreal: ACM.

Gerlach, J.M. 1994. Is this collaboration? In *Collaborative learning: Underlying processes and effective techniques. New directions for teaching and learning*, vol. 59, ed. K. Boswoth and S.J. Hamilton. San Francisco: Jossey-Bass.

Giles, J. 2005. Internet encyclopedias go head to head. *Nature* 438(7070): 900–901. Available at: http://www.nature.com/nature/journal/v438/n7070/full/438900a.html

Jones, Z., and B. Nuhfer-Halten. 2006. Uses of blogs in L2 instruction. In *Languages for today's world: Dimension 2006*, ed. M.L. Wilbur and C.M. Cherry, 25–35. Valdosta: Southern Conference on Language Teaching.

Lamb, B. 2004. Wide open spaces: Wikis, ready or not. *EDUCAUSE* 39(5). Available at: http://www.educause.edu/ir/library/pdf/erm0452.pdf

Larusson, J., and R. Alterman. 2009. Wikis to support the "collaborative" part of collaborative learning. *Computer-Supported Learning* 4: 371–402. Springer.

Lave, J., and Wenger, E. 1991. Situated Learning: Legitimate Peripheral Participation. Cambridge University Press.

Lim, C. 2005. Knowledge transfer between users and producers in the accumulation of technological capability. *Asian Journal of Technology Innovation* 12(2): 179–205.

Lot, C. 2005. *Introduction to the Wiki*. Distance Learning Systems. Center for Distance Education. Available at: http://distance.uaf.edu/dls/resources/present/cc-aug-04/wiki/index.cfm

McCombs, B.L., and J.S. Whisler. 1997. *The learner-centered classroom and school: Strategies for increasing student motivation and achievement*. San Francisco: Jossey-Bass.

Mindel, J.L., and S. Verma. 2006. Wikis for teaching and learning. *Communications of the Association for Information Systems (CAIS)* 18: 1–23.

Reiser, R.A., and R.M. Gagné. 1983. *Selecting media for instruction*. Englewood Cliffs: Educational Technology.

Salomon, G., D.N. Perkins, and T. Globerson. 1991. Partners in cognition: Extending human intelligent technologies. *Educational Researcher* 20: 2–9.

Tascott, D. 2009. *Grown up digital: How the net generation is changing your world*. New York: McGraw-Hill.

Wheeler, S., P. Yeomans, and D. Wheeler. 2008. The good, the bad and the wiki: Evaluating student-generate content for collaborative learning. *British Journal of Educational Technology* 39(6): 987–995.

Part III
Corpus-Based Approaches to/Applications for Teaching and Processing Languages

Chapter 9
A Genre-Based Approach to the Teaching of Legal and Business English: The GENTT Specialized Corpus in the LSP Classroom

Anabel Borja Albi, Natividad Juste Vidal, Pilar Ordóñez López, and Tomás Conde

9.1 Introduction

With this contribution we wish to put forward the results of an initiative of collaborative work between a team of teachers of Language for Specific Purposes (LSP) and teachers of specialized translation who decided to combine their efforts to design and implement two LSP courses which form part of the degree programme in Translation and Interpreting of the University Jaume I in Spain. On their third year, students have to take two courses of legal and business English, a prerequisite for their enrolment in the fourth year courses of legal and business Translation.

The practice of specialized translation requires not only a very high command of general English but also a high command of professional English. The texts specialized translators work with are characterized by stereotyped structures, complex syntax, standard phraseology and genre specific vocabulary. In fact, dictionaries and other terminology-based resources have proved insufficient, since they need to transfer from one language to another, texts patterns which are extremely conventionalized.

This problem prompted us to use authentic professional documents as a starting point to design a new teaching approach based on the hypothesis that the application of textual genres to the teaching-learning of LSP can provide both teachers and learners with culture-dependent codes in their progress towards the acquisition of language for special purposes. Each specialized genre presents its own features,

A. Borja Albi (✉) • N. Juste Vidal • P. Ordóñez López
Departamento de Traducción y Comunicación,
GENTT Research Group, Universitat Jaume I, Castellón, Spain
e-mail: borja@trad.uji.es; juste@trad.uji.es; mordonez@uji.es

T. Conde
Departamento de Filología Inglesa y Alemana,
Universidad del País Vasco, Vitoria-Gasteiz, Spain
e-mail: tomas.conde@ehu.es

E. Bárcena et al. (eds.), *Languages for Specific Purposes in the Digital Era*,
Educational Linguistics 19, DOI 10.1007/978-3-319-02222-2_9,

purposes and cultural conventions. Once learners know how to recognize and use genres (terminology, phraseology, macrostructure, rhetorical devices, etc.) they will be able to develop the necessary strategies to cope with new and unfamiliar text types. This is crucial in the context of current Information Society Technologies since genres, as well as reality, are constantly changing, evolving and appearing in new forms. They reflect the evolution of specific socio-cultural interactions and, therefore, of specialized linguistic performance and expertise.

In the following sections we will analyse the impact of corpora on LSP teaching, present the GENTT example corpus of specialized discourse full-text documents and discuss how LSP teachers and learners can efficiently exploit this tool.

9.2 The Use of Corpora in LSP Teaching: Contextualizing LSP

Until recently, language-teaching materials were based mostly on non-authentic sentence examples. However, access to authentic texts (in an electronic format) has improved significantly in the area of LSP thanks to the Internet and to the rapidly evolving electronic text and corpus analysis methodologies. Tribble (1997) shows how even small corpora of fewer than one million words can be of considerable benefit in the LSP context. The applications of corpus technologies to LSP range from the identification of high frequency lexis in a specific domain, collocation, colligation and semantic prosody, grammar and discourse, to the contrastive analysis of lexical items in different domains or the contrastive analysis of genres (text-types) in different sublanguages.

Since the 1980s, the application of textual genres to language teaching and, in particular, to LSP teaching, has become one of the most dynamic lines of research in the area of genre theory. Regarding the process of second language acquisition, Bazerman (1988), Bazerman and Russell (2002), Bhatia (1993, 2004) and Swales (1990, 2004), among others, emphasize the importance of understanding communication codes that are specific to the culture of individual fields of specialization and the structure of its textual genres to acquire linguistic expertise in a particular field of knowledge. In order to maximize the advantages of a genre-based approach to LSP learning, the large number of documents that can be found for each genre within the different fields of knowledge must be efficiently stored, classified and managed. Electronic corpora have proved to be useful and dynamic tools for specialized knowledge and collaborative information management within the LSP context.

Adolphs (2006) points out that a key advantage of the use of corpora within the context of LSP is that they can supply data regarding specific phraseology, word frequencies and distributions in different discourse contexts, thereby providing important information for the language learner and instructor. The co-text reveals information about the specific phraseology that surrounds a particular word and contributes to its functional interpretation. Word frequency information can be used to design syllabuses based on the needs of particular learners with regard to both the sequence of specific vocabulary items that are being taught and the overall size of the restricted vocabulary that is required to achieve an adequate coverage of a specialized domain. This kind of information derived from corpora provides LSP learners with a list of words that make up the core of the language domain and that can be used to analyse and deal with numerous vocabulary acquisition problems such as polysemous words, learnability or interference with the learner's first language and decontextualisation.

9.3 The GENTT Corpus of Specialized Genres

The GENTT Research Group has been working since 2000 on the concept of textual genre and its relevance to the drafting and translation of specialized texts in professional settings. The main focus of GENTT is the multilingual study of genres in professional legal, medical and technical contexts, three domains that occupy a central position in LSP Teaching and Translation Studies. The GENTT project has focused on mapping the textual performances of these fields and compiling a multilingual (English, Spanish, French, German and Catalan) example corpus of specialized discourse full-text documents in the fields of law, medicine and technology.

The following list shows the objectives (partly achieved at the moment) of a team of 14 people, who have been working together under the funding of various public institutions:

- To build up a catalogue (mapping) of the genres of law, medicine and technology (GENTT field trees).
- To relate, classify and define the features of the professional texts in these three fields, from a formal and communicative perspective (GENTT Genre Template).
- To build up a multilingual (Catalan, English, German, Spanish and French) example corpus of specialized discourse texts (GENTT Example Corpus).
- To provide LSP learners and other users of professional texts (translators and technical writers and proofreaders) with text models and templates that could be used as textual, conceptual, linguistic and terminological reference.
- To build up a repository of teaching materials with real life texts for LSP
- To create an electronic tool to manage all the information related to the genres contained in the corpus (GENTT Corpus Management System).

The GENTT Corpus includes currently more than 1,000 full-text documents, which contain over three million words in total, all fully searchable and easily retrievable in electronic format. In the creation of this corpus, an empirical-descriptive methodology has been applied. The identification and compilation of each genre and subgenre example is based on the analysis of "the function, the cultural context, the situational context and the existence of a differentiated linguistic performance" (Borja 2005: 16).

The representativeness of the corpus does not lie in the amount of texts or words it contains, but in the number of different genre examples provided. In fact, its design is intended to create a knowledge management system (a genre tree), similar to terminological knowledge representation systems, structured around the notion of genre, for learners and users of professional specialized genres (Borja 2005). As our project is open and dynamic, the corpus is constantly evolving subject to the creativity and input of those participating in its development.

9.3.1 Main Functionalities of the Corpus

Although the system distinguishes between various types of users (*Administrator, GENTT member, Basic User...*), here we shall approach it from a *Basic User learning LSP* point of view. The functions Basic Users can perform are the following:

- document search,
- document download,
- word and collocations search,
- subcorpora (smaller corpus document collections created attending to the individual needs of the user) creation and download and
- editing of the individual searches and findings.

GENTT members may also upload documents and modify genre classifications. In addition to the functions available to basic users, administrators can also create reports on the state of the corpus. Finally, users with higher privileges have the option of giving other researchers/students access to the corpus.

In order to log in to the corpus, participants in the LSP learning context (from now on, *users*) should have registered previously. A corpus Administrator can carry out the registration process. Alternatively, an invitation might be issued by another user. Once registered, users can log in to the system and perform different functions depending on their role. Users may also add collaborators, who can search, create, download and edit their subcorpora. This functionality enhances greatly collaborative work on the LSP classroom (Fig. 9.1).

Users can browse data according to their needs. The search may be either simple or advanced, but in both cases users can customise the results display by selecting the columns they wish to view. Searches may be narrowed down through the Advanced Search option by choosing among the categories shown in several drop-down menus: title, author, source, status, year of publication, genre, textual and language.

The system offers the option of saving searches, so that the user can later refine and exploit them as personal subcorpora. After saving the subcorpus, the column of operations in the results table allows the selection and de-selection of documents to modify subcorpus contents. Users can download the documents selected in several formats: plain text, HTML and jpg. One of the most interesting options for users

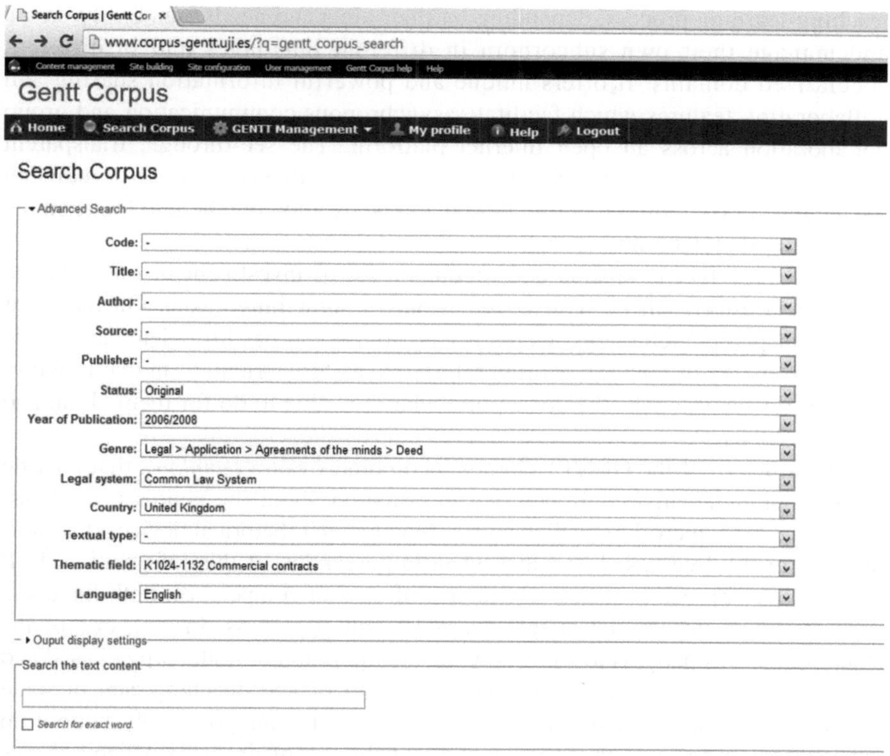

Fig. 9.1 The GENTT Corpus interface

is to upload documents into the corpus. Once a new document has been added, an identification card should be filled in (Country; Genre; Thematic field; Title; Author; Source; Year of publication; Translator; Suggested Genre; Related documents). All the documents in the corpus have been organized according to a hierarchical genre classification that can also be modified by users.

9.3.2 A See-Through Learning Approach

As stated by Adolphs (2006), in order to build up a suitable corpus or subcorpus for specific needs in the LSP context, it is essential to establish the basis for its design criteria, that is, what the role of the corpus is; who uses it; what the particular learning objective is; or what the particular genre that is being explored is. The GENTT Corpus embraces the web 2.0 philosophy, providing a collaborative environment that permits users interested in legal, medical and technical domains to browse, feed and manage a collection of texts on line so that participants in the teaching-learning process, depending on their aims and needs, can easily create and manage their own subcorpora in different languages and in different specialized domains. It offers unique and powerful information sharing and collaboration features which facilitate asynchronous communication and group collaboration across an open Internet platform. The see-through, transparent technology approach implemented affords users the added advantage of reducing the technical skill required to use these features, by allowing them to focus on the language and collaborative tasks.

Technology that is opaque and requires a lot of investment in time, mental energy and effort will be rejected in favour of something easier. On the other hand, transparent technology, which is easy to use and has little demands on the cognitive energy of the user, is often referred to as 'user friendly' in that it allows the user to 'see through' the device into what it is able to do for them (John and Wheeler 2008).

The structure of the GENTT Corpus incorporates *genre templates* that provide formal, communicative and cognitive information about the genres it contains, e.g. macro- and micro-linguistic features, function and rhetorical devices. Previous research in the area has shown that when in possession of this information, LSP learners can improve progressively their professional competence, both linguistic and extralinguistic, through a self-directed learning process. In fact, one of the objectives of this paper is to show how the incorporation of both corpus-based and genre-based approaches into text analysis as part of LSP teaching can, in some respects, overcome the criticism that corpus linguistic analyses apply bottom-up rather than top-down methodologies and that the use of decontextualized corpus data does not take into account the socio-cultural context.

The GENTT Corpus also provides learners of professional languages with *text models and patterns* to be used as cultural, conceptual, textual, linguistic and terminological reference. The possibilities of applying the work on genre-based corpora to LSP teaching are evident. Following Bhatia (1997), work with genres pertaining to the student's professional background and interests causes learners to develop an explicit desire for conscious participation in the professional community and a feeling of shared ownership of their communicative resources, rather than learning words and structures mechanically and out of context. According to Bhatia et al. (2008) learners of a specialized language need:

- to understand the specialist's communication code,
- to familiarize themselves with rhetorical resources and those that occur in specialized genres,
- to understand the various socio-cultural contexts in which specialized communication takes place, and
- to be capable of using specialized genres to respond to new and unexpected situations.

All these four skills can be enhanced by using the GENTT Corpus and by becoming familiar with the textual mapping and genre characterizations it provides.

Another advantage of this electronic tool, based on genres extracted from real life communication, is that language is learnt in its actual context and learning programmes can be designed with very specific needs in mind. It is possible, for example, to design a course focused on the discourse of a particular professional and communicative situation (e.g. the documents of a judicial process which might be of interest for a student of legal English), treating it as a single genre (a judgment) or as a system of genres that would include all the documents that accompany that particular genre (claim, counterclaim, injunction, judgment, appeal, etc.) and even the oral genres related to them (witness deposition transcripts).

Within this context learners become the centre of the process as they improve their linguistic and extralinguistic competences according to their own learning styles. Teachers, on the other hand, are facilitators of the instruction process and can also tailor their syllabus—from very controlled to more complex learning tasks design—towards the needs of a diverse range of learners. Both sides benefit from the use of corpus technologies by means of a hypothetical deductive approach, helping LSP students learn to communicate effectively and fully understand the realities of the world of specialized discourse.

Bearing these factors in mind, a constructive teaching-learning approach based on the concepts of corpus and genre can be implemented, applying a methodology in which learners use language actively in a given context, monitor their own learning progress and develop new skills and competences such as hypothesis testing and data analysis. This approach allows learners to explore language data and to derive patterns of language use, which promotes creativity and innovation in the language classroom.

In the following sections we present practical learning activities for the teaching of legal and business English using the GENTT Corpus, in which the teacher instructs students in analytic strategies, both rhetorical and textual. Both legal and business English serve very specific professional purposes and affect the daily lives of virtually everyone in our society. The activities and materials presented here are designed to give students a broader linguistic perspective including comparative insights into the particular knowledge systems and procedures of law and business, which are the basis of these two areas of specialized discourse.

9.4 The GENTT Corpus in the Legal English Classroom

9.4.1 Legal English

Among the various specialized languages, legal language is one of the most formulaic, frozen and conservative. The possibilities of language performance are considerably restrained given that legal language is subject to special rules which do not apply to general texts and which are limiting with respect to the possible forms of expressing terminology, phrases and even to the drafting and macrostructure of legal instruments. Legal language can be defined as (1) the language which is used in those communicative situations in which public power is enforced, regardless of whether the manifestation of this power (legislative, executive or judicial) is directed towards the citizen or is used by citizens to communicate with public institutions; and (2) the language employed by private parties in legally binding relations.

The legal system is, possibly, one of the most normativized systems and one which relies largely on words and texts: statutes are decreed, meetings are called to order, contracts are entered into, search warrants are issued, etc. In all these cases there is a fixed, conventional form of expression that is exceedingly precise and depends on the legal functions of these texts. The extreme formality of legal language can also be attributed to its long sentences, complex constructions, archaic and hyper-formal vocabulary and a focus on content to the exclusion of reader needs.

Despite claims about the precision and exactness of legal language, lawyers often opt for deliberate ambiguity—usually of a syntactic type—which the LSP learner must be able to recognize. The constructions that most lend themselves to ambiguity are nominalizations, passives and multiple adjectivation, as well as the distinction between adjective clauses being restrictive or non-restrictive. Many legal disputes revolve around textual ambiguity and the possible interpretations that any one sentence can have. In this context, learning objectives may include: getting familiar with legal lexis, understanding complex structures and rhetorical devices and learning to disambiguate vague constructions (where possible). Furthermore, legal language users will need to have an excellent command of genre conventions. The acquisition of these abilities and competences can greatly benefit from the analysis of the legal documents contained in the GENTT Corpus.

Linguists and social scientists that have turned their attention to legal language have remarked its complexity as a distinctive feature. However it should be noted that the complexity of this language does not come solely from the grammar, but is a consequence of the pragmatic aspects which contextualize it as authors like Danet (1985) and Gunnarsson (1984) uphold. Therefore, its apparent complexity cannot be attributed only to linguistic factors but rather to the combination of a complex conceptual structure that lends it a very sophisticated form of expression. As previously mentioned, the GENTT Corpus is built upon the idea of genre, which constitutes a key element to understand the legal conceptual framework.

An additional difficulty for students of legal English is the cultural anisomorphism between legal systems, meaning the losses and gains that always occur in interlinguistic transfer. Sometimes the legal terms and concepts do not exist in the students' mother tongue or the concepts are completely different (e.g., the term company limited by shares in English carries legal and commercial implications which are different from those of the Spanish *sociedad limitada*, the popular English *trust* is inexistent in Spanish legislation, etc.). The number of false friends is significant:

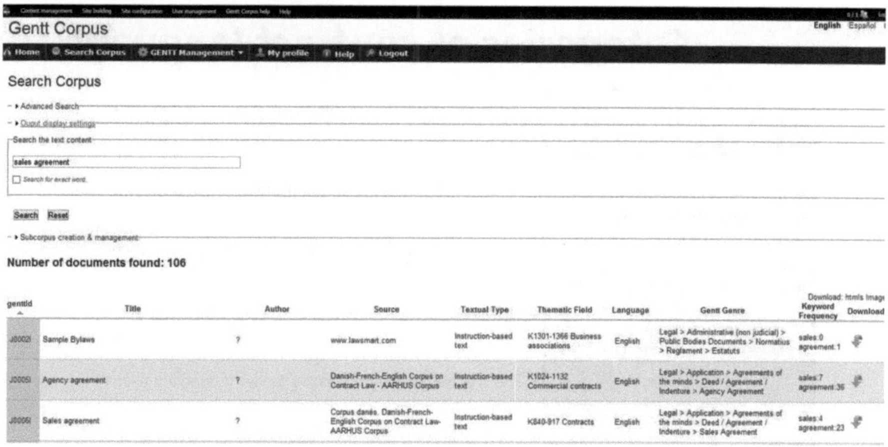

Fig. 9.2 Search findings for business agreements

in Spanish statute does not mean *estatuto* but rather *ley*; *ley* does not mean *law* but rather *statute* or *Act*, to name only a few English-Spanish cognates. The multilingual nature of the GENTT Corpus affords the possibility of using a comparative law approach to the study of legal concepts and language.

9.4.2 Corpus-Based Activities in the Teaching of Legal English

The activities proposed in the following sections are aimed at reinforcing receptive reading and productive writing. Of course, listening and speaking should also be considered when designing legal English course contents but our corpus is an excellent tool for reading and writing activities so we shall focus on the former. Regarding language systems, we propose two grammar activities, one on modals (Activity 1) and one on suffixed prepositions (Activity 2). The third activity deals with the macrostructure of legal instruments and is aimed at improving reading subskills, speed and comprehension (Activity 3).

9.4.2.1 Activity 1

Learning to identify expressions of obligation, permission and prohibition in business agreements.

Task: Students are asked to identify all the Business Agreements in the corpus and find clauses expressing three particular categories of language: obligation, permission and prohibition (Fig. 9.2).

Fig. 9.3 Hand-out 1. Categories of contract language

Aims: To make students aware of the importance of using the right verbs and categories of language to convey the exact meaning and purpose in legally binding agreements.
Methodology: The students are provided with tables containing one or more examples of a particular category of language, with each example being followed by variations on that example (e.g., obligation clauses using *shall, must, agrees to, undertakes, covenants, is obligated to*, etc.). The table is introduced by the teacher and discussed in the classroom to highlight the typical dysfunctions in the use of these expressions and the problems a deficient use may bring about. Students then work individually to identify and download the Business Agreements contained in the corpus and create a subcorpus. Working in small groups, they are asked to find examples in the subcorpus similar to the ones provided. Each group works on one category and presents its findings to the class (Fig. 9.3).

Teaching rationale: A clause or sentence in the body of the contract can serve a number of purposes. Each purpose requires its own category of language and each category raises its own issues of usage. Commercial litigation frequently has its roots in mishandled contract language and this activity is aimed at raising students' awareness of the importance of seeking consistency in written usages with very specific purposes (Fig. 9.4).

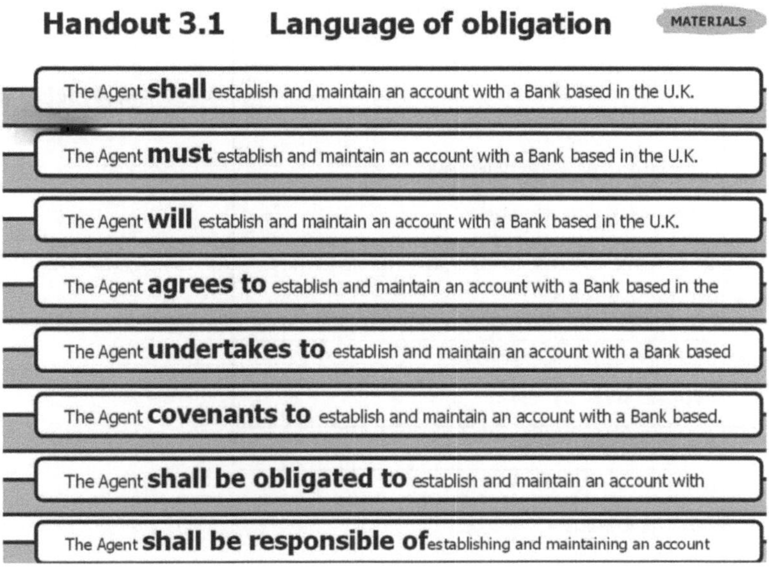

Fig. 9.4 Different forms of expressing obligation

9.4.2.2 Activity 2

Understanding and using suffixed prepositions (hereby, hereto, therein, thereto …).

Legal writing extensively uses archaic vocabulary, old words and phrases that were formerly quotidian language, but today exist mostly or only in law. A good example are *herein, hereto, hereby, heretofore, herewith, whereby* and *wherefore*. Pronominal adverbs occur in a number of Germanic languages, formed in replacement of a preposition and a pronoun by turning the latter into a locative adverb and the former into a prepositional adverb and joining them in reverse order: For that → *therefore*; In that → *therein*; By this → *hereby*; To this → *hereto*; In which → *wherein*. They are used frequently by lawyers primarily as a way of avoiding the repetition of names of things in the document (or sometimes as a reference to the document itself). Pronominal adverbs are considered as a feature of *legal jargon*.

Task: Students are asked to identify suffixed prepositions in the previously built subcorpus, extract ten examples in context and provide a translation into Spanish.

Aims: To enhance the acquisition and comprehension of complex specialized grammar compounds.

Methodology: Before starting the corpus activity, the teacher will introduce these archaic expressions and students will be provided with a hand-out including the main forms and meanings they can take (Fig. 9.5).

MATERIALS

Handout: ***Suffixed Prepositions 1***	
Hereafter	en lo sucesivo, a continuación
Hereby	Por el presente
Herein	En el presente, adjunto, que aquí se menciona
Hereinabove	Más arriba, previamente, anteriormente
Hereinafter	Más abajo, en los sucesivo, a continuación
Hereinbefore	Más arriba, anteriormente
Hereinbelow	Más abajo, en los sucesivo, a continuación
Hereof	Del presente, de este
Hereon	Sobre esto, relativo al presente
Hereto	Al presente
Heretofore	Hasta ahora, anteriormente
Hereunder	Más abajo, más adelante, a continuación
Hereupon	Sobre esto, por consiguiente
Herewith	Anexo, adjunto, que se acompaña
Thereabout	Aproximadamente
Thereafter	Posteriormente, en lo sucesivo
Thereat	Por tal motivo, a tal respecto

Fig. 9.5 Hand-out. Suffixed prepositions 1

Students work in pairs. A list of instructions is provided, explaining the steps that should be followed to carry out this activity. Once students are logged on to the corpus, they should browse the corpus to search for the term *hereto*. The screenshot in Fig. 9.6 shows the results of searching the term *hereto* in the corpus. It provides information about the frequency of appearance of *hereto* in each agreement. In the middle column the concordances contextualizing the term are displayed and on the right hand side we find the download link. By clicking on the green arrow the students get the complete text with the terms highlighted.

After performing searches such as this one for all the expressions, students are asked to translate individually several sentences containing suffixed prepositions. To conclude this activity, each pair is asked to present their results to the rest of students in the group.

Teaching rationale: The rationale behind this activity is to provide students with a new approach to the analysis of legal language in context (Fig. 9.7).

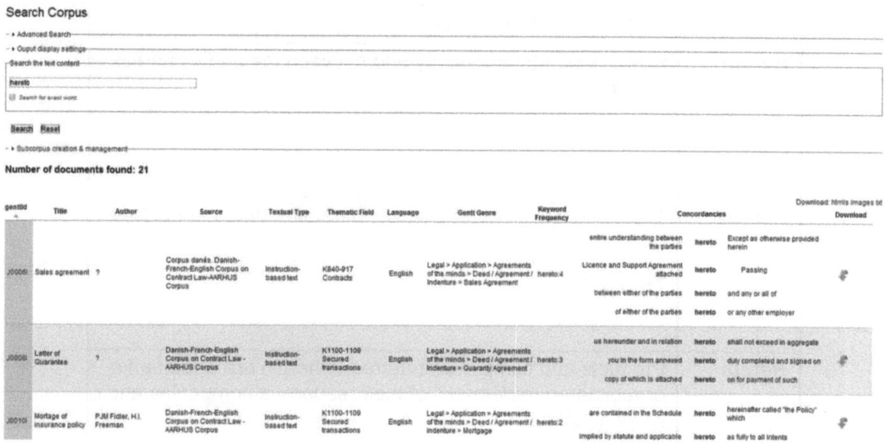

Fig. 9.6 Search findings for *Hereto*

9.4.2.3 Activity 3

Familiarizing themselves with the macrostructure of commercial agreements.

Task: Students are asked to identify the macrostructure of four business agreements, define a common macrostructure for all of them and compare them with the typical Spanish Agreements macrostructure.

Aims: To improve the different reading subskills: (1) predicting content of what we read; (2) identifying global meaning (GIST, skimming—terminology for reading only); (3) selecting specific detail from text (scanning—terminology for reading only); (4) inferring meaning from text; (5) guessing meaning of unknown vocabulary from text.

Methodology: Working in pairs, students are asked to analyse six commercial agreements from the corpus and decide whether they share or not a common macrostructure. Findings are presented to and discussed in the group. Figure 9.8 shows the potential results of this activity.

Teaching rationale: The rationale behind this activity is to make students aware of the importance of knowing the genre conventions affecting text structure. Becoming familiar with the typical sections of the most important legal instruments will help them to increase their reading speed and comprehension.

9.5 The GENTT Corpus in the Business English Classroom

9.5.1 *Business English: A Trendy Cover Term?*

Business English has experienced a steady growth in recent decades, becoming the main expansion area of ESP (Hewings 2002), due to various factors such as the

	Original and translation
Hereto	Now it is hereby agreed by and between the parties hereto as follows: **Translation:** ____________________
Hereby	The Vendor doth hereby agree to transfer unto the Purchaser… **Translation:** ____________________
Herein	Products and companies referred to herein are trademarks or registered trademarks of their respective companies and / or mark holders. **Translation:** ____________________
Hereinafter	The Member States of the ATA Organization hereinafter referred to as the Member States… **Translation:** ____________________
Thereto	An Agreement and a Protocol thereto between the Government of the and the Government of New Zealand for… **Translation:** ____________________
Hereunder	No rule hereunder shall be construed to repeal a former rule… **Translation:** ____________________
Hereunder	Explanations are provided hereunder on the description requirements of specification and actions of applicants... **Translation:** ____________________
Herein	Any application to the court hereunder shall be made and heard in the manner provided by law… **Translation:** ____________________

Fig. 9.7 Worksheet for suffixed prepositions activity

Business Agreement Macrostructure

1. Commencement : ***This Agreement is made this 3rd day of July between.....***

2. Recitals: ***Whereas...***

3. Operative part: ***Now it s here by agreed as follows***

Definitions
Conditions precedent
Other operative provisions
1) *Representations and Warranties*
2) *Termination clauses*
Boiler plate
1) *Force majeur*
2) *Confidentiality*
3) *'Time of the essence'*
4) *Anti-waiver clause*
5) *Amendments*
6) *Expenses*
7) *Notices*
8) *Assignment*
9) *Severability*
10) *Applicable law*

4. Conclusion formula: ***In witness whereof...***

5. Signature

6. Schedules

Fig. 9.8 Business agreement macrostructure

consolidation of English as a *lingua franca* and the expansion of local and national markets, leading to an increase of international business relationships.

Scholars such as Pickett (1986) or Dudley-Evans and St. John (1998) coincide in the difficulty of establishing a clear definition of *Business English*. On the one hand, business English is learnt for a wide variety of purposes; on the other, there exists considerable overlap between business English (ESP) and general English in strictly linguistic terms. Nevertheless, it is important to establish some defining features of business English in order to maximize the pedagogical outcome of the proposed classroom activities. Given the educational setting in which we are working, the most relevant characteristics are the following:

- Effective communication is the main concern (Dudley-Evans and St John 1998: 73).
- Language depends on status, power and how well established the business relationship is (ibid.: 73).
- Seven core communicative events are identified (ibid.: 63): telephoning, socializing, making presentations, taking part in meetings and negotiating (oral); and corresponding and reporting (written).

- The communicative events above, especially those that require the written form, are carried out by means of specific genres.
- Sharing other pragmatic features with general English, assertion and downtoning, as well as checking and confirming (Duckworth 1995) are key elements of business English.
- Combination of general, semi-specialized and specialized lexis.

9.5.2 Corpus-Based Activities in the Teaching of Business English

The following activities are designed for *Business and Administrative English for Translators*, an optional course that undergraduates in their second year should take if they are to specialise in legal and business Translation. This course is aimed at providing students with some basic knowledge of business communication (correspondence, types of corporations, reports, CVs and covering letters). For the vast majority of students, this is the first contact with business English. Furthermore, it is important to bear in mind that most of them are not familiar with corpus methodologies. This implies that some initial familiarization sessions are needed, in which students get acquainted with the terminology of corpus linguistics and with the GENTT Corpus itself. The students' average language proficiency is at an upper intermediate level.

9.5.2.1 Activity 1

Becoming familiar with the lexis of business correspondence.

Task: Students are asked to use the GENTT Corpus to browse the documents available in the genre *Letters* and to identify the most typical lexical elements of this genre.

Aims: To conduct a simple search by genre in the GENTT Corpus; to extract the most characteristic lexical elements of the genre.

Methodology: Students work in pairs. A list of instructions is provided, explaining the steps that should be followed to carry out this activity. Once students are logged on to the corpus, they should conduct a search to retrieve the information they are required to find. After retrieving the corresponding documents, it is their task to identify the relevant lexical elements, working in pairs. To conclude this activity, each pair is asked to present their results to the other students in the group.

Teaching rationale: The rationale behind this activity is to provide students with a new approach to the analysis of business language and, at the same time, to encourage them to take an active role in the study of the semi-specialized and specialized lexis of business correspondence.

9.5.2.2 Activity 2

Identifying typical business correspondence collocations.

Task: Students are asked to find the most frequent collocations in which the word *payment* occurs.

Aims: To introduce concordances; to make students reflect on the relevance of phraseology; to make students aware of genre conventions.

Methodology: Students work in small groups. First, students log on to the corpus. They are provided with instructions for every step. Students need to conduct a keyword search, explore the concordances they retrieve and analyse these results according to the task. Following this, students are expected to take part in a discussion to share their findings with the rest of the classroom.

Teaching rationale: The motivation for this activity is to raise students' awareness of the fundamental role of collocations, phraseology and genre conventions in specialized communication. Ultimately, the rationale behind this activity is to challenge students' restricted perception of specialized language, which is frequently equated with specialized lexis (Fig. 9.9).

9.5.2.3 Additional Activities

Once students have familiarized themselves with the corpus, additional activities are the identification of downtoning structures, the mapping of the business genre by means of identifying different subgenres and the analysis of more complex phraseological units.

9.6 Conclusions

After 2 years applying the teaching-learning approach described, we have found that the learning objectives initially established by the team of LSP and specialized translation teachers have largely been achieved and student satisfaction has increased. Not only does the implementation of this corpus and genre-based methodology enhance formal, communicative and cognitive learning within the LSP context, but it also promotes collaborative work and interaction between teacher and students and among students themselves.

keyword Frequency	Concordancies		
payment :4	time of its restitution to	**payment**	of fair and reasonable compensation
	the claim is brought	**payment**	of compensation to the possessor
	time of its return to	**payment**	by the requesting State of
	b to transfer ownership against	**payment**	or gratuitously to a person
payment :1	or your first claim for	**payment**	at this office Within this
payment :2	dated th October regarding your	**payment**	of in total We
	for using the Swift Transfer	**payment**	facility This charge is in
payment :2	our original letter January requested	**payment**	in days Please settle
	you have sent us your	**payment**	since this letter was written

Fig. 9.9 Search findings for the term *payment* collocations

The set of activities we have designed and implemented[1] ranges from very controlled to more complex and autonomous learning tasks. Typically, the teacher first provides students with a list of instructions. They then are asked to work individually or in pairs and present their work to the rest of the class. A group discussion usually follows.

The experience has revealed that through the use of the GENTT Corpus in the classroom a data-driven approach can be adopted. This approach contributes significantly to the development of autonomous learning, enabling students to identify the characteristic patterns of each genre, thereby increasing their capacity for performing critical analysis and decision-making.

[1] Learning to identify modals in business agreements; Understanding and using suffixed prepositions; Familiarizing with the macrostructure of commercial agreements; Becoming familiar with the lexis of business correspondence; and Identifying typical business correspondence collocations.

Our experience also shows how students take an active role in the study of specialized lexis since they analyse legal and business language in context and have to deal with authentic and real world professional texts. Their learning becomes meaningful and they develop an explicit desire for conscious participation in the professional community and a feeling of shared ownership of their communicative resources, rather than learning words and structures mechanically and out of context.

With the implementation of this type of tools, we are moving towards new expectations in language teaching, that is, towards a dynamic corpus and genre-based approach in which learner and teacher collaborate, participate and interact in the instruction process, thus incorporating creativity and innovation in LSP teaching.

In its previous versions, the corpus was managed through an Intranet within the Universitat Jaume I. With the new 3.0 version, the group has opted for opening the system, according to the Web 2.0 philosophy, so that we can evolve towards a more collaborative environment that will enable users to search, feed and manage the corpus on line. However, due to copyright issues, access to the corpus is limited and the Administrator must give permission. Those of you interested in searching the GENTT Corpus or taking part in our investigation should contact the GENTT team at www.gentt.uji.es.

References

Adolphs, S. 2006. *Introducing electronic test analysis. A practical guide for language and literary studies*. New York: Routledge.

Bazerman, C. 1988. *Shaping written knowledge*. Madison: University of Wisconsin Press.

Bazerman, C., and D. Russell. 2002. *Writing selves/writing societies: Research from activity perspectives. Perspectives on writing*. Fort Collins: The WAC Clearinghouse.

Bhatia, V.K. 1993. *Analyzing genre: Language use in professional settings*. London: Longman.

Bhatia, Vijay V.K. 1997. Translating legal genres. In *Text typology and translation*, ed. Anna Trosborg, 10–15. Amsterdam: Benjamin.

Bhatia, V.K. 2004. *Worlds of written discourse: A genre-based view*. London/New York: Continuum.

Bhatia, V.K., C.N. Candlin, and J. Engberg (eds.). 2008. *Legal discourse across cultures and systems*. Hong Kong: Hong Kong University Press.

Borja, A. 2005. Organización del conocimiento para la traducción jurídica a través de sistemas expertos basados en el concepto de género textual. In *El género textual y la traducción. Reflexiones teóricas y aplicaciones pedagógicas*, ed. I. García Izquierdo, 40–42. Bern: Peter Lang.

Danet, B. 1985. Language in the legal process. In *Handbook of discourse analysis*, vol. 1, ed. T. Van Dijk. London: Academic.

Duckworth, M. 1995. *Oxford business English*. Oxford: Oxford University Press.

Dudley-Evans, T., and M.J. St John. 1998. *Development in English for specific purposes: A multidisciplinary approach*. Cambridge: Cambridge University Press.

Gunnarsson, B.L. 1984. Functional comprehensibility of legislative texts. Experiments with a Swedish Act of Parliament. In *Studies of legal discourse*, Monographic issue: Text 4, ed. Danet Brenda, 1–3. Berlin/New York: Mouton Publishers.

Hewings, M. 2002. A History of ESP through English for specific purposes. *English for Specific Purposes World* 1(3). Retrieved July 5, 2010, from http://www.esp-world.info/Articles_3/Hewings_paper.htm

John, P.D., and S. Wheeler. 2008. *The digital classroom: Harnessing technology for the future*. London: Routledge.

Pickett, D. 1986. Business English. Falling between two stools. *Comlon* 26: 16–21.

Swales, J. 1990. *Genre analysis. English in academic and research settings*. Cambridge/New York: Cambridge University Press.

Swales, J. 2004. *Research genres. Explorations and applications*. Cambridge: Cambridge University Press.

Tribble, C. 1997. Improving corpora for ELT: Quick-and-dirty ways of developing corpora for language teaching. In *PALC'97 Proceedings*, eds. J. Melia and B. Lewandowska-Tomaszczyk. Lodz: Lodz University Press. Retrieved July 5, 2010, from http://www.ctribble.co.uk/text/Palc.htm

Chapter 10
Innovative Methods for LSP-Teaching: How We Use Corpora to Teach Business Russian

James Wilson, Serge Sharoff, Paul Stephenson, and Anthony Hartley

10.1 Introduction

In the last two decades much work has been carried out on corpus development; many large corpora, both general reference and specialised, have been created and user-friendly tools that allow non-specialist users to perform complex corpus queries and even build their own corpora have been developed. Consequently, we have seen an influx of corpus-based resources, in particular dictionaries, such as the *Collins Cobuild English Language Dictionary* (1995) and the *Cambridge Advanced Learners Dictionary* (2008), and grammars (Biber et al. 1999; Willis 2004), and the *indirect* impact of corpora in language learning and teaching has been considerable. Conversely, the *direct* impact of corpora in the language learning classroom has been less impressive, especially in Foreign Language Teaching (FLT), and we might argue that little progress has been made since Tim Johns' work on Data Driven Learning (DDL) in the 1980s and 1990s (see, for example, 1991a, b, 1993). That is, few tutors make active use of corpus-based exercises or use corpora in their classes. Despite the abundant general literature on corpora (e.g. McEnery and Wilson 1996; Biber et al. 1998; Adolphs 2006; Anderson and Corbett 2009; O'Keeffe and McCarthy 2010) and the rapidly growing literature on the application of corpora in language teaching (e.g. Sinclair 2004; Aston et al. 2004; Hidalgo et al. 2007; Aijmer 2009; Bennet 2010; Reppen 2010; Harris and Moreno 2010; Frankenberg-Garcia et al. 2011), the use of corpora for pedagogical purposes has not become an established practice. In fact, many language tutors are not sure what corpora are (Mukherjee 2004) or what they may be used for (McCarthy 2008). Tutors who use corpora in their teaching form a small and generally expert community, and even

J. Wilson (✉) S. Sharoff • P. Stephenson • A. Hartley
School of Modern Languages and Cultures, University of Leeds, Leeds, UK
e-mail: j.a.wilson@leeds.ac.uk; s.sharoff@leeds.ac.uk; a.hartley@leeds.ac.uk

E. Bárcena et al. (eds.), *Languages for Specific Purposes in the Digital Era*, Educational Linguistics 19, DOI 10.1007/978-3-319-02222-2_10,

they tend to use corpora predominantly as a source of reference for checking their language intuition and therefore do not exploit the available technology to the full. Most work has been done on the use of corpora in English Language Teaching (ELT) (e.g. Braun et al. 2006; O'Keeffe et al. 2007; Bennett 2010; Campoy et al. 2010; Frankenberg-Garcia et al. 2011) and, increasingly, on learner corpora (Aijmer 2009), while FLT has remained almost untouched by the corpus "revolution". Furthermore, even for ELT many works in the literature reflect corpus linguists' research interests in language use and many corpus-based examples are chosen because they are linguistically interesting, not because they are pedagogically relevant.

This is unfortunate in that a corpus-based approach to language learning and teaching has many benefits for both tutors and their students. Corpora can have a considerable positive impact on Language for Specific Purposes (hereafter, LSP) teaching, a rapidly growing market that is particularly relevant to the linguistic needs of industry but for which there is a lack of conventional printed teaching materials. Using corpora alongside established teaching practices, we can offer tuition in several LSP domains and tailor our curricula to the needs of industry and increase the employability of our graduates. Our case study is a business Russian class offered at the University of Leeds; we demonstrate how we use corpora in our language classes and in what ways a corpus-based approach is particularly well suited to business Russian and other LSP subjects.

The business Russian class is part of an applied Russian language module that is taken by students in their third year of study (having returned from a term or year in Russia) and it prepares students for work in industry. Several topics are covered on the course; these include: formal letter writing, CVs and covering letters, business presentations, sales pitches, and official telephone conversations. While such a module is of particular relevance to students intending to work in Russia upon completing their degree, tutors found it hard to structure and deliver because there are few relevant teaching materials. Similarly, students expressed that, unlike for their other subjects, there was not a (single) course book containing all or most of the materials relevant to the business Russian module. Students need access to notes on business-specific terminology and conventions in formal etiquette and style as well as sample official documents of various kinds (CVs, covering letters, letters of complaint, etc.) – documents which students are expected to produce in class tests and for homework assignments (as well as in "real-world" scenarios beyond the degree). Before introducing corpus-based materials to the module we relied heavily on web-based material, which was gleaned from many Russian-language websites and needed to be adapted for pedagogical purposes, and we also studied materials from books on business Russian and official written discourse produced in the Czech Republic (and intended primarily for Czech learners of Russian).[1] Although

[1] These books include several recent publications that focus on Russian in the spheres of commerce, law, international relations and administration (Dynda and Dyndová 1998; Kupcevičová and Vilímek 2006; Mrověcová 2007; Dlouhá 1998; Golčáková 2008; Rezková 2008).

concerns over the lack of adequate teaching materials were voiced specifically about business Russian, we might argue that there is a dearth of printed materials for other LSP subjects and for other languages, especially though not exclusively for less commonly taught ones.

Two principal skills that we look to train on the business Russian module are: (1) vocabulary acquisition and (2) register recognition and differentiation. Although students taking the applied Russian module have spent 9 months in Russia, the business Russian class is their first real experience of formal writing. The core lexicon of business Russian is different to that of other genres that students are already familiar with, and many important discipline-specific words and phrases are not found in standard dictionaries or other language learning resources that students use. Furthermore, even at the (upper-)intermediate level, students are not fully competent in recognising and successfully differentiating between different varieties of written Russian. They tend to struggle in formulating official documents, as they are unfamiliar with formal salutation and valediction, higher-level grammatical and syntactic constructions and generic or discipline-specific formal clichés. As the students already possess generic language learning skills and have a solid grounding in general written Russian (grammar, vocabulary and syntax) when they enrol on the course, the task of acquiring a discipline-specific lexicon and specific morphosyntactic constructions should be straightforward, provided that there is a reliable means of identifying the vocabulary and register of a particular LSP domain. In fact, assessment shows that students encounter few problems in learning terminology specific to business Russian; however, tutors' task of compiling lists of discipline-specific terminology and constructions, given the lack of resources, is time-consuming and laborious.

Our aim is therefore to use corpora to facilitate vocabulary acquisition and to enhance students' ability to recognise formal expressions and use them in an appropriate context. We describe herein how corpora can be used to compensate for the lack of printed materials, how they facilitate tutors' task of designing relevant materials and how a corpus-based approach is particularly relevant to LSP teaching. This study contributes to the literature on the application of corpora in language learning and teaching and, more specifically in FLT and in LSP domains, by showcasing the work we have done, both from a technological perspective to enhance possibilities for manipulating corpora for pedagogical purposes and from a pedagogical perspective to develop materials to utilise the technology more fully. We demonstrate how we have simplified our existing corpus-based tools and enhanced them to facilitate and enhance teaching and research across the arts and humanities. More specifically, we focus on the application of our tools in the business Russian class and describe how tutors and students may use our tools to:

1. generate frequency lists of business-related keywords;
2. automatically extract lists of business-related collocations;
3. search for affixed and compound forms;

4. automatically classify texts according to genre and domain;
5. rank concordance lines according to their level of difficulty;
6. collect their own corpora of business texts and official documents and analyze them using the functions that are available in our interface.

We then present examples of how the individual search options in the IntelliText interface (see Sect. 10.2) are used to train vocabulary acquisition and register recognition and differentiation – skills that are essential for any LSP domain – and to enhance students' language competence more generally. Finally, while our focus is on technological advances in corpus development and the application of corpus-based tools in LSP teaching, part of our chapter is devoted to material design and reports on our efforts to create corpus-based language exercises to complement and support our tools and that allow students to exploit the available technology more fully.

10.2 Simplifying and Enhancing Corpora for Teaching

In most cases, corpora are not conceived or designed for the language learning classroom but are usually intended for a specialist, technologically savvy target audience. This means that for pedagogical purposes corpora must be simplified and adapted in various ways in order to become established in the mainstream and to be accepted by language tutors. Large collections of electronically-stored texts, especially those that are not annotated, are of little practical value to language tutors or their students. The same holds for the output of a corpus search: other than for reference, a list of concordance lines is of little use. A corpus that is parsed and tagged is more useful; language learners can make more elaborate corpus queries and search for, say, a noun in a particular case, a verb in a particular tense or a multi-word expression. However, to perform more complex searches language learners often need to be familiar with complex regular expressions and competent in using computer syntax, as many interfaces require grammatical information to be typed in as a string code. Assume that a language learner wants to see which adjectives are commonly used in the expression *to make an impression* between the words *an* and *impression*. In our former interface (http://corpus.leeds.ac.uk/internet.html) he or she would have needed to enter the following string code (CQP syntax):

```
[lemma = "make"] [pos = "DT"] [pos = "JJ"] [word = "impression"]
```

The string tells the regular expression processor to look for any form of *make*, a determiner (DT) – this allows for an article before the adjective; a more specific search for examples that occur with the indefinite article could be achieved by replacing [pos="DT"] with [word="a"] – an adjective (JJ) and the word *impression*. Even one-word searches in which the search word is in a particular grammatical case may require a complex code in highly inflected languages. Take the Russian word *работа* "work" in the dative singular case (*работе*), for example. Users would need to know the following string code in order to search for this form:[2]

```
[lemma="работа"&pos="Ncfsgn*"] (or [lemma="работа"&pos="N..sg.*"])
```

Without clear and comprehensive instructions, these searches would be beyond the competence level of most untrained users and such a counter-intuitive method overwhelms many non-specialists. Moreover, until recent years the main target audience for the outputs of research on the development and use of corpora has been the immediate specialist community of computational and corpus linguists; therefore, user documentation is in some cases inaccessible to users from other disciplines.

A second and equally serious problem concerning the use of corpora for pedagogical purposes is that the content of many of the examples that the concordancer generates is too difficult for all but advanced students. This is certainly true in the case of languages that are taken up from the ab-initio level at British universities such as Russian, Arabic and Chinese. Or many examples that are generated are not pedagogically relevant, and in preparing their notes or exercises language tutors might have to sift through hundreds of examples to find just one or two appropriate ones. Therefore, tutors may find it quicker and easier to produce materials on the basis of their intuitions rather than taking examples from corpora. For teaching and learning purposes, tutors and their students need to be able to refine their search by filtering concordance lines according to several parameters (difficulty, genre, domain, grammatical features, and other categories). Language tutors and learners also require additional functions such as frequency lists, lists of useful collocations and the option to search for affixed forms, display their search word in various positions within a sentence, compare words and phrases within and across corpora, and so on.

It is evident from the above that there are two issues that need to be taken into account if corpora are to be enter the mainstream of language learning and teaching. First, corpus tools need to be made simple so that non-specialists can use them. Second, corpus-based tools and functions need to be developed specifically for a target audience of language tutors and learners. Language learners require specific options for building corpora and generating frequency lists, and they require a more elaborate, yet user-friendly, annotation system for classifying texts and individual concordances and collocations according to several parameters.

We have already taken steps to address these demands on the Intelligent Tools for Creating and Analysing Electronic Text Corpora for Humanities Research (IntelliText) project (Wilson et al. 2011) carried out at the Centre for Translation

[2] There is a reasonably high degree of syncretism in the Russian case system and *работе* is both the dative and preposition singular form. Users could not therefore simply enter *работе* as a word form, unless they did not need to restrict their search to a particular case.

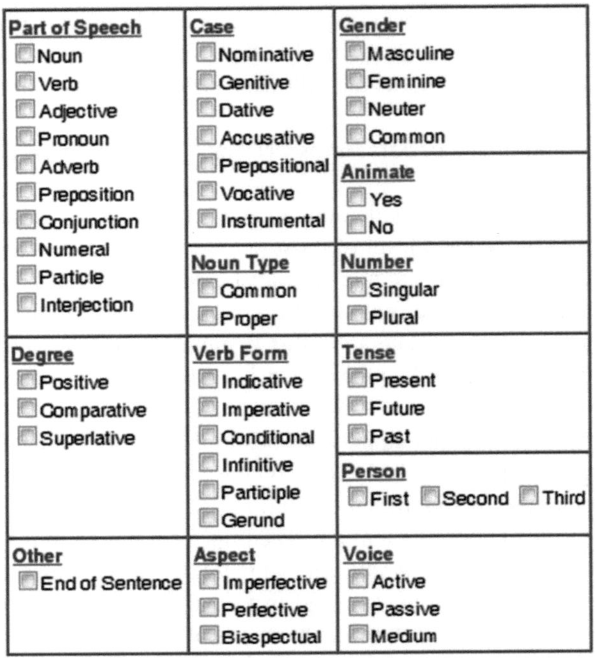

Fig. 10.1 Russian Part of Speech (POS) editor

Studies at the University of Leeds. The broad aims of the project were (1) to make our corpora and corpus-annotating software simple to use and accessible to a wide and diverse group of users and (2) to create a versatile and intuitive interface with tools and functions aimed at enhancing and facilitating the work of teachers and researches in various areas of the humanities. Our four targeted disciplines were language learning and teaching, translation studies, linguistics and history, and we liaised with academics from these disciplines to receive their advice and guidance on the features that should be implemented in our interface. Most of our collaborators, mainly academics with little or no experience in using corpora in their teaching or research, emphasised the importance of a simple and intuitive interface that is supported by clear and comprehensive documentation including discipline-specific tutorials.

With the aim of making our interface more intuitive and user-friendly, we have implemented a part-of-speech (POS) editor that allows users to add grammatical information to their search by ticking check-boxes (see Fig. 10.1), rather than by manually typing out complex string codes. We have also simplified multi-word searching by developing a search builder (see Fig. 10.2) that allows users to formulate complex queries, including searches involving specific and non-specific intermediates, and to specify whether their search word is a lemma or not. Other functions developed and implemented on the IntelliText project are discussed below in the context of their application in LSP teaching.

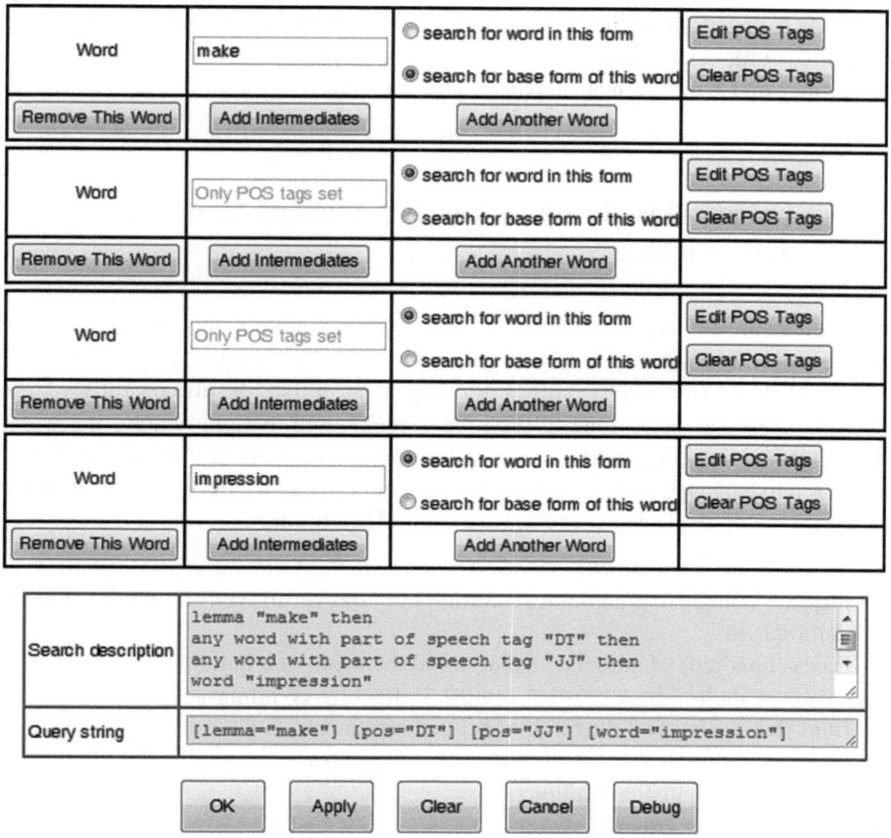

Fig. 10.2 Search builder

We are also tackling the second problem outlined above and, acting on the advice of language tutors, we have made several modifications to our interface that directly benefit language learning and teaching. Users may search for words in various places in a sentence, display their search words at the start, end or in the middle of a concordance line, search for affixed forms of words without needing to know string codes or symbols (see Sect. 10.3.1.3) and compare the use of two or more competing words or phrases. To support the general IntelliText user guide we have also created language-specific tutorials for English as a Foreign language, Japanese and Russian, which provide sample searches for and exercises on linguistic issues relevant to these languages.[3] With respect to developing a more sophisticated annotation system, we are researching possibilities for classifying texts and

[3] http://smlc09.leeds.ac.uk/itweb/cmsimple/?Sample_Corpus_Searches_%28Russian%29

individual concordance lines according to their level of difficulty and we have compiled corpora stratified according to topics studied by students at UK institutions at levels 2 and 3 for German, Japanese and Russian.

10.3 Corpus-Based Approaches to Language Learning and Teaching

As corpora are a fairly new addition to the teaching toolkit, many users are unaware how to use them, what to use them for or what benefits they bring to learning and teaching (McCarthy 2008). This is not surprising in that, despite recent progress in EFL, little has been done to promote corpus-based learning among the wider language learning community. This is unfortunate, as we believe that a corpus-based approach to language learning can supplement and extend the effectiveness of existing teaching materials. Using corpora, students and tutors can:

- view grammar in context;
- display complex grammatical forms not shown in conventional bilingual dictionaries;
- access hundreds of authentic examples at the touch of a button;
- view vocabulary in a broader context, extracting common and useful collocations that are beyond the remit of printed resources;
- grasp subtle differences between words and phrases;
- verify their linguistic intuition;
- achieve a better grasp of style;
- augment their vocabulary, in particular on themed topics and in specific domains;
- test controversial points of grammar and compare prescribed grammar with actual language use.

More specifically, in LSP teaching corpora can be used to train specific language skills and in some cases can go beyond the remit of printed resources. Here we look specifically at their application in the context of the business Russian module and how they may be used to train vocabulary acquisition and register recognition and differentiation. Even in the largest dictionaries and the most comprehensive grammar manuals only a few phrases, collocations and constructions are shown (in some cases out of context), and the information given may be insufficient for language learners to fully grasp how a particular word or grammatical feature is used in context. Corpora, on the other hand, are made up of hundreds of authentic language examples and collocations, thus language learners may view problematic words or grammatical forms in hundreds of sentences and in different types of text and context. Moreover, printed materials tend to cover only the main LSP domains, as it is financially impracticable to publish books on topics that do not have a wide target audience, and they cannot represent current affairs. From corpora, however, tutors may develop materials and create ad-hoc exercises for highly specific topics or to create vocabulary lists on current topics that students can use to describe events that are taking place at the present time. In fact, tutors may create materials for any topic, provided that enough written material is available for that topic. For example, for our final-year core Russian language module we created corpora of texts on the Tsunami that occurred in Japan in March 2011 and on the Libya Crisis and the death of Muammar Gaddafi from Russian-language newspaper articles available online. We use these and other corpora, built in the same way, and exercises based on their content to augment students' vocabulary and to train students to discuss topics, both orally and in writing, using sophisticated and stylistically appropriate words, phrases and constructions. In fact, tutors may create materials for any topic, provided that enough written material is available for that topic.

10.3.1 Vocabulary Acquisition

In this section, we shall focus on three corpus-based methods of vocabulary acquisition: (1) frequency lists, (2) collocation extraction and (3) compound and affix searching. We shall also describe how tutors and students can use our tools to create DIY corpora and use these corpora to extend their vocabulary on themed topics.

The acquisition of a core, discipline-specific vocabulary can provide a solid basis for creating materials for modules such as business Russian, French for lawyers, Spanish for medics, and other LSP-based subjects, whose core lexicon differs markedly from that required for "general" language learning and many key phrases of which are not found in standard bilingual dictionaries. Tutors can quickly build their own corpora for various LSP domains, no matter how specialised, and then generate frequency lists of the most common words and phrases in these corpora. The benefits of this approach were clearly demonstrated by Butler (1974). Butler used frequency lists extracted from a small corpus (94,000 words) of systematically selected chemistry papers to "permit second-year chemistry undergraduates (or postgraduates), with no previous knowledge of German, to read papers from German chemical journals for comprehension and, where necessary, for translation" (50). Using exercises built around the most frequent words and collocations from his "chemistry" corpus, Butler aimed to equip his students with the requisite reading skills within 10 teaching hours (plus 20 h of independent study). The results were "gratifyingly successful" (53). Butler's methodology can be extended to other languages and to other LSP domains.

We are currently testing a similar methodology on the AHRC-funded ReadingCorp (A corpus-based approach to achieving reading competence in Russian) project that is being carried out at the Universities of Leeds and Sheffield. Building on previous research carried out on the CEELBAS-funded Russian for

Research project,[4] on which we indentified that existing postgraduate (PG) language provision at many institutions is inadequate and many potentially good researchers are consequently slipping through the net, we aim to test whether a corpus-based and vocabulary-oriented approach can be used to provide PhD students with little or no knowledge of Russian the necessary reading skills to comprehend primary texts in their area of research. Keyword lists are extracted from two specialised corpora: a general academic corpus made up of academic articles in areas of interest specified on the Russian for Research project and a smaller corpus of texts directly relevant to the students' research topic. Besides producing an extensible methodology and discipline-specific exercises, we shall also deliver an online grammar of Russian specifically for researchers in which emphasis lies firmly on the identification of common grammatical structures in academic texts selected from corpus-based frequency data.

Quick acquisition of discipline-specific vocabulary is highly desirable in LSP teaching, as in the above-mentioned case of PhD students who need to learn a foreign language from scratch for their research. Intensive undergraduate ab-initio programmes are not suited to researchers' language needs; much of the material covered at Level 1 is of little relevance to researchers, while many important points of grammar and language use (from the researcher's perspective) are not covered. Gaining the necessary reading competence to understand academic texts is quite straightforward: academic texts are characterised by lexical and stylistic repetition; therefore, corpus-derived frequency lists can be particularly effective, as Butler demonstrated. The same holds for grammar: teaching can be structured around the grammatical constructions that occur most frequently in academic texts and training need not involve production and correct use of these forms, but simply the ability to recognise them and know what purpose they serve. As specialised intensive language for research courses are not practicable at many institutions (especially in the case of less commonly taught languages) and there are concerns over the sustainability of established courses, new, cost-effective modes of delivery are highly sought after. A corpus-based, vocabulary-oriented approach is a realistic and inexpensive way of training or improving reading skills quickly and effectively.

10.3.1.1 Frequency Lists

Until recently, tools for extracting frequency and keyword lists from corpora belonged to the exclusive domain of computational linguists and non-specialists needed technical assistance to produce them. Nowadays, however, a standard feature of many corpus interfaces is a built-in and easy-to-use frequency list generator. Users can use our tools to generate lists of single- or multi-word terms and they can generate both frequency and keyword lists from the corpora available through our

[4] http://www.ceelbas.ac.uk/research/networkprojects/funded2007 (project CN07SF-1).

Table 10.1 Russian keywords sorted by the Log-likelihood score of their significance

Single words	Multiwords
банк (bank)	ценные бумаги (securities)
предприятие (enterprise)	юридическое лицо (organisation)
кредит (credit)	денежные средства (monetary assets)
договор (contract)	федеральный закон (federal law)
товар (product)	заработный плата (salary)
рынок (market)	бухгалтерский учет (accounting)
финансовый (financial)	земельный участок (land plot)
налог (tax)	акционерное общество (public company)
страхование (insurance)	рынок ценных бумаг (capital market)
цена (price)	основные средства (fixed-capital assets)
учет (accounting)	фондовая биржа (stock exchange)
ценный (valuable)	процентная ставка (interest rate)
денежный (money-adj)	фондовый рынок (stock exchange)
имущество (property)	арбитражный суд (arbitrage)
налоговый (tax-adj)	недвижимое имущество (real estate)
прибыль (profit)	система управления (system of management)
государственный (state)	налоговые органы (tax authorities)
страховой (insurance-adj)	договор страхования (insurance contract)
стоимость (cost)	инвестиционный фонд (investment fund)

interface or from corpora that they upload to it. A frequency list is understood here as a list of the most common words or lemmas in a corpus; a keyword list as a list of words that appear in a corpus more often than we would expect by chance and that are extracted by statistical tests that compare their frequency against expected frequencies derived from larger reference corpora (as, for example, the words and phrases in Table 10.1). While the output of keyword lists is useful only for reference and passive language acquisition, tutors can create exercises around the output in order to promote active language acquisition (see Sect. 10.4).

Single-word terms from specialised corpora are detected by Log-likelihood scores for their frequencies against a reference corpus (Rayson and Garside 2000). An adaptation of the commonly-used Bootcat algorithm (Baroni and Bernardini 2004) is used for the extraction of multi-word terms. For example, we can start with the frequencies of Russian words in the overall Internet corpus (Sharoff 2006) and the frequencies from the business corpus to get the list of keywords. Then the list can be extended by finding commonly used sequences of several words that contain at least one of the words in the keyword list. The importance of multiword units can be highlighted by non-compositional expressions, like *ценные бумаги* (securities) which literally means "valuable papers". Users will be eventually be able to specify the length of the phrases generated in the lists and select to view keyword lists of specific parts of speech such as verbs, adjectives and nouns.

10.3.1.2 Automatic Extraction of Collocations

Tools for indentifying and displaying collocations in corpora are now well established in many interfaces. There is an unresolved issue with regard to the most appropriate score by which to rank the collocates (Evert and Kren 2001), but the Log-likelihood score (Dunning 1993) is generally considered as a reasonable choice, as it takes into account the ratio of frequencies as well as the actual number of examples, Our tools can rank collocations either by their joint frequency or by three statistical scores: Log likelihood, Mutual Information and T-Score. All three statistical methods are used to determine the statistical significance of two words occurring together; the default sorting order in the collocation tables is by log likelihood.

Language learners often produce odd collocations, usually because of interference from their native language (L1), and collocational information in most dictionaries is scant – obviously because space is limited (even in larger dictionaries). The automatic extraction of collocations is therefore another corpus-based function that can be used to good effect in learning and teaching and it exceeds the capabilities of existing printed resources. In keeping with the business theme of this paper, let us look at two examples from Russian: adjective + *рынок* "market" and *произвести* "to make, produce" + noun. Our tools allow users both to restrict the grammatical tag of the collocates and to select their position in relation to the search word; therefore, we can tell the corpus to show adjectives on the left of *рынок* (see Fig. 10.3) and nouns on the right of *произвести* (see Fig. 10.4). We used the Russian Business Corpus available via our interface for both queries. To get a better idea of how these collocations are used in context students can then click either on the collocations in the "Pair" column or on the number beside them in the "Count" column of the table and view a list of concordances.[5] A more detailed account of how we use the collocation search function on the business Russian module is given in Sect. 10.4.

10.3.1.3 Compound and Affix Searching

As the aims of IntelliText were to create a user-friendly and simple search interface, we have implemented a search type specifically intended for affixes that allows users to either enter an affix and see in which words that affix occurs or enter a lemma to generate affixed forms of that lemma (see Fig. 10.5). Our Affix Search function is a particularly valuable resource for vocabulary building in many languages, particularly those for which affixation is a productive source of word formation, such as for the Slavonic languages in the case of verbal prefixation. The lists in Fig. 10.6 show the outputs of both type of affix search.

[5] Users generate ten concordances by clicking on the collocation and a list of all occurrences of the collocation by clicking on the number.

Pair	Count	F1	F2	LL	MI	T
фондовый рынок	302	3543	5310	697.5	8	17.31
российский рынок	185	17829	5310	230.38	4.96	13.16
вторичный рынок	94	838	5310	229.7	8.39	9.67
мировой рынок	125	5542	5310	203.17	6.08	11.01
валютный рынок	110	4543	5310	182.61	6.18	10.34
внутренний рынок	111	4954	5310	179.98	6.07	10.38
внебиржевой рынок	47	266	5310	126.24	9.05	6.84
первичный рынок	58	1506	5310	109.67	6.85	7.55
финансовый рынок	85	14627	5310	81.79	4.12	8.69
страховой рынок	58	7026	5310	65.47	4.63	7.31
организованный рынок	27	356	5310	60.37	7.83	5.17
международный рынок	56	9956	5310	52.95	4.08	7.04
внешний рынок	39	3890	5310	47.66	4.91	6.04
межбанковский рынок	22	376	5310	46.24	7.45	4.66
междилерский рынок	12	19	5310	41.79	10.89	3.46

Fig. 10.3 Top ten adjective collocates to the left of *рынок* in the Russian Business Corpus

Pair	Count	F1	F2	LL	MI	T
произвести впечатление	332	6147	10171	908.81	9.28	18.19
произвести фурор	39	6147	115	155.34	12.65	6.24
произвести обыск	53	6147	1588	145.07	9.31	7.27
произвести эффект	66	6147	5943	144.1	7.72	8.09
произвести продукция	71	6147	11862	133.14	6.83	8.35
произвести посадка	30	6147	2839	64.71	7.65	5.45
произвести замена	30	6147	3200	62.92	7.48	5.45
произвести расчет	38	6147	9881	62.88	6.19	6.08
произвести сенсация	20	6147	938	50.18	8.66	4.46
произвести выстрел	23	6147	3694	43.54	6.89	4.76
произвести платеж	19	6147	2764	36.9	7.03	4.33
произвести расход	22	6147	8184	32.51	5.67	4.6
произвести ремонт	20	6147	5750	32.09	6.05	4.4
произвести пуск	14	6147	1012	32.08	8.04	3.73
произвести оплата	20	6147	5958	31.74	5.99	4.4

Fig. 10.4 Top ten noun collocates (Collocates are displayed in their lemma form) to the right of *произвести* in the Russian Business Corpus

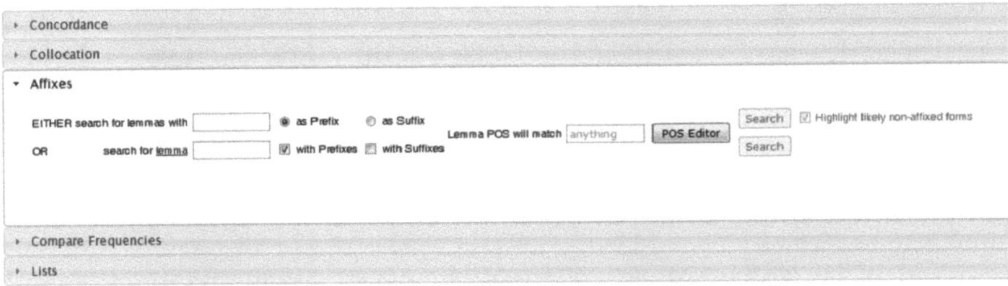

Fig. 10.5 The Affix Search page

Lemma	Count	Forms	Lemma	Count	Forms
передать	10248	65	считать	41768	78
перестать	9581	47	прочитать	6348	59
перейти	7949	37	предпочитать	4169	53
перевести	5892	57	рассчитать	3020	48
переходить	5856	63	почитать	2365	65
передавать	5424	60	посчитать	1666	40
переживать	4589	63	подсчитать	875	40
пережить	4379	63	пересчитать	609	34
перенести	3234	51	зачитать	497	37
переводить	2944	63	перечитать	494	27
переставать	2612	27	вычитать	478	46
перебить	2580	43	сосчитать	461	29
переехать	2351	38	просчитать	425	37
переносить	1999	51	причитать	352	22
перечислить	1873	43	дочитать	334	26

Fig. 10.6 Sample outputs of an Affix Search: verbs beginning with *пере–* (on *left*) and prefixed forms of *читать* (on *right*)

Unfortunately, the searching mechanism cannot distinguish between genuine affixed forms and non-affixed forms containing the same combinations of letters. For example, a search for the prefix *over* looks for all words beginning with over and so finds words such as *overt* and *overly* as well as genuine affixed forms such as *overdone* and *overlay*. Similarly, a search for affixed forms of the verb *do* generates words like *Nintendo* and *torpedo*. Users can try to improve the accuracy of the output by selecting the "Highlight likely non-affixed forms" option, which highlights in red forms that are not lemmas when the affix is removed. For example, *Nintendo* and *torpedo* can be filtered out, since the forms *Ninten* and *torpe* are not lemmas.

However, this function is unreliable for many languages and retagging is needed to knock out non-affixed forms from affix searches.[6]

Though called an Affix Search, this function can also be used to display lists of compound forms such as ***работодатель*** "employer", ***работодательница*** "female employer", ***работо****способность* "work capacity"; *клиенто****ориентированность*** "client-centeredness", *ренто****ориентированность*** "rent-centeredness", *бизнес****ориентированность*** "business-centeredness", *англо****ориентированность*** "English-centeredness".

10.3.1.4 Using DIY Corpora for LSP Teaching

Besides using existing corpora to generate frequency lists, lists of collocations, affixes and compounds, users may also compile their own collections of texts which are automatically lemmatised and grammatically tagged by our tools. DIY corpora are useful in both language and translation for specific purposes, in cases when tutors, students or translators need to work with specific types of language. In combination with the Frequency List Generator, DIY corpora offer a quick and easy means of extracting a core vocabulary list for any LSP domain. Users simply need to upload a set of texts, either as plain text, Microsoft Word or comprised files and they can then make full use of all the features built into our interface. With regard to the business Russian module, students may collect advertisements, CVs and covering letters, letters of complaint, political leaflets, etc., and then extract keywords from their corpus or look up specific words in concordance and collocation searches. This is a major benefit of corpus-based learning: while the lexicon of such a breadth of highly-specific domains cannot be represented in printed language-learning resources, which often take years to produce and generally cater for wider groups of users, corpus-derived frequency lists can be created within hours and, more importantly, can cater for the individual. Corpora also give students greater autonomy and allow them to extract their own frequency lists from and perform other searches on corpora that they have compiled – an activity that can be both fun and fulfilling.

10.3.2 Register Recognition and Differentiation: "Tagging for Teaching"

Many modern corpora are enriched with grammatical and domain information that allows users to refine their searches and look for specific word forms, select texts according to parameters like genre and topic and classify them in several other ways. Besides morphological and semantic tagging, now customary in many

[6] In the case of Russian, words like *президент* "president" and *предприятие* "enterprise" are correctly highlighted as non-affixed forms, as *зидент* and *дприятие* are not lemmas. On the other hand, words like *сон* "sleep; dream" and *сад* "garden" are not highlighted as non-affixed forms, as *он* "he" and *ад* "hell" are lemmas.

modern corpus interfaces, several other types of tagging can be used to enhance language learning. In this section, we look at three types of annotation that are relevant to LSP-teaching: (1) genre classification, (2) difficulty ranking and (3) the classification of texts according to the grammatical forms that they contain.

10.3.2.1 Genre Classification

Genre classification, a system by which genre categories can be automatically assigned to texts in non-annotated corpora, is a major advance in corpus development and allows us to show stylistic variation across texts. On the basis of previous research in which parameters for automatic genre detection and classification of texts from the Web (Sharoff 2010; Sharoff et al. 2010), we have been able to classify texts into such general genre categories as news items ('reporting'), legal texts ('regulations'), FAQs, advice ('instruction'), promotional materials ('advertising'), listings ('information') and everything else ('discussion').

Modern text classification (which covers genre and topic classification) is based on (1) detecting features which represent each individual document and (2) applying Machine Learning algorithms using a collection of documents with known labels. We used the Weka toolkit for the latter task (Witten and Frank 2005). Given a topically diverse document collection, the genre of documents can be successfully encoded by character n-grams, i.e., sequences of n characters (Mason et al. 2010; Sharoff et al. 2010). For example, the genre of news reports in English can be described by such n-grams as: rday week sday annou, which generalise over references to dates *(yesterday, Tuesday, Wednesday, Saturday),* while the genre of research articles can be described by such n-grams as s by; ly l; eris; naly, which generalise over some of the features of the formal language (including the greater use of adverbs and the passive voice). Such features are not absolute; Machine Learning algorithms (such as Naïve Bayes or Support Vector Machines) learn the strength of association between individual features and the labels, reaching the accuracy of 70–80 % on a topically diverse corpus.

In a similar fashion, for business Russian, we have been able to apply formality tags so that business clichés can be extracted to help students differentiate between formal and neutral language use as well as to help them achieve a better understanding of register and to allow them to compile their own lists of generic phrases used in official writing. Such stylistic tagging has a much wider application and can be used to display other features such as non-standard or regional use.

10.3.2.2 Difficulty Ranking

As we mentioned earlier (see Sect. 10.2), many language tutors have highlighted that the use of corpora in their language classes is limited in that students find it hard to understand the content of the concordance lines. This is not surprising: most corpora are made up of authentic texts and were not designed with the language

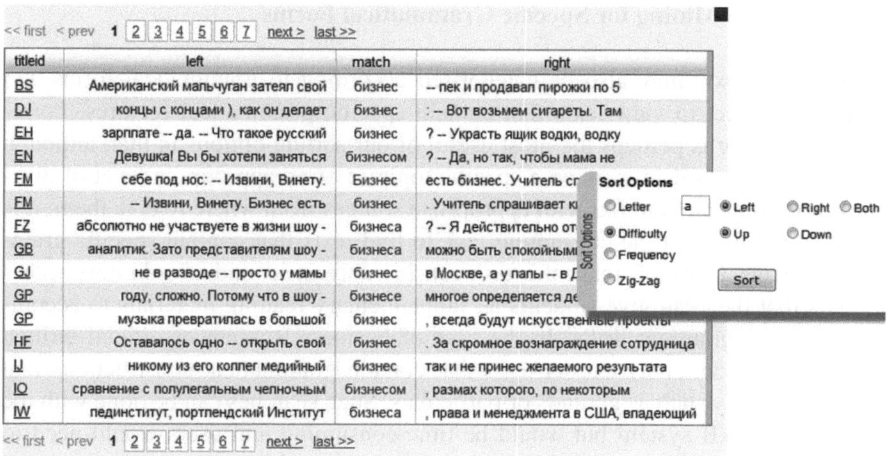

Fig. 10.7 Difficulty ranking in the IntelliText interface

learner and difficulty levels in mind. Most corpora were created for linguistic purposes, and while it is possible to develop tools to exploit these corpora for specific audiences, it is not possible to change their contents, and it is obviously time-consuming to create new pedagogically oriented corpora made up of graded texts and stratified according to content and other phenomena relevant to language learning. As a consequence, in the case of many languages, only advanced language learners have full access to corpus-based language learning, and even then tutors often need to sift through many examples to find just one or two appropriate ones.

Some recent advances have been made in this respect. Sharoff et al. (2008) established parameters for assessing the difficulty of texts and individual sentences in Russian (and other languages) and mapped the result to the CEFR levels.[7] Methods have also been developed for automatically ranking concordance lines according to their difficulty by measuring lexical and syntactic complexity and sentence similarity (Segler 2007; Kilgarriff et al. 2008; Kotani et al. 2008). As additional options for sorting the concordance lines we have integrated a relatively straightforward lexical match using the frequency-based CEFR-annotated lists (Kilgarriff 2010). This means that the difficulty level of the concordance lines displayed can be matched to the experience level of the students. Our user interface provides simple intuitive components, such as sliders, to ensure that setting the desired level of difficulty is easy. Even though, like other automatic processes, difficulty tagging is not completely accurate it still makes the tutors' task of selecting appropriate examples from the concordance lines much easier. Like all the processing features in our system difficulty tagging has been implemented in a plug-in fashion so that it can easily be replaced as better methods are developed (Fig. 10.7).

---

[7] http://www.coe.int/t/dg4/linguistic/cadre_en.asp

10.3.2.3 Text Mining for Specific Grammatical Forms

Corpus-held texts may also be categorised according to grammatical forms and users may select to view texts that contain specific grammatical features. Form-based searching is perhaps the most useful of our sorting options in that, although tutors can easily select texts on a specific topic or of an appropriate level of difficulty, once they are familiar with appropriate sources from where to take them, it is a very difficult and time-consuming task to find texts that contain specific grammatical forms. Our tools make this task considerably easier and afford tutors access to texts that they can give students as supplementary reading materials to accompany in-class grammar drills. In the case of business Russian or official written discourse, students may extract texts that contain grammatical constructions that occur frequently such as gerunds or participles. Such searches can be done with the underlying CWB system but would be time-consuming and users would need to have in-depth knowledge of the search syntax as well as some computational expertise. We provide a function in the interface that hides this complexity in a manner similar to the way in which we made affix searching more accessible.

10.4 Corpus-Based Exercises

So far in this chapter we have dealt only with corpus-based language learning and teaching from a technological perspective, describing how the tools and functions that we implemented on IntelliText can be used in LSP teaching. However, for these tools to be used effectively, pedagogically relevant and needs-driven materials and exercises need to be written to accompany the technology and a suitable methodology needs to developed for introducing corpora to existing teaching syllabi. Unfortunately, the pedagogical aspect of corpus-based learning and teaching has not been researched in equal measure to the technological side of the approach, and thus material design lags behind advances in the technology, and this is perhaps a reason that DDL has not reached the mainstream since the innovative work of Tim Johns in the 1980s and 1990s (1991a, b, 1993).

We have been developing corpus-based materials on two small projects: ReadingCorp, mentioned above (see Sect. 10.3.2.1), and WritingCorp – Corpus-based exercises for essay and précis writing in Russian – funded by the Teaching Enhancement and Student Success (TESS) fund at the University of Leeds. On ReadingCorp we are using a vocabulary-oriented approach and designing materials on the basis of frequency lists taken from texts that are directly relevant to the research topics of PhD students at the universities of Leeds and Sheffield. Our aim is to use these materials to equip students with skills for comprehending essential primary materials written in Russian. On WritingCorp we are designing corpus-based exercises on themed topics that students cover at Level 2 (crime, health, culture, society, etc.) to allow them to consolidate and expand on material covered in class and improve their written Russian by engaging with topic-related texts.

Tutors can make use of different types of corpus-based exercise. We either create exercises around the results of corpus searches and embed them in a broader pedagogical context or, to encourage learner autonomy, we design exercises that require students to actively work with corpora and perform their own searches, either in language lab sessions or as homework assignments. The former type of exercise has been termed the "hands-off" or "soft" approach to corpus-based language learning and the latter the "hands-on" or "hard" approach by Boulton (2008) and Gabrielatos (2005), respectively. By employing the hands-on or hard approach we not only look to enhance students' language competence but we also teach the students how to use corpora in learning a foreign language – a useful transferable skill that students can apply when learning other languages and an exercise that helps us in our endeavour to foster a culture of corpus use. The hands-on approach is particularly useful from a motivational perspective in that it allows students to work independently outside the classroom and gives them an opportunity to explore language-related issues that are of particular interest to them. Most in-class exercises are centred round the hands-off or soft approach and can be created on the fly for a specific lesson. We also provide hands-off exercises on our VLE system, either as Word documents or as interactive exercises created in Hot Potatoes. In sum, using a corpus-based approach, we aim not only to improve students' language competence but we also train them in using corpora to address language variation and other linguistic issues – a valuable skill that they can apply in other language modules and for languages other than Russian.

We introduce corpora and corpus-based exercises to existing modes of delivery. We believe that corpora should be used to support, not replace, existing teaching practices and we strive towards a blended learning approach, which is highly desirable in the modern-day language learning classroom. We use several types of exercise on the business Russian module, including: (1) a four-step approach to vocabulary building; (2) compound searching; (3) using collocations to find differences between near synonyms and problematic pairs of words; and (4) indentifying the more frequent of two or more expressions with similar usage.

In the first of these exercises, we give students a corpus of texts and ask them to perform several tasks. First, they generate a keyword list. Second, they perform a concordance search on the keywords to highlight their use in a broader context. Third, they perform a collocation search on the keywords to extract common collocations. Finally, they enter the collocations into a concordance search. Working with authentic data, they inevitably find other interesting cases of language use in carrying out these exercises.

For compound searching we identify potentially interesting compound forms, either the initial or end part of a compound form, and ask students to find words that contain these forms and then build on their initial search in various ways. Sample compound forms are given in Table 10.2.

The corpus generates business-related words such as *торгово-промышленный* "commercial and industrial", *налогооблагаемый* "taxable" and *агрофирма* "(an) agro-industrial firm". These words are of little use to students out of context, with respect to active vocabulary acquisition; therefore, we use the hands-on approach

Table 10.2 Sample "parts" of business-related compound forms

Search for as "prefix"	Search for as "suffix"
работо	
торгово	
валютно	
налого	
финансово	
	торговля
	фирма
	общество
	производство

titleid	left	match	right
>>	документами банка. — Является ли курсовая разница	налогооблагаемым доходом	? — Курсовая разница в целях налогового учета
>>	на доходы. Еще одна приятность: из вашего	налогооблагаемого дохода	вычитается миллион рублей и проценты по
>>	системе, то есть зависеть от получаемого	налогооблагаемого дохода	. В ту же инспекцию в срок до конца января
>>	, то у такого физического лица возникает	налогооблагаемый доход	. Таки образом, уплата страховых взносов
>>	пенсионные вклады работника вычитаются из	налогооблагаемого дохода	. После выхода на пенсию, когда накопленные
>>	ведение бизнеса, которые в США вычитаются из	налогооблагаемых доходов	). После появления первой аналоговой копии
>>	фирма не несет никаких расходов, уменьшить	налогооблагаемые доходы	она не вправе. Однако такая позиция контролирующих
>>	подтверждающим документам включается в его	налогооблагаемый доход	и подлежит обложению налогом с доходов физлиц
>>	earnings: совокупный доход. Персональный	налогооблагаемый доход	до проведения всех корректировок. После
>>	разрешалось максимально вычитать из своего	налогооблагаемого дохода	суммы до 40 000 ф. ст., а максимальный капитал
>>	индекс налога и цен): Степень повышения	налогооблагаемого дохода	, необходимая для компенсирования налогоплательщикам
>>	ступени налоговой шкалы): Предельные размеры	налогооблагаемого дохода	или богатства, в границах которых доход
>>	Налоговые декларации содержат сведения о	налогооблагаемых доходах	, таможенные декларации - о провозимых через
>>	предыдущие или последующие годы, чтобы уменьшить	налогооблагаемый доход	соответствующего года. Покупатель. (-0-
>>	прямые налоги, взимаемые в зависимости от	налогооблагаемого дохода	данного лица с учетом предоставленных ему

Fig. 10.8 Concordances generated from the collocation *налогооблагаемый доход*

and instruct them to perform concordance and collocation searches on some of the compound forms and submit their annotated sample sentences to us. A collocation search reveals that *торгово-промышленный* is used almost exclusively in the phrase *торгово-промышленная палата* "Chamber of Commerce and Industry" and that common collocations that contain *налогооблагаемый* are *налогооблагаемый доход* and *налогооблагаемая прибыль*, both meaning "taxable income". Students can then perform a concordance search on these collocations, by clicking on the collocation in the results table, to see them in a broader context. This type of task is particularly suited to homework assignments (Fig. 10.8).

By performing a collocation search on *налогооблагаемый* and then clicking on the concordances of *налогооблагаемый доход* students may also identify other words or phrases that are commonly found in its immediate context: *вычитать (из)* "to deduct (from)", *уменьшить* "to reduce", *предельные размеры* "threshold", etc. Therefore, from the initial word-forming exercise students would be able to commit words like *налогооблагаемый* to their passive vocabulary, while by performing collocation and concordance searches they are more likely to be able to apply them actively by using corpora to see how a word like *налогооблагаемый* is used both in specific collocations and in a broader context.

Corpora are particularly useful for understanding subtle differences in meaning and making distinctions between near synonyms or pairs of words that non-Russians

Pair	Count	F1	F2	LL	MI	T	Pair	Count	F1	F2	LL	MI	T
свой ремесло	134	644414	2003	146	4.48	11.06	розничный торговля	1079	4062	17990	3904.63	11.63	32.84
заниматься ремесло	33	45789	2003	55.56	6.27	5.67	внешний торговля	1029	27249	17990	2654.69	8.81	32.01
художественный ремесло	22	12017	2003	47.18	7.61	4.67	международный торговля	612	35306	17990	1334.56	7.69	24.62
этот ремесло	74	944692	2003	46.63	3.07	7.58	оптовый торговля	396	2358	17990	1327.06	10.97	19.89
народный ремесло	20	18268	2003	37.78	6.87	4.43	в торговля	821	426615	17990	902.47	4.52	27.4
какому-нибудь ремесло	11	559	2003	36.66	11.04	3.32	свободный торговля	414	28512	17990	864.87	7.44	20.23
писательский ремесло	11	1112	2003	32.86	10.05	3.31	биржевой торговля	218	2846	17990	639.08	9.83	14.75
столярный ремесло	8	217	2003	29.21	11.95	2.83	мировой торговля	246	29268	17990	446.22	6.65	15.53
и ремесло	141	5535765	2003	27.11	1.45	7.52	электронный торговля	189	16208	17990	373.51	7.12	13.65
традиционный ремесло	14	13226	2003	26.2	6.82	3.71	министерство торговля	170	14943	17990	333.83	7.08	12.94
актерский ремесло	9	1110	2003	25.98	9.76	3	беспошлинный торговля	69	225	17990	254.54	11.84	8.3
военный ремесло	18	41828	2003	25.71	5.53	4.15	сфера торговля	134	25538	17990	211.58	5.97	11.39
учиться ремесло	14	22040	2003	22.67	6.09	3.69	заниматься торговля	145	45789	17990	193.04	5.24	11.72
кузнечный ремесло	6	204	2003	21.21	11.62	2.45	организация торговля	156	69684	17990	181.47	4.74	12.02
развитие ремесло	18	75399	2003	20.56	4.68	4.08	биржевый торговля	57	585	17990	174.14	10.18	7.54

Fig. 10.9 Collocation-based comparison of the words *ремесло* and *торговля*

find hard to distinguish and for which conventional dictionaries and grammars offer little help. Some typical and more general examples are "crime" and "bed": *преступление* vs. *преступность* and *постель* vs. *кровать*. By viewing the collocates of these words students can achieve a better understanding of how they are used. They should be able to identify that *преступление* denotes a specific crime, whereas *преступность* is an abstract noun denoting crime in general. Likewise, by looking at the adjective collocates on the left of *постель* and *кровать* students should be able to identify that *постель* is a bed in both the physical and abstract sense (as well as bedding), while *кровать* is only a physical object or a bed frame. They can also use corpora to establish important distinctions between problematic pairs of phrases such as *в русском языке* vs. *на русском языке* "in (the) Russian (language)", *в автобусе* vs. *на автобусе* "in/on/by (the) bus) and *в самом деле* vs. *на самом деле* "in actual fact", which many learners of Russian fail to master. In a business context, words such as *business*, *trade* and *commerce* may cause students problems, as each has several translations in Russian. Let us look at *trade* to highlight this point (Fig. 10.9).

The results show that *ремесло* is a specific trade and *торговля* is an abstract term denoting the exchange of goods. Moreover, there are some interesting findings. Both words occur with *заниматься* "to do; be engaged in" and *военное* (*военный* "military") *ремесло* is potentially confusing, as it may be understood by some native speakers of English as meaning "arms trade". In the first case, *заниматься ремеслом* means "to ply a trade", while *заниматься торговлей* means "to be involved in trade; to work as/be a trader (of)". A concordance search of *военное ремесло* would show students that this term denotes the act of training to become a soldier and is therefore a specific trade, as we would expect; "arms trade" is *торговля оружием*, again with the expected Russian equivalent of trade (*торговля*). Therefore, by using a collocation search, if necessary in combination with viewing concordances, students can work out problematic distinctions between words and phrases that cause learners problems more effectively than by relying on (brief) descriptions offered in language manuals. Corpora also highlight anomalous cases in which actual language use does not correspond to the prescribed rules.

Fig. 10.10 Table of results for a frequency comparison of *международная фирма* (Query 1) and *международная компания* (Query 2)

Corpus	Query 1 Instances	Query 1 IPM	Query 2 Instances	Query 2 IPM
RNC2009-MOCKY	7	0.060	43	0.368
RNC2009-FULL	7	0.060	43	0.369
RS-MOCKY	0	0.000	1	0.172
NEWS-RU	10	0.129	82	1.056
I-RU	11	0.055	96	0.484
BIZ-RU	1	0.063	51	3.205
WIKI-RU	8	0.045	122	0.682
RU-SPOKEN	0	0.000	0	0.000
Totals	44	0.062	438	0.616

Frequency comparisons are useful for identifying the more common of two or more words or phrases that are semantically synonymous, as in: preposition + snail/postal/paper + mail. It is often the case that one of two or more words or phrases that differ neither in meaning (nor in register) is used considerably more. Tutors can give their students sets of examples to compare, and a subsidiary aim of this task is to improve students' analytical skills and for them to make such queries themselves on other pairs of words that they encounter in their own reading.

Two business-related examples are *международная фирма* vs. *международная компания* "international firm, company" and деловая женщина vs. бизнесменка "business woman". In the first case, *фирма* and *компания* are contextually synonymous; in the second, *бизнесменка* is a neologism and considered a colloquial form. A frequency comparison search will show only differences in the frequency of the words or phrases that are compared, not subtle differences in their use. Therefore, to make sure that words are in fact synonyms students are advised to perform a concordance search on each of them. Figures 10.10 and 10.11 show the results for a search performed on *международная фирма* vs. *международная компания*. Students can see from these results that *международная компания* is the more common of the two by a considerable margin – a perhaps surprising observation for learners of Russian. Frequency comparisons may also be used to compare (across different corpora) the use of words or phrases that are semantically synonymous but differ stylistically. A good example is *выйти из дома* vs. *выйти из дому* "to leave the house". The former is neutral, while the latter is colloquial; therefore, students can look at their use in corpora of various genres to achieve a better understanding of when it is appropriate to use one or the other form.

10.5 Conclusions

We have shown in this chapter several ways in which corpora can facilitate and enhance learning and teaching and that a corpus-based approach to business Russian, as well as to LSP teaching more generally, has many benefits and helps to

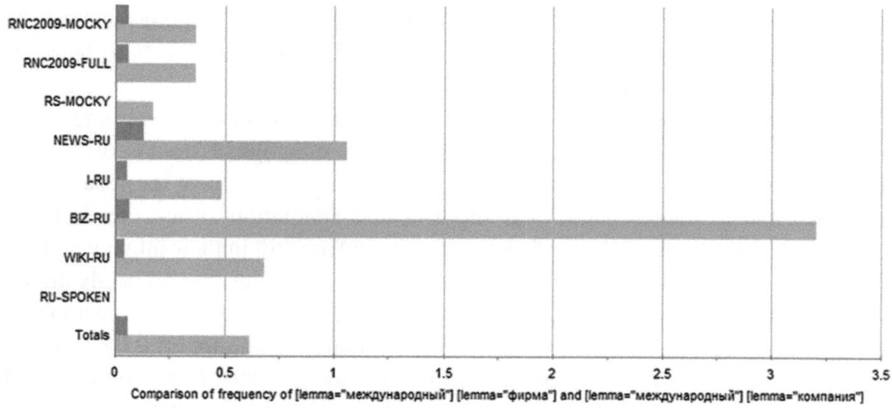

Fig. 10.11 Chart of a frequency comparison search of *международная фирма* (Query 1) and *международная компания* (Query 2)

compensate for the lack of printed teaching materials. We have also shown that corpora are well suited to training certain important LSP skills, such as vocabulary acquisition and register recognition and differentiation.

Corpus-derived frequency lists provide the basis for LSP courses and they can be created for most topics, provided that a large enough body of literature exists for these topics; importantly, a corpus-based approach can meet the needs of the individual language learner, such as a PhD student needing to acquire specialised reading skills in a short time. The breadth of LSP subjects cannot be covered by conventional printed course books, printed course books cannot cater for the needs of the individual and nor can they represent events taking place at the present time. Corpora can cater for all of these needs. Tutors, or even students, can use our tools to generate frequency, collocation and concordance lists, on the basis of which ad-hoc materials and exercises can be created. The materials (and the lists) can be stored electronically, in online repositories, and made available to other users; moreover, available in the format of a collaborative wiki, they can be updated and augmented at any time by their creators or by others. Collaborative learning is particularly important within ICT (Information and Communication(s) Technology) and the pooling and sharing of language resources has many benefits. First, collaboration can enhance language learning and teaching and facilitate tutors' work. Second, a collaborative approach can help provide support both for LSP or other specialised modules and for less-commonly taught languages for which student numbers may not warrant a taught programme but for which tuition can be offered cross-institutionally through a collaborative distance e-learning programme. A further advantage of corpora over printed language manuals is that they are not limited by space. Students can view hundreds of collocations or concordances as opposed to just one or two. A corpus-based approach to LSP teaching can also be used to facilitate register recognition and differentiation. We were able to utilise tools for automatic genre classification to tag business clichés and formal expressions to help students extract set phrases and use them in their own sample official letters. Other tags can be used in other LSP domains to help learners differentiate between genres and registers more accurately.

That said, for corpora to become a standard feature in LSP teaching more research is needed on both the technological and pedagogical strands of corpus-based learning and teaching. Corpus-based tools require refinement for pedagogical purposes and a more accurate and sophisticated annotation system needs to be developed. Such tools are being developed, yet they are still in their infancy and are in need of further refinement. With regard to pedagogy, relevant and needs-driven materials need to be developed, as does an extensible methodology for the application of corpora in learning and teaching. Without materials to support it the technology is of little practical use to the majority of language learners. More collaboration between computer scientists and researchers in other fields is needed to identify further tools and functions that language learners require. However, it is fair to say on the basis of existing evidence and expected technological advances that corpus-based tools will become easier to use and more functional, tagging will become more accurate and corpora will play an increasingly important role in research and teaching in various academic disciplines, including LSP teaching.

In sum, we believe that a corpus-based approach can make an important contribution to LSP teaching; corpora can facilitate the work of both tutors and their students and they can be used to create materials for highly specialised subjects, on current affairs and to meet the needs of the individual learner. However, specific conditions need to be met for a corpus-based approach to reach the mainstream. First, corpora should be used to support, not replace, existing teaching practices and should be incorporated into a blended learning package optimal for enhancing learners' language competence. Second, corpus-based exercises need to be created to accompany the technology. Third, more work is needed to promote, through workshops, seminars and practical demonstrations, corpus-based language learning in order to present its benefits and methods of application to tutors and students and to foster a culture of corpus use among the language learning and teaching community.

References

Adolphs, S. 2006. *Introducing electronic text analysis*. London: Routledge.

Aijmer, K. (ed.). 2009. *Corpora and language teaching*. Amsterdam: John Benjamins.

Anderson, W., and J. Corbett. 2009. *Exploring English with online corpora*. Basingstoke: Palgrave MacMillan.

Aston, G., S. Bernardini, and D. Stewart (eds.). 2004. *Corpora and language learners*. Amsterdam/Philadelphia: John Benjamins.

Baroni, M., and S. Bernardini. 2004. Bootcat: Bootstrapping corpora and terms from the web. In *Proceedings of LREC2004*, Lisbon.

Bennet, G. 2010. *Using corpora in the language learning classroom: Corpus linguistics for teachers*. Michigan: University of Michigan Press.

Biber, D., S. Conrad, and R. Reppen. 1998. *Corpus linguistics: Investigating language structure and use*. Cambridge: Cambridge University Press.

Biber, D., et al. 1999. *Longman grammar of spoken and written English*. London: Longman.

Boulton, A. 2008. DDL: Reaching the parts other teaching can't reach? In *Proceedings of the 8th teaching and language corpora conference*, ed. A. Frankenberg-Garcia. Associação de Estudos e de Investigação Cientifíca do ISLA-Lisbo.

Braun, S., Kohn, K., and Mukherjee, J. 2006. *Corpus Technology and Language Pedagogy*. Frankfurt: Peter Lang.

Butler, Christopher S. 1974. German for Chemists. In Teaching Languages to Adults for Special Purposes (CILT Reports and Papers 11), 50–53. Available online at http://www.eric.ed.gov/PDFS/ED100172.pdf

Campoy, M., B. Belles-Fortuno, and L. Gea-Valor (eds.). 2010. *Corpus-based approaches to English language teaching*. London: Continuum.

Dlouhá, O. 1998. *Ruština pro veřejnou zprávu*. Plzeň: Aleš Čeněk.

Dunning, T. 1993. Accurate methods for the statistics of surprise and coincidence. *Computational Linguistics* 19(1): 61–74.

Dynda, A., and E. Dyndová. 1998. *Česko-ruská obchodní korespondence*. Prague: Pragoeduca.

Evert, S., and B. Krenn. 2001. Methods for the qualitative evaluation of lexical association measures. In *Proceedings of the 39th annual meeting of the association for computational linguistics*, Toulouse.

Frankenberg-Garcia, A., L. Flowerdew, and G. Aston (eds.). 2011. *New trends in corpora and language learning*. London: Continuum.

Gabrielatos, C. 2005. Corpora and language teaching: Just a fling or wedding bells? *TESL-EJ* 8(4): 1–35.

Golčáková, B. 2008. *Ruština pro mezinárodní vztahy*. Plzeň: Aleš Čeněk.

Harris, T., and M. Moreno (eds.). 2010. *Corpus linguistics in language teaching*. Bern: Peter Lang.

Hidalgo, E., L. Quereda, and J. Santana (eds.). 2007. *Corpora in the foreign language classroom*. Amsterdam: Rodopi.

Johns, T. 1991a. Should you be persuaded: Two examples of data-driven learning. *English Language Research Journal* 4: 1–16.

Johns, T. 1991b. From printout to handout: Grammar and vocabulary teaching in the context of data-driven learning. *English Language Research Journal* 4: 27–45.

Johns, T. 1993. Data-driven learning: An update. *TELL&CALL* 2: 4–10.

Kilgarriff, A. 2010. Comparable corpora within and across languages: Word frequency lists and the Kelly project. In *Proceedings of the BUCC workshop*, Malta.

Kilgarriff, A., M. Husák, K. McAdam, M. Rundell, and P. Rychlý. 2008. GDEX: Automatically finding good dictionary examples in a corpus. In *Proceedings of EURALEX'08*, Barcelona.

Kotani, K., T. Yoshimi, T. Kutsumi, I. Sata, and H. Isahara. 2008. EFL learner reading time model for evaluating reading proficiency. In *Proceedings of CICLING*, Haifa.

Kupcevičová, J., and V. Vilímek. 2006. *Ruská řečová etiketa*. Ostrava: Philosophical Faculty of Ostrava University.

Mason, J., M. Shepherd, J. Duffy, V. Keselj, and C. Watters. 2010. An n-gram based approach to multi-labeled web page genre classification. In *Proceedings of 43rd Hawaii international conference on system sciences*, Hawaii.

McCarthy, M. 2008. Accessing and interpreting corpus information in the teacher education context. *Language Teaching* 41(4): 563–574.

McEnery, T., and A. Wilson. 1996. *Corpus linguistics*. Edinburgh: Edinburgh University Press.

Mrověcová, L. 2007. *Obchodní ruština*. Brno: Computer Press.

Mukherjee, J. (2004): "Bridging the gap between applied corpus linguistics and the reality of English language teaching in Germany", Applied Corpus Linguistics: A Multidimensional Perspective, ed. U. Connor & T. Upton. Amsterdam: Rodopi. 239–250.

O'Keeffe, A., and M. McCarthy (eds.). 2010. *The Routledge handbook of corpus linguistics*. London: Routledge.

O'Keeffe, A., McCarthy, M. and Carter, R. (2007). *From Corpus to Classroom. Language use and language teaching*. Cambridge: Cambridge University Press.
Rayson, P., and R. Garside. 2000. Comparing corpora using frequency profiling. In *Proceedings of the comparing corpora workshop at ACL*, Hong Kong.
Reppen, R. 2010. *Using corpora in the language classroom*. Cambridge/New York: Cambridge University Press.
Rezková, J. 2008. *Ruština pro právníky*. Prague: Univerzita Karlova.
Segler, T. 2007. *Investigating the selection of example sentences for unknown target words in ICALL reading texts for L2 German*. Unpublished Ph.D. thesis, University of Edinburgh.
Sharoff, S. 2006. Creating general-purpose corpora using automated search engine queries. In *WaCky! Working papers on the Web as corpus*, ed. M. Baroni and S. Bernardini. Bologna: Gedit.
Sharoff, S. 2010. In the garden and in the jungle: Comparing genres in the BNC and internet. In *Genres on the web: Computational models and empirical studies*, ed. A. Mehler, S. Sharoff, and M. Santini. Berlin/New York: Springer.
Sharoff, S., S. Kurella, and A. Hartley. 2008. Seeking needles in the Web haystack: Finding texts suitable for language learners. In *Proceedings of teaching and learning corpora conference*, Lisbon.
Sharoff, S., Z. Wu, and K. Markert. 2010. The Web library of Babel: evaluating genre collections. In: *Proceedings of the seventh language resources and evaluation conference*, Malta.
Sinclair, J. (ed.). 2004. *How to use corpora in language teaching*. Amsterdam: John Benjamins.
Willis, D. (ed.). 2004. *Collins cobuild – Intermediate English grammar*. Birmingham: University of Birmingham.
Wilson, J., A. Hartley, S. Sharoff, and P. Stephenson. 2011. Advanced corpus solutions for humanities researchers. In *Proceedings of Pacific Asia conference on language, information and Computation Sendai*, 2010.
Witten, I., and E. Frank. 2005. *Data mining: Practical machine learning tools and techniques*, 2nd ed. San Francisco: Morgan Kaufmann.

Chapter 11
Automatic Specialized vs. Non-specialized Text Differentiation: The Usability of Grammatical Features in a Latin Multilingual Context

M. Teresa Cabré, Iria da Cunha, Eric SanJuan, Juan-Manuel Torres-Moreno, and Jorge Vivaldi

11.1 Introduction

The differentiation between general and specialized texts has been a controversial question. Following the Communicative Theory of Terminology (Cabré 1999), it can be considered that a text is specialized only if it is written by a professional of the domain. For example, a text about cancer would be specialized if it is written by a doctor. Moreover, specialized texts can be divided in three specialization levels: high, medium and low. In all of them, the writer has to be a specialist of the domain, but the potential reader changes: other specialists, students or general public, respectively. Thus, newspaper articles are considered non-specialized texts, because they are written by journalists, not by specialists in economy, politics or medicine, for

M.T. Cabré • I. da Cunha (✉) • J. Vivaldi
Institut Universitari de Lingüística Aplicada, Universidad
Pompeu Fabra (UPF), Barcelona, Spain
e-mail: teresa.cabre@upf.edu; iria.dacunha@upf.edu; jorge.vivaldi@upf.edu

E. SanJuan
Departament Statistique et Informatique Décisionnelle, Laboratoire
Informatique d'Avignon, Université d'Avignon (UAPV), Avignon, France

Brain and Language Research Institute (BLRI), Avignon, France
e-mail: eric.sanjuan@univ-avignon.fr

J.-M. Torres-Moreno
Departament Statistique et Informatique Décisionnelle, Laboratoire
Informatique d'Avignon, Université d'Avignon (UAPV), Avignon, France

École Polytechnique de Montréal, Montreal, QC, Canada

Brain and Language Research Institute (BLRI), Avignon, France
e-mail: juan-manuel.torres@univ-avignon.fr

E. Bárcena et al. (eds.), *Languages for Specific Purposes in the Digital Era*, Educational Linguistics 19, DOI 10.1007/978-3-319-02222-2_11,

example. Journalists may know general aspects about these subjects, but they do not have the intimate knowledge (conceptual as well as lexical) of the domain.

Some researches about the differences between specialized and non-specialized texts exist. The majority of these works consider the lexicon as the most visible and differentiator aspect, in order to distinguish between these two kinds of texts. As Cabré (1999) states, terms are units of the lexicon with a precise meaning in a given domain, and they show the specialized information of that domain. Therefore, terms will appear in all the texts of their specialized scope.

As Kocourek mentions (1982), specialized language is a variety of language, whose resources (texts from all the linguistics levels) are marked by graphical characters, by syntactic tendencies, and, specially, by a set of lexical units having a metalinguistic semantic precision inside texts. Exactly, some works (Kocourek 1982, 1991) consider that grammatical features (both morphological and syntactic) are characteristic of specialized texts, as, for example, verbal tense, verbal mode and verbal flexion related to grammatical person. In the same line, there are some authors that have detected several grammatical phenomena that allow us to distinguish specialized texts. Nevertheless, they use small corpora and it is difficult to generalize their results: they use a very limited number of features of a unique category or they have analyzed a short number of documents manually. Hoffmann (1976) studies names and verbs frequencies in a non-specialized corpus vs. a specialized corpus. Coulon (1972), Cajolet-Laganière and Maillet (1995), and L'Homme (1993, 1995) have analyzed verbs in French specialized texts. More works where differences between general and specialized texts are shown can be found in Cabré (2007).

The question we want to answer is: Is it possible to find specific characteristics into specialized texts different from their discourse conditions (that are external to the text) or the terminology they have? In this paper we would like to show, using association rules mining (Borgelt and Kruse 2002), that certain grammatical features, besides lexicon, have a strong potential to differentiate specialized text content from non-specialized one. Although this subject has not been studied in depth in the literature, some preliminary works about it have been carried out (Cabré et al. 2010; Cabré 2007).

Cabré et al. (2010) present an analysis of the specific linguistic features of specialized discourse compared to the ones related to general discourse, from a corpus linguistics approach. They therefore focus their research on the contrast of the frequency rate of some lexical units in a textual corpus of Economics in Spanish, integrated by two different sub-corpora: on the one hand, a set of texts published by experts on this field and, on the other hand, articles published in Spanish in written press. This study is aimed to detect linguistic differences among multiple texts with a different degree of specialization concerning the same issue.

The developed automatic tool will be useful for some tasks, like automatic constitution of corpora of specialized texts and contextual information retrieval systems that need to discern between specialized and non specialized short queries, among others.

In Sect. 11.2 the methodology of our work is explained. In Sect. 11.3 the experiments and the results are shown. In Sect. 11.4 some conclusions are presented.

11.2 Methodology

The methodology to carry out this work has several stages. First, some linguistic features that may be characteristic of specialized texts and general texts have been pointed out. Second, these observations have been extended to combinations of grammatical features and lemmas. Last, a classifier based on these discriminative high level features has been built and evaluated.

11.2.1 Selection of Linguistic Features

A corpus has been compiled, divided into two sub-corpora:

- A sub-corpus of specialized texts (scientific papers, books, theses, etc.). It contains 11,453,458 tokens corresponding to 364,194 sentences and a vocabulary of 114,881 types.
- A sub-corpus with plain language from newspapers. It contains 5,871,961 tokens corresponding to 193,851 sentences and a vocabulary of 127,473 types.

The texts of both sub-corpora have been extracted from the Technical Corpus of the Institute for Applied Linguistics (IULA-CT) of the Universitat Pompeu Fabra of Barcelona.[1] This corpus contains texts in three languages (Catalan, Spanish and English). It includes texts of six specialized domains (economics, law, computing, medicine, genome and environment) and non-specialized texts from newspapers. All the texts of the corpus are tagged with POS tags, employing the well known tool TreeTagger locally trained and using a tagset developed in the IULA. The full meaning of the POS tags can be seen at the following URL: http://www.iula.upf.edu/corpus/etqfrmes.htm.[2] In this work, the tags have been simplified to keep only the linguistic information showed in Table 11.1 (ex. 'A' is a simplification of 'AMS', 'AMP').

The experiments where grammatical features characteristic of specialized texts and general texts were detected on this corpus are shown in Cabré et al. (2010) and Cabré (2007). Table 11.1 includes their results.

In the sequel the subset of documents from economics are also considered. This is a field where there is a large overlap between topics and vocabulary in specialized and non specialized publications, making the task even harder.

[1] http://bwananet.iula.upf.edu/

[2] For more details about these resources, see Vivaldi (2009).

Table 11.1 Linguistic features employed in our research

POS	Tag meaning	% in generalist text	% in specialized text
A	Determiner	10.00	9.90
C	Conjunction	6.79	7.62
D	Adverb	10.30	10.54
E	Specifier	4.39	5.49
JQ	Qualifier adjective	8.43	9.00
J	Adjective	4.56	4.48
N4	Proper noun	8.05	6.34
N5	Common noun	10.53	10.59
P	Preposition	10.35	10.34
R	Pronoun	6.34	7.03
T	Date	0.42	0.07
VC	Verb (participle)	4.51	4.47
V1P	Verb (first person, plural)	0.25	1.16
V1S	Verb (first person, singular)	0.13	0.24
V2	Verb (second person)	0.03	0.05
V	Verb	10.38	10.12
X	Number	4.54	2.56
Total	–	100.00	100.00

11.2.2 Combining Sequences of Linguistic Features and Lemmas

To highlight combinations of linguistic features that may also be characteristic of specialized texts, association rules were extracted mixing vocabulary and the above mentioned linguistic features. Indeed, association rules are well suited to detect relations among variables into large symbolic (i.e. non numerical) data (Amir et al. 2005) and express them in an intelligible way.

They are computed at sentence level instead of over entire documents. For that, documents are divided into sentences and association rules give the probability of a sentence comes from a specialized text or a non specialized one. Complete documents can be classified using contextual information about their structure or statistical information about their specific vocabulary. Since at sentence level none of this information can be used, resulting association rules rely on other features that may reveal relevant grammatical structures.

Therefore, the proposed application not only allows classifying texts, it also allows to look for technical statements inside non specialized documents. The resulting sentence classifier has a wide range of applications. It can be used in automatic summarization or restricted focused information retrieval to select sentences according to their level of speciality. It can also be used to classify queries into specialized or generalist.

To extract such association rules, sentences are encoded as a bag of lemmas and grammatical tags. The category of the text from where the sentence has been extracted is also added to this representation.

Table 11.2 Example of plain text and sentence single feature representation model

Plain text	*La comunidad internacional debe seguir esforzándose en abrir esos mercados*
POS tagged text	*La_el_A comunidad_comunidad_N5 internacional_ internacional_JQ debe_deber_V seguir_seguir_V esforzándo_esforzar_V se_pr_R en_en_P abrir_abrir_V esos_ese_E mercados_mercado_N5*
Representation	SPE V R deber seguir esforzar internacional el en abrir ese N5 JQ V comunidad mercado pr P D A D E

A literal sentence of a general text (plain text) and its related POS tagged text and its representation (that is, the detected lemmas and tags in this sentence) are included in Table 11.2. SPE shows that this sentence has been classified as part of a specialized document.

As already mentioned in Cabré et al. (2011), the form of our association rules is X= >D. The X is a set of at most five lemmas and/or tags and the D is the decision (SPE = specialized/GEN = general). A rule is valid if X is included in more than s% of the sentences (it is called "support" of the rule; normally 5 %) and more than c% of these sentences are in category D (it is called "confidence" of the rule; 80 % as usual default value). These rules are called "decision rules", because the right side of the rule is restricted to a few number of categories. Therefore, association rules may be defined as sequences of POS tags, lemmas and/or word forms that induce the presence in the sentence of another sequence or a discourse type, while the set of decision rules is the subset of association rules that only induce a discourse type. This type of rules can be computed employing standard GPL packages (like "Apriori" by Christian Borgelt[3]).

Note that, to compute decision rules over SPE and GEN categories based on this library, it is necessary to generate first all association rules, which is computer time and space consuming.

Such association rules have been computed on multiple samples of 9,000 sentences with more than six words from each corpus. Therefore, the association rule extraction has been carried out on sets of 18,000 sentences with an average total of 112,870 tokens.

Now, the main drawback of this first representation is that order of lemmas and grammatical tags is not considered, while n-grams experiments showed that short ordered sequences of characters can be highly discriminative (da Cunha et al. 2011) to detect sentences coming from specialized texts.

In this second model, sentences are represented as bags of lemma and tag sequences. Only sequences of 3 or less elements are considered, frequencies of longer sequences being far too low for classification purpose.

Table 11.3 shows an example of plain text (the same than in Table 11.2) and its corresponding POS tagged text and representation. Appendix I includes more examples of plain text passages and their corresponding representation.

[3] http://www.borgelt.net/apriori.html

Table 11.3 Example of plain text and sentence sequence feature representation model

Plain text	*La comunidad internacional debe seguir esforzándose en abrir esos mercados*
POS tagged text	*La_el_A comunidad_comunidad_N5 internacional_ internacional_JQ debe_deber_V seguir_seguir_V esforzándo_esforzar_V se_pr_R en_en_P abrir_abrir_V esos_ese_E mercados_mercado_N5*
Representation	SPE V_V_V R_P_V deber_seguir_esforzar internacional_deber el en en_abrir_ese N5_JQ_V V_E comunidad_internacional_deber N5_JQ esforzar_pr mercado P_V seguir_esforzar_pr deber_seguir en_abrir V_R V_V JQ_V N5_D pr_en_abrir internacional_deber_seguir deber ese_mercado ese abrir_ese_mercado A P_V_E D ese_mercado pr_en mercado E comunidad_internacional N5 comunidad V_R_P P JQ_V_V R JQ V seguir_esforzar E_N5 V_E_N5 seguir abrir abrir_ese esforzar_pr_en R_P E_N5_D internacional pr V_V_R

It is possible to extract association rules from such representation in the same way that for single feature representation. However, there is a combinatorial explosion since, by considering sequences together with all their sub-sequences, we introduce as many artificial association like R_P=> P. This can be avoided if inclusive sequences are eliminated by, for example, only considering sequences of a given length. Different lengths for lemmas and grammatical tags have been experimented.

11.2.3 Sentence Classifier and Evaluation Methodology

Once a set of association rules is extracted from data, building an efficient classifier based on them is not straightforward. Indeed, for a given sentence, often several rules can be applied, leading to different conclusions. For example, consider these two rules:

e1) JQ_V_V R_P_V => SPE (support=0.3 %, confidence=90.9 %)
e2) la N5_D => GEN (support=0.5 %, confidence=90.0 %)

Both can be applied to sentence in Table 11.3 but they lead to opposite classifications. The first one has a higher confidence but the second one has a larger support and, therefore, should be more robust.

To choose among overlapping rules, two strategies have been tried. The first one consisted of the extraction of all the association rules with support larger than 0.05 % and the classification according to the rule with higher confidence. Using this strategy, rule e1 would have been selected to classify the sentence in Table 11.3. The second one consisted of the extraction of all the association rules with support larger than 0.01 % and with a confidence higher than 90 % and the classification according to the rule with maximal support. With this strategy, rule e2) would have been used to classify sentence in Table 11.3.

These approaches will be formalized. This gives rise to an algorithm called ClR (Classification by Rules) and a variant ClR' of it.

Therefore, let us consider a set DR of decision rules. By default, a sentence S is considered as generalist. Then all decision rules that could be applied to this sentence are selected, i.e. all rules such that all the premises (sequences of lemmas or tags) are satisfied by the sentence. This set of rules is denoted by DR(S). If DR(S) is non empty, the subset cDR(S) of its rules having the highest confidence is extracted.

S will be reclassified as specialized only if there is a rule in cDR(S) that infers this category and it has the largest support among rules in cDR(S).

This algorithm can be formalized as follows. It will be named ClR.

Algorithm ClR

Input:

a set **DR** of decision rules inferring GEN or SPE categories
a sentence **S**

Output: a decision **D** among GEN or SPE

Step 0: D:= GEN [*by default S is considered as generalist*].
Step 1: DR(S):={R in DR : R = (p1,...,pn=> C) ; p1,..., pn in **S** } [*select the set of decision rules applying to R*].
Step 3: **If** DR(S) is non-empty, **then**
[*reclassifying S as specialised if there is a rule in DR(S) inferring SPE of maximal confidence and support*]

c:=max{confidence(R): R in DR(S)}
cDR={R in DR(S) : confidence(R) = c}
s:=max{support(R): R in DR(S)}
scDR={R in cDR(S) : support(R) = s}
If there exists (p1,...,pn => SPE) in scDR, **then**
D=SPE
endif
endif
Return D

Using a tree index structure, the complexity of this algorithm is linear over the number of rules. A variant of Step 3 is also experimented by first looking for rules maximizing the support instead of confidence. I.e. If DR(S) is non-empty, its rule having the highest support is used to re-classify S. Therefore Step3 becomes:

Step 3': **If** DR(S) is non-empty, **then**
s:=max{support(R): R in DR(S)}
sDR={R in DR(S) : support(R) = s}
c:=max{confidence(R): R in DR(S)}
csDR={R in cDR(S) : confidence(R) = c}
If there exists (p1,...,pn => SPE) in scDR, **then**

D=SPE
endif
endif
This variant will be named **ClR'**.

This classifier has been evaluated for different sets of rules based on its capacity to differentiate sentences coming from specialized texts from others over the mentioned test corpora (specialized and non-specialized).

For each sample, 90 % of its sentences (specialized and non-specialized) are used for training and the remaining 10 % of them for test, repeating this split over 30 samples at random to avoid overfitting.

In the next experimental section it is reported that most efficient rules are those combining individual lemmas and sequences of 1–3 grammatical tags, which tends to show that grammatical information is appropriate for this task.

11.3 Experiments and Results

The machine learning strategy based on association rules allows the combination of sequences of lexical features (lemmas) and of grammatical features (POS tags). Two kinds of experiments are reported. The first sub-section deals with single features revealing that using rules mixing lemmas and grammatical tags is more efficient than lemmas along. The second sub-section is devoted to sequences of features showing that considering grammatical sequences improves results and pointing out some pure grammatical rules.

11.3.1 Associations Within Single Features

This sub-section deals with combinations of single features. All reported results have being obtained on the sub-corpus in economics. Single feature strategy allows us to obtain an average of 46,148 decision rules per sample. It appears that:

- 60 % of the rules induce category SPE, which means that there are more implicit decision rules among specialized texts than non specialized ones.
- 78 % of the rules include at least one grammatical tag, which shows that this information is significant to distinguish between these two categories.

Table 11.4 gives the list of POS tags that are effectively used in the resulting decision rules. Tags meanings can be found in Table 11.1.

Ten decision rules from the total list are provided here, selected at random (the first five rules classifying as SPE and the last five rules classifying as GEN). The first part shows the elements included in the rule and the figures provide the confidence of the rule.

Table 11.4 Tags included in rules with the percentage of rules using them

POS	% of rules using them
A	17.36
C	12.26
D	17.72
E	6.81
J	6.69
JQ	14.91
N4	12.11
N5	17.88
P	17.77
R	11.26
T	0.17
V	17.20
VC	6.70
X	4.48

Table 11.5 Results of Classifier_1

	Precision	Recall	F-Score
GEN	0.7602	0.8875	0.8190
SPE	0.8671	0.7239	0.7890
Average	0.8137	0.8057	**0.8040**

C N5 hospital (100.0 %)
A comercio libre (100.0 %)
eficiencia N5 el (100.0 %)
N5 P output (100.0 %)
y VC financiero (100.0 %)
C N5 victoria (100.0 %)
a N5 pedir (100.0 %)
artista N5 P (100.0 %)
C P derecha (100.0 %)
casa P E (100.0 %)

These rules show the specific probability of a sentence to be general (GEN) or specialized (SPE), given the set of lemmas and tags contained in it. For example, the first rule indicates that if a sentence contains a conjunction, a common noun and the lemma "hospital", it will be classified as specialized (SPE), being the precision of this rule 100 %.

Our classification system includes the set of all the rules. Thus, the system takes each sentence, searches for the set of rules matching it and selects the rule with the highest confidence. The system is able to indicate if it cannot take a decision. Finally, for a given text under analysis, if more than half of the sentences it contains belong to a given category, the text is considered to belong to such category.

Traditional precision, recall and F-Score measures have been employed, in order to evaluate the results of this system (using the total set of decision rules). This version of the system is called Classifier_1. These results are shown in Table 11.5.

Table 11.6 Results of Clasifier_2

	Precision	Recall	F-Score
GEN	0.7582	0.8959	0.8213
SPE	0.8749	0.7182	0.7889
Average	0.8166	0.8071	**0.8051**

Table 11.7 Tags used in decisions and percentage of decisions using them

POS	% of decisions using each tag
C	4.62
D	3.30
E	1.67
J	1.17
JQ	3.21
N4	2.49
N5	8.71
P	9.63
R	2.9
T	0.11
V	2.05
VC	2.62
X	1.89

A second experiment has been performed. Only the association rules containing at least one grammatical feature (that is, POS tags) have been included in the system. This means a subset of 36,217 rules (78 %). This second version of the system is called Classifier_2. Results obtained by Clasifier_2 are shown in Table 11.6.

The F-score is slightly higher in the second experiment (from 0.8040 to 0.8050). These results indicate that the classifier's performance is not degraded significantly if rules only based on lemmas are eliminated. This shows that classifier performance mostly relies on rules with tags. Table 11.7 gives, for each tag, the percentage of decisions that used them.

11.3.2 Associations Within Sequences of Features

This sub-section deals with combinations of sequences of features. All the reported results have been obtained both over the entire specialized corpus and the economics sub-corpus.

Classifiers using different lengths of sequences of lemmas and grammatical tags (POS) have been experimented. Table 11.8 shows for each approach on the sub-corpus about economics the following information:

- the average total number of association rules among features,
- the average number of these rules being decision rules (they infer one of the categories SPE or GEN),
- the F-score for the SPE category reached by the classifier using them.

Table 11.8 Experiments on the economics corpus with sequences of features

Sequence length for:		Total number of rules	Number of decision rules	F-score for category SPE (%)
Lemmas	POS tags			
[1..3]	[1..3]	61,289,664	79,573	82.01
[1..2]	[1..2]	11,829,999	46,460	79.24
[1..3]	0	267,659	28,847	77.87
0	3	14,812	7,635	33.56

Results obtained using the RIC algorithm

The F-score on SPE category is only reported here since the RIC algorithm is used, which considers GEN category as default. Therefore, the F-score for the GEN category based on the RIC classifier is correlated to the F-score of the SPE category.

All the experiments are carried out using the same parameters: (i) support threshold = 0.05 %, (ii) confidence threshold = 80 % and (iii) maximal length of association rules = 4. By considering both sequences of lemmas and grammatical tags, the F-score over the SPE category is improved from 78.90 to 82.01 %, as reported in Table 11.5, above, while this F-score drops if one of the two types of sequences (lemmas or POStags) is omitted. Better results are achieved when longer sequences are considered, but the total number of association rules from which decision rules are extracted is 120 times higher.

This is the main drawback of considering all possible sequences and sub-sequences; a huge set of artificial dependences is generated between each sequence and all its sub-sequences. However, this redundancy also allows finding automatically the best compromise between rules maximizing precision using long sequences and those rules maximising support using more frequent features. It is mainly a space size optimization issue; more advanced data mining approaches based on Boolean Analysis or Rough Sets could compute the target decision rules without requiring the parsing of all possible association rules. However, the average RAM size of actual computers (4Go) make possible to store easily such amount of rules and thus to apply standard general libraries on association rules to compute specific decision rules.

Now the complete specialized corpus is considered. Samples of 9,000 sentences are still considered, but not necessarily from economics. The average vocabulary size of these samples is more than ten times wider. Rules based on vocabulary have smaller support, frequencies of triples or pairs of lemmas have very low support, thus leaving room for the emergence of grammatical rules.

Main results are reported in Table 11.9 for both algorithms: RIC favoring rules with high confidence and its variant RIC' favoring rules with larger support.

The best scores have been obtained by using uni-lemmas[4] and sequences of less than three grammatical tags. It appears that frequency distribution of triples of grammatical tags is similar to lemma distribution. By definition, association rules tend to use most specific features, therefore too specific vocabulary can hide

[4] An n-lemma is a subsequence of n lemmas from a given text sequence.

Table 11.9 Experiments on the complete corpus with sequences of features

Sequence length for:		Total number	Number	F-score for category SPE	
Lemmas	POS tags	of rules	of decision rules	RIC (%)	RIC'(%)
[1..3]	[1..3]	38,731,548	180,176	76.75	77.33
[1]	[1..3]	15,389,678	174,175	83.10	82.79
[1..3]	0	212,029	11,009	73.00	78.66

Results obtained using the RIC algorithm

Table 11.10 Pure grammatical rules used by RIC over the best experiment to predict category SPE

Feature 1	Feature 2	Feature 3
A	D_P_J	V_D_D
A	N5_D_D	V_P_E
C_A_N5	JQ_C_A	A_N5_C
C_A_N5	N4_N5_D	A_N5_JQ
D_D_D	A_N5_JQ	N5_P_V
D_V_JQ	J	N5_P_N5
D_V_V	JQ	D_C_D
D_X_D	X_D_V	N5_JQ_D
JQ_D_A	P_A_N5	P_JQ_N5
N5_JQ_C	C_V_A	N5_P_N5
N5_JQ_P	A_N5_P	C_JQ_D
P_N5_JQ	N5_JQ_JQ	N4
V_A_N5	N5_JQ_JQ	D_A_N5

rules involving more general features as grammatical tags. Similarly, sequences of lemmas will be much more specific than grammatical ones. In the present experiment, by combining uni-lemmas with sequences of POS tags, the total number of association rules is reduced without losing a significant number of decision rules.

It clearly appears that by considering sequences of grammatical tags as sentence features, the F-score for the SPE category on the complete corpus is significantly improved. This shows that grammatical structures are useful to detect sentences from specialized texts. Moreover, it is interesting to note that RIC' variant is more efficient than RIC on sets of association rules with triples of lemmas as features, but not when this kind of rules have been excluded. Again, this is due to the fact that rules with such specific features have very low support and thus they are not used by the RIC' algorithm, unless there is no other rule available. In other words, RIC' variant filters out these too specific rules.

To have an idea about the decision rules used by the best classifier, Appendix II contains the top 100 most frequently used decision rules by the RIC algorithm in the best experiment to predict the specialized category.

The rule precision is high (over 90 %). 62 % of these rules use sequences of grammatical tags. 14 % do not use any lemma and are pure grammatical rules. The ten most frequent rules combine three features, as it is shown in Table 11.10.

11.4 Conclusions

The end purpose of this paper was to show that it is feasible to differentiate specialized texts from non-specialized texts written in Latin languages by using not only the lexicon but also some grammatical features. This task has been proposed in the past by several researchers but their results has been limited: (i) usually they have considered only a very limited number of features and (ii) their proposals has been explored over scarce number of texts, manually analyzed.

Our proposal is a tool that can be easily and systematically applied to any number of texts. Such tool has been developed by using machine learning techniques using association rules based on lexical and grammatical features. The resulting classifier appears to be robust since it only use high level features. The learning process relying on random samples makes possible to apply it on the fly over textual streams. A main characteristic of this tool is that it computes such association rules by mixing vocabulary and linguistic features at sentence level. Complete documents can be classified using contextual information about their structure or statistical information about their specific vocabulary. Therefore, the proposed application not only allows classifying texts, it also allows looking for technical statements inside non specialized documents or vice versa (non technical statement in technical texts).

Other strategies could be used. Indeed, one advantage in using a classifier based on decision rules is that it can point out when it doesn't find any clue to classify a sentence. This happens when it has to classify a new sentence for which no learned rule can be applied. In that case instead of considering such sentence as generalist, it could be classified in a third extra class for "unknown" sentences. If later on, more rules are learned and added, some "unknown sentences" could be re-classified. This would be specially appropriated in an interactive context were experts users could classify or re-classify sentences.

Two kinds of experiments are reported. The first, based on single features, reveals that using rules mixing lemmas and grammatical tags is more efficient than lemmas alone. The second experiment is devoted to sequences of features showing that considering grammatical sequences improves results and pointing out some pure grammatical rules. The best scores have been obtained by using uni-lemmas and sequences of less than three grammatical tags.

In this application GEN (for general or non specialised texts) is chosen as default decision, but other strategies could be used. In particular, Hidden Markov Models (HMM) (Manning and Schütze 1999) and Probabilistic Models (El-Bèze et al. 2007) could be used, which would be a complementary approach. HMM are based on short sequences of tokens, while decision rules are based on small bags of tokens. This enhancement will be considered in the future.

The results of this research could be considered as a new perspective to investigate about subjects like terminology, specialized discourse and Natural Language Processing tasks. Some examples would be the optimization of search engines, the automatic summarization of specialized documents and the automatic building of Languages for Specific Purposes corpora.

As future work, more experiments will be carried out, employing new and bigger corpora, and working in different domains, as for example medicine, law and computer sciences. Further experiments will be conducted using other corpora in languages other than Latin ones. Moreover, further work is planned to evaluate if using more complex structures mixing lemmas and grammatical tags would make results improve even more.

Acknowledgments This work has been partially financed by the Spanish projects RICOTERM 4 (FFI2010-21365-C03-01) and APLE 2 (FFI2012-37260), and a Juan de la Cierva grant (JCI-2011-09665).

Appendix I. Examples of Plain Text Passages and Their Corresponding Representation

---

SENTENCE: Muchos países en desarrollo se han quedado rezagados en lo que respecta a la apertura al comercio mundial y no toman las medidas del caso porque perciben ciertos obstáculos al intercambio comercial.

SPE N5_JQ_C A_N5_JQ P_N4 N5_JQ_D P_N5 rezagar R_V_P P_A D_V desarrollo N4_R respectar país intercambio el V_A en mundial N5_R_V JQ_C JQ_D caso P_N4_R N5_JQ quedar V_J porque medida VC_VC V_VC_VC V_P N5_P_A N5_C R_V_VC N5_P N5_R C_D_V = haber A C D E P_N5_R de N4 N5 J J_N5_P C_V_J C_D A_N5_C V_VC VC_VC_P P R que JQ VC_P_N4 V A_N5_P C_V J_N5 percibir D_V_A a apertura V_J_N5 V_P_A mucho cierto A_N5 obstáculo lo V_A_N5 N5_P_N5 comercial VC no tomar JQ_C_D R_V N4_R_V comercio P_A_N5 y N5_C_V VC_P pr

---

SENTENCE: Sin embargo, algunos de estos temores son exagerados.

SPE V_VC_D P_E N4 N5 P_E_N5 P C E_N5_V N5_V D_N4_P D E este ser de sin embargo VC_D V temor N5_V_VC exagerar N4_P_E N4_P = VC D_N4 V_VC E_N5 algún

---

SENTENCE: Por ejemplo, actualmente los aranceles son mucho más bajos que cuando las economías asiáticas de reciente industrialización comenzaron a dar impulso a sus exportaciones en los años sesenta.

SPE A_N5_JQ ser exportación P_A reciente D_A_N5 N5_X_D N5_JQ_P JQ_N5 P_JQ el P_J en E_D_JQ JQ_C N5_D_D V_E N5_JQ P_V bajo por V_P JQ_P E_D N5_P_A V_N5 JQ_P_JQ N5_D N5_P_J arancel ejemplo P_V_N5 N5_V_E N5_P D_JQ_C V_N5_P N5_V N5_X = N5_V_P D_D_A A sesenta C D E impulso de C_A N5 industrialización J C_C D_JQ J_N5_P su más asiático P JQ_N5_V que JQ V P_JQ_N5 X dar J_N5 A_N5_V a A_N5_X C_A_N5 mucho A_N5 año P_J_N5 comenzar economía X_D cuando JQ_C_C D_A C_C_A D_D P_A_N5 V_P_V actual V_E_D

SENTENCE: Algunos obstáculos reales son de índole externa la propagación de las prácticas antidumping, la protección de los productos agrícolas y el Acuerdo Multifibras, que aún está vigente.

SPE N5_JQ_C A_N5_JQ P_N5 N5_JQ_D ser algún N4_D_R D_R V_P_N5 P_A D_V D_A_N5 N5_N5 agrícola el N5_D_A JQ_C N5_JQ_V N5_N5_D JQ_D V_JQ_D N5_JQ real A_N4_D JQ_D_D V_P N5_P_A JQ_V N5_D externo D_R_D V_JQ N5_P protección antidumping = práctica D_D_A A C D D_D_D de N4 C_A N5 producto JQ_V_P P R D_V_JQ que JQ V índole aún propagación A_N5_P P_ N5_JQ C_A_N4 estar R_D A_N4 acuerdo multifibras A_N5 obstáculo vigente R_D_V J Q_C_A A_N5_N5 D_A D_D P_A_N5 y N4_D

SENTENCE: La comunidad internacional debe seguir esforzándose en abrir esos mercados.

SPE mercado R_P A V_V_V JQ_V N5 el P D R_P_V abrir en E P_V V_R_P R V_E_N5 ese pr V_E V_R esforzar deber N5_JQ V = P_V_E JQ_V_V seguir V_V_R V_V internacional comunidad E_N5_D N5_D N5_JQ_V E_N5 JQ

SENTENCE: Por otra parte, el ajuste entraña un costo, y por eso es importante introducir reformas complementarias para controlarlo.

SPE P_N4 ser ajuste introducir D_A_N5 N5_JQ_P N4_V costo el N5_D_A N5_D_C N5_JQ V_J P_N4_V P_V V_N5_JQ controlar por JQ_P V_R D_C_P V_N5 JQ_V para N5_D V_JQ_V entrañar V_JQ ése importante uno N5_V_J reforma N5_V JQ_V_N5 = V_R_D J_N5_D A C D N4 JQ_P_V N5 J P_V_R P R complementario JQ V C_P parte J_N5 A_N5_V V_J_N5 R_D otro A_N5 N4_ N5_D N4_N5 D_A N4_V_JQ D_C C_P_N4 y pr

---

SENTENCE: Muchos países que no se han integrado del todo a la economía mundial dependen de las exportaciones de productos básicos.

SPE V_VC_P A_N5_JQ N5_R_D N5_JQ_D P_N5 exportación D_R VC_P_A P_A país el mundial N5_JQ_V JQ_D N5_JQ integrar V_P básico N5_P_A JQ_V R_V_VC N5_P N5_R = haber A D_R_V D depender E de N5 producto JQ_V_P V_VC P R que JQ V A_N5_P todo P_N5_JQ a V_P_A R_D mucho A_N5 R_D_R economía N5_P_N5 VC no R_V P_A_N5 VC_P pr

---

SENTENCE: Por último, una característica de los países que se han integrado con rapidez es su elevado nivel de inversiones en infraestructura, por ejemplo, producción de energía eléctrica, pavimentación de caminos e instalación de líneas telefónicas.

SPE telefónico V_VC_P N5_JQ_D ser P_N5 D_P P_A N5_C_N5 país N5_R_R JQ_N5 el en energía JQ_D J_JQ_N5 N5_JQ V_J instalación C_N5 N5_D_P por integrar D_P_N5 último JQ_D_E línea N5_P_A N5_C rapidez N5_D_N5 N5_D C_N5_P R_V_VC camino ejemplo N5_P P_N5_C P_N5_D N5_R producción uno N5_V_J nivel N5_V D_N5 = haber A C P_N5_P D elevado E de N5 P_N5_V J JQ_N5_P su V_VC P inversión JQ_D_N5 R D_N5_P que JQ V VC_P_N5 E_N5 pavimentación con A_N5_R R_R_V P_N5_JQ eléctrico característica A_N5 infraestructura J_JQ N5_P_N5 V_J_JQ VC R_R R_V D_E_N5 P_A_N5 D_E y VC_P E_N5_P pr

---

SENTENCE: En el caso de África al sur del Sahara, el elevado costo del transporte de las exportaciones demuestra que la falta de infraestructura apropiada puede ser un impedimento grave para la integración.

SPE poder P_N4 ser P_N5 transporte exportación africa N4_P P_A N4_P_A N5_JQ_P costo JQ_N5 el en N5_JQ_V V_C P_N4_P caso D_A_JQ N5_JQ V_J impedimento J_N5_JQ JQ_P A_N4_D V_C_A apropiado falta N5_P_A V_V JQ_V N5_D para N5_V_C JQ_P_A grave N5_P demostrar uno N5_V sur = A C D elevado de N4 C_A N5 J JQ_N5_P A_N5_D P JQ_V_V que V JQ sahara A_N5_P J_N5 P_N5_JQ A_N5_V a C_A_N5 V_J_N5 A_N4 A_N5 infraestructura N5_P_ N4 N5_P_N5 D_A N4_D_A integración V_V_J P_A_N4 P_A_N5 A_JQ A_JQ_ N5 N4_D

SENTENCE: Países de integración rápida y lenta

SPE lento rápido N5 C P y JQ_C_JQ N5_JQ_C de N5_JQ integración C_JQ JQ_C P_N5_JQ P_N5 JQ país

---

SENTENCE: De hecho, las tres cuartas partes del notable incremento registrado en la última década correspondió tan sólo a diez países.

SPE X_N5_D D_P P_A_JQ A_X VC_P_A P_A país JQ_N5 el N5_D_A en sólo V_D notable tan corresponder P_X hecho último N5_P_A N5_D tres X_E_N5 N5_V_D N5_P N5_VC N5_V = incremento A D E de N5 JQ_N5_VC D_D_P P JQ_N5_V V_D_D D_A_X V JQ E_N5 parte X cuarto X_N5 a A_X_E N5_VC_P P_X_N5 D_P_X X_E diez VC D_A década D_D A_JQ A_JQ_N5 VC_P E_N5_P registrar

---

Appendix II. Most Frequently Used Decision Rules by RIC Over the Best Experiment to Predict Category SPE

Rule	Precision (%)
A comercio libre	100.0
A D eficiente	100.0
A D_P_J V_D_D	100.0
A mediterráneo el	100.0
A N5_D_D V_P_E	100.0
A solución P_A_N5	93.8
A_JQ_N5 país N5_P_A	100.0
aumentar P_N5_D	100.0

(continued)

(continued)

Rule	Precision (%)
A_N4_D JQ ue	100.0
A_N5_D a JQ_V_P	93.3
A_N5_D comercio V	100.0
A_N5_D D activo	100.0
A_N5_D trabajador JQ	100.0
A_N5_R A_N5_P país	100.0
a X relación	100.0
C mayor P_N5_D	100.0
C N5 hospital	100.0
comercial D_A_N5 V	100.0
comercio el N5_P_A	100.0
creación	90.0
C_A_N5 JQ_C_A A_N5_C	100.0
C_A_N5 N4_N5_D A_N5_JQ	100.0
de A_N5_JQ marco	100.0
de función	100.0
desarrollo el país	100.0
diferencia N5_P_N5 V	100.0
= distinto N5_P_A	100.0
D_D_D A_N5_JQ N5_P_V	90.0
D_V_JQ J N5_P_N5	100.0
D_V_V JQ D_C_D	100.0
D_X_D X_D_V N5_JQ_D	100.0
éste C N5_P_N5	100.0
éste VC con	100.0
efecto N5_JQ_D	100.0
eficiencia N5 el	100.0
en desarrollo N5_JQ_D	100.0
en resultado este	100.0
estimación P pr	100.0
= ineficiencia	100.0
intercambio	100.0
J de consecuencia	93.8
J el libre	100.0
JQ región E	100.0
JQ_D_A P_A_N5 P_JQ_N5	100.0
mayor N5_P_N5 N5_JQ_D	100.0
medio num P_N5_D	100.0
N5 cooperación	100.0
N5 integración	100.0
N5 P output	100.0
N5 P ptas.	100.0
N5 tratar D_P_N5	100.0
N5_JQ_C C_V_A N5_P_N5	100.0
N5_JQ_D JQ_P_A mercado	100.0

(continued)

(continued)

Rule	Precision (%)
N5_JQ_D JQ_P_A política	100.0
N5_JQ_P A_N5_P C_JQ_D	100.0
N5_JQ_P estimación D	100.0
N5_JQ_V D_X_D el	100.0
N5_V_D P país	100.0
necesidad C N5_JQ_D	90.0
país JQ_D_V	100.0
P el argentaria	100.0
por conferencia V	100.0
= práctica	92.3
pr muestra	100.0
P_A_N5 A_N5_C económico	100.0
P_A_N5 A_N5_JQ asociación	100.0
P_A_N5 desarrollo N5_JQ_D	96.2
P_A_N5 D_A_N5 política	100.0
P_A_N5 N5_P_N5 hospital	100.0
P_N5_JQ D nivel	100.0
P_N5_JQ N5_JQ_JQ N4	100.0
que JQ ue	100.0
que país JQ_C_JQ	100.0
relativo A_N5_P	100.0
R N5_P_N5 coste	100.0
ser cada P_J_N5	93.3
ser éste N5_JQ_P	100.0
ser éste VC	100.0
ser N5_JQ_V JQ_V_P	100.0
socio=C	100.0
tal más JQ	100.0
uno gran N5_R_V	90.0
uno plazo N5_P_A	100.0
utilizar de N5_JQ_D	100.0
variable N5	100.0
VC comercio N5_P_N5	100.0
V_A_N5 N5 comercial	100.0
V_A_N5 N5_JQ_JQ D_A_N5	100.0
V_A_N5 paz P_A_N5	92.3
V_A_N5 P_A_N5 estados	100.0
V_P_A E relación	100.0
W D =	100.0
X desarrollo JQ_P_A	100.0
y VC financiero	100.0

References

Amir, A., Y. Aumann, R. Feldman, and M. Fresko. 2005. Maximal association rules: A tool for mining associations in text. *Journal of Intelligent Information Systems* 5(3): 333–345.

Borgelt, C., and R. Kruse. 2002. Induction of association rules: Apriori Implementation. In *Proceedings of the 15th conference on computational statistics* (Compstat 2002, Berlin, Germany). Heidelberg: Physika Verlag.

Cabré, M.T. 1999. *La terminología. Representación y comunicación*. Barcelona: IULA-UPF.

Cabré, M.T. 2007. Constituir un corpus de textos de especialidad: condiciones y posibilidades. In *Les corpus en linguistique et en traductologie*, ed. M. Ballard and C. Pineira-Tresmontant, 89–106. Arras: Artois Presses Université.

Cabré, M.T., C. Bach, I. da Cunha, A. Morales, and J. Vivaldi. 2010. Comparación de algunas características lingüísticas del discurso especializado frente al discurso general: el caso del discurso económico. In *Proceedings of the XXVII AESLA international conference: Ways and modes of human communication*(AESLA 2009), 453–460. Ciudad Real: Universidad de Castilla-La Mancha.

Cabré, M.T., I. da Cunha, E. SanJuan, J.M. Torres-Moreno, and J. Vivaldi. 2011. Automatic specialized vs. non-specialized texts differentiation: A first approach. In *Technological innovation in the teaching and processing of LSPs: Proceedings of TISLID'10*, ed. N. Talaván, E. Martín Monje, and F. Palazón, 301–310. Madrid: Universidad Nacional de Educación a Distancia (UNED).

Cajolet-Laganière, H., and N. Maillet. 1995. Caractérisation des textes techniques québécois. *Présence francophone* 47: 113–147.

Coulon, R. 1972. French as it is written by French sociologists. *Bulletin pédagogique des IUT* 18: 11–25.

da Cunha, I., M.T. Cabré, E. SanJuan, G. Sierra, J.M. Torres-Moreno, and J. Vivaldi. 2011. *Automatic specialized vs. Non-specialized sentence differentiation* (Lecture notes in computer science 6609), 266–276. Berlin: Springer.

El-Bèze, M., J.M. Torres-Moreno, and F. Béchet. 2007. Un duel probabiliste pour départager deux Présidents. *Revue des Nouvelles Technologies de l'Information* E-10: 117–126.

Hoffmann, L. 1976. *Kommunikationsmittel Fachsprache – Eine Einführung*. Berlin: Sammlung Akademie Verlag.

Kocourek, R. 1982. *La langue française de la technique et de la science* (2nd ed., 1991). Wiesbaden: Brandstetter.

Kocourek, R. 1991. *La langue française de la technique et de la science. Vers une linguistique de la langue savante*. Wiesbaden: Oscar Branstetter.

L'Homme, M.C. 1993. *Contribution à l'analyse grammaticale de la langue despécialité : le mode, le temps et la personne du verbe dans quelques textes, scientifiques écrits à vocation pédagogique*. Québec: Université Laval.

L'Homme, M.C. 1995. Formes verbales de temps et texte scientifique. *Le langage et l'homme* 31(2–3): 107–123.

Manning, C., and H. Schütze. 1999. *Foundations of statistical natural language processing*. Cambridge, MA: The MIT Press.

Vivaldi, J. 2009. Corpus and exploitation tool: IULACT and bwanaNet. In *A survey on corpus-based research. Proceedings of the I international conference on corpus linguistics (CICL-09)*, ed. P. Cantos Gómez and A. Sánchez Pérez, 224–239. Murcia: Universidad de Murcia.

Chapter 12
Exploring the Potential of Corpus Use in Translation Training: New Approaches for Incorporating Software in Danish Translation Course Design

Anne Lise Laursen and Ismael Arinas Pellón

12.1 Introduction

Technical knowledge grows exponentially and training specialized translation students within a very limited time requires that they build information processing skills linked to their future job reality: problem-solving strategies, self-directed learning, and team-work (Kastberg 2002). This teaching approach is, according to Kastberg, adaptative in the sense that it allows students to cope with translations selected for educational purposes, as well as with any future subject matter. In other words, there is a shift from teaching contents to teaching processes and methods. The advantage of this approach is that, once learned, these processes and methods can be applied efficiently by the postgraduates across professional translation tasks which were not specifically taught during their master's degree. For example, professional translators may have to work with new electronic textual genres which have emerged after their university period.

The translation master's program at the Faculty of Business and Social Sciences (formerly Aarhus School of Business or ASB) has a long tradition of translation training. From 2008, the new structure for the master's degree has included a language specific version of a common *introductory module* to translation and interpreting. The English, French, German, and Spanish language specializations are introduced to functional translation, personal knowledge management (Schreiber et al. 2004), terminology, interpreting, and translation quality. This introductory module has separate theory and applied classes. In this chapter we describe how the

A.L. Laursen (✉)
Department of Business Communication, Aarhus University, Aarhus, Denmark
e-mail: all@asb.dk

I. Arinas Pellón
Departamento de Lingüística Aplicada a la Ciencia y a la Tecnología, Universidad Politécnica de Madrid, Madrid, Spain
e-mail: ismael.arinas@upm.es

E. Bárcena et al. (eds.), *Languages for Specific Purposes in the Digital Era*, Educational Linguistics 19, DOI 10.1007/978-3-319-02222-2_12,

applied classes of the introductory module for the Spanish translation students have been coordinated with the tasks in the financial translation classes. The students are challenged to combine the use of functional translation strategies and corpus analysis when performing these tasks. The activities in the practical part of the introductory module and the financial translation classes specifically focus on the use of concordancing software for solving tasks related with functional translation, terminology, and translation quality.

When considering the application of software to train translation students, we are essentially taking into consideration the same viewpoint as those instructors who are using programming languages, computer assisted design (CAD) software, or simulation software to train engineering students. We are showing the students a practical application of functional translation theory through the use of some tools of the trade. In this way they can adapt their knowledge to new professional situations.

Although there are many software packs that can be used in translation training, there has been a certain reluctance to take steps towards their full didactic application. According to Bowker and Marshman (2011), "electronic tools for translators and terminologists have often been relegated to a small number of courses within translation programs." Kiraly (2000) argues that it is time to reconsider the conventional approaches in translation training which date back almost half a century. He actually recommends that the efforts to develop *translation competence* should be parallel to the development of a *translator competence* that involves the use of new software tools.

As Johansson (2003) reminds us, quoting Aijmer and Altenberg, the use of bilingual corpora:

- Provides insights that may remain unnoticed when studying only monolingual corpora.
- Increases the understanding of language-specific, typological, and cultural differences through comparison.
- Can be applied to lexicography, language teaching, and translation.

Johansson (2003) indicates that he found significant differences when he compared the distribution of certain verbs in Norwegian original texts with their distribution in texts translated to Norwegian. He attributes these differences to the source text of the translations and stresses the importance of the work with corpora to improve the studies of lexical and grammatical patterns from a contrastive point of view. Laviosa (2003) agrees with Johansson and specifically points to corpus-based research to provide evidence of "language pair- and translation-specific phenomena". Vinay and Dalbernet (1958/1995) and Korzen and Lundquist (2003) have also indicated that there are stylistic differences between language pairs which are not attributable to grammatical or lexical differences, but to predominant choices of structures and lexis among native speakers.

For the experience here described, we opted to introduce the use of comparable genre corpora instead of parallel corpora (Kenny 2007) for two reasons: (a) to avoid using translations influenced by the source text; and (b) to show the students how they can profit from corpus searches to detect stylistic choice differences between

Spanish and Danish. As a good example of the comparable corpora approach, we can mention the GENTT project[1] at the Spanish Universitat Jaume I but Danish is not one of the languages that they include. Our research focuses on a language pair (Danish/Spanish) that has not been studied for translation purposes within the annual report genre.

In the following section, we describe the corpus tools used with our students and the implemented methodology. Then, we present our findings regarding the contrastive use between Spanish and Danish of demonstratives and additive linkers in annual reports. The next section describes how the concordancing tools help the students in the lexicographic translation (applied to annual reports). The last section before the conclusions explains how our students use comparable corpora to assess the quality of their translations with examples from the annual reports corpus.

12.2 Tools and Methods Used

The introductory module of theory and methods consists of five two-hour sessions. In the Spanish department, we devote four of these sessions to teaching the use of a *concordancing software* for translation purposes. Vermeer's *SKOPOS functional translation theory* is the theoretical base for the course as described in Schjoldager (2008), which is the base material for the introductory module in all language departments (English, French, German, and Spanish). Specifically, during these four sessions devoted to teaching the use of concordancing software, we focus on its use for the following four purposes: identification of genre feature differences between Danish and Spanish, extraction of terminology, comparison of the use of terminology between Danish and Spanish, and assessing translation quality.

We have selected the concordancing software *Antconc3.2.1w* (from now on Antconc) because it is easy to use and the students can work with it independently. This software can be downloaded for free from Laurence Anthony's web-site: http://www.antlab.sci.waseda.ac.jp/software.html. Antconc can generate concordances (Key Word In Context or KWIC) and sorts the KWIC results. It can produce *n-grams* for one specific word or words. Antconc can yield the n-grams for the whole corpus according to minimum and maximum cluster length criteria. This software analyses statistically the collocations for specific words. It also generates a word list for the whole corpus and, with a reference corpus available, Antconc extracts keyword lists from the corpus under study.

To work with Antconc, we compiled six corpora of specialized language genres: a corpus of informed consents in Spanish, a corpus of Spanish company by-laws, a corpus of Spanish patient information leaflets, a corpus of Spanish purchase agreements, and two comparable corpora of annual report notes (one in Danish and one in Spanish). By comparable corpora (Teubert 1996), we mean that none of them are translations and are similar in terms of contents and length.

[1] http://www.gentt.uji.es/

Table 12.1 Data for the compiled Spanish reference corpus

	Spanish reference corpus
Number of tokens	4,080,101
Number of types	135,206
Type/token ratio	3.31 %
Number of documents	999

We also compiled a reference corpus of approximately four million tokens. This reference corpus includes the following types of Spanish texts from the twentieth and twenty-first centuries: e-mails, brochures, letters from the public administration, laws, newspaper articles, trade union bulletins, novels, press releases, cooking recipes, web sites, tender offers, blog articles, book reviews, telephone and internet service contracts, tales, readme files, jokes, and regulations. Our reference corpus was used to teach the students how to extract terms from the specialized genre corpora using Antconc's *Keyword* function in combination with the *clusters function.* Table 12.1 displays the essential characteristics of the Spanish reference corpus that we have compiled.

This general corpus was compiled to provide the students with a reference corpus that should be both large enough to perform the terminology extraction tasks and freely available to all students. Of course this corpus has several limitations: (a) its size is far from the 160 million words of the Corpus de Referencia del Español Actual (CREA) compiled by the Spanish Real Academia[2] or the 100 million words of Mark Davis' *Corpus del Español*[3]; and (b) its contents are not organized according to any proportional use in everyday communication. Nevertheless, our reference corpus serves well the purpose of providing a standard against which to compare the smaller genre corpora (Rayson and Garside 2000) because it is freely accessible to the students and large enough to show our students the basics of corpus use for term extraction. Sinclair (2005) and Reppen (2010) agree that general corpora have to be large. Sinclair (2005) sets some common criteria to build a corpus regardless of its size and that can be summarized as follows:

- Decide whether the corpus texts will be spoken, written, or electronic (in our general reference corpus they are written and electronic);
- Decide the type of texts (see above for a list of text types selected);
- Decide the domain of the texts (this corpus includes academic and popular domains);
- Decide the language of the corpus (our corpus uses only Spanish);
- Decide the regional variety of the texts (this corpus contains mostly Iberian Spanish samples although there are some Ibero-American texts too);

[2] http://www.rae.es/rae/gestores/gespub000019.nsf/voTodosporId/B104F9F0D0029604C1257164004032BE?OpenDocument&i=1 provides a description of the corpus characteristics in Spanish (Spanish language from the twentieth and twenty-first centuries).

[3] http://www.corpusdelespanol.org/x.asp (Spanish Language from the thirteenth till the twentieth centuries). Neither this corpus, nor the CREA can be downloaded by the students to use them as reference corpora.

Table 12.2 Annual report notes comparable corpora in Spanish and Danish

	Spanish corpus	Danish corpus
Number of tokens	434,144	145,337
Number of types	15,100	10,701
Type/token ratio	3.47 %	7.36 %
Number of documents	14	14

- Decide the date of the texts (our corpus contains exclusively texts from the twentieth and twenty-first centuries);
- Estimate the size so that the lexical items searched are statistically likely to appear.

Nevertheless, Nelson (2010) indicates that very large corpora are more useful for lexicographic purposes than for didactic ones. So the size of the corpus has to be adjusted to its purpose and the use of exemplar texts that match the fluency of the learners is recommended for didactic purposes when teaching them how to use a genre (Nelson 2010). Biber (2010) explains that in the analysis of genre corpora, "the focus is on the linguistic characteristics that are used to structure complete texts." Therefore, the purpose of our general reference corpus is to serve as a standard for the comparison with the smaller genre corpora. These, in their turn, have been compiled to familiarize the learners with the prototypical characteristics of specialized language genres. And as Handford (2010) claims, genre-based corpora can be smaller and still claim to be representative of the genre.

The Spanish specialized corpora are used to link the concept of *functional translation* with the concept of genre (Swales 1990; Bhatia 1993; Trosborg 1997, 2000) and applied by identifying with Antconc generic features, extracting terms, and creating recyclable knowledge maps of genre translations. The Spanish-Danish comparable corpora are used both in the introductory module and the Spanish financial translation courses for a translation quality exercise that involves using Antconc, the comparable corpora, and the translation strategies learned in the financial translation classes to assess and correct samples of former students' translations of annual reports.

In general, the common tools for translation, i.e. dictionaries, lack essential information for the translation of specialized texts. This insufficiency of linguistic and extra-linguistic information can be lessened by resourcing to less traditional tools, for example: genre corpora. Specially compiled genre corpora compare favorably to the Internet in the sense that they provide a focused information search whose results are more relevant for solving the communicative and cognitive problems that emerge in the translation process.

Bernardini and Castagnoli (2008) describe the role of corpora in translation teaching and practice as ideal for the identification of stylistic features, idiosyncrasies, and register and genre conventions. The characteristics of the comparable corpora used for identifying these issues from a cross-linguistic point of view in the Danish-Spanish training sessions are shown in Table 12.2.

It must be taken into account that Danish is more concise than Spanish, so even though both corpora contain the same number of documents, the Spanish one is wordier. To illustrate our work with the students, we will focus here on the work performed with the annual report notes comparable corpora.

A corpus meant for students of specialized translation should be customized to facilitate the search of terminology, collocations, and syntactic patterns within a given domain. As texts within a given domain may vary in terms of style and vocabulary, the ideal choice of texts collected for the corpus should be made as a function of the job the corpus shall fulfill (Bowker and Pearson 2002). Setting the choice of specific genres as the criterion for corpus composition within a given domain allows avoiding homonyms and polysemes not belonging to the domain. At the same time, the users can see the specific moves and linguistic devices that belong to the idiosyncrasy of specific genres. Comparable corpora (Spanish-Danish) will reveal cross-cultural and cross-linguistic differences in moves, linguistic devices, genre-restricted phraseology and terminology.

Antconc is a tool that successfully exemplifies the general features of corpus analysis software. The students are shown how to obtain concordances from corpora; how to obtain clusters and collocates; how to make word lists and keyword lists; and how to use *regular expressions* for each of the previously mentioned operations. Regular expressions are pattern matching alphanumeric strings that can both provide more efficient corpus queries and compensate some of the limitations of not using a Part-of-Speech (POS) annotated corpus. Just for illustrative purposes, Examples (1) and (2) below show some of the queries that can be performed with regular expressions:

(1) typing in Antconc's query box *famil(y|ies)* or *bec[ao]me* would generate results containing the singular and plural forms of *family* or the present and past forms of *to become*.
(2) typing in Antconc's query box *un(interest|excit)ing* or *retaliat[a-z]* would yield results containing both *uninteresting* and *unexciting* or all the verbal forms of *to retaliate* plus the nouns *retaliation* and *retaliations*, and the adjective *retaliative*.

Regular expressions can be far more sophisticated than what is illustrated by the previous two examples, but with some basic simple combinations, the results can already be very useful for the students[4]. Some disadvantages of regular expressions are related to the possibility of generating concordances with noise – queries which include undesired results – and the loss of some results if the corpus contains some irregular blank spaces between words. The reason for this is that regular expressions search for literal correspondences in the corpus: any extra space due to a mistype would exclude relevant concordances. In Example (2) above, if the students are only interested in the verbal forms, they would need to expand the regular expression to exclude the nouns as is shown in (3):

(3) a query with *retaliat[^onv]* would yield only results containing the string *retaliat* followed by any letter except 'o', 'n', or 'v'.

[4] For basic introductions to the use of regular expressions check the following tutorial: http://www.regular-expressions.info/tutorial.html

This implies that any regular expression has to be double checked before using the concordances that it generates. In fact, regular expressions can become complex and they may lack transparency as Example (4) shows:

(4) *\bthat\W+(?:\w+\W+){1,6}?was\b* would produce concordances of the word *that* and the word *was* at a distance of between 1 and 6 words.

To extract term candidates from the Spanish annual report notes corpus with Antconc's *keyword* function, the students first make a word list of this corpus and then load the reference corpus. Antconc offers two statistical measures to detect keywords in a corpus: the *Chi-squared test* and the *Log-likelihood test*. Rayson and Garside (2000) and Rayson et al. (2004) recommend the log-likelihood test on the grounds that it accounts better for the fact that word-types do not appear in a normal distribution across different texts in a corpus. The log-likelihood test first makes a word list of the reference corpus. This reference word list provides an expected standard frequency for each word. This expected frequency is first compared to the observed frequency in the whole analyzed corpus and then individually for each of the documents contained in the corpus. Those words that are far more frequent in the analyzed corpus that what is expected are selected as positive keywords. Those words which are far less frequent than expected are selected as negative keywords. From this keyword list, the students can manually select one-word terms.

To find multi-word terms, Antconc's *clusters-function* detects unexpectedly frequent co-occurrences to the right and left of the terms searched. Once again, the students can select manually from among these frequent co-occurrences those which are multi-word terms. Let us illustrate this with one example from the annual report notes corpus. The first ten keywords provided by Antconc after analyzing the corpus are (in order of keyness): *A, S, Grupo, Euros, El, miles, activos, La, ejercicio, valor*. The first two correspond to the acronym of *Sociedad Anónima* (*S.A.*) which is translated into English either by *Inc.* or *plc*. A promising starting point could be the word *valor* (value) as it is in singular and seems itself as a word that can be combined with others to provide several multi-word term candidates. Performing a search with this word using the clusters function provides the following list of multi-word term candidates (limiting the frequency to a minimum of 25 and setting the size of the cluster between two and five elements):

Valor razonable (697 occurrences)	[= *fair value*]
Valor neto (128 occurrences)	[= *net value*]
Valor actual (79 occurrences)	[= *present value*]
Deterioro de valor (71 occurrences)	[= *depreciation*]
Valor nominal (66 occurrences)	[= *nominal value*]
Valor en libros (62 occurrences)	[= *book value*]
Valor de mercado (60 occurrences)	[= *market value*]
Valor contable (59 occurrences)	[= *book value*]
Valor neto contable (39 occurrences)	[= *net book value*]
Valor en uso (33 occurrences)	[= *value in use*]
Valor recuperable (31 occurrences)	[= *recoverable amount*]
Valor neto realizable (28 occurrences)	[= *net realization value*]

In fact, on a closer look, the above candidates prove to be terms belonging to the specific genre of annual accounts or terms originating from the adjacent financial genres. The final task for the terminology session consists in extracting terms from one of the corpora and then creating a dictionary entry according to the template shown below in the *applied lexicographic approach* section.

Once the students have learned the basics of regular expressions for their searches, identified some stylistic features using a corpus, and extracted term candidates from a genre corpus, they have compiled enough information to build a knowledge map. Knowledge mapping has been defined by Ditlevsen and Kastberg (2009) as a graphical technique to visualize structured information that points to the sources of that information. In other words, this technique maps what the students have learned by representing graphically the links to the sources of their knowledge. These maps evolve in density and structure as the students get more translation experience. An example of such a map can be seen on http://www.intralinea.it/uploads/specialised/Ditlevsen_Kastberg_appendices.pdf (page 6). For this mapping task the students used the *open source* software IHMC CmapTools[5] whose electronic maps can be shared on-line and may contain links to websites, e-mail addresses, and files. Most of the students created a knowledge map for the translation of annual reports so they could use it for their class exercises. Their knowledge maps included people who could help them with the understanding of the genre (e-mails, phone numbers); links to folders containing their corpora; links to files of corrected exercises; grammars and dictionaries; reference books; links to legislation and regulations referring to the contents of annual reports; and links to files containing the use of regular expressions for queries on Antconc.

In parallel with the introduction of software and corpora, we tested the tools in the first semester module of financial translation. Our intention was to use the authenticity of the comparable corpora to highlight certain contrastive features between Danish and Spanish as well as specific terminological and lexicographic aspects involved in translations within this domain.

12.3 Stylistic Contrasts Between Spanish and Danish

Contrastive features have for many years been illustrated by examples and by comparing one pair of languages, typically involving English, and furthermore without no genre-specific focus. The seven methods or strategies of translation developed by Vinay and Darbelnet (1958/1995) constitute an (implicit) evidence for the existence of certain contrastive features between the specific language pair rather than a taxonomy of contrasts. One type of contrastive feature, however, can be generalized, namely the predominance of French nouns compared to English, which can be

[5] http://cmap.ihmc.us

observed at different structural levels. Scholars at the Copenhagen Business School have set up a theoretical framework based on text corpora compiled from several European languages, within which contrastive features of the Germanic and Romance languages can be described (2003; Korzen 2005). The specific empirical research with focus on Scandinavian and Romance languages points to the same preference for verbal versus nominal style in the two language families, which affects the sentence as well as the textual structure.

Another stylistic contrast between members of the two language families are observed by López Ciruela (2003) and Alcaraz Varó and Hughes (2002), who point to a difference between English and Spanish when it comes to the realization of anaphoric relations. According to their observations, Spanish texts are characterized by expressing anaphors in terms of lexical variation while English anaphors are typically expressed by lexical reiteration (Alcaraz Varó and Hughes 2002; López Ciruela 2003). Alcaraz Varó and Hughes (2002) show an example of what they call "stolid repetition" in a fragment of an English legal text on insider trading, which contains successive reiterations of the term within or between sentences (*insider trading* restrictions – prohibiting *insider trading*, etc.). A literal translation would break with Spanish conventions, and a Spanish translator would have to resort to devices like for instance partial synonyms or demonstrative summaries (*said conduct, activities of this kind*, etc.). A similar contrast is found between Spanish and Danish. Here, the use of devices of variation in a Spanish source text would cause confusion or at least be spectacular for a Danish audience if translated literally. By way of example, the conventional Spanish palette of synonyms for the Spanish central bank (i.e. *el Banco de España – el banco emisor – la entidad emisora – la autoridad monetaria – el organismo que dirige Luis María Linde*), which the Spanish audience might meet in one text, would have to be toned down if translated into Danish.

The linking aspect is also briefly commented by Vinay and Darbelnet, who point to asymmetry – again between English and French – in the use of structural markers for signaling logical connections between sentences. French texts tend to explicit connections by means of connectors, while English texts show a tendency towards mere juxtaposition.

Apart from the studies of the Copenhagen scholars mentioned above, contrastive features have for many years been illustrated by examples and by comparing one pair of languages, typically involving English, and furthermore without a genre-specific focus. Until now, there have been no empirical contrastive studies of the language use of Danish and Spanish and therefore we have based our teaching of translation strategies on own observations, being convinced of the possibility to draw parallels to different contrastive studies of two major languages, like for instance those of Vinay and Darbelnet. However, with the electronic corpora it is now possible to demonstrate to what extent these features can actually be observed in authentic texts within specific genres and between the two languages that we are working with.

Table 12.3 Spanish Demonstrative adjective occurrences used as cohesive ties

Masculine singular	Feminine singular	Masculine plural	Feminine plural
ESTE (661)	ESTA (628)	ESTOS (324)	ESTAS (365)
ESE (40)	ESA (26)	ESOS (4)	ESAS (16)
AQUEL (4)	AQUELLA (5)	AQUELLOS (101)	AQUELLAS (73)
2247 demonstratives: 0,517 %			

Table 12.4 Danish demonstrative adjective/pronoun occurrences used as cohesive ties

Dual	Neutral	Plural
DENNE (89)	DETTE (71)	DISSE (150)
310 demonstratives: 0,213 %		

In the following paragraphs we shall focus especially on the contrastive features mentioned above, i.e. the use of nouns versus verbs and the linking aspects and the extent to which these features can be attested by the genre corpora used in the translation training to support the translation strategies.

In the first place, we have found that due to the high occurrence of technical terms, the note corpora do not specifically reflect the contrast between nominal and verbal style. The high level technical content leaves relatively little opportunity for making paradigmatic choices between verbs and nouns, as opposed to other subgenres within the financial domain, for instance market reports.

However, in our note corpora we have found attestation for various facets connected to this preference for noun phrases in Spanish which in fact combine the two contrastive features, i.e. the preference for nouns, and the tendency of marked linking.

For one part, we have found that the structure *demonstrative article plus noun* is a recurrent feature in the Spanish texts and is used to a much larger extent as a cohesive device than in the Danish comparable texts. This can immediately be attested by a mere count of the demonstrative items in the two corpora. The findings in the Spanish corpus are shown in Table 12.3.

The findings in the Danish corpus are shown in Table 12.4.

In the second place, the Danish demonstratives are not orthographically marked in terms of functions. A manual count of the Danish neutral *dette* in the Danish corpus shows that only 25 % of the occurrences are accompanied by a noun. So the distribution of this salient cohesive device is even less pronounced in the Danish corpus than it appears at first sight. A few instances from the two corpora show that, in fact, it is rather difficult to find matches of this anaphoric device, which is shown in Table 12.5.

The salient Danish anaphoric device or the conventional pattern in this connection seems to be the demonstrative pronoun *this* (i.e. not accompanied by a noun).

Table 12.5 Compared deictic references between Spanish and Danish corpora

Este importe (20 out of 1627 occurrences) 1.22 % [=This amount]	Dette beløb (1 out of 283 occurrences) 0.35 % [=This amount]
Este tipo de + noun (23 out of 1023 occurrences) 2,24 % [= This type of ...]	Denne type/denne slags + noun (0) 0 % [= This type of ...]
Este ejercicio (19 out of 2053 occurrences) 0.92 % [= This fiscal year]	Dette regnskabsår (0 out of 178 occurrences) 0 % [= This fiscal year]
Esta modificación/estas modificaciones (84 out of 318 occurrences) 26.41 % [= This change/these changes]	Denne ændring/disse ændringer (4 out of 517 occurrences) 0.77 % [= This change/these changes]
Esta interpretación (43 out of 77 occurrences) 55.84 % [= This interpretation]	Denne fortolkning (1 out of 95 occurrences) 1.05 % [= This interpretation]
Esta norma (32 out of 95 occurrences) 33.68 % [= This standard]	Denne standard (0 out of 25 occurrences) 0 % [= This standard]

Table 12.6 Typical cohesion in a comparable Spanish and Danish sentence found in note corpora

S1: El Grupo aplicará también la NIIF 1 (modificada) desde el 1 de enero de 2009 ...	S1:I henhold til den nye standard skal der ikke længere præsenteres oplysninger for geografiske segmenter
S2: Esta modificación no tendrá ningún efecto en los estados financieros del Grupo	S2: Dette medfører ændret præsentation af segmentoplysninger fra og med 2009 ...
[=The Group applies also the IFRS 1 (changed) from 1th January 2009. This change will not have any effect on the financial statements of the Group]	[=According to the new standard, there shall no longer be presented information on geographical segments... This involves changes of the presentation of segment information...]

This also tends to be the case in the comparable note corpora, here exemplified by the following comparable examples from the corpora: (Table 12.6).

Finally, the corpus data concerning the logical linking between sentences in itself confirms the observations of Vinay and Darbelnet when it comes the subcategory of additives. As we see it, this subcategory is the most likely to be subject to choices between implicit and explicit linking. As it appears in Table 12.7, the additives found in the Spanish note corpus likewise make frequent use of nouns or noun phrases in additives:

Table 12.7 Spanish additives including noun phrases

Additives	
En este sentido (33) (7.6 per 10^5 tokens) [=in this sense/connection]	Por otra parte (37) (8,52 per 10^5 tokens) [= besides]
En este contexto (2) (0.46 per 10^5 tokens) [= in this context/connection]	Por su parte (28) (6.44 per 10^5 tokens) [= for his, her, etc. part]
A este respecto (7) (1.61 per 10^5 tokens) [= in this respect]	Por otro lado (39) (9.0 per 10^5 tokens) [= besides]
Asimismo + así mismo (204) (46,98 per 10^5 tokens) [= likewise]	Además (86) (19.8 per 10^5 tokens) [= furthermore]
Igualmente (29) (6,67 per 10^5 tokens) [= likewise]	De igual forma/de igual modo (3) (0,69 per 10^5 tokens) [= in the same way]
También (155) (35.7 per 10^5 tokens) [= also]	A su vez (22) (5,06 per 10^5 tokens) [= in (his, her, etc.) turn]
Paralelamente (1) (0,23 per 10^5 tokens) [= parallel to ...]	
Number of additives in Spanish corpus: 613 (141,19 per 10^5 tokens)	

Table 12.8 Danish additives

Additives	
I den/denne forbindelse (4) (2,75 per 10^5 tokens) [= in this connection]	Herudover (36) (24,77 per 10^5 tokens) [= apart from this]
Ligeledes (28) (19.26 per 10^5 tokens) [= likewise]	Desuden (20) (13,76 per 10^5 tokens) [= furthermore]
Også (32) (22.01 per 10^5 tokens) [= also]	
Number of additives in Danish corpus: 120 (82,56 per 10^5 tokens)	

The Danish preference for shorter versions of additives, if any, without any NPs, is shown by the corpus findings in Table 12.8.

The normalised numbers above give us a picture of the relative distribution within this genre in terms of occurrences, in terms of variation, and in terms of complexity. It should be noted that the interpretation as Spanish additives – as well as their English translations – in the more controversial cases, such as *por otra parte*, *por otro lado*, and *a su vez*, comes from the Spanish dictionary *Diccionario de partículas discursivas en español* accessed on http://www.dpde.es/

12.4 An Applied Lexicographic Approach

Apart from the demonstration of these textual contrasts, various terminological and lexical issues involved in the different tasks of translation training can benefit from the introduction of software.

In the first place, the comparable corpora can supply the trainees with a range of authentic solutions to their immediate translation problems. In the particular case of company notes, the thematic content is structured by a common international framework and is therefore – to a certain extent – similar although the degree of details might be different. In this way, the linguistic realization of descriptions of e.g. the accountable treatment of assets and income can be contrasted.

Furthermore, in the Spanish language group we work with a lexicographic product, a students' dictionary, initiated in 1996 as part of the dissertation program at the end of the translation studies and subsequently maintained by new groups of trainees as an aspect of their training. The purpose of the project has been two-legged. The intention has been for one part, in view of the lack of adequate Danish-Spanish LSP dictionaries in the market, to compile a dictionary within the field of economics as a tool for future trainees and at the same time, by applying modern lexicographical principles in the dictionary design, turn the trainees into competent future designers of corporate terminological databanks or corporate dictionaries (for a description of the concept of this particular dictionary – see Laursen and Duvå 2005). Currently there are around 3,000 terms (until now mainly focused on stock exchange terminology) and recently we have managed to convert it into an electronic version that can be accessed from the web at http://børsordbog.asb.dk/. In this context, the authentic data from the comparable corpora serve as an ideal supplement. Again, the initial steps to the software have been taken in the introductory module. Here, on the basis of the term extraction processed by AntConc, the trainees have been taught to make their own dictionary articles according to the theory of lexicographic functions (e.g. Tarp 2004). The specific focus on the accounting domain has then been taken care of in the financial translation classes, where it has seemed logical to record as much of the genre-specific more or less subtle features captured along the line or in the translation process in favor of future translations.

It should be added that, apart from the list of terms and equivalents, the concept includes a number of collocations and extended definitions or explanatory notes designed for translators. For the young translation trainee, there are no previous schemata to be invoked when meeting with the subject matters of the LSP texts. The extended definition inserted as an information category is inspired by Temmerman's (2000) idea of building up templates of information in order to structure the relevant explanations or additions according to the nature of the term to be defined and in this way open up for a sufficient use-value for the intended type of user, *in casu* the translation trainees. A description of the particular design of the template of information related to the genre of annual accounts can be found in Laursen 2010. By using the dictionary as a tool on a daily basis, it can assist the trainees in building up their schemata of the domain in question or in other words supply their world knowledge with both lexical and cognitive elements from the domain. Classroom discussions as to how much the explanation should include can – combined with raw data from the corpora – generate dictionary entries like the one on the term *afskrivning* [= *depreciation*] shown in Example (5) that includes corpus-based data:

(5) ***afskrivning***

amortización

Afskrivning af et aktiv betyder, at anskaffelsesprisen udgiftsføres over en årrække. Dette sker systematisk, således at der fratrækkes en bestemt procentdel af anskaffelsesværdien hvert år. Afskrivningen afspejler normalt den værdiforringelse, der sker ved brug af aktivet, og det antal år, afskrivningen fordeles over afspejler aktivets formodede levetid, for maskiner og andre anlægsaktiver typisk 20 år.

[= A depreciation of an asset means that the cost of the asset is recognized as an expense in the income statement over a number of years. This is done systematically by means of deducting a certain percentage of the cost every year. The depreciation reflects the decrease in value during the expected useful life of the asset – typically 20 years for machines and other tangible assets]

afskrivning over forventet levetid	*amortización en base a la vida útil estimada*
foretage afskrivning af et aktiv	*proceder a la amortización de un activo*
foretage afskrivning af et aktiv	*realizar la amortización de un activo*

→ afskrive
→ nedskrivning

The obvious advantages of corpus-based lexicography compared to the traditional method of introspection is described by Hunston, who emphasizes the elements of value added in terms of attestation of frequency, collocations/phraseology, variation and authenticity (Hunston 2002). These elements are of utmost importance for LSP translation from a genre perspective, and the genre corpora have proven their value in this context.

Finally, according to our experience, the note corpora can be used successfully as a benchmark when taking a critical view on existing dictionaries and parallel texts. The implementation of the framework of the International Accounting Standards (IAS) within the EU has implied certain changes in the accounting terminology. New lexical units have been introduced in accounting vocabulary. Some of them originate from basic general vocabulary and are used here with a particular meaning. This is for instance the case of the verbs *measure* and *recognize*, which in this new context mean *evaluate* and *include*, respectively. The young trainees will meet words in the LSP dictionary which they know from their basic everyday vocabulary of the L2, and therefore they will have reasonable doubts about the actual use in this specific genre. Furthermore, the huge amount of EU parallel texts in the area of financial reporting, especially the fourth and seventh Directive, currently used as a terminological resource by the trainees, is not always terminologically consistent with the IAS terminology. Therefore, again, there might be doubts about whether a specific term is used in the real world. We have outlined in Tables 12.9 and 12.10 three dictionary examples and three parallel text examples which illustrate how the corpora can be used in this situation – here in a translation from Danish to Spanish. In Table 12.9, the intervention of the English as relay language is due to the lack of a Danish-Spanish accounting dictionary.

Table 12.9 Checking existing dictionaries against note corpora

Danish ST	Danish-English accounting dictionary	English-Spanish accounting dictionary	Spanish note corpus	Conclusion
'indregne'	Recognize	Reconocer	Search word: 'gastos' Example: "Los gastos de investigación se reconocen como gastos .."	Use of 'reconocer' is correct (Frequent occurrences in corpus)
'måle'	Measure	Medir	Search word: 'coste amortizado' Example: "Los pasivos financieros a vencimiento se valoran por su coste amortizado"	No occurrences of 'medir' in note corpus TL equivalent: 'valorar' (Frequent occurrences in corpus)
'ændring i lagre af færdigvarer'	Changes in inventories of finished goods	Cambios en inventarios de bienes terminados	Search word: 'terminados' Example – accounting item: "variación de existencias de productos terminados"	TL equivalent: 'variación de existencias ...' (Frequent occurrences in corpus)

Table 12.10 Checking parallel text terminology against note corpora

4th Directive – Danish version	Danish note-corpus	4th Directive – Spanish version	Spanish note-corpus
aktiver [= assets]	aktiver	activo	activo
anlægsaktiver [= non-current assets]	anlægsaktiver	activo inmovilizado	activo no corriente
omsætningsaktiver [= current assets]	omsætningsaktiver	activo circulante	activo corriente

12.5 Corpus Assisted Quality Assessment

The last exercise in first semester parallel lectures of the introductory module and the ordinary financial translation module has been a quality assessment of translations on a note made by two trainees from a *pre-corpus* translation class. Table 12.11 shows extracts of the individual comments on errors and the various ways in which the trainees have resorted to the corpora in this exercise:

Table 12.11 Corpus-based assessment: errors and comments

(Checking on use of verbs): måles til dagsværdi på overtagelsestidspunktet: [= recognised at fair value at acquisition date] Verbos utilizado en las traducciones: se miden al valor razonable a la fecha de adquisición se ajustan a los valores razonables según la fecha de adquisición	Hice búsquedas de "se mide+" y "se ajusta+" pero no salió nada utilizable en este contexto. La colocación correcta es "valorarse a/por". La búsqueda "se valora+" resultó en 155 hits de concordancia. Luego busqué la colocación "valor razonable" (regex, Level 1, 3L, sort) y salieron muchas colocaciones buenas: '... las cuales figuran en el activo del balance de situación consolidado <u>valoradas por</u> su valor razonable, ...' '... inmuebles que previamente se encontraban en el inmovilizado material y que fueron <u>valorados a</u> su valor razonable a dicha fecha ...' [= I searched for 'se mide+ and 'se ajuste+ but nothing useful came up in this context. The correct collocation is 'valorarse a/por'. The search for 'se valora+' showed 155 concordance hits. Then I searched for the collocation 'valor razonable' (regex, Level 1, 3L, sort) and there came many useful collocations]
(Checking on use of preposition): hensættelse til [= provisions for] Preposición utilizada en las traducciones: "provisiones a" + sustantivo'	Una búsqueda en Antconc muestra que no existen ejemplos de esta composición 'a'. En cambio, una preposición muy utilizada con provisiones y un sustantivo es "para", por ejemplo "La política seguida respecto a la contabilización de provisiones <u>para</u> riesgos y gastos ..." "Provisiones <u>para</u> pensiones y obligaciones similares ..." [A search in Antconc shows that there are no examples with this composition. In turn, a frequent preposition is 'para', for instance ...]
(Checking on use of term from EU directive): Immaterielle aktiver [= intangible assets] Termino usado en las traducciones: Inmovilizaciones inmateriales	Éste es un término que se utiliza muy poco en comparación con el nuevo término que es inmovilizado intangible. En Antconc inmovilizaciones inmateriales aparece 3 veces e inmovilizado intangible 38 veces. [This is a term which is used very little compared to the new term which is 'inmovilizado intangible'. En Antconc 'inmovilizaciones inmateriales' appears 3 times and 'inmovilizado intangible' 38 times.]

(continued)

Table 12.11 (continued)

(Checking on orthography): Mayúsculas/minúsculas: el grupo vs.el Grupo	En ambos textos han puesto "el grupo" en vez de "el Grupo", pero a ver qué pasa si busco las colocaciones en Antconc. Hago clic sobre las casillas de verificación "Words" y "Case" para que el programa encuentre exactamente lo que le pido que encuentre: El Grupo: 757 El grupo: 62 [In both translations they have used 'el grupo' instead of 'el Grupo' but let's se what is happening when I search collocations in Antconc. I clic at 'Words' and 'Case' in order that the program finds exactly that I am asking it to do.]

Table 12.11 illustrates a variety of strategic opportunities that the trainees have discovered in this new tool in terms of localization and documentation of errors or unidiomatic strings in the revision of translation made by others. As to their own translations, it is possible to trace improvements if we compare the output of first semester translations of strings from the company notes before and after the introduction of the software. In Table 12.12 we have underlined some problematic strings of the 2008 trainees and the more successful strings of the 2009 translation, where the trainees have leant on the Spanish note corpus in terms of syntax, terminology, collocations and genre-specific expressions:

In general, we have experienced a great interest for using the corpora in the daily translation training based on the comparable genre corpora and the skills acquired in the introductory module. Lee and Swales (2006) point to the quality of a genre corpus in language learning. According to interviews with their students, the corpus use seems to be confidence-building and empowering. The students do not have to recur to native speakers' intuitions or grammar books. They even sometimes prefer corpora to grammars or textbooks and they find that the exemplification is closer to their actual needs. When it comes to LSP translation training, similar arguments can be found. Genre corpora are operational because they don't present long lists of concordance lines that can make the students loose overview at first sight. Furthermore, the exemplification of vocabulary and contrastive features is abundant and authentic compared to text books and lecture notes built on the trainers' experience. Likewise, doubts about the terminology of parallel text and dictionaries can be clarified. Or as Beeby et al. remind us: "the teacher is no longer the sole source of information and authority, the only specialist available to the students. Corpus methodology reinforces autonomy and responsibility" (Beeby et al. 2009).

Table 12.12 Before and after-examples of strings of translation of company notes

Source text strings	Translation 2008 trainees (no use of software) Non-idiomatic strings underlined	Translation 2009 trainees (after introduction of software) Idiomatic strings underlined
Materielle anlægsaktiver Grunde og bygninger.... måles til kostpris **[Tangible fixed assets]** *[Land and buildings ... are measured at cost price]*	**Inmovilizaciones corporales** Se miden terrenos y construcciones ... al precio de coste ... **Inmovilizaciones materiales** Terrenos y construcciones ... se contabilizan a su (precio de) coste ... **Activos materiales** Terrenos y construcciones ... se valoran a su coste histórico ...	**Inmovilizado material** Los terrenos y construcciones ... se reconocen por su coste ... **Inmovilizado material** Los terrenos, construcciones ... se valoran por su coste ... **Inmovilizado material** Los terrenos y construcciones ... figuran valorados por su coste ...
Der foretages lineære afskrivninger baseret på følgende vurdering af aktivernes forventede brugstider og restværdi herefter: [*There are made linear depreciations based on the following estimation of the expected life of the assets and the residual value hereafter*:]	Se efectúan amortizaciones, [calculadas] según el método lineal, basándose en la siguiente evaluación de las vidas útiles previstas y el valor residual correspondiente de los bienes. Amortizaciones lineales se realizan basándose en la evaluación siguiente de la vida útil prevista de los bienes y su valor residual tras de esta. Se hacen amortizaciones lineales basadas en la siguiente valoración de la vida útil y el valor residual previstos de los activos después de esto	La amortización se realiza de forma lineal, basada en una estimación de la vida útil y el valor residual previsto, según el siguiente detalle: La amortización se realiza de forma lineal basada en la siguiente estimación de la vida útil de los activos y su valor residual tras este periodo: Se realizan amortizaciones lineales basadas en una estimación de la vida útil y el valor residual previstos, según el siguiente detalle:

12.6 Conclusions

The short time available (four semesters) for the training of specialized translation MA students requires adaptive teaching strategies. One approach to maximize the didactic outcomes under these conditions is to focus the teaching on methods and processes that can be applied successfully to a wide range of translation scenarios. In this chapter, we have combined functional translation strategies, corpus analysis, and genre analysis to increase the learners' autonomy in the field of specialized translation.

Similarly to what is seen in the training of engineers, teaching the use of software tools to future translators serves not only to illustrate how theory applies to translation tasks but also to introduce them to the tools of the trade. We have selected examples of contrastive features that illustrate how Danish and Spanish fulfill the communicative purposes of the same genre through different stylistic choices. More specifically, the students can see that the use of demonstratives and linking expressions presents stylistic differences between Spanish and Danish. The validity of these examples can be easily tested by the students with the use of the corpus and Antconc and they can extrapolate the corpus analysis techniques to other genres that they may encounter in their professional lives.

Regular expressions can compensate some of the information gaps in corpora lacking POS tags, but they must be double-checked to make sure that they are not retrieving unwanted concordances. Probably a selection of useful and checked regular expressions should be included in the course instead of only teaching the fundamentals of their construction.

We have shown how functional lexicography can provide more accurate information through the use of corpus analysis and considering the purpose and speaker-reader relationship in the genre analyzed. We have also presented some examples of how corpus-based dictionaries for specialized translation should be organized.

As a result of this experience we have noticed that the students are using the annual reports notes corpus to carry out their translation quality tasks. They cite in their course papers corpus queries as criterion to decide whether an expression is correct or not.

In short, we find that the integration of comparable corpora is a valuable didactic supplement to translation training and deserves to be further explored.

References

Alcaraz Varó, Enrique, and Brian Hughes. 2002. *Legal translation explained*. Manchester: St. Jerome.

Beeby, Allison, Patricia Rodríguez Inés, and Pilar Sanchez Gijon (eds.). 2009. *Introduction to: Corpus use and translating*. Amsterdam/Philadelphia: John Benjamins, B.V.

Bernardini, Silvia, and Sara Castagnoli. 2008. Corpora for translator education and translation practice. In *Topics in language resources for translation and localisation*, ed. Elia Yuste Rodrigo, 39–55. Amsterdam/Philadelphia: Benjamins.

Bhatia, Vijay. 1993. *Analysing genre: Language use in professional settings*. London: Longman.

Biber, Douglas. 2010. What can a corpus tell us about registers and genres. In *The Routledge handbook of corpus linguistics*, ed. Anne O'Keeffe and Michael McCarthy, 241–254. Abingdon: Routledge.

Bowker, Lynne, and Elizabeth Marshman. 2011. Better integration for better preparation: Bringing terminology and technology more fully into translator training using the CERTT approach. In *Teaching and learning terminology*, ed. Amparo Alcina, 61–88. Amsterdam/Philadelphia: John Benjamins B.V.

Bowker, Lynne, and Jennifer Pearson. 2002. *Working with specialized language. A practical guide to using corpora*. London/New York: Routledge.

Ditlevsen, Marianne G., and Peter Kastberg. 2009. Personal knowledge management. Knowledge mapping techniques in the training of LSP translators. *Intralinea, Special Issue: Specialised Translation*. http://www.intralinea.it/specials/specialised/eng_more.php?id=844_0_45_0. Accessed 14 May 2013.

Handford, Michael. 2010. What can a corpus tell us about specialist genres? In *The Routledge handbook of corpus linguistics*, ed. Anne O'Keeffe and Michael McCarthy, 255–269. Abingdon: Routledge.

Hunston, Susan. 2002. *Corpora in applied linguistics*. Cambridge: Cambridge University Press.

Johansson, Stig. 2003. Contrastive linguistics and corpora. In *Corpus-based approaches to contrastive linguistics and translation studies*, ed. Sylviane Granger, Jacques Lerot, and Stephanie Petch-Tyson, 31–44. Amsterdam: Editions Rodopi B.V.

Kastberg, Peter. 2002. Information and documentation management in the training of technical translators – as opposed to teaching technical science. *LSP & Professional Communication* 2: 57–65.

Kenny, Dorothy. 2007. Translation memories and parallel corpora: Challenges for the translation trainer. In *Across boundaries: International perspectives on translation studies*, ed. Dorothy Kenny and Kyonjoo Ryou, 192–208. Newcastle: Cambridge Scholars Publishing.

Kiraly, Don. 2000. *A social constructivist approach to translator education*. Manchester: St Jerome Publishing.

Korzen, Iorn. 2005. Endocentric and exocentroc languages in translation. *Translation. Perspectives: Studies in Translatology* 13: 21–37. doi:10.1080/0907676050866896l.

Korzen, Iorn, and Lita Lundquist. 2003. *Sprogtypologi og oversættelse: Endocentriske og exocentriske sprog*. Copenhagen: Samfundslitteratur.

Laursen, Anne Lise. 2010. Explanatory notes in LSP dictionaries. *Reconceptualizing LSP*. Online proceedings of the XVII European LSP Symposium 2009. http://www.asb.dk/fileadmin/www.asb.dk/isek/fileexplorer_fetchfile-aspx-file-16801.pdf. Accessed 14 May 2013.

Laursen, Anne Lise, and Grete Duvå. 2005. Cyberlexicography in LSP: New aspects of components and structures in the dictionary. In *Symposium on lexicography XI*, ed. Henrik Gottlieb et al., 337–350. Tübingen: Max Niemeyer Verlag.

Laviosa, Sara. 2003. Corpora and translation studies. In *Corpus-based approaches to contrastive linguistics and translation studies*, ed. Sylviane Granger, Jacques Lerot, and Stephanie Petch-Tyson, 45–54. Amsterdam: Editions Rodopi B.V.

Lee, David, and John Swales. 2006. A corpus-based EAP course for NNS doctoral students: Moving from available specialized corpora to self-compiled corpora. *English for Specific Purposes* 25: 56–75.

López Ciruela, Andrés. 2003. *Una Defensa Crítica de las Memorias de Traducción*. Panace@ Vol. IV, n°. 12: 180–182. http://www.medtrad.org/panacea/PanaceaPDFs/Junio2003.htm. Accessed 14 May 2013.

Nelson, Mike. 2010. Building a written corpus: What are the basics? In *The Routledge handbook of corpus linguistics*, ed. Anne O'Keeffe and Michael McCarthy, 53–65. Abingdon: Routledge.

Rayson, Paul, and Roger Garside. 2000. Comparing corpora using frequency profiling. *WCC'00 proceedings of the workshop on comparing corpora – Volume 9*. http://www.comp.lancs.ac.uk/~paul/publications/rg_acl2000.pdf. Accessed 14 May 2013.

Rayson, Paul, Damon Berridge, and Brian Francis. 2004. Extending the Cochran rule for the comparison of word frequencies. *JADT 2004: 7es Journées Internationales d'Analyse statistique des Données Textuelles*. http://eprints.lancs.ac.uk/12424/1/rbf04_jadt.pdf. Accessed 14 May 2013.

Reppen, Randi. 2010. Building a corpus: What are the key considerations? In *The Routledge handbook of corpus linguistics*, ed. Anne O'Keeffe and Michael McCarthy, 31–37. Abingdon: Routledge.

Schjoldager, Anne. 2008. *Understanding translation*. Aarhus: Academica.

Schreiber, Trine, Karen Harbo, Marianne G. Ditlevsen, and Peter Kastberg. 2004. *Personal knowledge management eller personlig videnstyring – en metode til at udvikle og understøtte den enkeltes informationskompetence*. Århus: Nyhedsbrev Fra Handelshøjskolens Bibliotek I Århus.

Sinclair, John. 2005. Corpus and text – Basic principles. In *Developing linguistic corpora: A guide to good practice*, ed. Martin Wynne, 1–16. Oxford: Oxbow Books.

Swales, John. 1990. *Genre analysis: English in academic and research settings*. New York: Cambridge University Press.

Tarp, Sven. 2004. How can dictionaries assist translators? In *Translation and bilingual dictionaries*, ed. Chan Sin-wai, 23–38. Tubingen: Niemeyer.

Temmerman, Rita. 2000. *Towards new ways of terminology description: The sociocognitive approach*. Amsterdam: John Benjamins.

Teubert, Wolfgang. 1996. Comparable or parallel corpora? *International Journal of Lexicography* 9: 238–264.

Trosborg, Anna (ed.). 1997. *Text typology and translation*. Philadelphia: John Benjamins.

Trosborg, Anna (ed.). 2000. *Analysing professional genres*. Amsterdam: John Benjamins.

Vinay, Jean-Paul, and Jean Darbelnet. 1958/1995. *Comparative stylistics of French and English. A methodology for translation*. Amsterdam/Philadelphia: John Benjamins.

Part IV
Processing Natural Languages

Chapter 13
Representing Environmental Knowledge in EcoLexicon

Pamela Faber, Pilar León-Araúz, and Arianne Reimerink

13.1 Introduction

EcoLexicon[1] is a multilingual terminological knowledge base (TKB) on the environment. The knowledge base was initially implemented in Spanish, English, and German. Currently, four more languages are being added: Modern Greek, Russian, French, and Dutch. So far it has 3,527 concepts and 18,596 terms. It targets different user groups, such as translators, technical writers, environmental experts, etc., who wish to expand their knowledge of the environment for the purpose of text comprehension or generation. These users can freely access EcoLexicon, and are able to find the information needed, thanks to a user-friendly visual interface with different modules for conceptual, linguistic, and graphical data.

Each entry in EcoLexicon provides a wide range of interrelated information. Figure 13.1 shows the entry for GROYNE. Users are not obliged to view all this information at the same time, but can browse through the different windows and resources, depending on their needs.

Under the tag 'Dominios' an ontological structure shows the exact position of the concept in the class hierarchy. For example, GROYNE *is_a* Construction (bottom-left corner of the window). The concept definition is shown when the cursor is placed on the concept. All definitions are formulated according to a category template (Faber et al. 2007) that constrains definitional information.

This research has been funded by project FFI2008-06080-C03-01/FILO, from the Spanish Ministry of Science and Innovation

[1] http://ecolexicon.ugr.es

P. Faber (✉) • P. León-Araúz • A. Reimerink
Departamento de Traducción e interpretación, Universidad de Granada, Granada, Spain
e-mail: pfaber@ugr.es; pleon@ugr.es; arianne@ugr.es

E. Bárcena et al. (eds.), *Languages for Specific Purposes in the Digital Era*, Educational Linguistics 19, DOI 10.1007/978-3-319-02222-2_13,

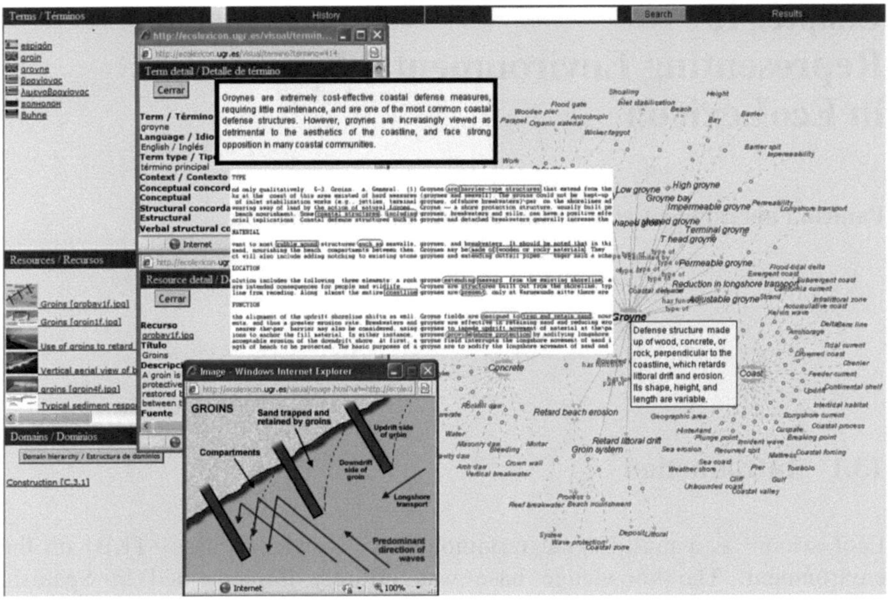

Fig. 13.1 EcoLexicon user interface

The definition for GROYNE, as a physical artificial object or "defense structure made of wood, concrete or rock, perpendicular to the coastline, which retards littoral drift and erosion" is the linguistic expression of conceptual relations such as *is_a* [DEFENSE STRUCTURE], *made_of* [WOOD, CONCRETE, or ROCK], and *has_function* [RETARDS LITTORAL DRIFT AND EROSION]. Contexts (top window with black contour) and concordances (center window) appear when clicking on the terms. They give information to the users on conceptual and linguistic aspects of the specialized knowledge unit. Graphical resources are displayed when clicking on the links in the box 'Recursos' (in the left-hand margin towards the middle). These visual resources have been selected so that the type of image is in direct relation with the conceptual relations activated in the definition (Faber et al. 2007; Faber 2012).

At a more fine-grained level, conceptual relations are displayed in a dynamic network of related concepts (right-hand side of the screen). Users are free to click on any of these concepts and thus further expand their knowledge of this sector of the specialized domain. The terminological units, under the tag 'Términos' provide linguistic information, and show the designations of the concept in English and Spanish: '*groyne*' and its diatopic variant '*groin*', and '*espigón*', respectively (top left-hand corner).

EcoLexicon provides an internally coherent information system, organized according to explicit conceptual and linguistic premises at the macro- as well as micro-structural level. This organization is described in detail in the following sections. Section 13.2 deals with the macrostructure and microstructure of the TKB.

Section 13.3 explains how current trends in cognitive science, such as situated cognition, have inspired the representation of conceptual dynamism in EcoLexicon. Finally, Section 13.4 summarizes the conclusions that can be derived from this research.

13.2 Macrostructure and Microstructure

In EcoLexicon, great care has been taken to create an internally coherent information system with sufficient dynamism and flexibility to represent the multidisciplinary field of the environment and facilitate information retrieval by the end users. At the macrostructural level, the information is organized in a prototypical domain event and stored in a relational database as well as a domain ontology. A closed inventory of conceptual relations makes the microstructure of the resource consistent with its macrostructure. A set of definitional templates based on the prototypical domain event and these conceptual relations constitute a definitional grammar for the creation of the meaning definitions of specialized concepts. Finally, additional information, such as concordances and images are provided to enhance knowledge acquisition.

13.2.1 Macrostructure: The Environmental Event and the Domain Ontology

At the macrostructural level, all knowledge extracted from our multilingual corpus of specialized texts is organized in a frame-like structure or prototypical domain event, namely, the Environmental Event (EE; see Fig. 13.2).

The EE is a basic template applicable to all levels of information structuring. It is conceptualized as a dynamic process that is initiated by an agent (either natural or human). This process affects a specific kind of patient (an environmental entity), and produces a result in a given geographical area. These macro-categories (agent → process → patient/result, and location) are the semantic roles characteristic of this specialized domain, and the EE provides a model to represent their interrelationships at a more specific level.

The data in EcoLexicon are primarily hosted in a relational database (RDB). This type of modeling initially allowed for a rapid deployment of the platform and fed the system in its early stages. Nevertheless, relational modeling has certain limitations. One of the most evident is its limited capacity to represent real-world entities, which makes it impossible to draw inferences about them. This is why ontologies have become so popular. They allow reasoning processes, and are thus a more powerful representational model. In our approach, we emphasize the importance of storing semantic information in the ontology, while leaving the rest in the relational database. In this way, we can use the new ontological system, and at the same time continue feeding the legacy system.

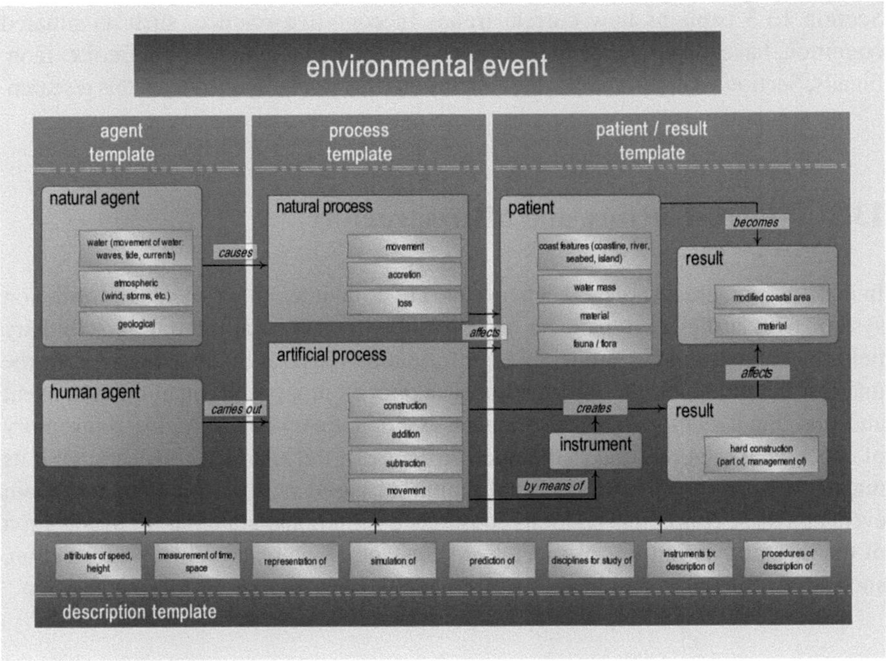

Fig. 13.2 The Environmental Event (EE, Faber et al. 2005, 2006, 2007)

Upper-level classes in our ontology correspond to the basic semantic roles described in the EE (agent-process-patient-result-location). As shown in Fig. 13.3, all classes constitute a general knowledge hierarchy derived from each of them. This structure enables users to gain a better understanding of the complexity of environmental events, which provide a process-oriented general overview of the domain.

These ontological classes are fed with the information stored in the database. This is accomplished with the D2RQ tool, which provides a usage scenario where relational databases are maintained as non-legacy applications (Bizer and Seaborne 2004). D2RQ is a declarative language that describes mappings between both systems. Moreover, these mappings can be conditional, which allows for feeding each class only with its corresponding instances (León Araúz and Magaña Redondo 2010).

Our inventory of conceptual relations (see Sect. 13.2.2), specifically conceived for EcoLexicon, can be enhanced by an additional degree of OWL semantic expressiveness. This expressiveness is provided by property characteristics, such as transitivity and symmetry, and restrictions, such as allValuesfrom and someValuesfrom, which enhance user searches (Smith et al. 2004). As previously mentioned, one of the main advantages of ontologies is that they make reasoning and inferences possible. However, domain ontologies need a set of systematized criteria for conceptual description, because a high degree of generalization jeopardizes accurate inferences.

Fig. 13.3 Ontological classes

Generally speaking, apart from the obvious transitive relation *is_a*, the *part_of* relation could also benefit from transitivity. Nevertheless, this is only possible under certain conditions. It is true that not all parts have the same implications in regard to their wholes and, in certain cases, transitivity may turn out to be misleading. For example, a RIVER HEAD is *part_of* a RIVER and a RIVER is *part_of* the HYDROSPHERE. However, a RIVER HEAD cannot be considered a *part_of* the HYDROSPHERE, since this does not reflect how things are related in the real world.

Consequently, before considering transitivity, partonymy should be divided into subrelations, which only apply to certain types of conceptual classes. More specifically, at least one relation is needed for processes, which are clearly divided into subprocesses (SCREENING < PRELIMINARY TREATMENT < WASTEWATER TREATMENT, SO SCREENING < WASTEWATER TREATMENT), and another relation is needed for physical objects that have clear spatial boundaries, as shown in Fig. 13.4.

In Fig. 13.4, a SPARQL query is made to retrieve the concepts that are *part_of* Concept 3262, which refers to SEWER. On the right side, DRAINAGE SYSTEM is retrieved as a direct *part_of* relation, whereas SEWAGE COLLECTION AND DISPOSAL SYSTEM and SEWAGE DISPOSAL SYSTEM are implicitly inferred with the Jena reasoner.

Thus, terminological resources have found a powerful representational model in ontologies. In turn, the design of ontologies can benefit from linguistic theory, especially from cognitive approaches (León et al. 2009; Faber 2012). Meyer et al. (1992) were among the first terminologists to perceive that term bases would be more

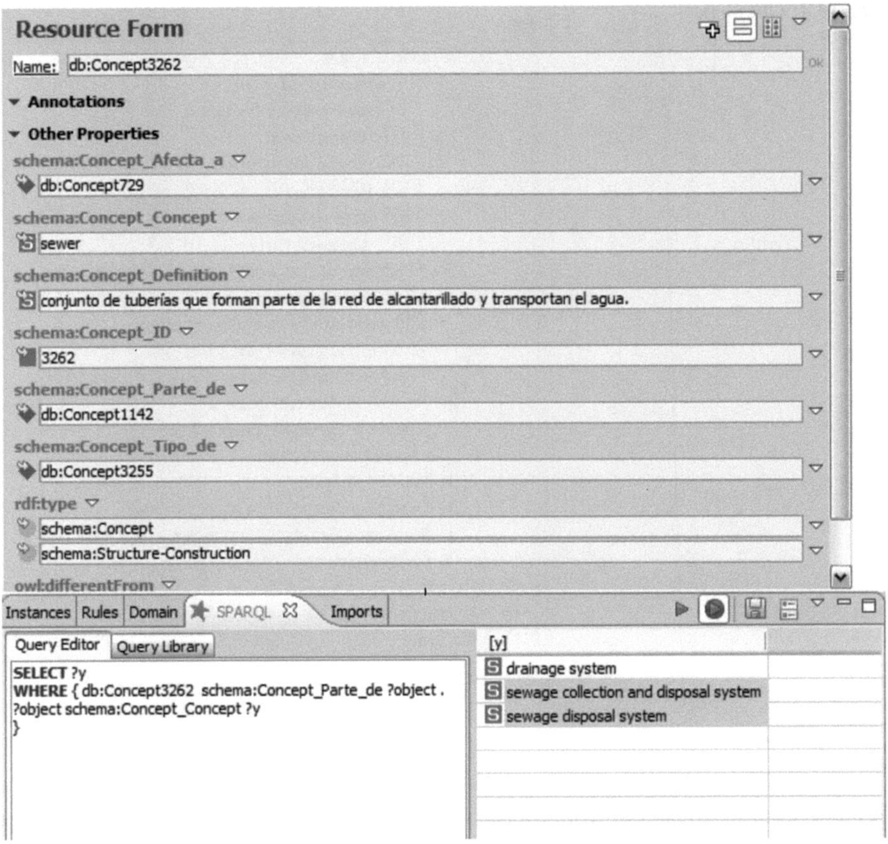

Fig. 13.4 The concept SEWER in the ontology and inferred transitivity

useful if their organization resembled the way concepts are represented in the mind. As a result, simple repositories of terms gradually were transformed into terminological knowledge bases (TKBs), and thus became real information systems that highlight conceptual interrelatedness and multidimensionality.

13.2.2 Conceptual Relations and Networks

From a visual perspective, concepts appear in conceptual networks that link them to all related concepts by means of a closed inventory of semantic relations, especially conceived for the environmental domain. Figure 13.5 shows the network of GROYNE. As can be observed, GROYNE is associated with other concepts in a two-level hierarchy by means of vertical relations (*type_of*, *part_of*, etc.) and horizontal relations (*has_function, located_at*, etc.).

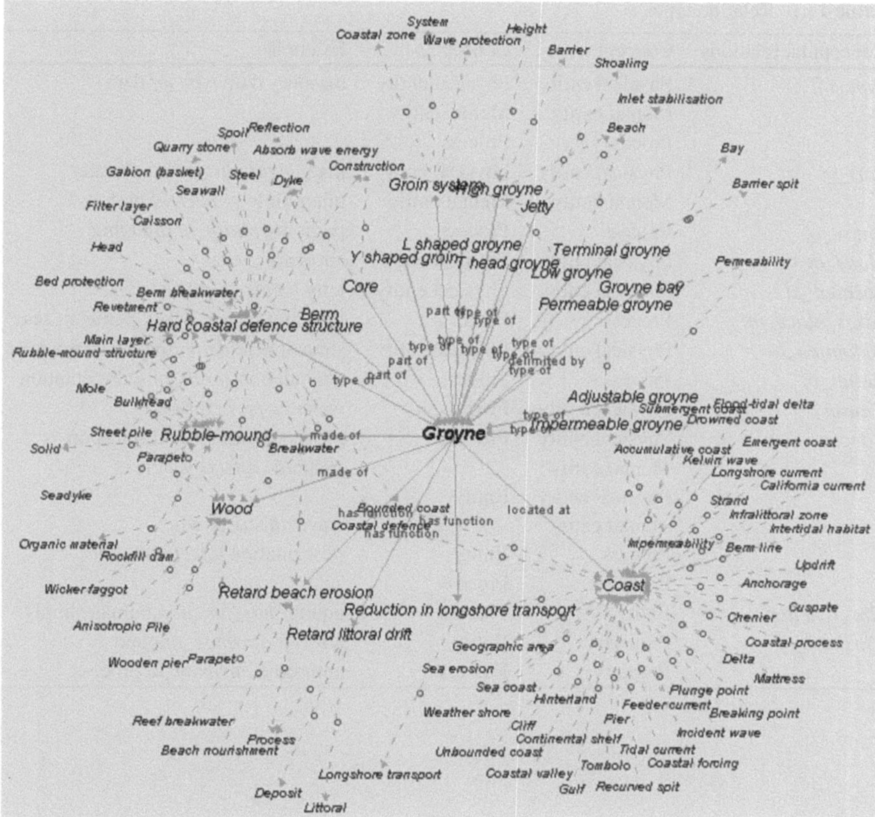

Fig. 13.5 Conceptual network of GROYNE

According to our corpus data, conceptual relations depend on concept types and their relational power. Table 13.1 shows the inventory of conceptual relations associated with the types of element that they can link in each conceptual proposition (León Araúz 2009; León Araúz and Faber 2010).

Apart from the relations shown in Table 13.1, there are others that have their own hierarchy. For example, *has_function* and *affects* include more specific knowledge, which is codified in domain-specific verbs: *studies*, *represents*, *measures*, *effected_by* (as functions of mental entities or instruments), and *erodes*, *changes_state_of*, etc. (for processes or entities that affect other entities in a more concrete way).

According to these criteria, the potential activation of certain semantic relations is determined by the nature of the concept. Nevertheless, this action is reciprocal since at the same time, semantic relations determine which kind of concepts can be part of the same conceptual proposition. This gives rise to all the combinations in Fig. 13.6.

Table 13.1 Relation types

Conceptual relations	Concept 1	Concept 2	Examples
Type_of	Physical entity	Physical entity	masonry dam *type_of* dam
	Mental entity	Mental entity	
	Process	Process	
Part_of	Physical entity	Physical entity	main layer *part_of* breakwater
	Mental entity	Mental entity	microbiology *part_of* biology
Phase_of	Process	Process	pumping *phase_of* dredging
Made_of	Physical entity	Physical entity	air *made_of* gas
Located_at	Physical entity	Physical entity	jetty *located_at* canal
Takes_place_at	Process	Process	littoral transport *takes_place_at* sea
Delimited_by	Physical entity	Physical entity	stratosphere *delimited_by* stratopause
Result_of	Process	Process	aggradation *result_of* sedimentation
Causes	Physical entity	Process	water *causes* erosion
Affects	Physical entity	Process	groyne *affects* littoral transport
	Mental entity		pesticide *affects* water
	Physical entity	Entity	
	Mental entity		wave *affects* groyne
	Process	Entity	precipitation *affects* erosion
	Process	Process	
Has_function	Entity	Process	aquifer *has_function* human supply
Attribute_of	Property	Entity	abyssal *attribute_of* plain
	Property	Process	anthropic *attribute_of* process

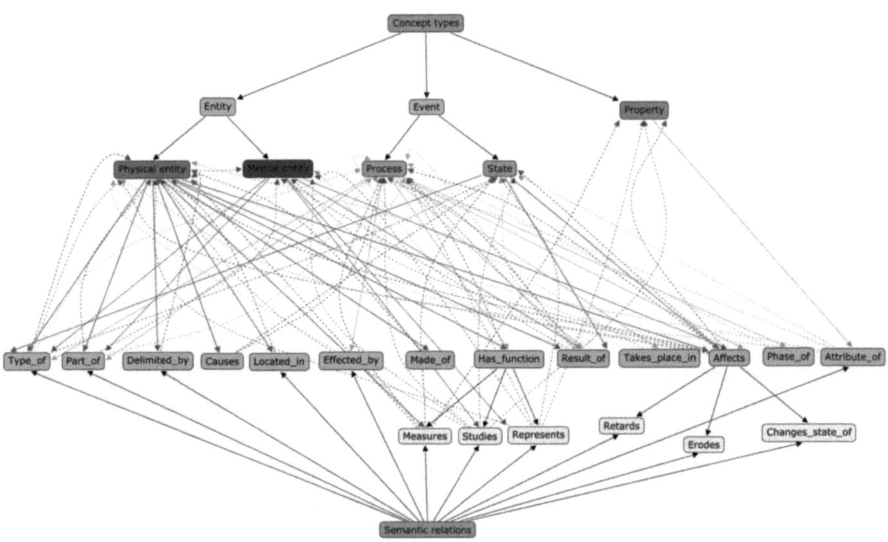

Fig. 13.6 Combinatorial potential

This combinatorial potential represents certain constraints associated with the specific nature of concepts. For instance, a process may activate the relation *affected_by*, but only if it is associated with a physical entity. However, if it activates *affects*, it can be linked to entities, events, and properties.

To enhance the coherence of EcoLexicon, we applied the premises of the Generative Lexicon to the conceptual relations within the context of the environmental domain. As is well known, the Generative Lexicon (GL) describes lexical items in terms of their *qualia* structure, which is composed of the following roles:

1. Formal role: the basic type distinguishing the meaning of a word;
2. Constitutive role: the relation between an object and its constituent parts;
3. Telic role: the purpose or function of the object, if there is one;
4. Agentive role: the factors involved in the object's origins or "coming into being". (Pustejovsky et al. 2006:3)

GL and *qualia* structure have been successfully applied to the SIMPLE ontology, where an extended version of the *qualia* structure was developed (Lenci et al. 2000). It is also the basis of the Brandeis Semantic Ontology (BSO, Pustejovsky et al. 2006). In the BSO, lexical items consist of three major types: entity, event and property. Each of these types is subdivided into three further hierarchies: natural, artifactual, and complex:

1. Natural types: natural kind concepts consisting of reference only to formal and constitutive *qualia* roles;
2. Artifactual types: concepts making reference to purpose, function, or origin.
3. Complex types: concepts integrating reference to a relation between types. (Pustejovsky et al. 2006:1)

In the same way as the *extension of the qualia structure*, we have related our concept typology and, their *qualia* roles, to the inventory of conceptual relations elaborated for our specialized domain. Conceptual relations are associated with a particular *qualia* role, depending on each concept type. As a result, the macrostructure and microstructure of all concepts in the domain are represented in terms of these possible combinations (see Fig. 13.7).

The most recurrent concepts of the domain (PHYSICAL OBJECTS and PROCESSES) are the ones that can be linked to others through a greater number of relations. However, there are also certain relations exclusive of a single type, such as *attribute_of*, for properties, and *studies* (for sciences and disciplines). For natural PHYSICAL OBJECT types, apart from the relations traditionally linked to formal and constitutive roles, two non-hierarchical relations have been added. The conceptual relations, *has_location* and *made_of*, are necessary in the description of environmental entities. The *material* that an object is *made_of* and its *location* are key properties of subordinate concepts, and can even be the most essential feature. For instance, a GROYNE is not a GROYNE if it is not *located in* the SEA.

Concept nature triggers or restricts the activation of a set of possible relations, but at the same time it determines which other concept types can be linked by each relation. For instance, if a PROCESS activates the relation *part_of*, it can only be

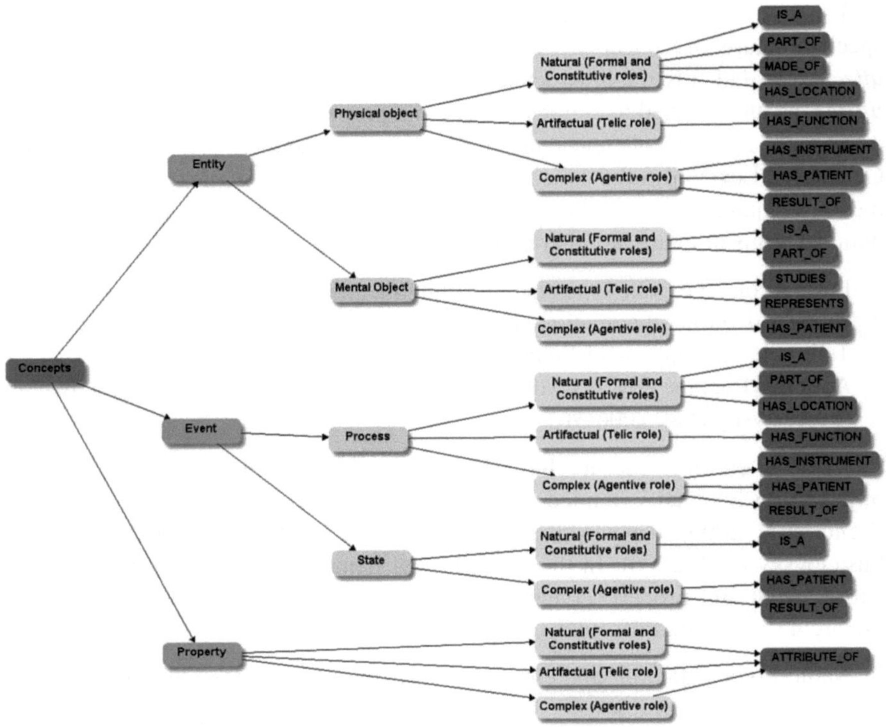

Fig. 13.7 Concept types, *qualia* roles, and conceptual relations

related to another PROCESS since this concept type can never be divided into physical entities. However, relations can also constrain the second concept in a proposition. For example, *made_of* can only activate physical concepts on both sides of the proposition.

13.2.3 Definitions

In accordance with the Environmental Event (EE), the elaboration of concept definitions is systematically related to the macrostructure of concepts which, in turn, complements their conceptual system. We have thus opted for a definitional format that accomplishes the following: (1) it makes category membership explicit; (2) it reflects a concept's relations with other concepts within the same category; (3) it specifies essential attributes and features. The first two principles are achieved through the *genus* – the *is_a* relationship of the formal role or the *part_of* relation of the constitutive role – because it maps back to the superordinate concept in its hierarchical inheritance. The third principle is based on the *differentiae*, which are

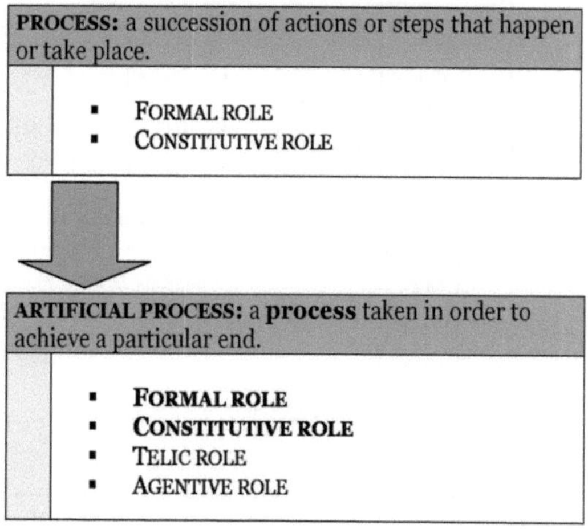

Fig. 13.8 Definitional templates of PROCESS and ARTIFICIAL PROCESS

the properties that distinguish more specific and coordinate concepts and are conveyed by the non-hierarchical relations that reflect the telic and agentive roles.

The notion of *qualia* is also applied to the definitional templates of EcoLexicon. For example, even though a PROCESS can activate all the relations in Fig. 13.8, the prototypical definitional structure is constrained. Natural processes and entities usually activate the formal role, distinguishing the basic meaning of the word, since this is the minimum information needed for description. Additionally they may include the constitutive role if the concept is significantly related to any part or phase. In contrast, artificial concepts have been created with a purpose in mind. Therefore their definitional templates will be far more complex. An artificial process, such as DREDGING, has a function, which means that it must also have a telic role. Moreover, artificial processes within an engineering context will frequently be carried out with an instrument, which makes the agentive role also necessary. Thus, our definitional templates are shared by all concepts belonging to the same conceptual category. Figures 13.8 and 13.9 and Tables 13.2 and 13.3 show the definitional templates associated with most recurrent concepts in an artificial context: artificial processes, instruments, and functional entities.

In EcoLexicon, the linguistic expression of the definitional template results in a definition, such as the one in Table 13.2. A PROCESS (e.g. DREDGING) has all four roles with different fillers. The same category template can be applied to other processes in the same paradigm (PIPING, PUMPING, etc.).

For concepts belonging to the category INSTRUMENT, such as DREDGER, the definitional template necessarily focuses on the formal and telic roles, since function or purpose is the essential information that necessarily defines any instrument. Moreover, the constitutive role can also be optionally included, given the fact that an instrument often has well-differentiated parts (see Table 13.3).

As can be seen in Table 13.4, DREDGER is mainly defined on the basis of its telic role.

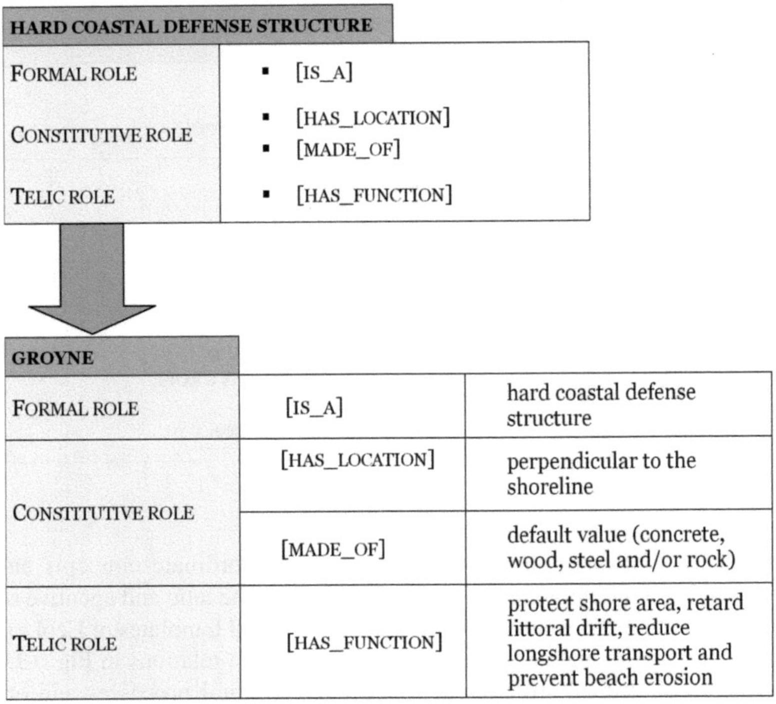

Fig. 13.9 Activation of the HARD COASTAL DEFENSE template in the definition of GROYNE

Table 13.2 Definition of DREDGING

Dredging		
Formal	[IS-A]	Artificial process of subtraction: removal
	[HAS_LOCATION]	Underwater
		Rivers
		Canals
		Harbors
CONSTITUTIVE	[HAS_PART]	Pumping
		Excavation
		Piping
		Material placement
		Sand placement
TELIC	[HAS_FUNCTION]	Construction
		Maintenance of water depths
		Beach nourishment
AGENTIVE	[HAS_PATIENT]	Material
		Sand
	[HAS_INSTRUMENT]	Dredger

Table 13.3 Definitional template of INSTRUMENT

INSTRUMENT: an object used to accomplish a purpose
• FORMAL ROLE • [CONSTITUTIVE ROLE] • TELIC ROLE

Table 13.4 Definitional template of DREDGER

Dredger		
FORMAL	[IS-A]	Instrument
CONSTITUTIVE	---------------	
TELIC	[HAS-FUNCTION]	Dredging
AGENTIVE	---------------	

Since DREDGER is an artifactual concept, its description does not need an agentive role to be complete. As for the constitutive role, there are no components found in all types of dredgers because they vary in accordance with their subtypes. Some types have a shovel or a clamshell, whereas others have a bucket or a hopper. As a result, the definitional templates of specific instances of dredgers make use of this constitutive role, but this is not the case for the generic concept. The formal role, through the *is_a* relation, marks the category membership of the concept, whereas the telic role helps to evoke the previous definitional template (DREDGING).

The following example is more specific and thus noticeably lower in the conceptual hierarchy. A HARD COASTAL DEFENSE STRUCTURE is neither a process nor an instrument. Nevertheless, since it is an artificial functional entity, it shares the formal and telic roles with the instrument template. In this case, because of its degree of specificity, the constitutive role is no longer optional, as the material that it is made of and its location are essential to its definition (Fig. 13.9). The definitional statement of GROYNE is based on its *qualia* structure and the number and type of conceptual relations defined for the category template HARD COASTAL DEFENSE STRUCTURE.

The coordinate concepts of GROYNE make use of the same template. As functional agentive entities, all HARD COASTAL DEFENSE STRUCTURES require the following information for their description: (1) the *is_a* relation marking category membership (formal role); (2) the material they are *made_of*, complemented with the values of the CONSTRUCTION MATERIAL class (constitutive role); (3) their location, since a GROYNE is not a GROYNE if it is not *located_at* the SEA (formal role); and (4) the purpose for which they were built (telic role).

In this way, definitions have a uniform structure that enhances the information encoded in the conceptual system, and directly refer to and evoke the underlying event structure of the domain. These templates can be considered a conceptual grammar that reflects category membership throughout the environmental domain, and thus ensures a high degree of systematization at the micro-structural level.

Table 13.5 Linguistic context of GROYNE

Groynes are extremely cost-effective coastal defense measures, requiring little maintenance, and are one of the most common coastal defense structures. However, groynes are increasingly viewed as detrimental to the aesthetics of the coastline, and face strong opposition in many coastal communities.

13.2.4 Linguistic and Graphical Information

Context-based information is not only included in the representation of conceptual relations, but is also expressed linguistically. Apart from concepts, conceptual networks, definitions, and terms, EcoLexicon provides the user with additional information in the form of linguistic contexts, concordances, and images.

Linguistic contexts help the user achieve a certain level of understanding of a specialized domain. The linguistic contexts included in the TKB go beyond the relations expressed in the definition. In Table 13.5, for example, GROYNE is not only defined as a HARD COASTAL DEFENSE STRUCTURE. Other relevant information is included as well, such as the fact that groynes are cost-effective and many coastal communities prefer other solutions.

Three types of concordances are included in each entry of EcoLexicon: conceptual, phraseological, and verbal. These concordances allow users to enrich their knowledge from a wide range of different perspectives. Conceptual concordances show the activation of conceptual relations in the real use of terms in texts. Phraseological concordances help the user to acquire knowledge of the most frequent phrasemes in specialized discourse. Thirdly, verbal concordances highlight the most frequent verbal collocations, which provide both linguistic and conceptual information.

Figure 13.10 shows the conceptual concordances in the entry of GROYNE. Linguistic markers such as *designed to* and *provide* explicitly relate the concept to its function, *shore protection* and *trap and retain sand.*

Finally, the third type of contextual information added to the entry is graphical resources or images. Previous research has shown that definitions that effectively combine visual and verbal information have a great potential (Faber et al. 2007; Prieto 2008). The visual contexts that enhance the definition are chosen, depending on their most salient functions (Anglin et al. 2004), and in terms of their relationship with the real-world entity they represent. In EcoLexicon, the image typology is based on the parameters of iconicity, abstraction, and dynamism (Prieto 2008):

- Iconicity refers to the representation of real-world objects through the abstraction of conceptual attributes.
- Abstraction, a matter of degree, refers to the cognitive effort required for the recognition and representation of the concept.
- Dynamism implies the representation of movement; either through explicit movement (e.g. video and animation) or through the illustration of the steps that make up a process (e.g. images showing different stages of a process).

```
TYPE

od only qualitatively.  5-3. Groins.  a. General.  (1) Groynes (are) [barrier-type structures] that extend from the
ks at the  coast of this area existed of hard measures (groynes and seawall). The groins could not be  kept-up
 of inlet stabilization works (e.g., jetties, terminal groynes, offshore breakwaters)\par  on the shorelines ad
wearing away of land by the action of natural forces.  Groyne -- a shore protection structure, usually built pe
 beach nourishment. Some [coastal structures], (including) groynes, breakwaters and sills, can have a positive effe
ocial implications  Coastal defence structures such as groynes and detached breakwaters generally increase the

MATERIAL

vant to most [rubble mound] structures (such as) seawalls, groynes, and breakwaters. It should be noted that in thi
sand, nourishing the beach  compartments between them. Groynes may be (made of) [wooden or rocky materials]. They
ct will also include adding notching to existing stone groynes and extending outfall pipes.  Unger said a sche

LOCATION

olution includes the following  three elements: a rock groyne (extending) [seaward  from the existing shoreline], a
are intended consequences for people and wildlife.     Groynes are structures built out from the shoreline, typ
line from receding. Along  almost the entire [coastline] groynes are (present), only at Warnemunde mitte there are

FUNCTION

the alignment of the updrift shoreline shifts as well. Groyne fields are (designed to) [trap and retain sand], nour
ents, and thus a greater erosion rate. Breakwaters and groynes are effective in retaining sand and reducing ero
 nearer the\par  barrier may also be considered, using groynes to impede updrift movement of material at the\pa
ions to anchor the fill material. In either instance,  groynes (provide) [shore protection] by modifying longshore
acceptable erosion of the downdrift shore. At first, a groyne field interrupts the longshore movement of sand i
ngth of beach to be protected. The basic purposes of a groyne are to modify the longshore movement of sand and
```

Fig. 13.10 Conceptual concordances in the entry of GROYNE

GROYNE			
FORMAL ROLE	hard coastal defence structure [IS_A]		
CONSTITUTIVE ROLE	*default value* (concrete, wood, steel, and/or rock) [MADE_OF]		
FORMAL ROLE	perpendicular to shoreline [HAS_LOCATION]		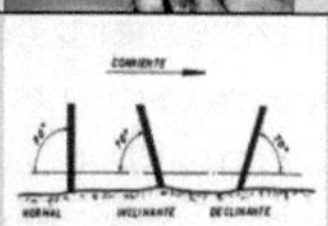
TELIC ROLE	protect a shore area, retard littoral drift, reduce longshore transport and prevent beach erosion [HAS_FUNCTION]	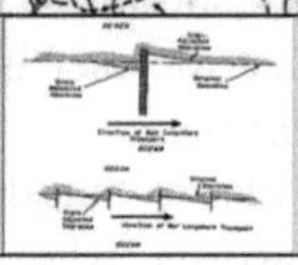	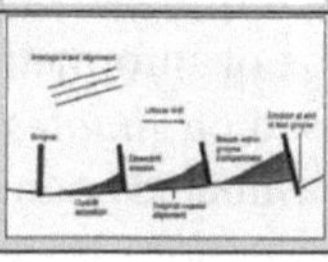

Fig. 13.11 The convergence of linguistic and graphical descriptions of GROYNE (Faber et al. 2007:57)

These criteria are applied to the selection of images included in the definition of concept-entries. Figure 13.11 shows an example of how various images are explicitly related to the conceptual relations expressed in the definition of GROYNE.

The analysis of the conceptual relations activated in the definition helps to select the most suitable images for Fig. 13.11. Iconic images are especially relevant for the representation of generic-specific and meronymic relations. The realistic depiction of the real-world entity allows the user to identify the object in question, by inferring its basic characteristics and linking them to previously stored knowledge structures. For example, the first image is an iconic image and shows that a GROYNE can be *made_of* CONCRETE. Abstraction facilitates the understanding of conceptual relations, such as *location_of*. For the concept GROYNE, location refers both to the position of the coastal structure in reference to the shoreline, and in reference to the sea-bottom.

The abstract image to the left illustrates the location of the GROYNE in reference to the shoreline. The non-hierarchical relation *has_function* is generally represented by dynamic images. Dynamism is conveyed by the use of symbols, such as arrows (representing movement), and textual information (linking the pictures to the real world) (Faber et al. 2007). Images illustrating the telic role of GROYNES have the abstract lines and labels of the images showing *location*.

13.3 Situated Cognition and Conceptual Dynamism in EcoLexicon

The previous sections have described EcoLexicon in terms of the systematic procedures implemented in conceptual description and representation. However, a high degree of systematization can sometimes impair the flexibility of knowledge resources. An environmental TKB should also account for the natural dynamism of concepts. On the one hand, the conceptual networks in EcoLexicon are not static maps. Instead, they provide the user with the chance to surf across different entries and see how conceptual structures change when another concept is focused on and is thus at the center of the network (Sect. 13.3.1). Nevertheless, the problem of an excessive information load in certain networks has made it necessary to reconceptualize general concepts so that only the information relevant to a certain context appears in the network. In this case, users do not surf across different entries. Instead, they are able to access different networks of the same central concept (Sect. 13.3.2). Each of these networks shows the concept in a different setting, depending on the type of information that the user is most interested in. This reconceptualization is based on *situated cognition.*

Situated cognition claims that understanding is equated with sensory and motor simulation. In other words, when we encounter a physical object, we partially capture property information on sensory modalities so that this information can later be reactivated (Damasio and Damasio 1994).

Since categorization itself is a dynamic context-dependent process, the representation and acquisition of specialized knowledge should certainly focus on contextual variation. From a neurological perspective, Barsalou (2009:1283) states that a concept produces a wide variety of situated conceptualizations in specific contexts. Context includes external factors (situational and cultural) as well as internal cognitive factors, all of which can influence one another (House 2006:342). This view goes hand in hand with the perception of language as a kind of action, where the meaning of linguistic forms is understood as a function of its use (Reimerink et al. 2010). In other words, a given utterance does not have a meaning, but rather a meaning potential that will always be exploited in different ways, depending on the discourse context (Evans 2009). The following sections explain the dynamics of knowledge in EcoLexicon, as reflected in situated and contextual conceptualizations.

Situated conceptualizations highlight the fact that concepts are not processed in isolation, but are typically situated in background situations and events (Barsalou 2003).

At any given moment in the perception of the entity, people also perceive the space surrounding it, including the agents, objects, and events present in it (Barsalou 2009:1283).

To date, brain-imaging experiments have largely involved the conceptualization of everyday objects such as cups, hammers, pencils, and food, which, when perceived, trigger simulations of potential actions. For example, the handle of a cup activates a grasping simulation (Tucker and Ellis 1998, 2001). Such re-enactments not only occur in the presence of the object itself, but also in response to words and other symbols. Although few neuropsychological experiments of this type have ever been performed with specialized concepts, there is no reason to suppose that the brain would work any differently (Faber 2011).

When it comes to individuals with different knowledge levels, Holt and Beilock (2006) found that hockey experts produced motor simulations absent in novices. In all likelihood, a similar result would be obtained if the object were a tide gauge, pluviometer, or anemometer. The expert's brain would show motor simulations in brain areas that would not be activated in the case of non-experts. Thus simulated interaction is a vital part of conceptual meaning. In EcoLexicon, the situated nature of both events and objects is highlighted through the representations of those non-hierarchical conceptual relations that express dynamism and simulation (*affects*, *causes*, *effected_by*, *measures*, etc.).

13.3.1 Dynamism Across Conceptual Networks

In EcoLexicon, the situated nature of conceptualization is partly reflected in dynamic networks. For example, this can be seen in the representation of the concept of EXTREME EVENT (Fig. 13.12) in its sense of natural disaster. This concept is very complex since it is a natural agent that initiates a process (i.e. earthquakes or volcanic eruptions can produce tsunamis), but it can also be the process itself, which occurs in time and space.

All of the concepts closest to the central concept are connected to it by a series of conceptual relations that are explicitly named (e.g. *type_of*, *causes*, *affects*, etc.). Since EXTREME EVENT is a very general concept, the only mental image that can be associated with it is that of its subtypes (HURRICANE, TORNADO, EARTHQUAKE, FLOOD, etc.). Its principal attribute is risk; it affects the environment; and it causes an environmental impact. As for the majority of relations (*type_of*), they can be regarded as access routes to more prototypical base-level concepts (Rosch 1978), which do have a mental image, and can activate specific scenarios. This set of subtypes take the form of constellations, each with their own set of subordinate concepts and conceptual relations, which encode more specific sub-event knowledge.

This general event can thus be situated in any of the more specific sub-events. For example, the conceptual network of HURRICANE is shown in Fig. 13.13.

Besides communicating the fact that HURRICANE is a type of EXTREME EVENT, this new representation highlights the fact that WIND and FLOODING are crucial

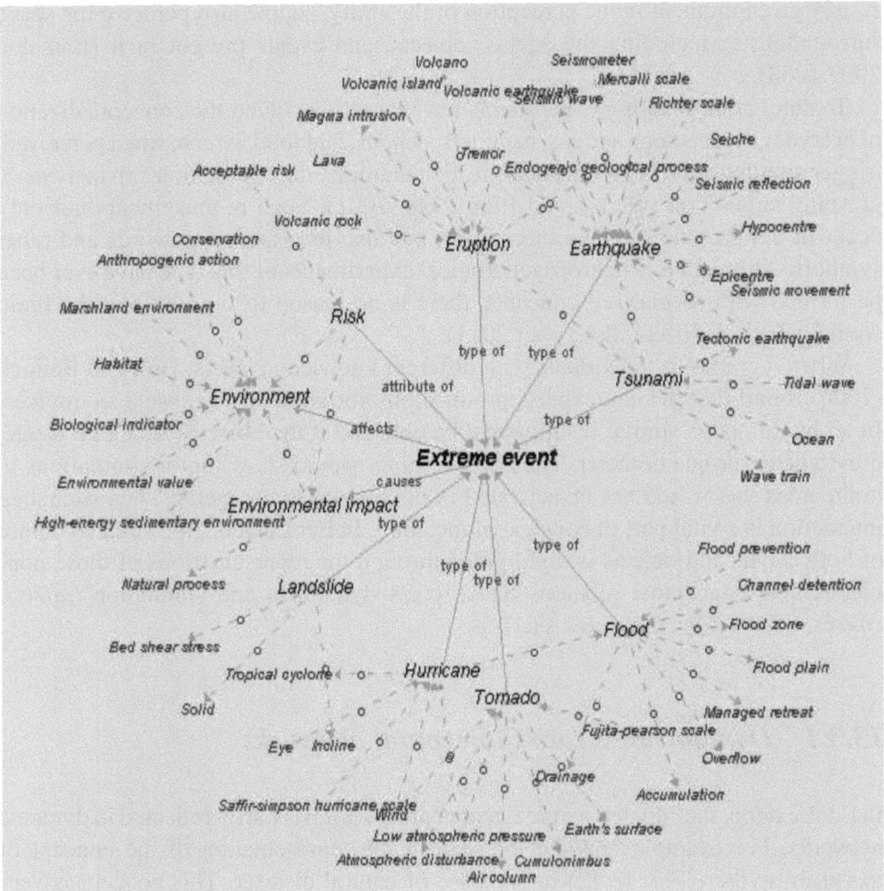

Fig. 13.12 Representation of EXTREME EVENT in EcoLexicon

participants in the event. WIND is *part_of* a HURRICANE, and a HURRICANE *causes* FLOODS. Not surprisingly, WIND and FLOOD are concepts that are susceptible to simulation since they can directly affect human life and health. It also mentions the attribute of LOW ATMOSPHERIC PRESSURE as well as the scale used for hurricane measurement (SAFFIR-SIMPSON HURRICANE SCALE), which codifies an important aspect of expert interaction with a hurricane.

Objects can also be represented dynamically as parts of events. One of the basic characteristics of objects is knowledge of whether and how they can be manipulated. In the case of man-made objects, another important property is their function. This would mean that an important part of the information in the representation of specialized engineering instruments would evidently involve how they are used by humans, for what purpose, and what is the result of the manipulation.

For example, a RECORDING INSTRUMENT (e.g. MARIGRAPH, PLUVIOGRAPH, ANEMOGRAPH, etc.) is a subtype of INSTRUMENT. As a man-made manipulable artifact,

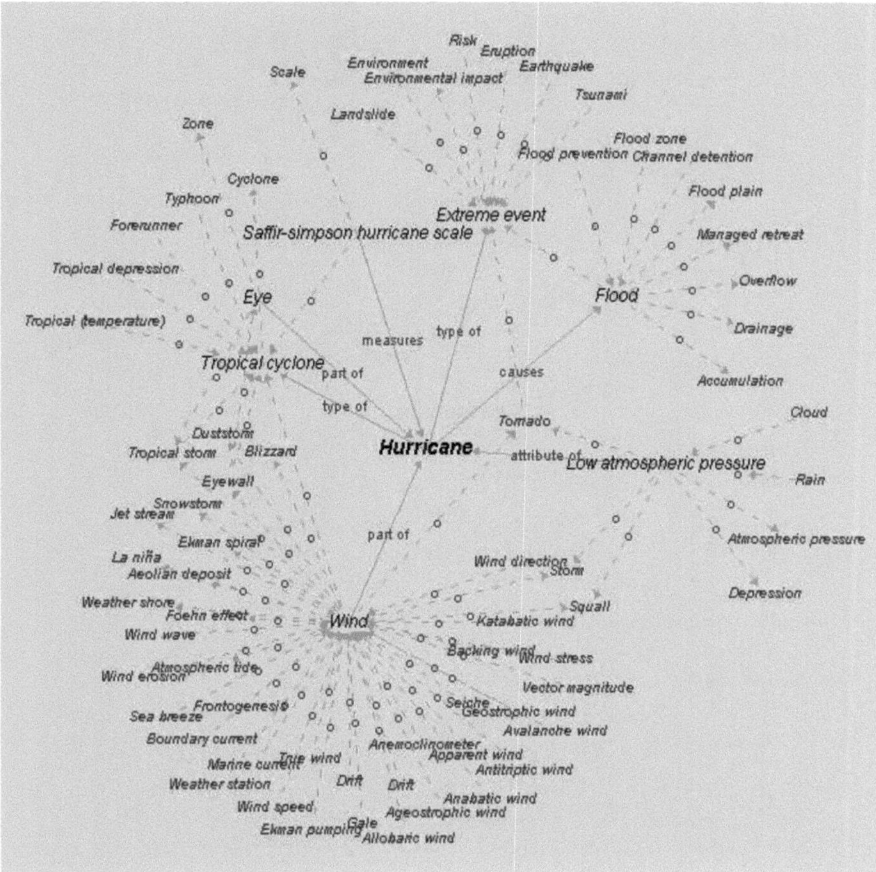

Fig. 13.13 Representation of HURRICANE in Ecolexicon

a RECORDING INSTRUMENT has a function (i.e. RECORDING) as well as an object that is recorded (TIDES, RAIN, WIND, etc.). As a tool, it is strongly susceptible to human interaction, and activates a simulation frame in which much of the perceiver's knowledge of the artifact involves his/her ability to handle it. For instance, Fig. 13.14 shows the representation of PLUVIOGRAPH.

The representation of PLUVIOGRAPH, of course, includes *type_of* information. A PLUVIOGRAPH is a RECORDING INSTRUMENT, and has subtypes, such as DIGITAL PLUVIOGRAPH and PORTABLE PLUVIOGRAPH. However, it is also part of what might be called a recording event in which a human agent causes the machine to record and generate a representation of something (RAINFALL). The RECORDING INSTRUMENT used in this event is a PLUVIOGRAPH, which produces (or *effects*) a PLUVIOGRAM. As can be observed in Fig. 13.14, this process is reflected in the non-hierarchical relations *represents* and *effected_by*.

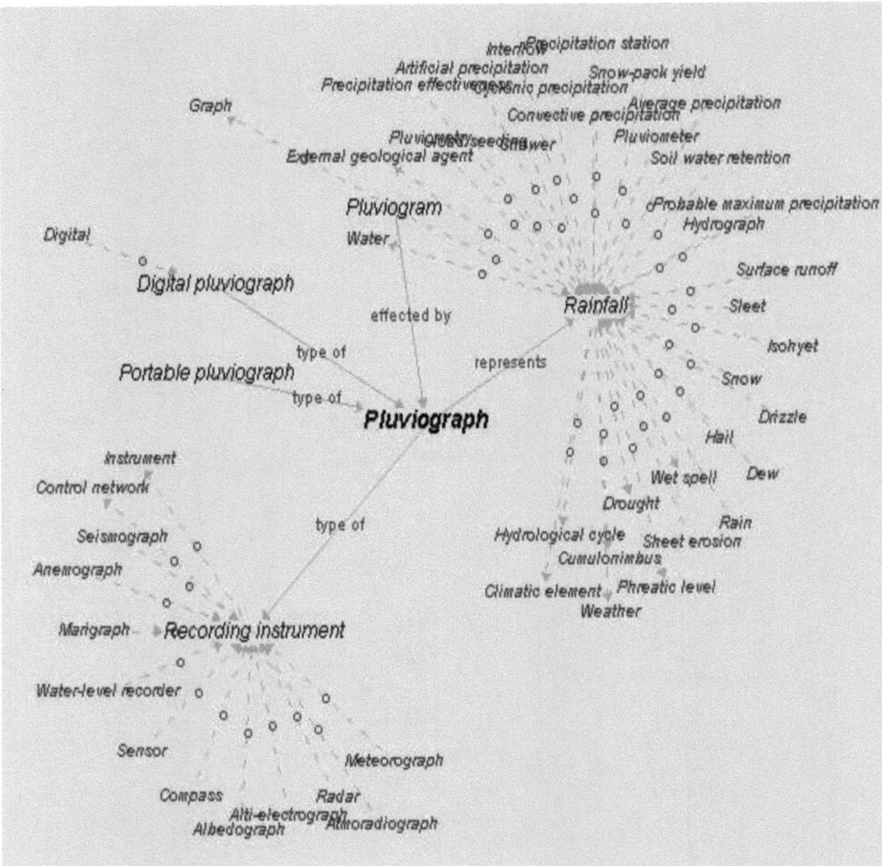

Fig. 13.14 Representation of PLUVIOGRAPH in EcoLexicon

13.3.2 Dynamism Within Conceptual Networks

In knowledge representation, concepts are very often classified according to different facets or dimensions. This phenomenon is widely known as *multidimensionality* (Kageura 1997). The representation of multidimensionality enhances knowledge acquisition providing different points of view in the same conceptual system. For instance, GROYNES can be classified according to their length (LONG GROYNE or SHORT GROYNE), their shape (ZIG-ZAG GROYNE, L-SHAPED GROYNE, Y-SHAPED GROYNE, T-SHAPED GROYNE), their position (STRAIGHT GROYNE, DEFLECTING GROYNE, DECLINED GROYNE) or the material they are made of (RUBBLE-MOUND GROYNE or SHEET PILE GROYNE). A thorough representation of GROYNE should include all these facets in order to give a complete overview of the concept.

Moreover, the environmental domain shows a high degree of multidimensionality. This is related to the fact that the same concept can act as an agent or a patient, as a

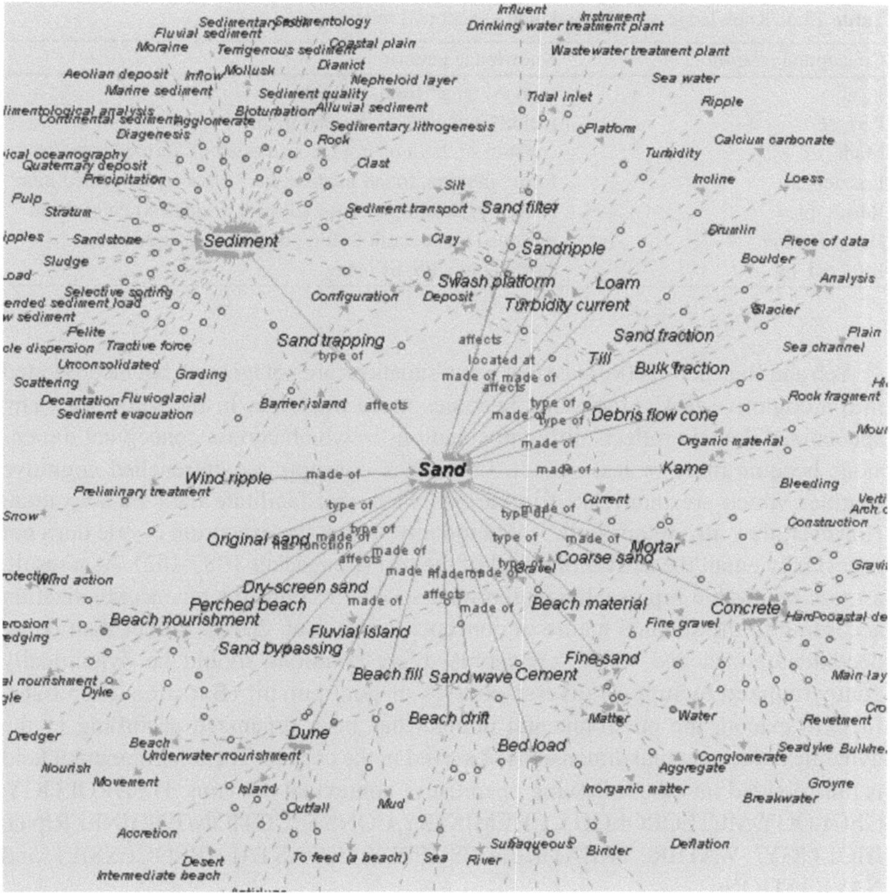

Fig. 13.15 Information overload in the network of SAND

process or a result, which increases the number of possible activated relations. However, all dimensions cannot always be represented at the same time, since their activation is context-dependent. In EcoLexicon this has led to a great deal of information overload (see Fig. 13.15), which jeopardizes knowledge acquisition.

Unlike specific concrete concepts such as DREDGING or GROYNE, there are certain general concepts, such as SAND, which can be involved in a myriad of incompatible events. Obviously, it is difficult for users to acquire any meaningful knowledge when all dimensions of SAND are shown in the same network. In Fig. 13.15, SAND is simultaneously linked to diverse natural and artificial concepts (i.e. TILL, BEACH FILL, and CONCRETE) through the *made_of* relation. However, they are not really coordinate concepts, because they belong to different environmental paradigms that rarely coincide in the same scenario. The same applies to SAND as an agent in BEACH NOURISHMENT or as a patient in a WATER TREATMENT PLANT.

Table 13.6 Knowledge patterns and their conceptual relations

Conceptual relation	Knowledge pattern
Is_a	such as, rang* from, includ*
Part_of	includ*, consist* of, formed by/of
Made_of	consist* of, built of/from, constructed of, formed by/of/from
Located_at	form* in/at/on, found in/at/on, tak* place in/at, located in/at
Result_of	caused by, leading to, derived from, formed when/by/from
Has_function	designed for/to, built to/for, purpose is to, used to/for
Effected_by	carried out with, by using

Yeh and Barsalou (2006) state that when situations are not ignored, but incorporated into a cognitive task, processing becomes more tractable. In the same way, any specialized domain reflects different situations in which certain conceptual dimensions become more or less salient. Of course, concepts are entrenched cognitive routines which are interrelated in various ways that facilitate their co-activation. However, they also retain sufficient autonomy so that the execution of one does not necessarily entail the activation of all of the rest (Langacker 1987:162). As a result, a more believable representational system should account for reconceptualization according to the situated nature of concepts (León et al. 2013). Rather than being decontextualized and stable, conceptual representations should be dynamically contextualized to support diverse courses of goal pursuit (Barsalou 2005:628). In EcoLexicon, the environmental domain has been organized according to the dynamics of conceptual dimensions observed in the corpus. The environmental field is thus divided into the following open list of contextual domains: HYDROLOGY, GEOLOGY, METEOROLOGY, CHEMISTRY, CONSTRUCTION/ENGINEERING, BIOLOGY, WATER TREATMENT/SUPPLY, COASTAL PROCESSES and NAVIGATION.

Reconceptualization requires the manual identification of relations and dimensions through Knowledge Patterns (KPs) and direct key term searches. The most reliable patterns identified in our corpus are listed in Table 13.6. Searching for these patterns in the corpus allows us to find new conceptual propositions, whereas direct key term searches show how the behavior of versatile concepts changes across different domains.

In Figs. 13.16, 13.17, 13.18 and 13.19, SAND is shown as a highly context-sensitive concept assigned to different conceptual dimensions according to its surrounding KPs. The concept SAND is generally (or prototypically) defined as a kind of sediment located in the sea, rivers, or soil layers. A specialized definition could even include information about its grain size. However, in real texts, SAND activates many other relations. In a more general domain, such as GEOLOGY (see Fig. 13.16), the concept is linked to the following: *type*, as a kind of SEDIMENT or MATERIAL; *attribute*, related to grain size as a classification parameter; and *material*, linking the concept to the natural elements of which it is part (VALLEY, SOIL, AQUIFER, DESERT, etc.).

These relations complement those activated in a prototypical definition. However, some of them are not compatible in other contexts. In the COASTAL PROCESS

```
GEOLOGY

TYPE

, suspended sediment has been categorized as suspended sand, silt, and  clay. The transport of each class is
ot drain by gravity and earthen material such as rock, sand, gravel,   or clay. This means that a 10 unit drop

MATERIAL

consisting  of a heterogeneous mixture of clay, silt, sand, gravel, and boulders ranging  widely in size and
n Maine. Sediments are composed of fine clays,   silt, sand and organic matter. Sediments are supplied to the
s have been proposed to classify sediments composed of sand-silt-clay mixtures in natural systems without, how
arbonate) areas or where soils and aquifers consist of sand and gravel. These natural features enable rapid in

ATTRIBUTE

 Petri parallel at  a depth of 200 m in muddy and fine sand sediments,  representing 2 % of the total assembla
 A comprises sandy sediments sites (medium  and coarse sand) with a low percentage of fines  and total volatil
 decelerated, sediments ranging from medium boulder to sand-sized were deposited. Sedimentation was controlled
```

Fig. 13.16 SAND in the GEOLOGY domain

```
COASTAL PROCESS

MATERIAL

  A beach is an area of sediment accumulation (usually sand) exposed to wave  action along the coast. Beache
 was designed along the entire  stretch of SR-105 as a sand berm with crest elevation  at +30 feet MLLW. Sand
sion and producing broader beaches.  Spits and bars  A sand spit is one of the most common coastal landforms.
e  sedimentary terraces or "raised beaches" containing sand and gravel deposits. The coastline  forms a chain
lluvium (debris from valley sides),   channel deposits (sand and gravel), and vertical accretion deposits (cla
f medium to coarse sand. Channel banks are composed of sand and  mud (silt-clay content averaging 30-40%) and

PATIENT

by sand  bars, which are formed by wave action moving sand onto and along the beach. The  river is then only
 level factors.\par  Most storms move large amounts of sand from the beach to offshore; but after the storm, t
ngle. The longshore current can carry large amounts of sand along the coast and can form spits (narrow peninsu
  longshore drift. Longshore drift erodes and deposits sand continuously along the  beach. The sand that is r
 different  areas of the continental shelf and slope. Sand being the largest, is transported  by waves towar
 action. During the summer months when waves are low,  sand is deposited on the beach, forming a high and wide
```

Fig. 13.17 SAND in the COASTAL PROCESS domain

```
COASTAL DEFENCE

MATERIAL

 them recover  naturally. (See also Case 2.) However, sand fences can be erected to help dune recovery after
ss impacts associated with construction of a nearshore sand berm. Baseline condition descriptions included dis
andward 550 ft of the west jetty were constructed as a sand-fill dike, with a crown elevation of +4 ft mlt and

FUNCTION

e also important to many beaches because they act as a sand  source. Many fish actively feed on the coral. Fo
important beneficial effects. First, beach nourishment sand directly protects the natural dune-bluffs from wav
 sources of sand.  Sand Sources for Beach Nourishment  Sand for nourishment projects is from a variety of envi
icate a highly variable environment. Thus, before this sand body is used for beach nourishment, further coring

PATIENT

der to restore it to its former width. The addition of sand  to the beach by dredging and pumping sand from of
ng wave energy in the case of breakwaters and trapping sand in the case of groins, thus influencing the sand m
jacent beaches, artificial sand bypassing can be used. Sand bypassing is the hydraulic or mechanical movement
movement of sand generally can  be restored by pumping sand from the side where sand accumulates through a  pi
urishment for the\par  beach.\par  offshore dumping of sand by hopper dredge was carried out at Long Branch, N
```

Fig. 13.18 SAND in the COASTAL DEFENSE domain

domain (see Fig. 13.17), salient dimensions are *material*, although natural elements are restricted to coastal ones (SAND BARRIER, SAND BERM, SAND SPIT, BEACH, etc.) and *patient*, where the concept is involved in certain natural processes (WAVE ACTION, STORMS, LONGSHORE CURRENT, DEPOSITION, etc.).

If context is again restricted to a COASTAL DEFENSE domain (Fig. 13.18), its dimensions are still the same, but this time, values focus on artificial elements (FENCE, BERM, DIKE) and processes (TRAPPING, PUMPING, DUMPING). Furthermore, there is a new dimension, highlighting the functional nature of the concept in this

```
WATER TREATMENT

INSTRUMENT

e water column. This equipment is called a detritor or sand  catcher. Sand grit and stones need to be removed
 5 l of water were collected after filtration  through sand filters. Chlorine concentration used in  the exper
d grit removal  Primary treatment typically includes a sand or grit channel or chamber where the   velocity of
first nitrifying the wastewater by passage through the sand filter, then recirculating the nitrified effluent

FUNCTION

lso called   "effluent polishing".  [edit] Filtration  Sand filtration removes much of the residual suspended
water-treatment plants in the Kingdom utilize imported sand for filtration. The objectives of this research pr
beds for wastewater sludge require a specific type of sand in order to dewater the sludge quickly. Author War
```

Fig. 13.19 SAND in the WATER TREATMENT domain

specific context (SAND *protects* DUNE-BLUFFS, SAND BODY *is used for* BEACH NOURISHMENT, etc.). Thus, when a telic role is added to a natural entity, the concept becomes an artifact and thus has an expanded description.

The previous three domains are closely related and can even be said to form a hierarchy (GEOLOGY → COASTAL PROCESS → COASTAL DEFENSE). However when the domain is completely different, the changes are even more striking (see Fig. 13.19).

In the WATER TREATMENT domain, SAND acquires a new dimension since it is linked to a particular instrument used in WATER TREATMENT PLANTS. The functional dimension now has a different value (FILTRATION) and *patient* and *material* are no longer representative conceptual dimensions.

Accordingly, in EcoLexicon, concepts with an information overload are reconceptualized in terms of domain membership. Our contextual domains are allocated in much the same way as in the European General Multilingual Environmental Thesaurus, whose structure is based on themes and descriptors, reflecting a systematic, category or discipline-oriented perspective (GEMET 2004). They provide a way to simplify the background situations in which concepts can occur in reality.

Domain membership restricts the relational behavior of concepts in terms of how their referents interact in the real world. Contextual constraints are not applied to individual concepts or to individual relations, since one concept can be activated in different contexts or use the same relations but with different values. Constraints are instead applied to conceptual propositions (León Araúz et al. 2009).

For instance, SAND is linked to CONCRETE through a *made_of* relation. Nevertheless, this proposition is irrelevant if users only want to know how SAND naturally interacts with the landscape or how it is transported to an ALLUVIAL FAN. Consequently, the proposition CONCRETE *made_of* SAND only appears if users select the CONSTRUCTION/ENGINEERING context. As a result, when constraints are applied, SAND only shows relevant dimensions for each contextual domain.

In Fig. 13.20, SAND is framed within the COASTAL PROCESSES domain, whereas in Figs. 13.21 and 13.22, it shows its prototypical structure in ENGINEERING/CONSTRUCTION and WATER TREATMENT contexts.

The number of conceptual relations changes from one network to another, as SAND is not equally relevant in all contextual domains. Furthermore, relation types also differ, which also highlights the changing nature of SAND's internal structure. Apart from the traditional formal role, in the COASTAL PROCESSES contextual domain,

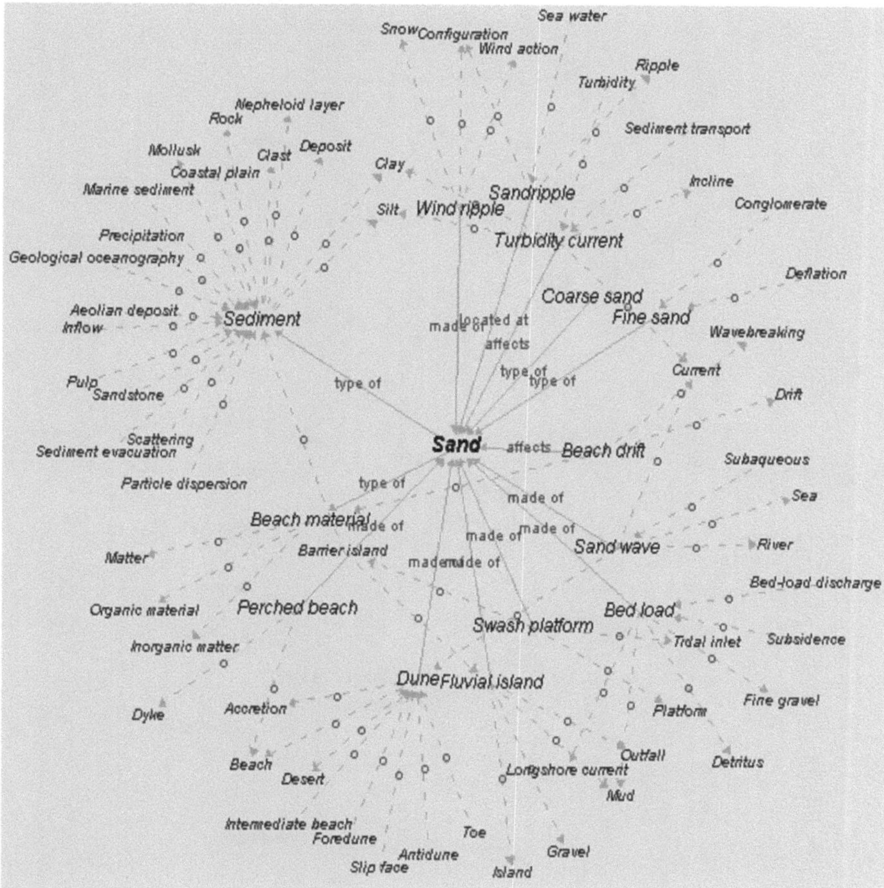

Fig. 13.20 SAND in the COASTAL PROCESSES domain

the dominant relation is *made_of.* The most important role of SAND is the constitutive one, as it is prototypically related to beach forms.

In contrast, in ENGINEERING/CONSTRUCTION and WATER TREATMENT domains, *affects* is one of the prominent relations reflecting the passive nature of SAND in artificial contexts. Nevertheless, in the ENGINEERING/CONSTRUCTION domain, SAND has a dual perspective as both an agent and a patient, since the *has_function* relation describes it as a telic artifact involved in BEACH NOURISHMENT.

Furthermore, SAND is not always related to the same concept types. In COASTAL PROCESSES, SAND is only linked to natural entities (DUNE, SAND WAVE, BED LOAD), whereas in WATER TREATMENT and ENGINEERING/CONSTRUCTION it is primarily related to artificial ones (BEACH NOURISHMENT, BEACH FILL, SAND TRAPPING). In addition, the second-level networks that appear in each contextual domain are also different. In the COASTAL PROCESSES DOMAIN the largest

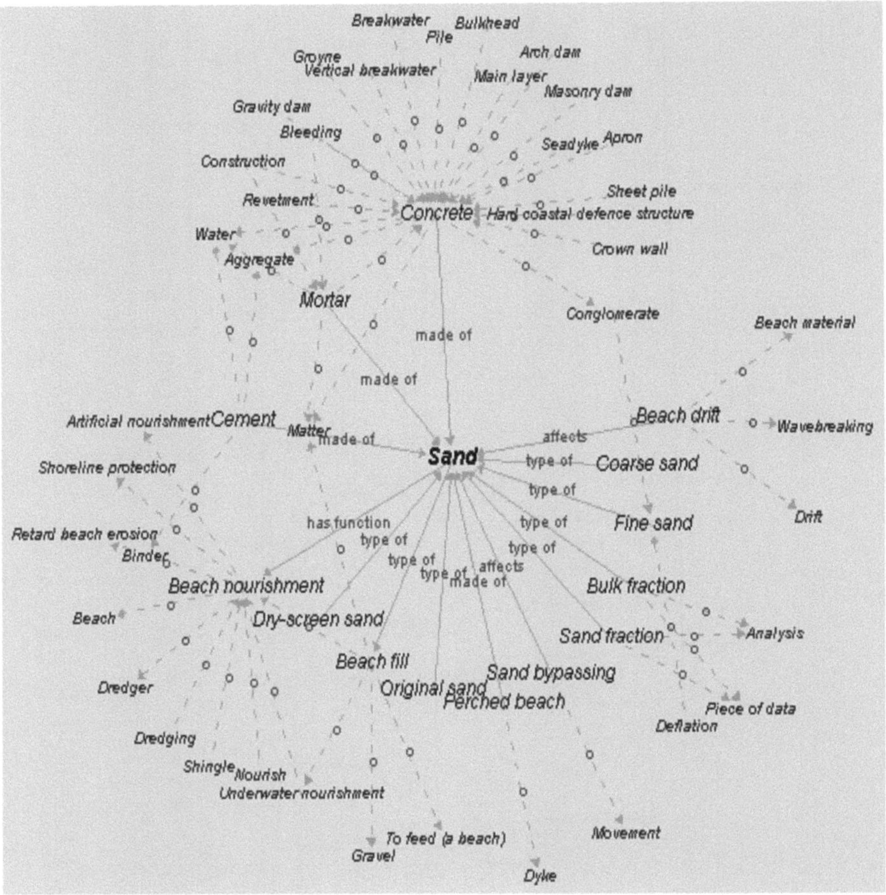

Fig. 13.21 SAND in the ENGINEERING/CONSTRUCTION domain

second-level networks linked to SAND are those activated by SEDIMENT and DUNE. Similarly, in a WATER TREATMENT context, SEDIMENT is also the concept with the widest network. Nevertheless, the second-level is composed of very different concepts: AEOLIAN DEPOSIT, and SCATTERING in the first case, and DECANTATION and SLUDGE in the second one. In the ENGINEERING/CONSTRUCTION domain, two new central concepts arise: BEACH NOURISHMENT and CONCRETE.

SAND subtypes differ from one network to the other since not all subtypes are coordinate concepts. Sand subtypes may vary from COARSE and FINE SAND (present in all domains) to BEACH FILL and ORIGINAL SAND (only present in coastal ENGINEERING) or DRY-SCREEN SAND (typical of WATER TREATMENT processes).

This type of multidimensionality is not only reflected in its subtypes, but also in its categorization. In the COASTAL PROCESSES domain, SAND is categorized both as SEDIMENT and BEACH MATERIAL. In contrast, in ENGINEERING/CONSTRUCTION

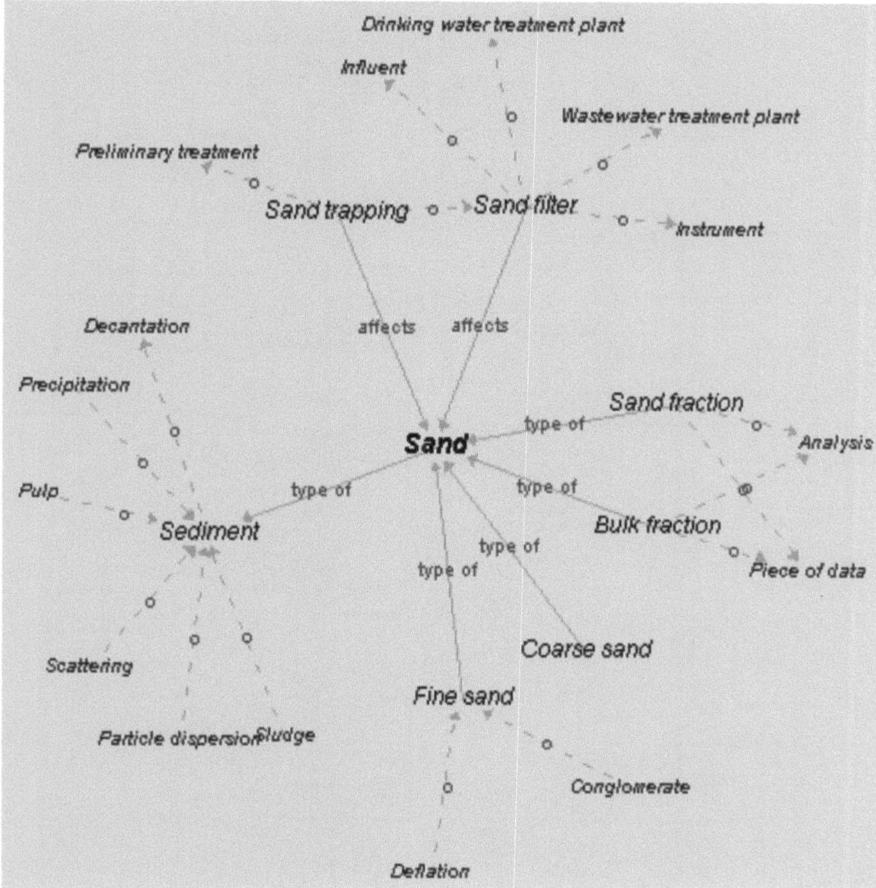

Fig. 13.22 SAND in the WATER TREATMENT domain

and WATER TREATMENT, the concept is described as a kind of BEACH FILL or again as SEDIMENT, respectively, although this time SEDIMENT is the result of DECANTATION and not DEPOSITION (as in a NATURAL COASTAL PROCESS). This reflects that multiple inheritance is also variable. Generally speaking, because of multiple inheritance, many concepts inherit different properties linked to various superordinate concepts. However, all those properties are not always equally important in each context.

SAND is overloaded mainly because of its link with the concepts at the second level of the network. However an even more general concept, such as WATER, can also be overloaded at the first level. Even after applying the domain-based constraints, certain resulting networks are still overloaded. Figure 13.23 shows WATER in the HYDROLOGY domain, which is obviously the most prototypical context for WATER. This is why the network still appears to be overly complex and in need of simplification.

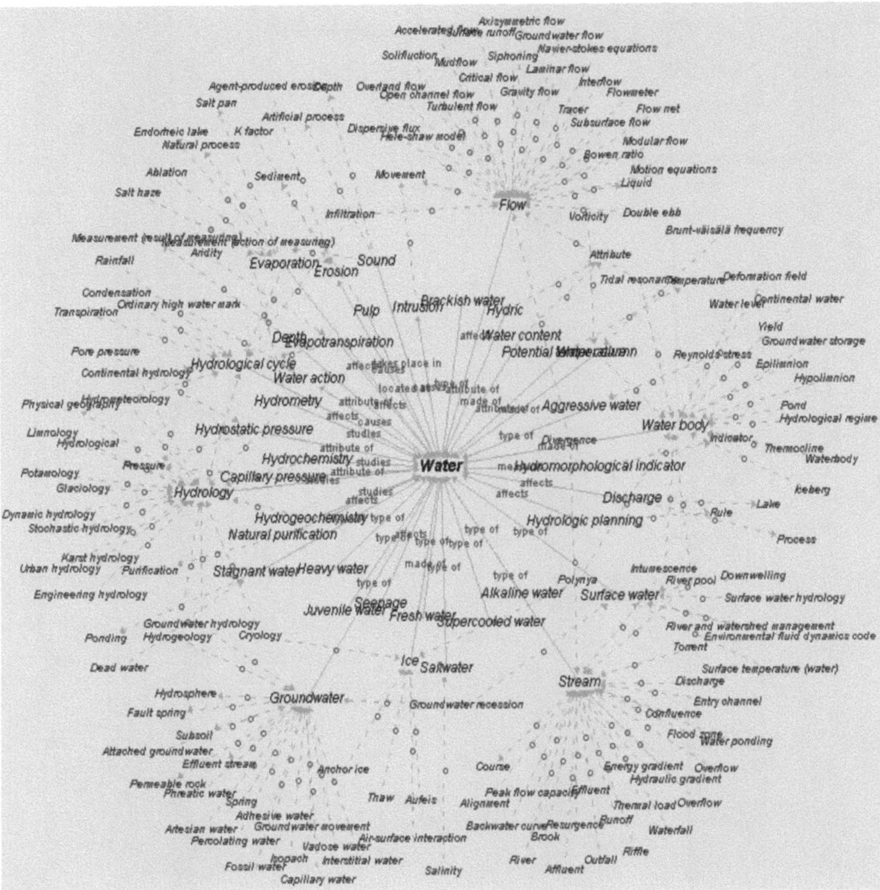

Fig. 13.23 Water in the HYDROLOGY domain

To solve this first-level overinformation, we apply relational constraints to individual concepts based on their semantic roles in a given proposition. For example, in WATER CYCLE *affects* WATER, WATER is a patient. However, if a role-based domain were to be associated with WATER CYCLE, this would require the application of agent-based constraints. Role-based constraints only generally apply for non-hierarchical relations since formal and constitutive roles are always activated. For example, WATER is composed of the same elements whether it acts as an agent or a patient (León Araúz and Faber 2010). Moreover, such constraints can only be applied to the first hierarchical level, since they are focused on a particular concept and not on the whole conceptual proposition. The overloaded network of WATER (Fig. 13.24) is restricted according to the agent role (Fig. 13.25).

Actually, role-based domains by themselves are not sufficient to reconceptualize knowledge in a meaningful way. In the role-free network, WATER appears linked

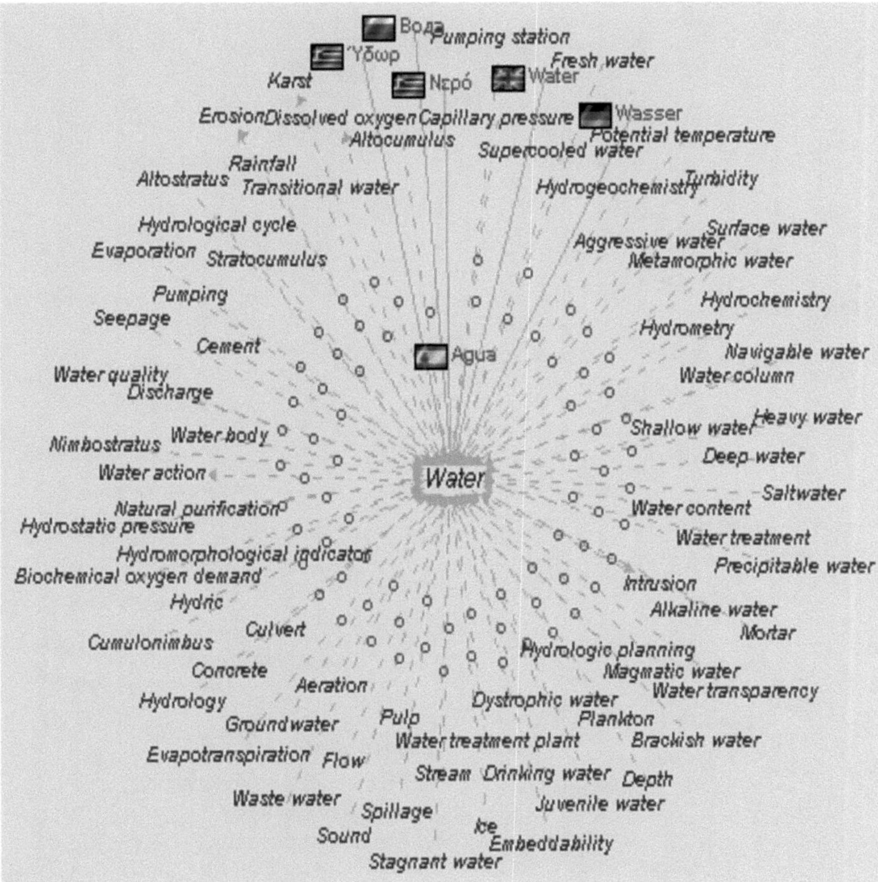

Fig. 13.24 Role-free network of WATER

to 72 concepts, whereas in the role-based network, WATER is related to 50. Despite the difference, the concept still appears overloaded, especially when the second hierarchical level is displayed. However, contextual domains, although usually dominated by one role, restrict the relational power of versatile concepts in a more quantitative way. This is why a new reconceptualization can take place with the intersection of role-based constraints and contextual domains. For example, WATER can be framed as an agent (Fig. 13.26) or a patient (Fig. 13.27) or even both (Fig. 13.28) within HYDROLOGY.

Now, the first level appears constrained according to different roles in a particular contextual domain, which at the same time applies to the second level. It is worth noting that Fig. 13.28 only shows hierarchical relations (*type_of, attribute_of, made_of*), because these are the only ones shared by concepts that can be agents

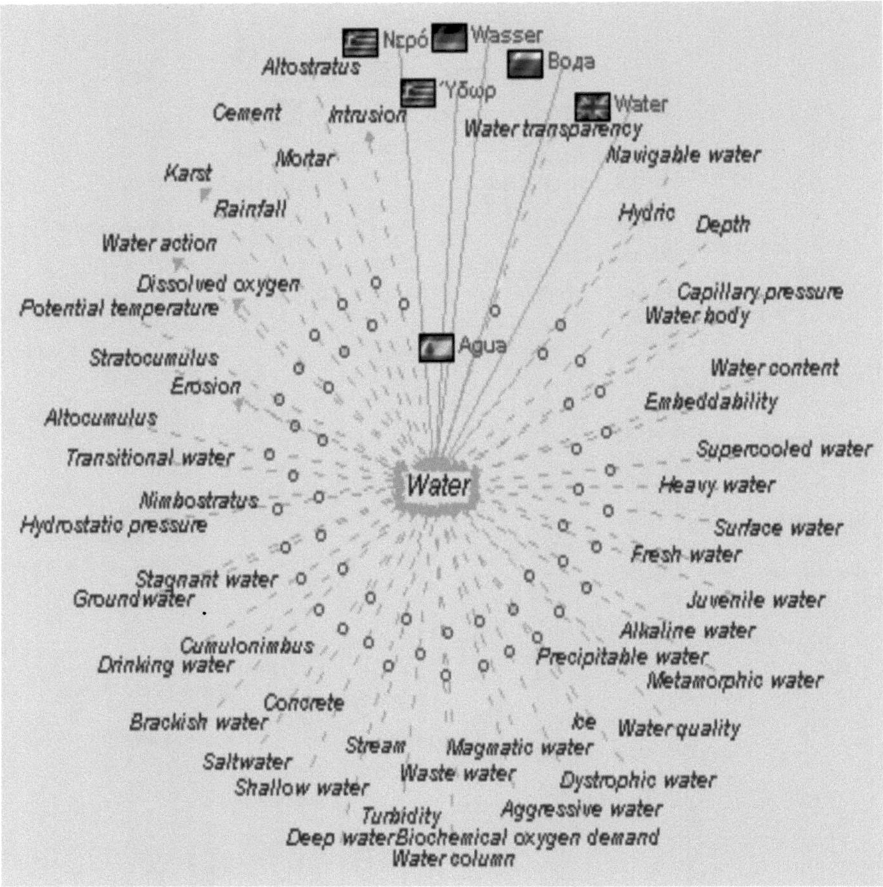

Fig. 13.25 Agent-based network of WATER

or patients. In Fig. 13.26, however, the representation adds the relation *causes*, typical of agents, and in Fig. 13.27, it adds propositions where WATER is *affected_by*, *measured*, *studied* or *located_at*.

13.4 Conclusions

In this chapter we have presented EcoLexicon from several perspectives. We have briefly explained the methodology applied for knowledge representation, and we have shown how all this information is presented to the end user. The internal

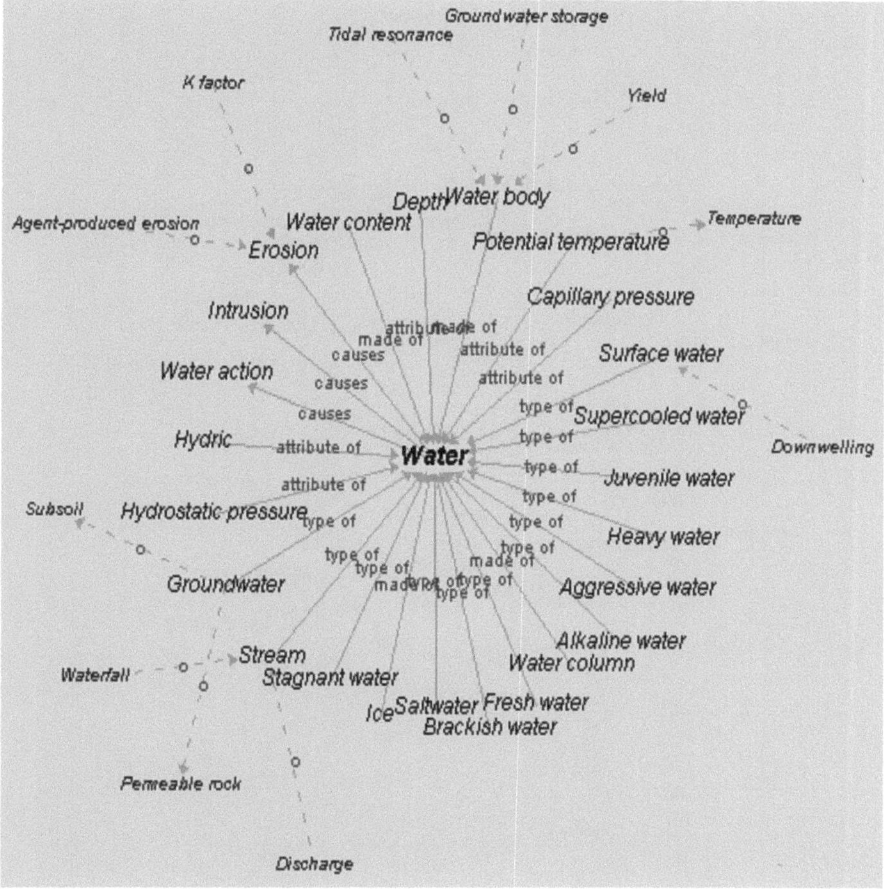

Fig. 13.26 WATER as an agent in HYDROLOGY

coherence at all levels of a dynamic knowledge representation shows that even complex domains can be represented in a user-friendly way. EcoLexicon combines the advantages of a relational database, allowing for a quick deployment and feeding of the platform, and an ontology, enhancing user queries. Reconceptualization provides a way of representing the dynamic and multidimensional nature of concepts and terms. It offers a qualitative criterion for the representation of specialized concepts in line with the workings of the human conceptual system. Moreover, it is a quantitative solution to the problem of information overload, as it significantly reduces irrelevant context-free information.

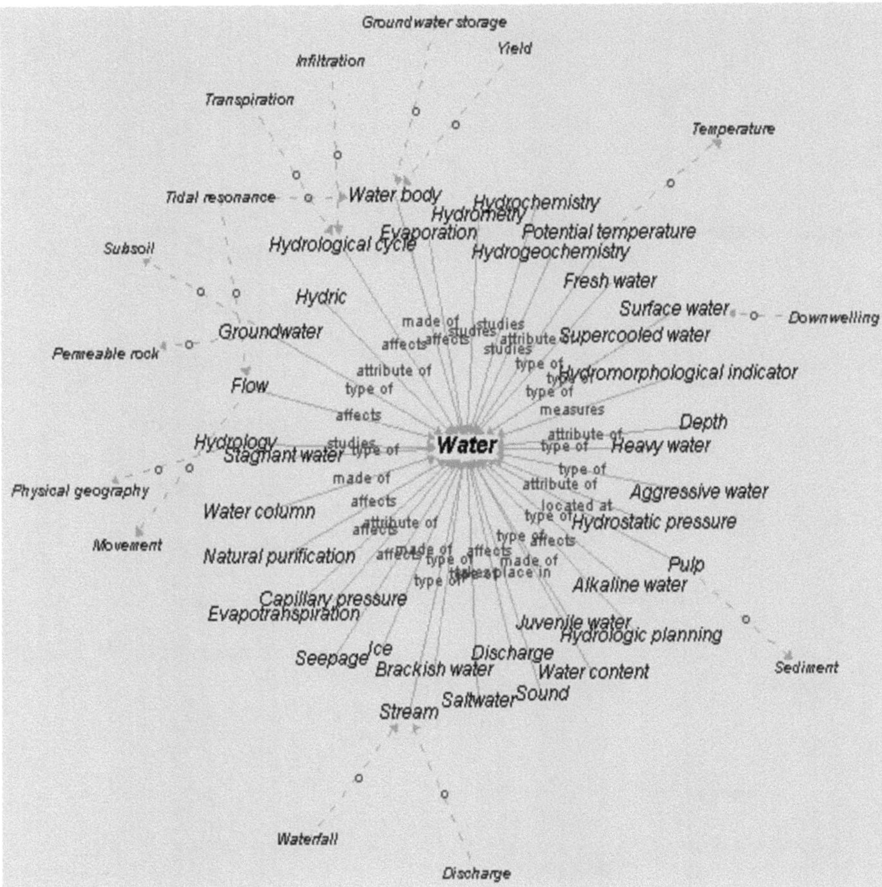

Fig. 13.27 WATER as a patient in HYDROLOGY

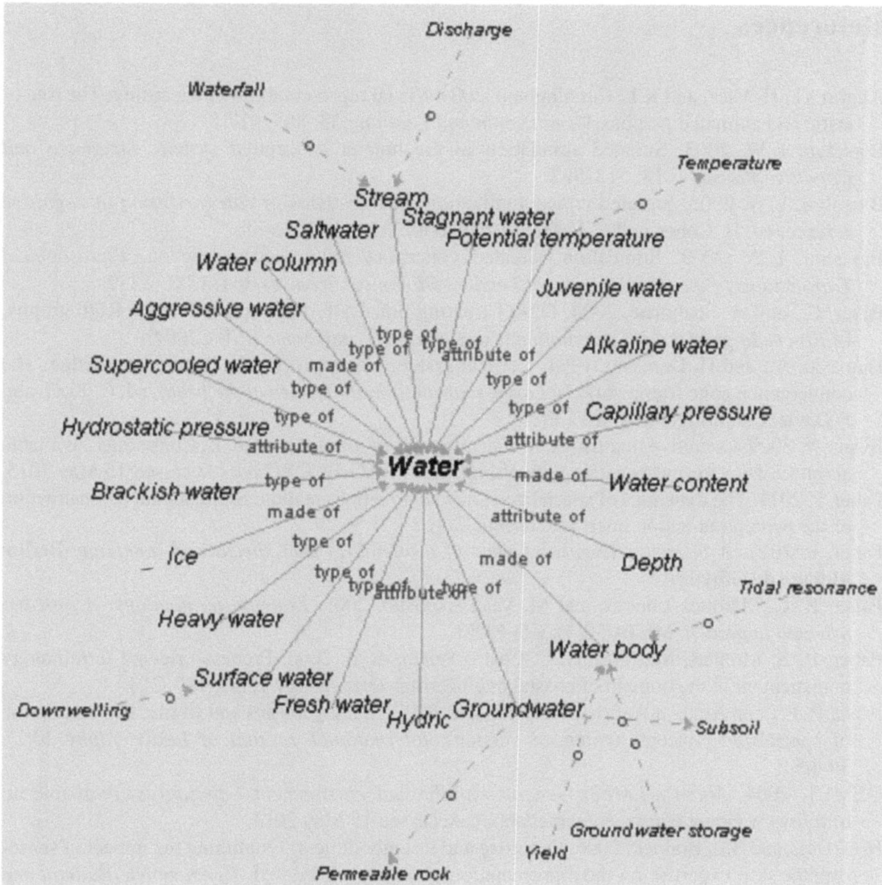

Fig. 13.28 WATER as an agent and patient in HYDROLOGY

References

Anglin, G., H. Vaez, and K.L. Cunningham. 2004. Visual representations and learning: The role of static and animated graphic. *Visualization and Learning* 33: 865–917.

Barsalou, L.W. 2003. Situated simulation in the human conceptual system. *Language and Cognitive Processes* 18: 513–562.

Barsalou, L.W. 2005. Situated conceptualization. In *Handbook of categorization in cognitive science*, ed. H. Cohen and C. Lefebvre, 619–650. St Louis: Elsevier.

Barsalou, L.W. 2009. Simulation, situated conceptualization and prediction. *Philosophical Transactions of the Royal Society of London: Biological Sciences* 364: 1281–1289.

Bizer, C., and A. Seaborne. 2004. D2RQ-treating non-RDF databases as virtual RDF graphs. In *Proceedings of the 3rd international semantic web conference (ISWC2004)*.

Damasio, A., and H. Damasio. 1994. Cortical systems for retrieval of concrete knowledge: The convergence zone framework. In *Large-scale neuronal theories of the brain*, ed. C. Koch and J. Davis. Cambridge, MA: MIT Press.

Evans, V. 2009. Cognitive linguistics. In *Encyclopedia of pragmatics*, ed. L. Cummings. Available at: http://www.vyvevans.net/cognitiveLinguisticsPRAG-ENCYC.pdf. Accessed 15 May 2013.

Faber, P. 2011. The dynamics of specialized knowledge representation: Simulational reconstruction or the perception-action interface. *Terminology* 17(1): 9–29.

Faber, P. 2012. *A cognitive linguistics view of terminology and specialized language*. Berlin: Mouton de Gruyter.

Faber, P., C. Márquez Linares, and M. Vega Expósito. 2005. *Framing terminology: A process-oriented approach*. META 50(4): CD-ROM.

Faber, P., S. Montero Martínez, M.C. Castro Prieto, et al. 2006. Process-oriented terminology management in the domain of coastal engineering. *Terminology* 12(2): 189–213.

Faber, P., P. León Araúz, J.A. Prieto Velasco, et al. 2007. Linking images and words: The description of specialized concepts (extended version). *International Journal of Lexicography* 20(1): 39–65.

GEMET. 2004. *About GEMET. General multilingual environmental thesaurus*. Available at: http://www.eionet.europa.eu/gemet/about. Accessed 15 May 2013.

Holt, L.E., and S.L. Beilock. 2006. Expertise and its embodiment: Examining the impact of sensorimotor skill expertise on the representation of action-related text. *Psychonomic Bulletin and Review* 13: 694–701.

House, J. 2006. Text and context in translation. *Journal of Pragmatics* 38: 338–358.

Kageura, K. 1997. Multifaceted/multidimensional concept systems. In *Handbook of terminology management: Basic aspects of terminology management*, ed. S.E. Wright and G. Budin, 119–132. Amsterdam/Philadelphia: John Benjamins.

Langacker, R.W. 1987. *Foundations of cognitive grammar: Theoretical prerequisites*, vol. 1. Stanford: Stanford University Press.

Lenci, A., N. Bel, F. Busa, et al. 2000. SIMPLE: A general framework for the development of multilingual lexicons. *International Journal of Lexicography* 13(4): 248–263.

León Araúz, P. 2009. *Representación multidimensional del conocimiento especializado: el uso de marcos desde la macroestructura hasta la microestructura*. Ph.D. thesis, University of Granada, Granada, Spain.

León Araúz, P., and P. Faber. 2010. Natural and contextual constraints for domain-specific relations. In *Proceedings of semantic relations. Theory and applications*, Malta.

León Araúz, P., and P.J. Magaña Redondo. 2010. *EcoLexicon: Contextualizing an environmental ontology*. In *Proceedings of the terminology and knowledge engineering (TKE) conference 2010*, Dublin City University, Dublin.

León Araúz, P., P.J. Magaña Redondo, and P. Faber. 2009. *Managing inner and outer overinformation in Ecolexicon: An environmental ontology*. In *Proceedings of the 8th international conference on terminology and artificial intelligence*, Toulouse.

León Araúz, P., A. Reimerink, and A. Garcia-Aragón. 2013. Dynamism and context in specialized knowledge. *Terminology* 19(1): 31–61.

Meyer, I., L. Bowker, and K. Eck. 1992. *COGNITERM: An experiment in building a knowledge-based term bank.* In *Proceedings of Euralex '92*, 159–172

Prieto Velasco, J.A. 2008. *Información gráfica y grados de especialidad en el discurso científico-técnico: un estudio de corpus*. Ph.D. thesis, University of Granada, Granada.

Pustejovsky J, C. Havasi, J. Littman, et al. 2006. Towards a generative lexical resource: The brandeis semantic ontology. In *Proceedings of LREC 2006*, Genoa.

Reimerink, A., M. García de Quesada, and S. Montero Martínez. 2010. Contextual information in terminological bases: A multimodal approach. *Journal of Pragmatics* 42(7): 1928–1950. doi:10.1016/j.pragma.2009.12.008.

Rosch, E. 1978. Principles of categorization. In *Cognition and categorization*, ed. E. Rosch and B.B. Lloyd, 27–28. Hillsdale: Erlbaum.

Smith, M., C. Welty, and D. McGuinness (eds.). 2004. *OWL Web ontology language guide*. W3C Recommendations.

Tucker, M., and R. Ellis. 1998. On the relations between seen objects and components of potential actions. *Journal of Experimental Psychology: Human Perception and Performance* 24: 830–846.

Tucker, M., and R. Ellis. 2001. The potentiation of grasp types during visual object categorization. *Visual Cognition* 8: 769–800.

Yeh, W., and L.W. Barsalou. 2006. The situated nature of concepts. *American Journal of Psychology* 119: 349–384.

Chapter 14
New Approaches to Audiovisual Translation: The Usefulness of Corpus-Based Studies for the Teaching of Dubbing and Subtitling

Juan Pedro Rica Peromingo, Reyes Albarrán Martín, and Blanca García Riaza

14.1 Introduction

The use of translated audiovisual products is a routine activity in our daily lives. It is a relevant and consistent economic activity and one of the most important and representative channels of cultural transmission. These are the main reasons why audiovisual translation (AVT) is one of the fastest growing areas in the field of Translation Studies. New training and research topics have been developed as Translation Studies turn their attention to audiovisual translation. Initial approaches focused on the professional stages of the different AVT modes and on the dilemma between the convenience of dubbing or subtitling audiovisual materials. Nowadays, audiovisual translation is studied from many different perspectives. Interest in this area is still growing considerably and audiovisual translation has become an established academic field across the globe. As a result of this, AVT is now offered at several universities at undergraduate levels, as well as in postgraduate or specialized courses. Spanish universities are not an exception to this trend and they have introduced AVT training together with more traditional areas such as literary or legal translation.

Several areas of research have arisen in the last decades. On the one hand, we find those studying the characteristics of AVT (by and large subtitling and dubbing).

J.P. Rica Peromingo (✉)
Departamento de Filología Inglesa I, Universidad Complutense de Madrid, Madrid, Spain
e-mail: juanpe@filol.ucm.es

R.A. Martín
Departamento de Traducción e Interpretación, Universidad de Salamanca, Salamanca, Spain
e-mail: reyes.albarran@usal.es

B.G. Riaza
Departamento de Filología Inglesa, Universidad de Salamanca, Salamanca, Spain
e-mail: bgr@usal.es

E. Bárcena et al. (eds.), *Languages for Specific Purposes in the Digital Era*, Educational Linguistics 19, DOI 10.1007/978-3-319-02222-2_14,

On the other hand, there are those that are focused on the professional dimension or the development of the didactical and pedagogical aspects of the field.

In this study, we propose that the empirical methodology put forward by corpus linguists and its computing tools can be used to analyze translations of media content, namely films, as Romero Fresco (2009) has advanced in his corpus–based study on the naturalness of the Spanish dubbing language, where he focuses on the television series Friends and its Spanish dubbing.

In this respect, and as Toda (2005: 128) asserts, the specific jargon present in cinema discourse is one of the most quickly evolving features of lexicon, a fact that has to be taken into account when analyzing audiovisual discourse. In this sense, and bearing in mind the applicability of corpus linguistics methodology and tools, we have compiled a corpus of bilingual subtitles in English and Spanish to study the formulae and structures present in the American films selected to form the corpus. As Pearson (1998: 44–45) claims, the only way of identifying specific terminology is to analyze a specific corpus, or domain-specific corpus which "do not contribute to a description of ordinary language, either because they contain a high proportion of unusual features, or their origins are not reliable as records of people behaving normally" (EAGLES 1994 as quoted in Tognini-Bonelli 2001: 8).

In the first part of this work, we will deal with the main characteristics of AVT, focusing on its two main forms: subtitling and dubbing. Then, we will analyze how AVT is taught at Spanish universities and what software tools are frequently used. Afterwards, we will present corpus linguistics as an adequate approach for the study of audiovisual discourse and we will include part of the analysis of the CORSUBIL corpus we have carried out. In so doing, we will be able to present the results and conclusions we have reached after our research, which has the main objective of presenting Corpus Linguistics as a very useful tool for audiovisual text analysis.

14.2 What Is Meant by AVT?

AVT is a special translation method which deals with two channels: auditory and visual. It is often called "constrained translation" (Titford 1982) because it is conditioned by extralinguistic elements, since several restrictive aspects need to be considered for the target text production.

AVT involves active engagement with social, cultural, political and technological changes because it requires increased specialization and greater diversification on the part of practitioners, trainers, and researchers alike.

The two most widely established and also the most popular forms of AVT are dubbing and subtitling. There are clearly established preferences among viewers in favour of one or the other according to the tradition in each country. France, Spain, Italy and Germany are among the European countries that prefer dubbing, while Portugal, the Netherlands, Greece and the Nordic countries choose subtitling. It is important to state that the decision on which method to use (dubbing or subtitling) is absolutely independent from the translator's personal preferences and it is essentially based on commercial issues.

Apart from dubbing and subtitling, we have identified (Rica et al. 2010) other minor forms of AVT such as:

- Voice-over (mainly used in documentaries).
- Localization (translation of web pages and video games).
- Subtitling for the deaf and hard of hearing (TDT).
- Audio description for the blind and partially sighted (DVD formats).
- *Fandubbing* and *fansubbing* (that is to say, dubbing and subtitling carried out by non-professionals).

Audiovisual translators have to cope with the same problems that any other translator may find. However, AVT restrictions and the difficulties in the oral to written transposition have to be included in the translation process. That is the main reason why AVT portrays specific characteristics and drawbacks to translators, since an audiovisual text represents a way of communication that is different from the written and the oral modes. Translation is constrained by nonverbal elements which may be intended to carry meaning or to complete the meaning of the words. Subtitling as well as dubbing is conditioned by the image (what is said or shown on the screen must not be contradictory to what characters do) and the time (the length of the translated message has to be the same as the original message).

As a result, and according to what has been stated by Díaz Cintas:

> The translator must be aware for each scene, for each frame almost, of which are the most important and relevant items (verbal or otherwise) in the meaning(s) and function(s) of the (AV) source text so as to make informed, context-sensitive, function-oriented, audiovisually-coherent decisions so as to the words that will be the most appropriate for the task at hand (2008: 33).

Audiovisual texts, due to their textual nature, can be characterized by their meaning density and their rhetorical complexity. It must also be taken into account that the linguistic characteristics of the audiovisual text are not the ones which normally appear in spontaneous oral language, since we are dealing with a previously established text.

> One more unhinging peculiarity of spoken dialogue is precisely that: it is spoken and not written. More accurately, it is written to sound spoken. People pause, collect their thoughts, begin again, clear their throats, change paths halfway down the syntactical road. Such anacolutha, deemed bad style and poorly thought out in a written text, are exactly what make a spoken dialogue animated, credible, authentic and human (Whitman-Linsen 1992: 31–32).

We are then talking about a prefabricated oral message, thought and structured following some particular conventions. Mason states this idea when he says that "Screen dialogue is not natural dialogue: any comparison of a screenplay with a transcribed sequence of naturally occurring conversation will demonstrate the point" (1989: 16).

14.2.1 Some Characteristics of Dubbing

Dubbing can be defined as the process of replacing the original soundtrack of a film with a translation of the message into another language. However, at the same time there must be a synchronization process of the sounds and lip movements between the original text and the translated one, in order to reduce the differences between both languages at a maximum and to create the illusion for the audience that the actors speak the same language they do.

Dubbed texts take an intermediate position between the written and the spoken language. As we have previously mentioned, they are texts "written to be spoken". Film language differs from that of spontaneous conversation in a number of ways. For example, there are features that in spontaneous speech result from performance-related factors such as pauses or hesitations or there are overlaps that are typically absent from film dialogue.

The dubbing process is composed of different stages: the script translation and subsequent adjustment, actors' direction, the multiple takes of a recording, etc. Professionals belonging to different fields and with specific profiles take part in each of these stages. There is, for example, a translator who is a specialist in dubbing, the dubbing director, a sound technician, a supervisor, and the dubbing actors.

Among the several parts of dubbing, the script translation is possibly one of the less appreciated aspects. It is important to point out that, unfortunately, in most translations for dubbing, the translator's role is just restricted to propose a first draft of the script for the dubbed version. That first translation is often modified due to technical or adjustment requisites, which implies a manipulation and alteration of the translator's work. Consequently, there exists the possibility of introducing translation mistakes, even some serious ones. Nonetheless, the translation activity constitutes an essential piece without which the smooth running of the whole process would not be possible. Therefore, we consider that, instead of doing without the translator, he/she should be present in the whole process of dubbing so that the quality of the linguistic elements is guaranteed.

Among the main features of this form of AVT are the following (Rica et al. 2010):

- Lip and prosodic synchrony: there is not usually a phonetic link between the sounds of the two languages, but there is an illusion that the character on the screen speaks the spectator's language, due to the coincidence of lip movements.
- A tendency toward written formality typical of written discourse: a more idiomatic language is sometimes needed.
- Stylistic imbalance due to the continuous switches from formal to informal language and vice versa.
- Cohesive factors are neglected.
- The translator has to use adaptation techniques through processes of naturalization (translating with a clear, fluid and acceptable style for the target culture receiver, deleting all the possible difficulties derived from its foreign nature), foreignization (opaque style for the target culture receptor), standardization (dialect levelling), euphemization (toning down language that might be offensive), simplification, etc.

Among the main characteristics of dubbing we find some of the most important drawbacks that this form of AVT reveals, for instance:

- Adapting language to the lip movements of a foreign language: (*What?* vs. *¿Qué?*)
- Re-acting a scene with different talents and voices.

- Accents and dialects: they are usually dubbed into a standard variety. However, they may reflect the characters' position in the plot and there is a loss of a character's fidelity. There is a need, then, to verbalize the origin of the speaker if it is important for the story, that is to say, if accents or dialects play a role.
- Switch the register according to the situation and social position.
- The use of voice quality is frequently used to hint stereotypes, for example, a refined upper class person or a rude working class one.
- Finally, some paralinguistic aspects normally hide some problems: speech, pauses, volume, gestures, body movement, etc.
  (Rica et al. 2010).

14.2.2 Some Characteristics of Subtitling

Subtitling consists of introducing a translation of the dialogue of a foreign-language film at the bottom of the screen. But subtitles not only include dialogues between actors, but also each text that appears on the screen (letters, signs, newspapers' pages) and the soundtrack (songs).

Experts on the field seem to agree with the idea that subtitling is addressed to play a more important role in the area of audiovisual translation. The use of subtitles is justified because it is cheaper and faster than dubbing (as we have already seen, dubbing requires the presence of more professionals working in a more complex technical context). Subtitles must be synchronized with image and dialogues and must remain on the screen enough time for the audience to read them easily. Among the advantages of subtitling we find, for instance, that the spectator may listen to the original voices of actors and therefore, is able to appreciate the characters' performance better. By contrast, one of the most important disadvantages of subtitling is that subtitles spoil part of the image and distract the audience's attention.

Subtitles tend to follow the standard punctuation rules, but they also use some specific punctuation conventions which may vary from company to company and from place to place.

Subtitling implies a change of medium from oral to written speech, which is a notable modification. In fact, dialogue in subtitles is not exactly the same as in a conventional oral exchange, but at the same time it also has to show a series of characteristics that distance it from written discourse, such as unfinished sentences, repetitions, scarce subordinated clauses and a predominance of juxtaposition. Nevertheless, subtitles cannot show all these aspects due to space and time limitations.

Some of the main characteristics of subtitling are:

- There are differences (overall in the number of characters per line) between subtitling for TV (TDT), DVD, movies, or other minor forms (opera, theatre, etc.).
- Due to obvious space restrictions and according to the average reading speed, there is a maximum number of characters per line and a maximum number of lines per subtitle. The so-called *six seconds rule* is used to estimate the length of a subtitle. It is claimed that in that time an average spectator is able to read and understand the information contained in a two-lined subtitle (each one of about 35 keystrokes with some variations for cinema, DVD or TV formats).

- There is a need to follow some general subtitling norms or conventions (Díaz Cintas 2003) or the client's own norms or conventions with respect to the use of swearwords, abbreviations, italics, hyphens in dialogues, capital letters, suspension dots, inserts, etc.
- The spotting (also known as 'timing' or 'cueing') consists of dividing the original dialogue into units to be subtitled and indicates the time when a subtitle should appear and disappear. Subtitles should keep temporal synchrony with the utterances, that is to say, the subtitle has to appear on the screen at the very moment when the character starts speaking and disappear when the character stops talking.
- Subtitling also involves the omission of several elements from the original linguistic message because spatial limitations have to be taken into account (32–35 keystrokes per line and a maximum of two lines).
  (Rica et al. 2010).

There are some important drawbacks or problems with subtitling such as:

- Possible interferences between the original language and the target language.
- The translator must adapt the information to the space provided and that entails the deletion of unnecessary elements.
- Temporal synchrony (the "golden rule" in subtitling): this means that subtitles must appear when the actor starts speaking and disappear when he/she stops speaking.
- Time conventions: subtitles must be produced according to time rules (between 1 and 6 s).
- Image "contamination": part of the screen is devoted to subtitles.
- Interpretation, intonation and non-verbal information are not transmitted through subtitles (on the contrary, that information is needed when dealing with subtitles for the deaf and hard of hearing).
- Adjustment usually influences the translation of cultural references.
- The main difficulties for translators focus on the translation of cultuvre-bound terms, slang and colloquialisms, taboo words or swearwords, puns or plays on words, humour examples and songs.
  (Rica et al. 2010).

14.3 Audiovisual Translation Training at Spanish Universities

At the beginning of the present study we already stated that research of audiovisual translation has developed considerably in the last decades and nowadays is being implemented at a university level. AVT is a relatively new area in the academic curriculum of Translation and Interpreting studies. Previously, AVT professionals had self-taught training. Therefore, not until very recently did the audiovisual translator enter the profession with practice, due to the fact that few educational institutions taught the most used audiovisual translation modes (subtitling, dubbing and above all, voice-over).

Training in subtitling and dubbing started to be part of the curricula of some institutions in the last decades of the twentieth century with the emergence of many academic courses at undergraduate levels as well as at postgraduate ones. In the last few years there has been considerable growth of AVT in the area of teaching and learning of languages for specific purposes.

In Spain, for example, there has been a huge proliferation in the number of universities teaching AVT in Translation and Interpreting studies, mainly dealing with aspects like:

- Historical information
- Characteristics of the audiovisual text and language
- Subtitling and dubbing conventions and norms
- Translation problems
- Professional aspects
- Resources and software
- Subtitling for the deaf and hard of hearing and audio-description

In the last few years, we have witnessed the development of a considerable number of masters and postgraduate courses specifically on audiovisual translation. Some of the best-known postgraduate programs offered by Spanish public universities dealing with AVT are, for instance, the Master in Audiovisual Translation offered by the Universitat Autònoma de Barcelona, or the Postgraduate Program in Audiovisual Translation of the Universitat Pompeu Fabra (Barcelona). Moreover, some private universities offer AVT studies as well, with the Universidad Europea de Madrid or Universidad Alfonso X el Sabio, among others.

Modules on AVT, whether compulsory or optional, are also common in undergraduate programs of several Spanish universities. The importance of this area can also be seen if we look at some recent research on AVT including: dissertations, general books, articles, or seminars. As Mayoral (2001) observes, more research articles, doctoral theses, books, conferences, courses and workshops have been produced in the last few years on the field.

The teaching and learning of the different AVT modes have been developed and at present are well-established components of postgraduate courses. One of the main challenges of introducing AVT at universities programs has been technology. High quality training requires students to familiarize themselves with the equipment and software that they will be using in their professional careers. The two main problems are that standard subtitling/dubbing programs are very expensive for most universities and that technology in this field evolves quickly and it soon becomes obsolete.

14.4 Resources and Software for AVT

Translation these days is unavoidably linked to technology and to a highly competitive professional market. Therefore, the study of these two aspects would be essential for the professional development of students. When it comes to audiovisual translation, this idea is even more important than in other translation fields.

To start with, the Internet has become a basic resource for audiovisual translators. Some basic online resources include: databases, mailing lists, free movie scripts and transcripts, blogs on AVT, as well as online dictionaries and glossaries or professional associations for subtitling and dubbing, etc.

Among the tools for audiovisual text analysis, we can find two different categories:

- Professional subtitling software: some of the most popular programs commercialised in the market are *Fab, Poliscript, EZTitles, Swift, Titlevision, Cavena Tempo, SoftNi.*
- Freeware subtitling software: *Subtitle Workshop* (a free program used by several universities), *Subtitle Ripper* or *Subtitle Processor.*

The technology and software used for dubbing is much more expensive and it is sometimes restricted to recording studios. Nevertheless, some software like *Virtual Dub* or *AV Video Morpher* is available for the general public.

14.5 New Approaches to AVT: Corpus Linguistics

Discourse analysis has traditionally been the appropriate approach to study language in depth, but it is a reality that new approaches to the study of language have been born in the last decades, providing linguists with new methodologies and new insights. That is the case of Corpus Linguistics, a discipline that develops a scientific analysis of language and is inserted into an empirical approach that operates with verifiable data, obtained by means of observation and examination, not focusing its studies on intuitions or speculations (Lyons 1981: 38).

According to McEnery and Wilson (2001), corpus linguistics is a methodology that can be applied in almost every area of linguistics, rather than to a mere branch; and has been defined as "[…] a way of investigating language by observing large amounts of naturally-occurring, electronically-stored discourse, using software which selects, sorts, matches, counts, and calculates" (Hunston and Francis 2000: 14–15). The development of corpus linguistics has meant both a quantitative and a qualitative change in the study of language, which can now be observed in greater quantities. As Sinclair (1991: 101) asserts, "language looks rather different when you look a lot of it at once", and it is precisely the compilation of corpora that has enabled the perspective over a great quantity of language. Corpora provide researchers with real instances of language in context, valuable data to get meaningful results in the frame of corpus linguistics; discourse analysis has meant a qualitative change to our understanding of language by enabling researchers to analyze vast quantities of real data in a systematic way, as Kennedy notes:

> Corpus linguistics, like all linguistics, is concerned primarily with the description and explanation of the nature, structure and use of language and languages and with particular matters such as language acquisition, variation and change. Corpus linguistics has nevertheless developed something of a life of its own within linguistics, with a tendency sometimes to focus on lexis and lexical grammar rather than pure syntax (Kennedy 1998: 8).

Thanks to the use of scientific data in the analysis of written and spoken language, linguists are able to make objective accounts on different language varieties and text types, leaving aside previous analytical procedures where assertions were based on subjective, individual perceptions (McEnery and Wilson 2001: 103). The work of language engineers and linguists has made important advances in the generation of resources and tools in the field of language description; improved corpora are now being built as well as computer software being developed to assist the linguist in his/her work. Benefits brought by computerized analysis of data to text processing are both innumerable and invaluable, as we have to consider that not only the processing of data is accelerated and improved, but also the quality of the evidence obtained are favored by the help of computers in information managing. As it is stated by McEnery and Wilson (2001: 17), computers have meant the turning of the discipline from a pseudo-procedure to a feasible methodology: *computational corpus linguistics,* where the computer is the basic tool to assist the analysis and description of language and meaning as they are contained in texts collected in a corpus. Computational corpus linguistics has, for this reason, accomplished a variety of techniques to retrieve, search for and compute data, to provide linguists with information about language that can be very varied and, at the same time, to empower them to solve problems that had been haunting language research for years.

The main object of study in corpus linguistics is the corpus, a collection of texts which implies not a mere gathering of language, but a purposeful assemblage of texts intended to be analyzed looking for some linguistic pattern. As McEnery and Wilson posit, although any collection of texts may be called a corpus, linguistics has made use of this word in specific contexts where has acquired specific characteristics:

> In principle, any collection of more than one text should be called a corpus: the term 'corpus' is simply the Latin for 'body', hence a corpus may be defined as any body of text. It need imply nothing more. But the term 'corpus' when used in the context of modern linguistics tends more frequently to have more specific connotations [Sampling and representativeness, finite size, machine readable form and standard reference] than this simple definition provides for (McEnery and Wilson 2001: 29).

Among the principles that rule corpus compilation, we would like to highlight those of Representativity, Authenticity and Sampling. Texts collected in a corpus should be representative of the text type studied; they should be as well authentic, taken from real instances of discourse production and constitute a sample big enough to obtain significant results from its study, as can be seen in Fig. 14.1 below.

14.6 Corpus and AVT: Empirical Approach to the Study of Audiovisual Discourse

In nowadays society, mass media are not only producers of information, but also important institutions which present culture, politics and social life, together with the way in which they are linguistically built. The discourse of media does not only reflect the textual features that are conventional practice at a given community

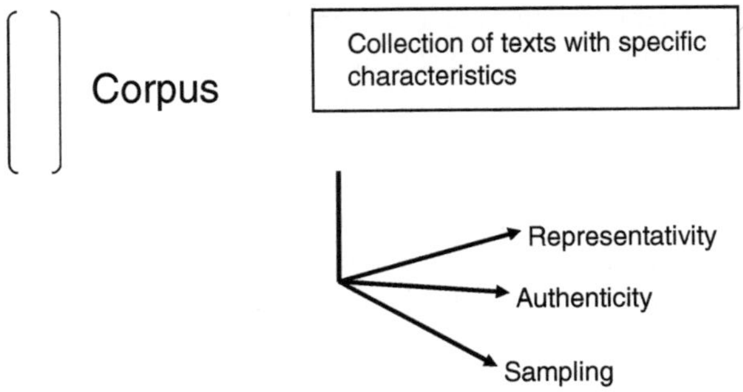

Fig. 14.1 Representativity, authenticity and sampling characteristics of corpora

(Kim and Thompson 2010: 54), but also how values are encoded in society (Bell and Garret 1998: 64–65). As Bell (1991: 1) points out, the audience dimension is one of the main defining characteristics of mass media, and articulates this relationship between audience and media outputs in six different features:

- The audience is larger than in other communicative events.
- Mass media content is publicly more accessible in relation to other contents.
- The audience is heterogeneous.
- There exists simultaneous contact with diverse individuals.
- The flow of communication is unidirectional and impersonal.
- The mass audience can be considered a creation of the modern society.

Many studies have focused their attention on the language of mass media. Newspaper discourse has been broadly studied (Calsamiglia and López Ferrero 2003; García Riaza 2010a, b) and the discourse of film and television broadcasting companies has also received the attention of linguists. Corpora of audiovisual discourse were already compiled in the eighties (Herbst 1987; Delabastita 1989; Whitman-Linsen 1992) to perform analyses on the translations of dialogues, and more recent research has devoted its attention to the examination of specific grammatical patterns in the language of films, such as Beltrán-Palanques analysis of refusals in contemporary American cinema (2010).

14.7 *CORSUBIL* Corpus: Analysis and Characteristics

CORSUBIL (*Corpus de Subtítulos Bilingües ingles-español*) is a bilingual corpus which includes bilingual subtitles in English and Spanish. It contains 18 million words distributed in two subcorpora: CORSUBILIN (*Corpus de Subtítulos Bilingües en Inglés*) and CORSUBILES (*Corpus de Subtítulos Bilingües en Español*) with its translations (see Fig. 14.2 below). The number of words in each of the subcorpora is practically the same: around nine million words with a selection of the most important movies in the history of the American movie world. The variety of English in the corpus is American English, since all the movies included in the CORSUBIL correspond to American movies. This bilingual corpus can nevertheless be extended to other varieties of English (British cinema, for example) in the future.

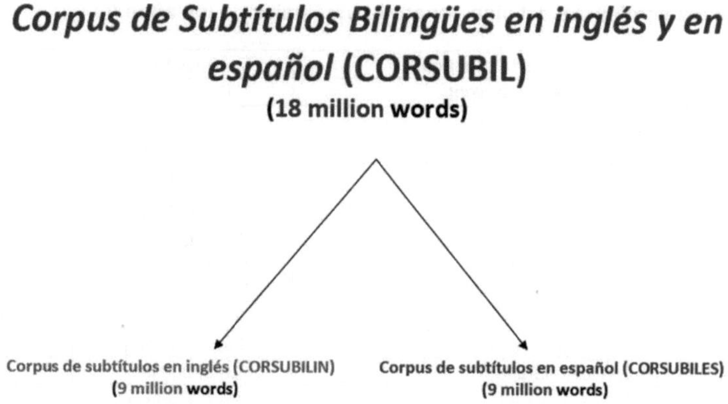

Fig. 14.2 Number of words in the CORSUBIL

This corpus has been compiled along 2010 and 2011 (Rica 2011a). The compilation process has been long and tedious because there are around 100 movies in each of the periods of the American film history among which those included in the corpus have been selected. The subtitles files have been extracted from the original DVDs using some software appropriate for this purpose: SubRip: http://subrip.softonic.com/ or DVD Subtitle Ripper: http://sourceforge.net/projects/subtitleripper/. The files obtained are .txt files which can be analyzed by corpus software such as Wordsmith Tools 3.0.

Each file has a code (Sub), an order number (000X), followed by "a" (for those original English subtitles) or "b" (for those translated subtitles into Spanish): for example, for the movie *It happened one night* (Fran Capra, 1934), the two files obtained are coded as follows: Sub0001a for the original English version and Sub0001b for the translated version in Spanish.

At the beginning of this process the distribution of movies into different movie styles was considered. That idea was discharged because there seems not to be a clear agreement on the distribution of American movies into different styles in some of the American movie databases consulted. That is why the distribution into different historical periods was used. The five periods in which the CORSUBIL is distributed are stated as follows: from the beginnings of the "talking films" in the USA to the 40s; the 50s and the 60s; the 70s and the 80s; the 90s; and, finally, the cinema in the twenty-first century. We followed some of the most important bibliographical references on the issue (Aguilar et al. 2002; Alsina Thevenet 1993a, b; Caparrós Lera 2009; Finler 2010). This distribution was considered more functional and practical for the analysis of the subtitles.

For each of the subcorpora a table with all the details of each movie chosen has been designed. This table includes, firstly, the file code, the original title of the movie in English and the translated title into Spanish, the movie director and the number of words in the file (see Fig. 14.3 for an example of the information included in this table).

A) Desde los comienzos del cine sonoro hasta finales de los años 40

Código	Año	Título película	Director	N.º palabras
Sub0001a	1934	*It happened one night*	Fran Capra	17372
Sub0001b	1934	*Sucedió una noche*	Fran Capra	16162
Sub0002a	1932	*Grand Hotel*	Edmund Goulding	18327
Sub0002b	1932	*Gran Hotel*	Edmund Goulding	17229
Sub0003a	1933	*Dinner at eight*	George Cukor	20657
Sub0003b	1933	*Ceno a las ocho*	George Cukor	19431
Sub0004a	1933	*Flying down to Rio*	Thornton Freeland	11071
Sub0004b	1933	*Volando hacia Río de joneiro*	Thornton Freeland	10224
Sub0005a	1933	*Gold diggers of 1933*	Mervyn LeRoy	18738
Sub0005b	1933	*Gold diggers of 1933*	Mervyn LeRoy	16965
Sub0006a	1929	*The love parade*	Ernst Lubitsch	14152
Sub0006b	1929	*El desfile del amor*	Ernst Lubitsch	11836
Sub0007a	1930	*Montecarlo*	Ernst Lubitsch	13301
Sub0007b	1930	*Montecarlo*	Ernst Lubitsch	11174
Sub0008a	1931	*Dr. jeckyll and Mr, Hyde*	Rouben Mamoulian	13122
Sub0008b	1931	*El hombre y el monstruo*	Rouben Mamoulian	12053
Sub0009a	1939	*Gone with the wind*	Victor Fleming	39281
Sub0009b	1939	*Lo que el viento se llevó*	Victor Fleming	33220

Fig. 14.3 Information about the movie subtitles in the CORSUBIL

After each of the periods collected a summary of all the words included in the subcorpora is also included: each of the periods contains approximately three million words (1.5 million words in the CORSUBILIN and 1.5 million words in the CORSUBILES), as can be seen in Fig. 14.4 below.

Regarding the methodology, we have used computer software (specifically Wordsmith 3.0 and, as mentioned before, software for extracting the subtitles from the original DVDs: SubRip y DVD Subtitle Ripper) for data gathering, for lexical searchings and for the quantitative analysis of the data. Software of this type has allowed us to obtain data in a reliable and fast way, and apply the statistical analysis needed for getting significant results. We have also used Microsoft Excel to carry out the T-test for the statistical analysis of some of the results obtained. Finally, we have applied the formulae proposed by Biber et al. (1994, 1998) called "norming", especially to avoid any possible influence in the results of the differences in the number of words in each of the periods and in each of the subcorpora. These formulae allow us to verify whether the results are statistically significant. It consists of the summation of all the tokens obtained in the searchings, divided by the total number of words in the corpus (or subcorpora) and, finally, multiplied by 10,000 words for its norming.

Our intention, in the end, will be to quantitatively and qualitatively analyze the data in order to obtain a bilingual list of lexical units used in English and their appropriate translation in Spanish. We believe that quantitatively analysis alone does not explain how language works. As Conrad (2002: 78) states: "numbers alone give little inside about language. Even the most sophisticated quantitative analysis must be tied to functional interpretations of the language patterns".

Sub0098a	1949	*Adam's rib*	King Vidor	18840
Sub0098b	1949	*La costilla de Adán*	King Vidor	18153
Sub0099a	1949	*It's a great feeling*	David Butler	16363
Sub0099b	1949	*El amor no puede esperar*	David Butler	15364
Sub0100a	1947	*Magic Town*	William A. Wellman	15229
Sub0100b	1947	*Ciudad mágica*	William A. Wellman	18633

Number of words English (a)	**1.630.376**
Número de palabras español (b)	**1.481.137**
TOTAL	**3.111.513**

Fig. 14.4 Total number of words in each of the periods collected

We have decided to use Wordsmith Tools 3.0 because it is one of the most accepted software programs among linguists for corpus analysis,[1] especially because it is user-friendly in its visual distribution and it also includes the most useful functions for lexical unit analysis: concordance lines, wordlists, keywords, collocations and phraseological units' analysis, etc. It allows us at the same time to apply all necessary statistical analysis and frequencies for the quantitative analysis of the data.

14.8 CORSUBIL Corpus: An Example of Analysis

As an example of all possibilities we have for linking corpus linguistics and our analysis of the bilingual subtitles compiled, we have taken the taxonomy for lexical units proposed by Biber et al. (1999, 2003) used in oral discourse. For the purposes of the present research we have concentrated our analysis on the polite speech-act formulae included in the taxonomy (see Table 14.1 below). These formulae include expressions for thanking, apologising, requesting and congratulating.

We have searched in the CORSUBILIN for all those terms and in the CORSUBILES for their translated counterparts. The final goal is to analyze the translation of such terms and build up a bilingual list of oral lexical units in English and Spanish. Our final goal is threefold:

– See whether the terms are translated correctly in Spanish or not.

[1] Both versions 4.0 and 5.0 are available (Scott 2003). Among their new functions we find the *WebGetter* which allows users to build up a corpus using web pages with the grammatical or lexical unit that is being analyzed. For the purposes of the present study, since the .txt files have already been collected, we are not in the need of using an updated version of the program with the *Webgetter* function.

Table 14.1 Polite speech-act formulae in the taxonomy

Please	That's okay
Please?	Sorry
Thank you	Beg your pardon?
Thank you very much	Pardon me
Thanks	Pardon?
Thanks a lot	Excuse me
You're welcome	Excuse me?
Good luck	Congratulations
No problem	Thank you for + ING
	Sorry to + INF

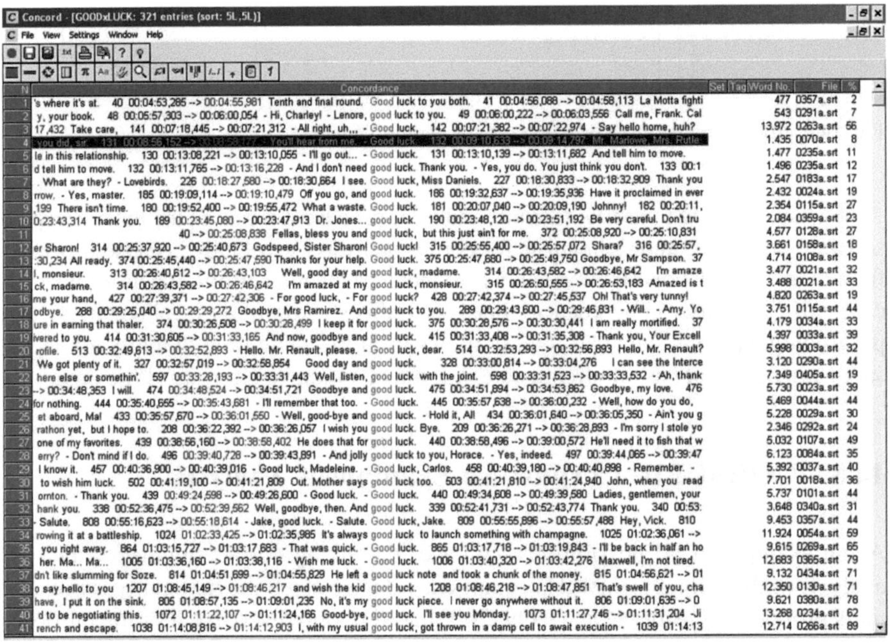

Fig. 14.5 "Good luck" in the CORSUBILIN

- See whether there are different possible translations for the same terms in Spanish.
- See whether all these oral lexical units are translated in the Spanish subtitles or omitted (as it normally happens with this kind of formulae) in the oral discourse.

For example, we have searched for the lexical unit "good luck" in the CORSUBIL: 321 tokens have been found in the CORSUBILIN for such lexical unit in the subtitles in English (see Fig. 14.5 below).

Searching for the lexical unit in the Spanish translated subtitles, 311 tokens were found in the CORSUBILES corpus (see Fig. 14.6 below).

Fig. 14.6 "Buena suerte" in the CORSUBILES

This means that for some reason there is a number of 11 tokens of difference between one subcorpora and the other. A deeper and more qualitative analysis of the data is needed to figure out the reasons of this difference: analyzing the data with concordance lines (see Figs. 14.5 and 14.6 above) only gives us the total numbers of tokens, but not the reasons why the logical translation for "good luck" in Spanish ("buena suerte") does not always appear as such in the Spanish subtitles.

If we take the files individually and locate the terms searched we notice that in 5 of the movies subtitled in Spanish (7 of the tokens) the lexical unit has been omitted

Table 14.2 Speech-act formulae *good luck* in English and in Spanish

Speech-act formulae	English subtitles	Spanish subtitles
Good luck	Good luck	Buena suerte ¡Suerte! Ø

and in 2 other movies (4 of the tokens) the translation in Spanish has been "¡Suerte!" and not "Buena suerte". Therefore, in our future bilingual list of this speech-act formulae it will be necessary to include the three possibilities found, as stated in Table 14.2 below.

It has been extensively proved in later years that for second language acquisition (SLA) or foreign language acquisition (FLA) and teaching the use of linguistic corpora constitutes a very useful tool (Rica 2010; Granger 2004; Hunston 2002). We believe that through a linguistic analysis of the subtitles in English and in Spanish, then, we may attain a better knowledge of the lexical networks that have been more frequently used in the translation of some films; we also have precisely and quickly access to specific terms; and, finally, we may be able to assess, either in a positive or negative way, the role of the translator in the translation of the film.

14.9 Practical Applications

The application of corpus studies to the analysis of AVT can mean a wide variety of changes in different fields of study in language teaching and research, such as lexicographic or translation studies.

Lexicographic studies benefitted from empirical data long before the discipline of corpus linguistics was established as a source of samples for linguistic research, but it has been the development of corpus linguistics which has triggered the compilation of more corpora for lexicographic purposes, collections of texts that have been used to study specific characteristics of the lexical elements of the language under study, and which have mainly given birth to important dictionaries that mean a step forward in the classification and description of language. The study that we have carried out can also be a step forward in the elaboration of dictionaries, providing lexicographers with up-to-date information and more complete and precise definitions, derived from the use of real examples extracted from actual uses of the language. Glossaries and dictionaries are essential tools for translators, data reservoirs of audiovisual language that can also benefit from corpus analyses on AVT. Specific translations shown in film subtitles can constitute a database for translators, who, from now on, do not depend exclusively on their knowledge to carry out audiovisual translations, but also on previous occurrences of the word, and how it has been translated.

Another of the most straightforward practical applications that corpus linguistics has is language teaching. New insights into the shape, meaning, beha-vior or company words keep can be immediately transported to the teaching field, thus obtaining real input coming from actual instances of language in use. Including real instances of language was an essential premise for corpus building and has now a direct repercussion on the outcomes and data that can be extracted from corpora, thus being based on actual use and reliable to be presented to learners.

A further step in this process is to include corpora as resources to learn the language in the classroom as reservoirs of information that students can analyze to discover the rules of language or the meanings of new words, especially in the area of languages for specific purposes, a field where corpora of particular linguistic varieties, like CORSUBIL, have been compiled to exploit them as sources of information about domain-specific language, including quantitative data about vocabulary and accounts of uses that can be especially relevant for learners of specific areas of language rather than examples taken from general corpora (McEnery and Wilson 2001: 121).

Translation studies are a fruitful field of application for corpus linguistic advances, a place to implement new theories and to use the tools that the discipline provides linguists with. Many of the corpora compiled nowadays include texts in more than one language, and some of them are used as tools to compare specific elements across different languages. We have a clear reflection of the use of corpora in translation in the alignment of concordance lines (Scott and Tribble 2006), outcomes from corpora that are compared in order to improve translation techniques or to assess if a translation process has been correctly carried out, and, more specifically, to be used as a learning resource in the audiovisual translation class.

An additional feature that has to be borne in mind about corpora is that, besides the opinion of some linguists, who consider them 'unreal' examples of language and not valid sources of evidence for corpora, translated texts are genuine communicative events that should not be considered inferior to texts in the original language they were written. However, they are slightly different, and are precisely these differences which have to be observed and described through corpus analysis (Baker et al. 1993: 234).

14.10 Conclusions

AVT is constantly evolving and offers multiple research possibilities. That is the reason why it has to be considered as a discipline benefitting from complementary approaches that should not be taken in isolation.

Corpus-based studies constitute a fairly new approach for the study of the audiovisual text. In this particular case we have chosen subtitling as the core element of our study. From the examples showed in this article we can conclude that Corpus Linguistics reveals itself as a fruitful approach to better know the audiovisual discourse in the original movies in English and in their translated versions in Spanish.

Through linguistic analysis in both languages, we can assess the translator's role as well as some of the main problems that this professional may find. We can also analyze the inconsistencies in register or style in both versions and we can confirm the differences in translation between films according to the specific period of time when a translation took place. In so doing, we will be able to draw some conclusions regarding language evolution (such as, for instance, words that are no longer used, new words that are extensively used or in vogue at present, etc.).

This study is the starting point for building up a bilingual list of lexical units used in English and their appropriate Spanish translation, more specifically, as an example for this paper, of polite speech-act formulae that include expressions for thanking, apologising, requesting and congratulating.

By analysing the translation of such terms and building up a complete bilingual list of oral lexical units in English and Spanish, we will be able to test, on the one hand, if some terms have been correctly translated into Spanish in the subtitles of the films contained in the corpus. On the other hand, we intend to portray the omission of lexical units that may appear in the English versions but are not translated into Spanish, an analysis that has provided us with a result of 11 tokens of difference between one subcorpora and the other. The analysis we have carried out using concordance lines gives us the total number of tokens, but a deeper and more qualitative analysis of the data is needed to figure out the reasons for this difference. More specifically, we want to benefit from the use of Corpus Linguistics to know why the logical translation for "good luck" in Spanish does not always appear as such in the Spanish subtitles. We have elaborated a temptative first classification for the speech-act formula to wish good luck, taking into account that five of the movies subtitled in Spanish (seven of the tokens) the lexical unit has been omitted and in two other movies (four of the tokens) the translation in Spanish has been "¡Suerte!" and not "Buena suerte". We think that one of the reasons why some of the lexical units may be absent in the Spanish subtitles could be because audiovisual translators tend to "sacrifice" those units which are, firstly, identified by the visual context in which the unit has been uttered and, secondly, due to the need to adjust the information contained in a subtitle to the space provided on the screen (Díaz Cintas 2008). With this example we intend to show that a deeper -and more qualitative- analysis of all the lexical units analyzed will be necessary in order to account for the initial differences found between the original English subtitles and the translated Spanish ones. An extensive study of all these lexical units will shed some light on the strategies used when translating audiovisual texts for dubbing and subtitling purposes: firstly, the same lexical units may be translated in different ways (i.e., *Sorry* translated as *Perdón*, *Lo siento, Perdona* or *Perdóneme*); secondly, the same lexical unit in the Spanish subtitles corresponds to different lexical units in the English subtitles (i.e., *¿Qué pasa?* in the Spanish subtitles is found to be the translation of lexical units in English such as *What's the matter?, What is it?* or *What's wrong?*); and, finally, the absence of such lexical units in the Spanish translations that we have already commented (Rica 2011b).

We believe that our main achievement in this article has been the presentation of an interdisciplinary study by blending AVT and Corpus Linguistics and showing some of the potential possibilities they offer, but this field of work still deserves further attention, and a deeper analysis will be carried out in forthcoming stages of the research.

References

Aguilar, C., et al. 2002. *Diccionario de películas del cine norteamericano: Antología crítica*. Madrid: T&B Editores.

Alsina Thevenet, H. 1993a. *Historia del cine americano I: desde la creación al primer sonido (1893–1930)*. Barcelona: Laertes.

Alsina Thevenet, H. 1993b. *Historia del cine americano II: el esplendor y el éxtasis*. Barcelona: Laertes.

Baker, M., G. Francis, and E. Tognini-Bonelli (eds.). 1993. *Text and technology: In Honour of John Sinclair*. Amsterdam/Philadelphia: John Benjamins.

Bell, A. 1991. *The language of news media*. Oxford: Blackwell.

Bell, A., and P. Garret. 1998. *Approaches to media discourse*. Oxford: Blackwell.

Beltrán-Palanques, V. 2010. Analising refusals in films". In *Current trends in anglophone studies: Cultural, linguistic and literary research*, Colección Aquilafuente nº72, ed. Ruano García et al., 70–84. Salamanca: Ediciones Universidad de Salamanca.

Biber, D., S. Conrad, and R. Reppen. 1994. Corpus-based approaches to issues in applied linguistics. *Applied Linguistics* 15(2): 169–189.

Biber, D., S. Conrad, and R. Reppen. 1998. *Corpus linguistics. Investigating language structure and use*. Cambridge: Cambridge University Press.

Biber, D., S. Johansson, G. Leech, S. Conrad, and E. Finegan. 1999. *The Longman grammar of spoken and written English*. Londres: Longman.

Biber, D., S. Conrad, and G. Leech. 2003. *The Longman student grammar of spoken and written English*. Londres: Longman.

Calsamiglia, H., and C. López Ferrero. 2003. Role and position in scientific voices: Reported speech in the media. *Discourse Studies* 5(2): 147–173.

Caparrós Lera, J.M. 2009. *Historia del cine mundial*. Madrid: Ediciones RIALP.

Conrad, S. 2002. Corpus linguistic approaches for discourse analysis. *Annual Review of Applied Linguistics* 22: 75–95.

Delabastita, D. 1989. Translation and mass-communication: Film and TV translation as evidence of cultural dynamics. *Babel* 35–4: 193–218.

Díaz Cintas, J. 2003. *Teoría y práctica de la subtitulación. Inglés-Español*. Madrid: Ariel.

Díaz Cintas, J. 2008. *The didactics of audiovisual translation*. Amsterdam/Philadelphia: John Benjamins Publishing Company.

Finler, J.W. 2010. *El cine americano. Historia de Hollywood: un viaje completo por la historia de la industria americana del cine*. Barcelona: Ediciones MaNonTroppo.

García Riaza, B. 2010a. Explicit attribution sources expressed by 'according to' in a corpus of science popularization articles from The Guardian. *Interlingüística* XXI: 157–168.

García Riaza, B. 2010b. *Mapping Attribution across texts: The particle 'according to' in science popularizations and editorials from The Guardian*. Paper presented at Mapping Language across Cultures Conference (MLAC10), Salamanca, 5–7 July 2010.

Granger, S. 2004. Computer learner corpus research: Current status and future prospects. In *Applied corpus linguistics: A multidimensional perspective*, ed. U. Connor and T. Upton, 123–145. Amsterdam: Rodopi.

Herbst, T. 1987. "A pragmatic translation approach to dubbing", EBU review. *Programmes, Administration, Law* 38–6: 21–23.

Hunston, S. 2002. *Corpora in applied linguistics*. Cambridge: Cambridge University Press.

Hunston, S., and G. Francis. 2000. *Pattern grammar. A corpus-based approach to the lexical grammar of English*. Amsterdam/Philadelphia: John Benjamins.

Kennedy, G. 1998. *An introduction to corpus linguistics*. London/New York: Longman.

Kim, C.K., and G. Thompson. 2010. Obligation and reader involvement in English and Korean science popularizations: A corpus-based cross-cultural text analysis. *Text & Talk* 30(1): 53–73.

Lyons, J. 1981. *Language and linguistics: An introduction*. Cambridge: Cambridge University Press.

Mason, I. 1989. Speaker meaning and reader meaning: preserving coherence in screen translating. In *Babel: The cultural and linguistic barriers between nations*, eds. Kölmel, Rainer y Jerry Paine, 13–24. Aberdeen: Aberdeen University Press.
Mayoral, R. 2001. Campos de estudio y trabajo en traducción audiovisual. In *La traducción para el doblaje y la subtitulación,* ed. M. Duro, 19–45. Madrid: Cátedra.
McEnery, T., and A. Wilson. (2001) [1996]. *Corpus linguistics. Edinburgh textbooks in empirical linguistics*. Edinburgh: Edinburgh University Press.
Pearson, J. 1998. *Terms in context*, Studies in corpus linguistics 1. Amsterdam/Philadelphia: John Benjamins.
Rica, J.P. 2010. Lingüística de corpus en la enseñanza del inglés como lengua extranjera (ILE), In *Los caminos de la lengua. Estudios en homenaje a Enrique Alcaraz Varó,* ed. J.L. Cifuentes, A. Gómez, A. Lillo, J. Mateo y F. Yus, 1405–1427. Alicante: Publicaciones de la Universidad de Alicante.
Rica, J.P. 2011a. *CORSUBIL: Corpus de Subtítulos Bilingües inglés-español*. Madrid: Universidad Complutense de Madrid. Documento sin publicar.
Rica, J.P. 2011b. *Audiovisual translation: A bilingual list of oral inserts in English and Spanish movie subtitles*. Communication presented at the 4th international conference media for all. Audiovisual translation: Taking stock, Imperial College London, London, 30th June.
Rica, J.P., R. Albarrán, and García Riaza, B. 2010. *LSP Software tools and resources for teaching linguistic aspects in audiovisual translation.* Communication presented at the first international workshop on technological innovation for specialized linguistic domains: Theoretical and methodological perspectives. UNED, Madrid (Spain), 21st October.
Romero Fresco, P. 2009. *A corpus-based study on the naturalness of the Spanish dubbing language: The analysis of discourse markers in the dibbed translation of Friends*. Unpublished Ph.D. thesis. Heriot-Watt University, School of Management and languages, Edinburgh.
Scott, M. 2003. Wordsmith Tools 4.0. and Wordsmith Tools 5.0. Available at: http://www.lexically.net/wordsmith/index.html. Last access: Jan 2011.
Scott, M., and C. Tribble. 2006. *Textual patterns. Key words and corpus analysis in language education. Studies in corpus linguistics 22*. Amsterdam/Philadelphia: John Benjamins.
Sinclair, J. McH. 1991. *Corpus, concordance, collocation*. Oxford: Oxford University Press.
Titford, C. 1982. Sub-titling: Constrained translation. *Lebende Sprachen* 3: 113–116.
Toda, F. 2005. Subtitulado y doblaje: Traducción especial(izada). *Quaderns, Revista de Traducció* 12: 119–132.
Tognini-Bonelli, E. 2001. *Corpus linguistics at work*, Studies in corpus linguistics 6. Amsterdam/Philadelphia: John Benjamins.
Whitman-Linsen, C. 1992. *Through the dubbing glass*. Frankfurt am Main: Peter Lang.

Chapter 15
The Pragmatic Level of OntoLingAnnot's Ontologies and Their Use in Pragmatic Annotation for Language Teaching

Antonio Pareja-Lora

15.1 Introduction

Pragmatics is a relatively young area of Linguistics. It was not until the mid-80s when Leech (1983) stated an effective set of postulates that helped discern the objects of Semantics from the objects of Pragmatics. Yet, according to Crystal (1992), at the beginning of the 90s, 'no coherent pragmatic theory' had 'been achieved, mainly because of the variety of topics it has to account for', such as (i) speech acts (Searle 1975); (ii) deixis, presuppositions and implicatures (Levinson 1983; Grice 1975 [1989]); or (iii) pragmatic coherence relations (Hovy and Maier 1995; Romera 2004; Asher and Lascarides 2003; Prévot 2004).

Thus, to some extent, until the beginning of the 90s, the different approaches to Pragmatics focused on a particular set of pragmatic phenomena. From this perspective, it could be said that a global and comprehensive view of Pragmatics was still missing. Such a global and comprehensive view can be found later on in Yule (1996), for example, who defines **Pragmatics** as the study of four areas: (1) *speaker meaning*, that is, what the speaker has in mind when s/he speaks; (2) *contextual meaning*, *i.e.*, 'what people mean in a particular context and how the context influences what is said'; (3) *invisible meaning*, or 'how more gets communicated than is said' (or intended meaning); and (4) *relative distance expression*, namely, how much needs to be said, according to the physical, social or conceptual (subjective) closeness between the speaker and the listener.

Nowadays, (a) the scope, the phenomena and the components of the pragmatic level of language, and (b) the interface of this linguistic level with the remaining ones (the morphological, the syntactic, the semantic and even the discourse-related) are rather clear (Prévot 2004). This allows for a precise and complete specification

A. Pareja-Lora (✉)
Departamento de Sistemas Informáticos y Computación/ATLAS,
Universidad Complutense de Madrid/UNED, Madrid, Spain
e-mail: apareja@sip.ucm.es

E. Bárcena et al. (eds.), *Languages for Specific Purposes in the Digital Era*,
Educational Linguistics 19, DOI 10.1007/978-3-319-02222-2_15,

of the phenomena that a pragmatic annotation scheme should contemplate and make explicit. And this, in turn, is exactly the final aim of the research presented here: the creation of a comprehensive pragmatic annotation scheme, suitable for the pragmatic annotation of texts and dialogues by, for example, undergraduate and graduate students of Linguistics and/or Philology taking a Pragmatics course or module.

Accordingly, this chapter shows the formalization of the pragmatic (annotation) level integrated into the OntoLingAnnot annotation framework. In particular, it presents the different pragmatic categories that can be used to annotate texts and dialogues using the framework. These pragmatic categories are included in the set of ontologies (Gruber 1993; Borst 1997) associated to OntoLingAnnot. Indeed, the OntoLingAnnot framework comprises six different ontologies (Pareja-Lora and Aguado de Cea 2010): a Linguistic Unit Ontology (LUO), a Linguistic Attribute Ontology (LAO), a Linguistic Value Ontology (LVO), a Linguistic Relationship Ontology (LRO), a Linguistic Level Ontology (LLO) and an Integration Ontology (IO).

This chapter has been organized as follows. Section 15.2 states the background and the main assumptions underlying the OntoLingAnnot annotation framework. Then, the pragmatic units of its pragmatic level and the taxonomical relations holding between them are presented in Sect. 15.3. The *attributes* and *values* characterizing them are included in Sect. 15.4, and the *relationships* that hold between pragmatic units are discussed in Sect. 15.5. Section 15.6 shows the evaluation results and the main contributions of the framework achieved so far. Finally, Sects. 15.7 and 15.8 show, respectively, the work that still needs to be done and some conclusions regarding this research.

15.2 Background and Assumptions of the OntoLingAnnot Annotation Framework

Linguistics and linguistic annotation are very wide fields, and, therefore, usually require being partitioned somehow for their study and/or research. Therefore, the traditional and most usual criterion to partition them is based on the concept of level, which divides Linguistics into, for example, Morphology, Syntax, Semantics, Discourse or Pragmatics. This partition of Linguistics and its applications has given rise to several good separate models of its different levels, which, nonetheless (and unfortunately), cannot interoperate and do not benefit from the advances of the others in most of the cases. This is due to the fact that this partition has also led to a somewhat poor communication between the resulting sub-areas and a lack of a global perspective of Linguistics and, in particular, of linguistic annotation.

Even the standardisation processes being carried out by the ISO TC37/SC4 subcommittee on linguistic annotation suffer somehow from this type of bias. Indeed, a great amount of the projects being developed within this ISO subcommittee have focused on delimiting separated and specific standard schemes for particular levels

Table 15.1 A summary of the annotation levels included in OntoLingAnnot and their scope

Annotation level	Annotation scope
Morphological	Up to word structure and meaning (including morph-related annotation)
Syntactic	Up to sentential structure (including multiword token, phrasal and clausal structure)
Semantic	Up to propositional structure and sentence meaning (including phrase and clause meaning), that is, propositional meaning
Discourse	Up to discourse structure (including coherence relation-based structure) and the supra-sentential and locutionary meaning[a] of texts (including anaphora resolution)
Pragmatic	Focuses on the illocutionary and perlocutionary structure and meaning[b] of texts (including deictic resolution and the annotation of other pragmatic relations)

[a]According to Yule (1996), producing an utterance entails three related acts: the locutionary act (*i.e.*, producing a meaningful expression), the illocutionary act (*i.e.*, the function that the utterance is expected to carry out or the purpose according to which it is uttered), and a perlocutionary act (*i.e.*, the effect that the utterance is intended to produce). Therefore, the **locutionary meaning** of a text corresponds to its straightforward interpretation, without considering any further contextual information
[b]As pointed out in the previous footnote, the illocutionary meaning and the perlocutionary meaning of a text have to do, respectively, with the purpose and the effect that the text is expected to perform and produce, and therefore, can be considered a contextualized interpretation of the text

of annotation, such as ISO/MAF (2008) [for morpho-syntactic annotation], ISO/SynAF (2010a, b, c, d) [for syntactic annotation], ISO/SemAF-Time (2009a, b), ISO/SemAF-Space (2010a, b, c, d), ISO/SemAF-Dacts (2009a, b) or ISO/SemAF-DS (2010a, b, c, d) [for the semantic annotation of discourse].

Much on the contrary, the OntoLingAnnot framework has been developed following a comprehensive and complementary approach, which considers all these levels of annotation altogether, not separately. Nevertheless, neat frontiers between the scopes of these levels had to be defined as well, in order to (i) avoid redundancy; and (ii) identify clearly the interfaces between these levels. The levels of annotation defined in the OntoLingAnnot framework, together with their scope, have been summarized in Table 15.1 (see next page).

As commented in Pareja-Lora and Aguado de Cea (2010), this comprehensive approach allowed comparing these different levels and "finding the differences and similarities between them, so as to bear a general and uniformed (level-independent) annotation framework across levels. In this comparison process, some regularities and uniformities across levels were found, which help structure and formalize all of them".

Some of these regularities and uniformities can be specified as follows (*cf.* Pareja-Lora and Aguado de Cea 2010):

1. The first step towards the annotation of a text at any level is identifying the ***units*** of that level included in the text, that is, segmenting the text into its constituent units (according to the level considered). This is referred to as its Segmentation (Sub-)Layer.
2. Then, these units must be further characterized by sub-classifying them and/or accompanying them with the ***features*** (*i.e.*, the pairs <***Attribute***, ***Value***>) that

they present in the text. This is referred to as the Paradigmatic Labelling (Sub-)Layer of the level in question.

3. To improve the annotation of the text at this level, the ***relations*** holding between its constituent units at this level should be identified as well afterwards. This is done within the corresponding Syntagmatic Relation Identification (Sub-)Layer.
4. The annotation of these relations can be further (and optionally) refined, as with units, sub-classifying and/or characterising them by means of their corresponding features in the text. This has been termed the Syntagmatic Relation Labelling (Sub-)Layer.
5. Finally, a full annotation of a text at a given level includes, apart from the annotation of the sub-layers mentioned above, the annotation of the higher-rank units that result from the composition or aggregation of other units, by means of one or more relations of that level (already identified and annotated). This is known as the Resulting Unit (Sub-)Layer of the level. Since linguistic levels cannot be considered disjoint, the units that constitute the ***interface*** between two or more levels must be detailed in this Layer too.

This constitutes the backbone of the OntoLingAnnot annotation framework. In addition, the following assumptions were made when it was developed:

1. Not all annotators and/or annotation tools might perform all the layers of annotation specified above for a given level. In fact, most of them may annotate only a particular set of linguistic phenomena of a certain layer of a given level and, towards this end, they may use only a specific subset of ***categories*** (*i.e.*, units, attributes and/or values). However, some others might annotate every phenomenon of all the layers of a given level, for example. Hence, eventually, the framework had to (i) maximize the coverage as for the phenomena that it contemplated and the categories that it included; and (ii) be flexible and scalable enough to allow its users to select the set of categories included in their annotations.
2. Maximizing the coverage and the scalability of the framework requires (a) following an eclectic and/or non-theory-biased approach for the selection of the categories that had to be finally included in the framework; (b) defining a coherent and theory-neutral terminology for the representation of the categories; (c) accompanying each term with as many synonyms as needed (that is, when several theories referred to the same phenomenon in a different way); and (d) adding many new terms as needed, in order to link the terms coming from different and complementary theories or approaches.
3. All linguistic phenomena, independently of their level and layer, can be represented and/or annotated by means of triples <LinguisticSubject, LinguisticAttribute, LinguisticValue>, where LinguisticSubject can be either a Linguistic Unit or a Linguistic Relationship.
4. These triples <LinguisticSubject, LinguisticAttribute, LinguisticValue> can be implemented by means of *RDF* triples <*Subject*, *Predicate*, *Object*> in which the corresponding linguistic units (*i.e.*, subjects), attributes (*i.e.*, predicates), and values (*i.e.*, objects), are conveniently formalized as ***classes*** or ***instances*** of one or more ontologies.

This completes the specification of the main pillars and assumptions underlying the OntoLingAnnot framework. The following sections present the different classes and instances that have been included in the pragmatic modules of OntoLingAnnot's ontologies. They represent the different categories that can be used for the pragmatic annotation of texts according to this framework. Each type of pragmatic categories, namely pragmatic units, pragmatic attributes, pragmatic values and pragmatic relationships is presented in a dedicated section.

15.3 The Pragmatic Units of OntoLing-Annot

This section introduces the classes of the LUO that formalize the pragmatic units contemplated in OntoLingAnnot. It also shows the taxonomical relations that hold among these concepts (*i.e.*, classes). First of all, the top-level concepts of the pragmatic module of the LUO will be defined here; then, their corresponding sub-classifications will be presented each in a dedicated sub-section. In addition, for readability reasons, the contents of this whole section have been summarized graphically as well in Fig. 15.1.

Concerning the top-level concepts of the pragmatic module of the LUO, they represent the principal types of pragmatic units within OntoLingAnnot, namely Macroproposition, Pragmateme and Pragmatic Functional Unit.

A ***Macroproposition*** is both a Pragmatic Unit and a complex Discourse Unit that stands on the Discourse-Pragmatics interface and that serves as a unitary construction block at the Pragmatic Level. Macropropositions can also be regarded as the linguistic units that result from the aggregation of some interrelated propositions at the Discourse Level (Dijk 1997). The Apology ('Excuse me'), the Query ('can you tell me where the nearest police station is, please?') and the Begging Act ('please') in Example 15.1 and in Fig. 15.3 are examples of this type of units. Macropropositions can be related by means of pragmatic relations, in order to build pragmatemes.

The unit ***Pragmateme***, hence, represents in OntoLingAnnot the main resulting unit of a text pragmatic analysis. The role of this kind of Pragmatic Unit in pragmatic annotation can be better understood in the light of the units that sub-classify it, which are presented in Sect. 15.1.2. Example 15.1 constitutes a particular type of Pragmateme, *i.e.*, a Macroproposition Aggregation Pragmateme, which consists of a Query and its corresponding Answer, (a) separated by a change of Turn at the Discourse Level; (b) marked orthographically and morpho-syntactically by means of a Question Mark; and (c) linked at the Pragmatic Level by a type of Adjacency Pair Relation (see Sect. 15.5 and Fig. 15.5).

Finally, a ***Pragmatic Functional Unit (PFU)*** signals a Pragmatic Coherence Relation (pragmatic coherence relations are discussed in Sect. 15.5). Thus, PFUs are the linguistic units that make explicit pragmatic relations in text or in dialogue. This unit extends the concept of Discourse Functional Unit (DFU) included in Romera (2004) to the Pragmatic Level. For this reason, PFUs are to the Pragmatic Level and to pragmatic coherence relations as DFUs are to the Discourse Level and

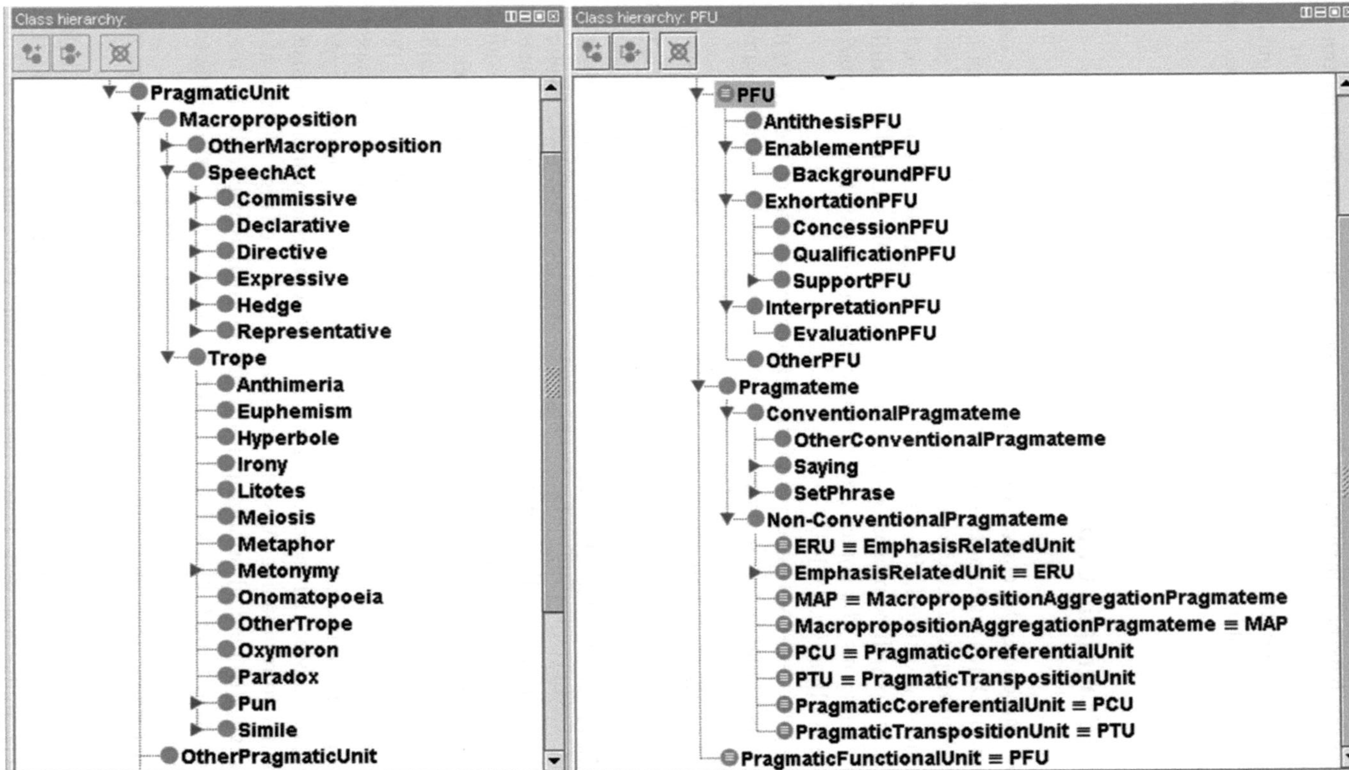

Fig. 15.1 The pragmatic units included in OntoLingAnnot (*i.e.*, in the LUO)

Person A:	'Excuse me, can you tell me where the nearest police station is, please?'
Person B:	'Go down the street and turn left at the traffic lights. I think it's on the right.'

Example 15.1 An excerpt of a short dialog

to discourse coherence relations. Accordingly, a PFU is the marker of a pragmatic relation that holds between two (adjacent) pragmatemes. The change of Turn mentioned above is an instance of an Answer PFU.

As commented, the next three sub-sections describe in detail the sub-classification of each of the pragmatic units introduced up to this point.

15.3.1 The Macroproposition Class and Its Subclasses

The main subclasses (that is, types) of Macroproposition included in OntoLingAnnot are Speech Act, Trope and Other Macroproposition.

Firstly, Speech Act represents all types of illocutionary acts (Searle 1975; Levinson 1983). Hence, the main subclasses of Speech Act in OntoLingAnnot are the following: Declarative ('I now pronounce you husband and wife'), Commissive ('I'll be right back'), Directive ('Go down the street'), Representative ('It's on the right'), Expressive ('I'm so sorry') and Hedge (such as 'I think' in Example 15.1, above). According to the relevant literature, they constitute an *Exhaustive-Decomposition* of this concept.[1] As can be observed, this *Exhaustive-Decomposition* includes the concept Hedge (Yule 1996), although it was not present in the works cited.

This results from the fact that a Hedge stands for an utterance that contains an implicit performative verb. According to Levinson (1983), a performative verb is an explicit form of a Speech Act and, therefore, Hedge was added as a *Subclass-Of* Speech Act into the pragmatic module of the LUO. All these subclasses have been further detailed and subspecified in OntoLingAnnot, following the ideas of Crystal (1992), Yule (1996), Mairal and Faber (1999), Roget (1852 [1982]) and OALD (2006), among others. This subclassification, with more than 135 classes, has not been included here for the sake of space.

Secondly, the Trope concept has been included in the LUO to account for (at least) the most important figurative uses of language, which have to be interpreted pragmatically. Hence, the main subclasses of Trope included in the pragmatic

[1] `Declarative` was originally referred to as `Declarative` in Searle (1975) and lately determined by Yule (1996) for coherence reasons.

module of the LUO are Anthimeria[2] ('I'll *unhair* thy head.'), Euphemism (such as using '*deceased*' instead of 'dead'), Hyperbole ('I have been waiting *for years*'), Irony (for example, saying '*You're a pretty sight*' to a mud-splattered child), Litotes ('Moreover, the attempt is ***not un****successful.*'), Meiosis[3] (for instance, referring to a generous gift as '*a small token of esteem*'), Metaphor ('*to keep the flag flying*'), Metonymy [as well as its subclasses, *i.e.*, Antonomasia, as using '*The Bard*' to refer to William Shakespeare and Synecdoche, as using '*boards*' for 'stage'], Onomatopoeia ('*hiccup*', '*zoom*', '*Bang!*'), Oxymoron ('*cruel kindness*'), Paradox ('*too funny not to be taken seriously*'), Pun ('Atheism is a *non-prophet* institution', instead of *non-profit*) and Simile ('*as busy as a bee*'). They constitute a *Disjoint-Decomposition* of the Trope concept. This *Disjoint-Decomposition* of Trope, as well as many of the examples that accompany them above, have been derived from collaborative and consensual sources, such as SIL (2013).

Finally, Other Macroproposition has been included as a subclass of Macroproposition in order to guarantee an *Exhaustive-Decomposition* of the latter concept. Broadly speaking, it accounts for those expressions which are pragmatically neutral, that is, which do not communicate anything else than is being said.

15.3.2 The Pragmateme Class and Its Subclasses

Regarding the Pragmateme class, it has been divided into two main *subclasses*, namely Non-Conventional Pragmateme and Conventional Pragmateme. These two *subclasses* have also been sub-specified by means of several *subclasses*, which have been determined mostly from the different types of pragmatic non-coherence-related relations presented in Sect. 15.5, below.

Thus, on the one hand, a Non-Conventional Pragmateme can be sub-specified as (i) a Macroproposition Aggregation Pragmateme (MAP), which is a complex Pragmatic Unit that consists of two (or more) pragmatic units, and the pragmatic relation that links them – as mentioned above, the whole Example 15.1 is an instance of MAP; (ii) a Pragmatic Transposition Unit (PTU), which represents a Linguistic Unit that has been moved to a non-conventional position in its context for pragmatic (*e.g.*, emphatic) reasons; (iii) a Pragmatic Co-Referential Unit (PCU), also referred to as a Deictic Unit, which describes a Pragmatic Unit that is used to point out a person, or a given location in time or in space, for example – several instances of this type of unit are shown in Fig. 15.3 and in Fig. 15.4 (below); and (iv) an Emphasis-Related Unit (ERU), which is a type of Pragmatic Unit that is used to stress (or which is stressed by) a particular element or aspect of the discourse (for instance, when saying 'I *do* speak English'). An ERU can also be further subclassified as

[2] `Anthimeria` is defined in SIL (2013) as the use of a member of one word class ('hair' in the example above, which is a noun) as if it were a member of another, thus altering its meaning.

[3] `Meiosis` can be defined as the minimization of the importance of a referent by the use of an expression that is disproportionate to it (SIL 2013).

either an Emphasized Unit (such as 'I speak English' in the example above) or an Emphatic Unit (such as '*do*' in the example above). The remaining subclasses of Pragmateme have not been further subspecified, since the pragmatic phenomena that they represent are better characterized according to the pragmatic relationships in which they are involved.

On the other hand, a Conventional Pragmateme can be subspecified as a Saying, a Set Phrase (such as an Idiom) or else as Other Conventional Pragmateme in OntoLingAnnot. All these subclasses are rather familiar concepts and do not require being described here.

15.3.3 The Pragmatic Functional Unit (PFU). Classes and Subclasses

There are as many types of PFUs as pragmatic coherence relations (see Sect. 15.5). These types (or subclasses) of PFU have been derived from a taxonomy of coherence relations included in Hovy and Maier (1995). This taxonomy is the result of an extensive study of nearly 30 other works on Discourse and Pragmatics, which were combined and interlinked by these authors. Therefore, both the concepts and the part of the taxonomy of this work dealing with Pragmatics are being reused in OntoLingAnnot's ontologies.

Hence, the subclasses of PFU are Interpretation PFU (and its *subclass*, Evaluation PFU), Enablement PFU (and its *subclass*, Background PFU), Antithesis PFU, Exhortation PFU (and its *subclasses*, that is, Concession PFU, Qualification PFU and Support PFU and its manifold *subclasses*).

15.4 The Pragmatic Features of Onto-LingAnnot

As any other linguistic feature, a pragmatic feature consists of an ordered pair ⟨*attribute, value*⟩; however, what characterises a pragmatic feature in OntoLingAnnot is that the *attribute* and the *value* of the pair belong to the pragmatic modules of the LAO and the LVO, respectively. Even though pragmatic attributes and pragmatic values are included in separate ontologies, they are presented here together, since the former can be properly understood only in the light of the latter.

Hence, on the one hand, the pragmatic module of the LAO (dealing with pragmatic attributes) consists of five main concepts, namely the top-level concept Pragmatic Attribute and the concepts Macropropositional Attribute, PFU Attribute, Markedness Attribute and Other Pragmatic Attribute. These last four concepts constitute a *Partition* of Pragmatic Attribute, since (i) they do not share any instance and (ii) the inclusion of the class Other Pragmatic Attribute guarantees covering the whole set of Pragmatic Attribute instances. In addition, in OntoLingAnnot, a Macropropositional Attribute can be subclassified as a Speech Act Attribute or a Common Macropropositional

Example 15.2 A LAO axiom

$$\forall x,y\ ((Speech\_Act(x) \wedge Speech\_Act\_Attribute(y)) \rightarrow Has\_Linguistic\_Attribute(x,y))$$

Attribute, whereas a Markedness Attribute can be subclassified as a Typographic Markedness Attribute[4] or a Common Markedness Attribute. Lastly, the Pragmatic Co-Referential Attribute class subclassifies the Other Pragmatic Attribute class.

All these classes have been linked to their corresponding pragmatic units in the LUO by means of suitable axioms, such as the one shown in Example 15.2.

Thus, (a) Speech Act Attribute (which is a LAO concept) and its *instances* have been linked to the Speech Act LUO concept (by means of the axiom shown in Example 15.2); (b) Common Macropropositional Attribute and its *instances* have been linked to Macroproposition; (c) Markedness Attribute, its *subclasses* and their corresponding *instances* have been linked to Pragmatic Unit; (d) PFU Attribute and its *instances* have been linked to the PFU class of the LUO; and, finally, (e) Pragmatic Co-Referential Attribute and its *instances* have been linked to the Pragmatic Co-Referential Unit LUO concept. The resulting pragmatic attributes and their links to pragmatic units in OntoLingAnnot are shown in Fig. 15.2 (see next page).

The LAO includes also the following *instances*: (1) isIndirectSpeech and has-PerformativeType, which are *InstancesOf* the class Speech Act Attribute; (2) has-FaceValue, isMitigatingDevice and hasAddressingType, which are *InstancesOf* Common Macropropositional Attribute; (3) isExtractable, which is the only *Instance Of* the class PFU Attribute so far; (4) hasPositionMarkedness, hasFormatMarked-ness, hasSizeMarkedness, hasStyleMarkedness and hasColourMarkedness, which are *InstancesOf* Typographic Markedness Attribute; (5) hasRegisterMarkedness, hasPolitenessMarkedness, hasAbbreviationalMarkedness, hasAppreciativeMarked-ness and hasPreferentialMarkedness, which are *InstancesOf* Common Markedness Attribute; and (6) hasProximity, which is the only *InstanceOf* the class Pragmatic Co-Referential Attribute thus far.

On the other hand, the pragmatic module of the LVO (dealing with pragmatic values) has been structured following the same criteria applied to the subclassification of pragmatic attributes. Accordingly, each of the classes of the pragmatic module of the LAO has a related (and near-homonym) class in the LVO. For instance, the Macropropositional Attribute class of the LAO relates to the Macropropositional Value class of the LVO, and the Typographic Markedness Attribute class of the LAO relates to the Typographic Markedness Value class of the LVO.

Analogously, each *InstanceOf* the pragmatic attributes included in the LAO has a corresponding class in the LVO, which represents its set of possible values; these possible values, in turn, have been included as *instances of* the last classes

[4] This attributes and the sub-hierarchy hanging below it can simply be ignored if the material being annotated relates to oral discourse. The `Markedness` of oral discourse can be better handled by means of *`Common`* `Markedness` attributes and also, to some extent, by means of ERUs.

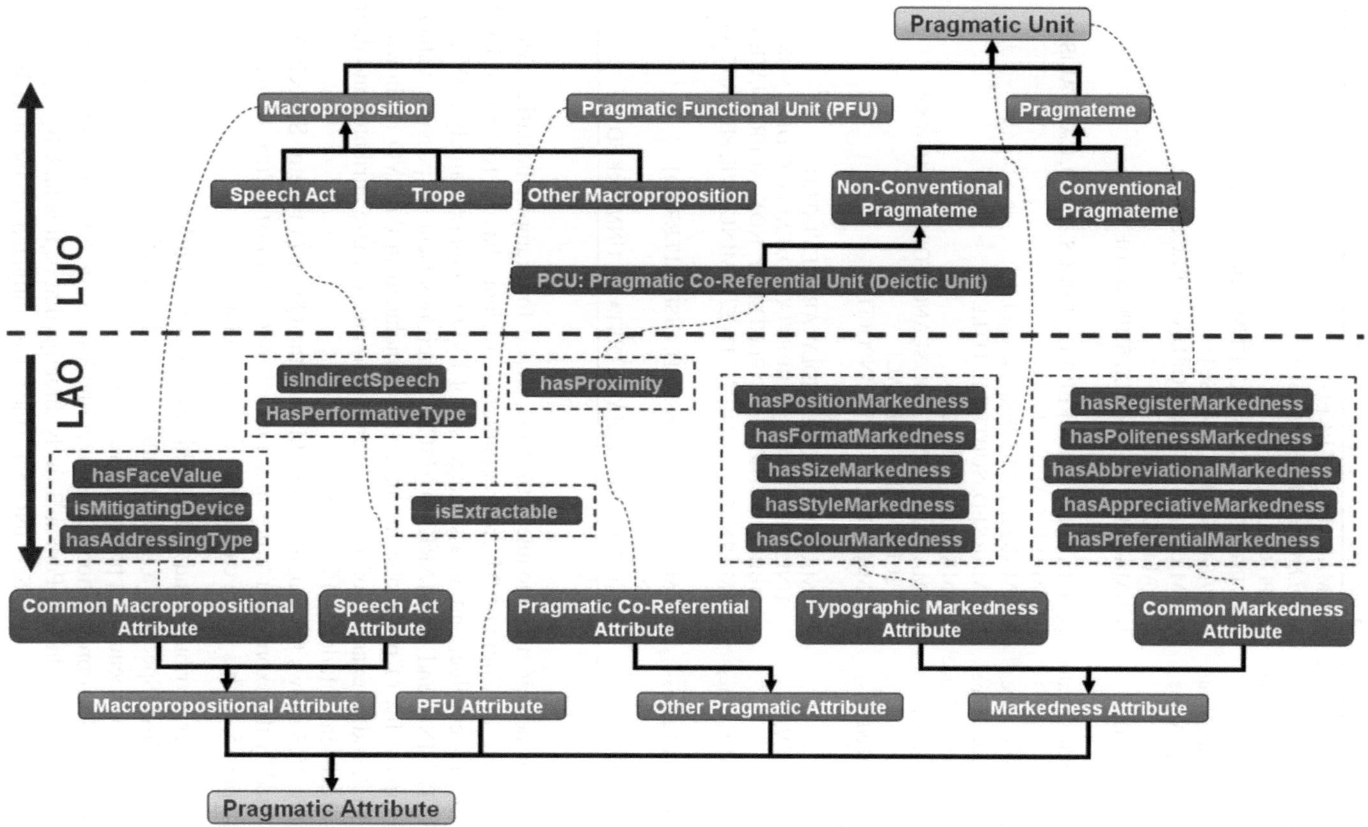

Fig. 15.2 The correspondences between pragmatic units and features in OntoLingAnnot

Table 15.2 The list of pragmatic instance values included in the LVO

Concepts	Instances
Common Pragmatic Value	{UNMARKED, MARKED}
Indirect Speech Value	*BOOLEAN*={TRUE, FALSE}
Performative Type Value	{EXPLICIT, IMPLICIT}
Face Value	{SAVING, THREATENING, UNMARKED_FACE}
Mitigating Device Value	*BOOLEAN*={TRUE, FALSE}
Addressing Type Value	{UNMARKED, OFF_RECORD, ON_RECORD, BALD_ON_RECORD}
Position Markedness Value	{UNMARKED, SUBINDEX, SUPERINDEX}
Format Markedness Value	{UNMARKED, UNDERLINED, ITALICS, BOLD, CAPITALISED, SMALL_CAPITALISED}
Size Markedness Value	{UNMARKED, BIGGER, SMALLER}
Style Markedness Value	{UNMARKED, SUBTITLE, TITLE}
Colour Markedness Value	{UNMARKED, MARKED}
Register Markedness Value	{UNMARKED, FAMILIAR, SLANG, FORMAL, JARGON, TECHNICAL, OFFICIAL}
Politeness Markedness Value	{UNMARKED, POLITE, UNPOLITE}
Abbreviational Markedness Value	{UNMARKED, EXPECTEDLY_ABBREVIATED, UNEXPECTEDLY_ABBREVIATED, EXPECTEDLY_NON_ABBREVIATED, UNEXPECTEDLY_NON_ABBREVIATED}
Appreciative Markedness Value	{UNMARKED, AUGMENTATIVE, DIMINUTIVE, PEJORATIVE}
Preferential Markedness Value	{UNMARKED, PREFERRED, DISPREFERRED}
Proximity Value	{CLOSE, INTERMEDIATE, DISTANT, UNMARKED}

mentioned in the pragmatic module of the LVO. Hence, for example, the hasFaceValue LAO *instance of* Common Macropropositional Attribute has its respective LVO *class*, *i.e.*, Face Value, and an associated set of LVO *instances*, namely SAVING, THREATENING and UNMARKED_FACE, which represent its possible values. The complete list of pragmatic instance values included in the LVO is shown in Table 15.2, and an example of pragmatic annotation using these attributes and their values has been included in Fig. 15.3.

Figure 15.3 shows the pragmatic labelling of the Query (a type of Speech Act) constituted by the expression *'can you tell me where the nearest police station is'* as in Example 15.1. This figure can be explained as follows:

1. [Speech Act Attributes and Values] this expression is *not* of an *indirect speech* type (isIndirectSpeech is a Boolean attribute) and its performative type is made EXPLICIT by means of a performative verb (*'tell'*);
2. [Common Macropropositional Attributes and Values (*cf.* Yule 1996)] this Query, even though it addresses Person B fairly directly (that is, it is an ON_RECORD speech act[5]), is a FACE SAVING act, since it is mitigated by the introductory

[5] As opposed to (1) `BALD_ON_RECORD` speech acts, which are usually realised by means of an imperative form; and to (2) `OFF_RECORD` speech acts, which address the interlocutor indirectly.

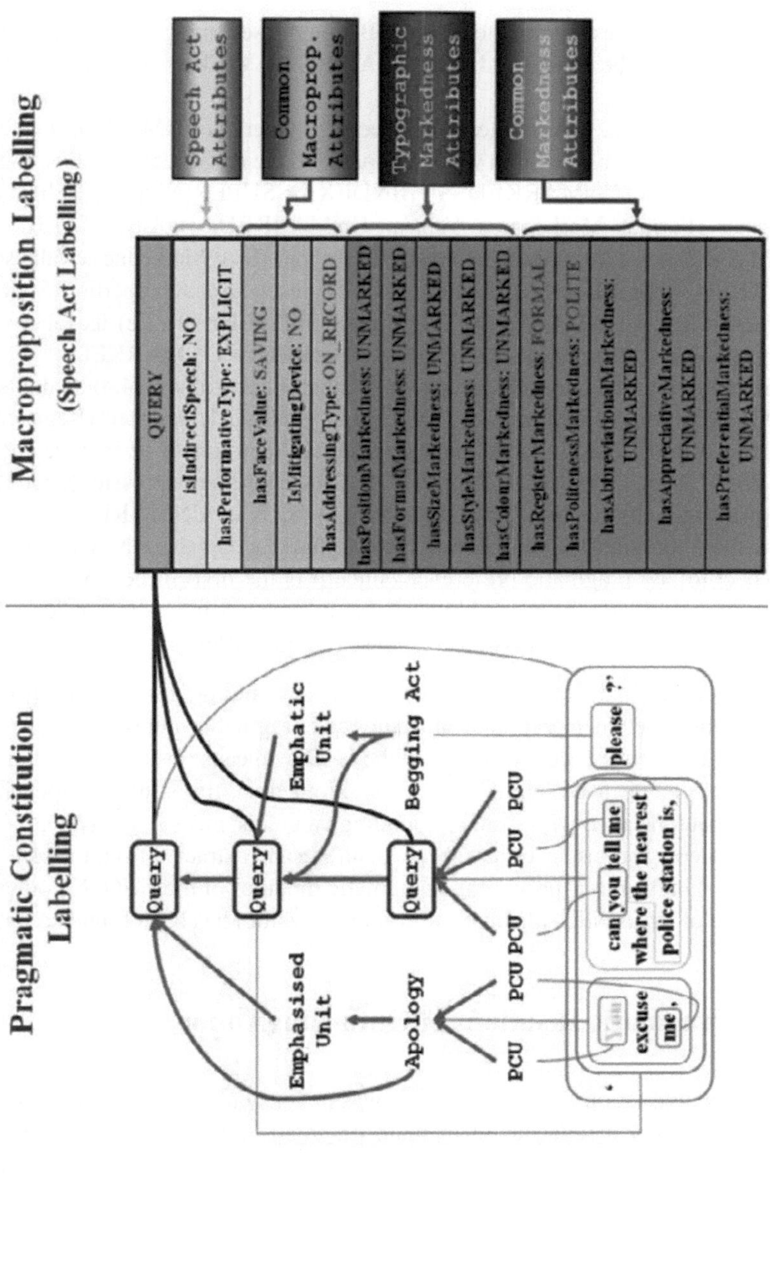

Fig. 15.3 Annotation of features (attributes and values) of a Query (a type of Speech Act)

Example 15.3 An LVO axiom

$$\forall y\ (Takes\_Linguistic\_Value(isIndirectSpeech,\ y) \rightarrow Indirect\_Speech\_Value(y))$$

'can' and, hence, it does not threaten Person B's public self-image. However, the whole Query cannot be considered a MITIGATING DEVICE as such, as shown in the figure;

3. [Typographic Markedness Attributes and Values] the Query is UNMARKED with respect to (3.a) its relative position when compared to the rest of the text (Position Markedness Values: UNMARKED, SUBINDEX or SUPERINDEX); (3.b) its font format (Format Markedness Values: UNMARKED, BOLD, ITALICS, UNDERLINED, etc.); (3.c) the relative size of its font (Size Markedness Values: UNMARKED, BIGGER or SMALLER); (3.d) its presentational properties (Style Markedness Values: UNMARKED, TITLE or SUBTITLE); or (3.e) its relative colour properties (Colour Markedness Value: MARKED or UNMARKED).
4. Lastly, in relation to [Common Markedness Attributes and Values] (4.a) it entails a POLITE (Politeness Markedness Value) and FORMAL register (Register Markedness Value), (4.b) it shows no Appreciative Markedness (it includes no AUGMENTATIVE, DIMINUTIVE or PEJORATIVE form or expression), and it is not [pragmatically] abbreviated anyhow, that is, it is UNMARKED with respect to the Abbreviational Markedness feature, and (4.c) it is also UNMARKED with respect to any pragmatic preference, since it is the first Speech Act of an *adjacency pair* and only the second Speech Act in such a pair can be considered a PREFERRED or DISPREFERRED response (*cf.* Yule 1996).

As with the correspondences between pragmatic units and pragmatic attributes, the correspondences between pragmatic attributes and pragmatic values (all of them included in Fig. 15.2) have been formalized in the LVO by means of suitable axioms, such as the one shown in Example 15.3. This axiom links the isIndirectSpeech pragmatic attribute instance with its corresponding value instances in the LVO.

All these concepts and instances have been identified and extracted from the same works mentioned in the description of the pragmatic modules of the LUO. No other type or example of Pragmatic Attribute (or Pragmatic Value) has been found so far.

15.5 The Pragmatic Relations of Onto-LingAnnot

As far as pragmatic relations are concerned, it was not easy to group, structure and subclassify them under a reduced set of main pragmatic relations. Much on the contrary, there seems to be a huge variety of pragmatic relations, according to their nature and properties. In fact, some of them are not even identified as such in the literature: they are rather disguised as units and/or features instead. In addition, they had to be gathered from several different (somewhat partial) research studies, since none of them covered all of them.

Accordingly, the main pragmatic concepts included in the LRO are the following:

- Pragmatic Coordination, Pragmatic Subordination and Pragmatic Constitution (some examples are presented in Fig. 15.4);
- Exophora and its manifold *subclasses*, which formalize the different types and subtypes of Deixis (that is, Social Deixis, –such as the one signalled by 'I' or 'you' in discourse–, Spatial Deixis *–id.* 'here' or 'there'–, Time Deixis *–id.* 'now' or 'yesterday'–, Discourse Deixis *–id.* 'as commented above' or 'as explained below'– and their corresponding *subclasses*) as well as Homophora (that is, for instance, using '*the President*' for 'The current President of the United States' or 'President Obama');
- Pragmatic (or Interpersonal) Coherence Relation[6] and its *subclasses*, such as Evaluation, Background or Justification (amongst others[7]);
- Pragmatic Realisation and its *subclasses*, such as Tropological Realisation (and its respective *subclasses*, one for each type of Trope in the LUO), Pragmatic Abbreviation, Presupposition Relation and Entailment Relation, which make explicit the implicit meaning underlying a particular Pragmatic Unit;
- Pragmatic Interpretation and its two *subclasses*, that is, Illocutionary Meaning Interpretation and Perlocutionary Meaning Interpretation, which detail how a certain Pragmatic Unit must be understood (*i.e.*, by means of either its literal meaning or its intended meaning, respectively); and,
- A bunch of other miscellaneous pragmatic relations, such as Adjacency Pair Relation, Hedging, Mitigation, Pragmatic Transposition, or Pragmatic Redundancy and Emphatic Redundancy (see some examples in Fig. 15.5).

As mentioned above, many of these classes have been sub-specified by means of suitable *subclasses* and characterized by several (ontological) *attributes*, which have not been included here for space restrictions.

15.6 Evaluation and Contributions of the Present Work

The work presented here has been evaluated against the following six criteria: linguistic coverage, degree of formalisation, ontological gap-filling, scalability, extensibility, interoperability, standard compliance and usability.

Regarding the **linguistic coverage** of the pragmatic level of OntoLingAnnot, as mentioned in the Introduction, all the main approaches to Pragmatics followed thus far lack some degree of generality: (1) Searle (1975) deals barely with speech acts; (2) Grice (1975 [1989]) with presuppositions and implicatures; (3) Levinson (1983) and Yule (1996) do not account for pragmatic coherence relations; (4) Schiffrin (1987), Hovy and Maier (1995) and Romera (2004) only include these last pragmatic

[6]Referred to as `Interpersonal Coherence Relation` in Hovy and Maier (1995) and as `Participation Framework Relation` in Schiffrin (1987) and in Romera (2004).

[7]Extracted from the taxonomy included in Hovy and Maier (1995).

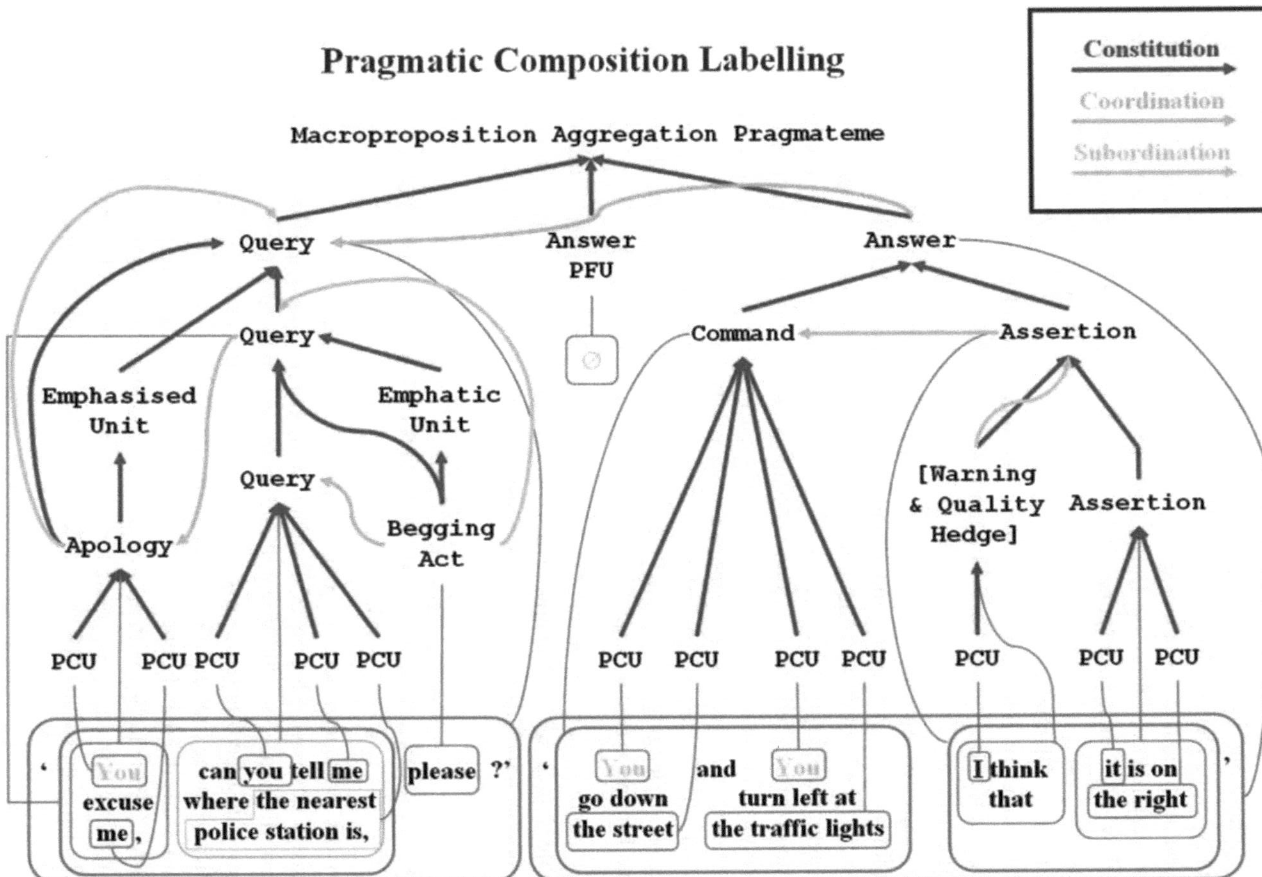

Fig. 15.4 Some examples of Pragmatic Composition (Constitution, Coordination and Subordination), according to OntoLingAnnot

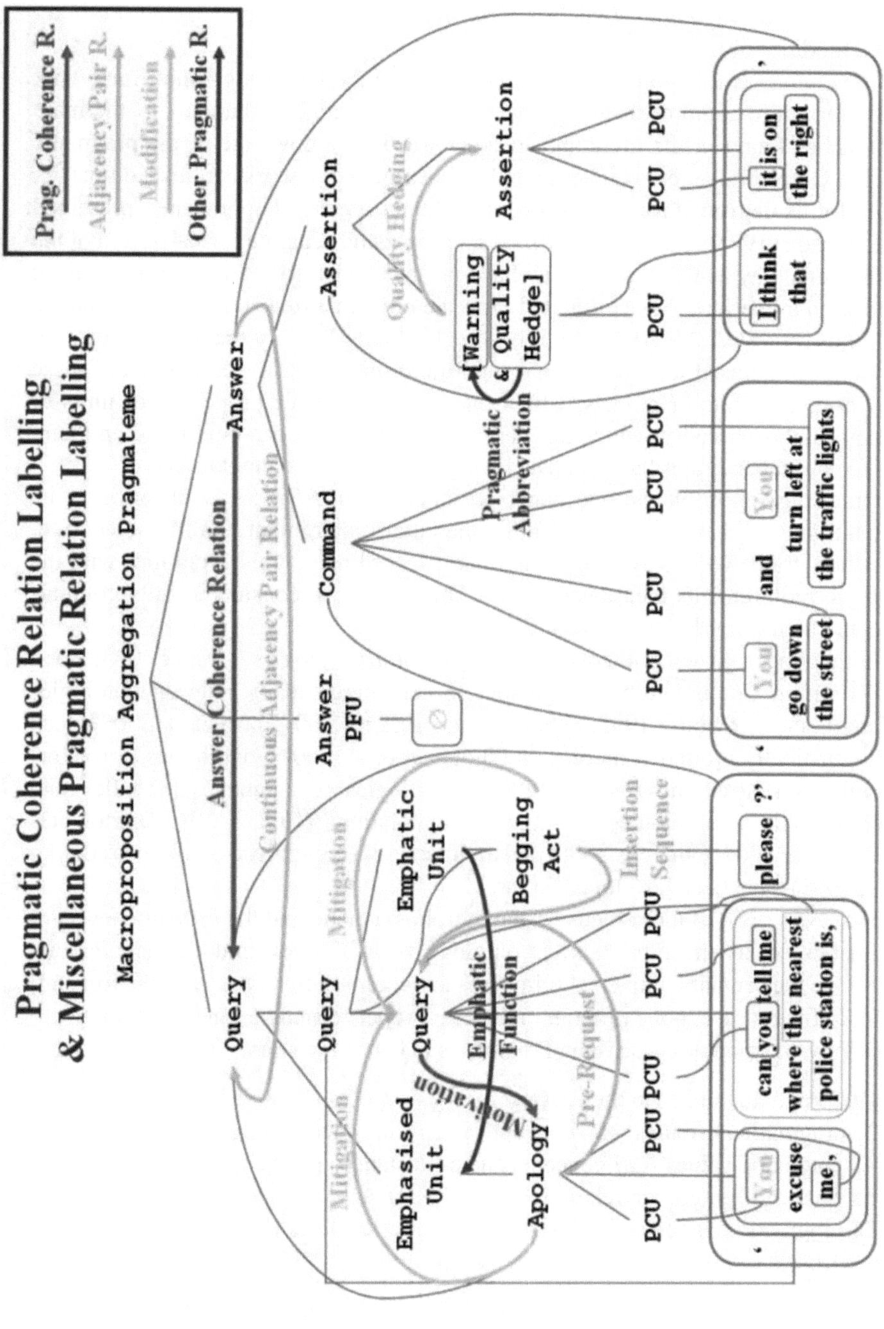

Fig. 15.5 Other examples of pragmatic relations according to OntoLingAnnot

relations; (5) Asher and Lascarides (2003) focus on the semantic-pragmatic interface; and (6) none of them extends the notion of Markedness (Martín Arista et al. 2002) to Pragmatics, which is a rather salient element underlying the pragmatic modules of the LAO and the LVO.

To summarize this point, the pragmatic level of the OntoLingAnnot framework is, by far, more comprehensive, global, detailed and general than any of the main approaches found in the literature. In other words, the coverage of the pragmatic level of OntoLingAnnot is higher than the coverage of the works published thus far.

As for its **degree of formalisation**, even the most general approaches, presented by Levinson (1983) and Yule (1996), lack a proper and accurate formalization of the phenomena they analyze, since they have not been encoded at all. For a linguistic annotation framework to be considered conveniently formalized, it must be computable and, thus (*cf.* ISO/LAF 2009a, b), it has to (1) detail precisely the different categories that can be used for annotation within the framework; (2) state which of these categories are units or objects, which ones are features or properties of units or objects, and (optionally) which ones are relationships that can hold between them; and (3) provide a graph-based mechanism to implement its annotations.

OntoLingAnnot, on the one hand, presupposes an *RDF(S)* serialization of its annotations and, hence, it clearly fulfils the latter requirement. On the other hand, the whole framework is ontology-based and, accordingly, it also complies with the first two requirements mentioned above. Thus, it can be considered fully computable and *conveniently formalised.*

In this line, a growing interest has lately risen in ontologies (Gruber 1993; Borst 1997) within Computational Linguistics. Some linguistically relevant ontologies (Mahesh and Nirenburg 1995; Schalley and Zaefferer 2007; Java et al. 2007), such as linguistically grounded ontologies (Buitelaar et al. 2009), ontologies of (or for) Linguistics (Farrar and Bateman 2005), ontologies of languages (Schalley and Zaefferer 2007), ontologies of linguistic annotations (GOLD 2013; OntoNotes 2013; Farrar 2007; Chiarcos 2008) and architectures of linguistic ontologies (Buyko et al. 2008) have been developed so far.

However, most of them focus on the morphosyntactic and the semantic levels of linguistics or, as the FunGramKB ontology (Mairal Usón and Periñán Pascual 2009), on the semantic universal primitives and their relationships with the [mental] lexicon. In any case, none of them includes a proper formalization of Pragmatics.

Briefly, the modules describing Pragmatics in OntoLingAnnot's ontologies contain

- 192 pragmatic units (in the LUO);
- 26 pragmatic attributes – 10 concepts and 16 instances (in the LAO);
- 81 pragmatic values – 27 concepts and 54 instances (in the LVO);
- 86 classes of pragmatic relations (in the LRO); and
- 24 pragmatic concepts relating the pragmatic level, its layers and substrata (in the LLO).

They amount to 409 pragmatic terms: 339 concepts and 70 instances. There are also several other ontological terms concerning Pragmatics (*attributes*, *SubclassOf*,

PartOf and *ad hoc* relations, rules and axioms), but, as mentioned, they are not discussed here for space reasons.

Thus, the ontological modules presented here can be regarded as the first attempt to formalize and structure coherently this linguistic level in an ontology. Therefore, the **ontological gap-filling** of the pragmatic level of OntoLingAnnot is irrefutable.

Concerning the **scalability** of the approach, as commented in Section 344 (Assumption 1), the whole framework was developed to be as flexible and scalable as possible. This was fulfilled by means of (1) the independence of the pragmatic categories (included in the ontologies) from the final annotation scheme; and (2) the implementation of annotations by means of *RDF(S)* ontology-based triples. This, in turn, (a) allows for the customization of the pragmatic category subset being applied in each particular pragmatic annotation scheme developed according to OntoLingAnnot; and (b) makes this framework highly scalable.

As far as the **extensibility** of the framework and its pragmatic annotation level is concerned, it is also assured by means of the principles mentioned in the previous paragraph. If ever needed, extending the framework (to cover a new phenomenon or to specialize and/or refine its set of categories) can be easily achieved by means of a suitable extension of OntoLingAnnot's ontologies, which is a very simple process.

The **interoperability** of the model is guaranteed by the implementation of annotations in standoff documents using the ontology-based *RDF(S)* triples commented above. These triples can be viewed as the basic components of a directed graph, which is the formalism promoted by ISO/LAF (2009a, b) to provide annotation interoperability. The resulting framework is, thus, fairly interoperable.

Analogously, to this extent, the whole OntoLingAnnot framework is already **standard-compliant**. However, no pragmatic annotation standard has been issued yet. Only the ISO/SemAF-Dacts (2010a, b, c, d) project deals tangentially with Pragmatics, since it includes a reduced list of speech acts. Therefore, in order to go a step further in the standardisation of the pragmatic level of OntoLingAnnot, it is intended to introduce and map the pragmatic concepts and instances of its ontologies into/onto the ISO Data Category Registry (DCR[8] – Kemps-Snijders et al. 2009).

Finally, with reference to the **usability** of the annotations presented here, the pragmatic level of OntoLingAnnot has been developed as part of the OntoLingAnnot annotation framework. This framework is currently being applied to the annotation of corpora in conjunction with the OntoLingAnnot Annotizer tool (Montalvo-Martínez 2009). This tool reuses and extends AKTive Media,[9] an open-source tool from the Natural Language Processing Group of the University of Sheffield. This application is helping find inconsistencies and gaps in the representation of the associated pragmatic phenomena, as well as some usability problems of the framework. This has led to a process of continuous but minor updating of OntoLingAnnot's ontologies. Accordingly, new usability tests should be carried out afterwards, possibly with a different annotation tool and in a different scenario, to have a real measure of the usability of the framework.

[8] http://www.isocat.org

[9] http://www.dcs.shef.ac.uk/~ajay/html/cresearch.html

15.7 Further Work

The last criterion of the previous paragraph shows clearly that the usability evaluation of OntoLingAnnot requires finding a new scenario for this purpose. This is where teaching Pragmatics to both undergraduate and graduate students of Linguistics and/or Philology comes into play. Indeed, the pragmatic annotation level of OntoLingAnnot seems to be a very useful tool *a priori* for this type of students and courses. Therefore, it is envisaged using it in conjunction with a CALL (Computer-Assisted Language Learning) system, such as COPPER or I-AGENT[10] for Spanish students of English Philology. In this new scenario, they could annotate English and Spanish texts and dialogues of different domains and genres and, later on, make a contrastive study of the pragmatic features that characterize, differentiate and/or share these two languages.

Besides, as mentioned above, the introduction and mapping of OntoLingAnnot's pragmatic categories into/onto the DCR is still pending.

15.8 Conclusions

This chapter has introduced the pragmatic annotation level of the OntoLingAnnot (linguistic) annotation framework, focusing on its pragmatic categories, which are included as concepts and instances of its ontologies. The corresponding ontological modules of OntoLingAnnot formalize the different pragmatic units, features and relationships identified in the literature so far, and constitute a coherent distribution and structuring of these pragmatic categories as for their use in (pragmatic) annotation.

As shown in the previous sections, this is the first ontological (and, hence, computable) conceptualization of Pragmatics thus far and, hence, it is an important contribution *per se* to the areas of Ontological Engineering, Pragmatics and Linguistic Annotation. Besides, no other pragmatic model or framework accounts globally and coherently for such a number of pragmatic phenomena and categories as those formalized and included in OntoLingAnnot's ontologies, which is another important contribution to the areas aforementioned. In addition, as discussed in Sect. 15.6, this approach is also scalable, extensible, interoperable, standard compliant and highly (re)usable.

For these reasons, it is more than ready for its incorporation as a new and innovative resource within English and/or Spanish Philology undergraduate and graduate courses, for example, in conjunction with an (I)CALL system. It is highly likely that its use by the students taking these courses helps them understand more easily their content.

[10] Developed by the ATLAS research group (http://portal.uned.es/portal/page?_pageid=93,8842771&_dad=portal&_schema=PORTAL& idContenido=3).

Appendix: List of Acronyms and Abbreviations

CALL	Computer-Assisted Language Learning
ERU	Emphasis-Related Unit
ICALL	Intelligent Computer-Assisted Language Learning
IO	Integration Ontology
LAO	Linguistic Attribute Ontology
LLO	Linguistic Level Ontology
LRO	Linguistic Relationship Ontology
LUO	Linguistic Unit Ontology
LVO	Linguistic Value Ontology
MAP	Macroproposition Aggregation Pragmateme
PCU	Pragmatic Co-Referential Unit
PFU	Pragmatic Functional Unit
PTU	Pragmatic Transposition Unit

References

Asher, Nicholas, and Alex Lascarides. 2003. *Logics of conversation*. Cambridge, UK: Cambridge University Press.

Borst, Willem N. 1997. *Construction of engineering ontologies*. Ph.D. thesis, University of Twente, Enschede.

Buitelaar, Paul, Philipp Cimiano, Peter Haase, and Michael Sintek. 2009. Towards linguistically grounded ontologies. In *The semantic web: Research and applications* (Lecture notes in computer science, Vol. 5554/2009). Berlin/Heidelberg: Springer.

Buyko, Ekaterina, Christian Chiarcos, and Antonio Pareja-Lora. 2008. Ontology-based interface specifications for an NLP pipeline architecture. In *Proceedings of LREC 2008*, Marrakech, May 2008.

Chiarcos, Christian. 2008. An ontology of linguistic annotations. *LDV Forum (GLDV-Journal for Computational Linguistics and Language Technology)* 23(1): 1–16.

Crystal, David. 1992. *A dictionary of linguistics and phonetics*, 3rd ed. Oxford: Blackwell.

Farrar, Scott. 2007. Using 'Ontolinguistics' for language description. In *Ontolinguistics: How ontolinguistic status shapes the linguistic coding of concepts*, ed. Andrea C. Schalley and Dietmar Zaefferer. Berlin/New York: Mouton de Gruyter.

Farrar, Scott, and John A. Bateman. 2005. *OntoSpace project reports – Deliverable D3 – Linguistic ontology baseline*. University of Bremen, Germany. http://www.ontospace.uni-bremen.de/pub/FarrarBateman05-i1-d3.pdf. Accessed 15 June 2013.

GOLD. 2013. http://linguistics-ontology.org/. Accessed 15 June 2013.

Grice, Herbert P. 1975 (1989). Logic and conversation. Ibid. *Reprinted in studies in the way of words,* ed. H.P. Grice, 22–40. Cambridge, MA: Harvard University Press.

Gruber, Thomas R. 1993. A translation approach to portable ontologies. *Journal on Knowledge Acquisition* 5(2): 199–220.

Hovy, Eduard, and Elisabeth Maier. 1995. *Parsimonious or profligate: How many and which discourse structure relations?* http://www.isi.edu/natural-language/people/hovy/papers/93discproc.pdf. Accessed 15 June 2013.

International Organization for Standardization. 2008. ISO/DIS 24611. *Language resource management – Morpho-syntactic annotation framework (MAF)*.

International Organization for Standardization. 2009a. ISO/DIS 24612. *Language resource management – Linguistic annotation framework (LAF)*.

International Organization for Standardization. 2009b. ISO/DIS 24617-1. *Language resource management – Semantic annotation framework (SemAF) – Part 1: Time & events.*
International Organization for Standardization. 2010a. ISO/DIS 24617-2. *Language resource management – Semantic annotation framework (SemAF) – Part 2:* Dialogue acts.
International Organization for Standardization. 2010b. ISO/PWI 24617-5. *Language resource management – Semantic annotation framework (SemAF) – Discourse structures.*
International Organization for Standardization. 2010c. ISO/PWI 24617-6. *Language resource management – Semantic annotation framework (SemAF) – Static spatial information.*
International Organization for Standardization. 2010d. ISO/FDIS 24615. *Language resource management – Syntactic annotation framework (SynAF).*
Java, Akshay, Sergei Nirenburg, Marjorie McShane, Tim Finin, Jesse English, and Anupam Joshi. 2007. Using a natural language understanding system to generate semantic web content. *International Journal on Semantic Web and Information Systems* 3(4): 50–74.
Kemps-Snijders, M., M. Windhouwer, P. Wittenburg, and S.E. Wright. 2009. ISOCat: Remodelling metadata for language resources. *International Journal of Metadata, Semantics and Ontologies* 4(4): 261–276.
Leech, Geoffrey. 1983. *Principles of pragmatics*. London: Longman.
Levinson, Stephen C. 1983. *Pragmatics*. Cambridge: Cambridge University Press.
Mahesh, Kavi, and Sergei Nirenburg. 1995. A situated ontology for practical NLP. In *Proceedings of the workshop on basic ontological issues in knowledge sharing, International Joint Conference on Artificial Intelligence (IJCAI-95)*, Montreal, August 1995.
Mairal Usón, Ricardo, and Pamela Faber. 1999. *Constructing a Lexicon of English verbs*. Berlin: Mouton de Gruyter.
Mairal Usón, Ricardo, and Periñán Pascual José Carlos. 2009. The anatomy of the lexicon within the framework of an NLP knowledge base. *RESLA: Revista española de lingüística aplicada* 22: 217–244.
Martín Arista, Javier, Elisa González Torres, Laura Caballero González, and Beatriz Martínez Fernández. 2002. Markedness and the hierarchy of subject prototypicality. *Revista Electrónica de Lingüística Aplicada (RAEL)* 15: 93–112.
Montalvo-Martínez, Martín. 2009. *OntoLing Annotizer: Una herramienta de ayuda a la anotación*. M.Sc. thesis, Universidad Complutense de Madrid, Madrid.
OALD. 2006. *Oxford advanced Learners' dictionary*. Oxford: Oxford University Press.
OntoNotes. 2013. http://www.bbn.com/ontonotes/. Accessed 15 June 2013.
Pareja-Lora, Antonio, Guadalupe Aguado de Cea. 2010. Modelling discourse-Related terminology in OntoLingAnnot's ontologies. In *Proceedings of the TKE 2010 workshop "Establishing and using ontologies as a basis for terminological and knowledge engineering resources*", Dublin, Aug 2010.
Prévot, Laurent. 2004. *Structures sémantiques et pragmatiques pour la modélisation de la cohérence dans des dialogues finalisés*. Thèse de doctorat de l'université Paul Sabatier, Toulouse, France.
Roget, Peter M. 1852 (1962, 1982). Roget's thesaurus. In *Burnt mill*, ed. Susan M. Lloyd. Harlow: Longman Group Limited.
Romera, Magdalena. 2004. *Discourse functional units: The expression of coherence relations in spoken Spanish*. Munich: LINCOM.
Schalley, Andrea C., and Dietmar Zaefferer. 2007. Ontolinguistics – An outline. In *Ontolinguistics: How ontolinguistic status shapes the linguistic coding of concepts*, ed. Andrea C. Schalley and Dietmar Zaefferer. Berlin/New York: Mouton de Gruyter.
Schiffrin, Deborah. 1987. *Discourse markers*. Cambridge/New York: Cambridge University Press.
Searle, John. 1975. Indirect speech acts. In *Syntax and semantics, 3: Speech acts*, ed. P. Cole and J.L. Morgan, 59–82. New York: Academic Press.
SIL. 2013. *Glossary of linguistic terms,* eds. Eugene E. Loos, Susan Anderson, Dwight H. Day (Jr.), Paul C. Jordan, and J. Douglas Wingate. http://www.sil.org/linguistics/GlossaryOfLinguisticTerms/. Accessed 15 June 2013.
van Dijk, Teun. A. (ed.). 1997. *Discourse studies*, 2 vols. London: Sage.
Yule, George. 1996. *Pragmatics*. Oxford: Oxford University Press.

Chapter 16
Reflections on the Future of Technology-Mediated LSP Research and Education

Jorge Arús, Elena Bárcena, and Timothy Read

In the introduction to this volume, we promised to present a state-of-the-art of technological and methodological innovation in the teaching and processing of specialized linguistic domains. It is our belief that the chapters included in this compilation have not only offered valuable insights into the promised state-of-the-art but also opened a number of approaches that will help to shape the future of CALL and LSP research, teaching and learning.

In the case of a book dealing with applied technologies, as is the case here, the future starts even before it is published, since technological evolution is faster than the typical process of publishing a book. This means that as soon as the last pages of this book are finished, a number of new technologies and products will already be either in the market, or in the labs of research institutions and universities, waiting to be presented to the academic community. This is particularly true for areas not included in the present volume which have recently gained attention, such as the Web 2.0, open educational resources and practices like MOOCs (Massive Open Online Courses), gamification, and mobile and augmented devices and applications.

J. Arús (✉)
Departamento de Filología Inglesa I, Universidad Complutense de Madrid, Madrid, Spain
e-mail: jarus@ucm.es

E. Bárcena
Departamento de Filologías Extranjeras y sus Lingüísticas, Universidad Nacional de Educación a Distancia, Madrid, Spain
e-mail: mbarcena@flog.uned.es

T. Read
Departamento de Lenguajes y Sistemas Informáticos, Universidad Nacional de Educación a Distancia, Madrid, Spain
e-mail: tread@lsi.uned.es

E. Bárcena et al. (eds.), *Languages for Specific Purposes in the Digital Era*, Educational Linguistics 19, DOI 10.1007/978-3-319-02222-2_16,

The potential of the Web 2.0 for LSP processing and learning is staggering. The Web is full of sites devoted to the illustration and/or discussion of different possible uses of the social media: blogs, microblogs like Twitter, general social networks like Facebook, etc. Some of the most popular sites at the time of writing are *Edudemic, Effective Web 2.0 Tools for the Classroom* and Larry Ferlazzo's *Best Web 2.0 Applications for Education* (see URLs in bibliography below). Researchers have for some time now looked into all these possibilities trying to bring a rationale to the use of these tools. Among the most recent publications on the educational uses of the Web 2.0, we can cite the papers by Benett et al. (2012), Pilgrim and Bledsoe (2013), Sadaf et al. (2013), and Saurabh and Sairam (2013); specifically applied to FLT (Foreign Language Teaching) are Friedman (2012) and Wang and Vasquez (2012); and even more closely related to the interests of the LSP community are the papers by Garrett (2009) and Papadima-Sophocleous and Yerou (2013).

Another area of educational technology that is receiving considerable attention is that of open educational resources (or OERs) and practices (Geser 2012), and MOOCs (McAuley et al. 2010; Read and Bárcena 2013). Such resources and open online environments with potentially very large student numbers are argued to be highly flexible and effective ways of potentiating social interaction and involving students in their own learning (Beetham and Sharpe 2013), while flattening the hierarchical control typically present in standard online courses. Furthermore, the *openness* (Hilton et al. 2010) of course access and the resources therein frees the students to work more actively, thereby potentiating their ability to summarize, synthesize and adapt to the learning activities being undertaken. Given that an important part of language learning involves improving competences beyond strict comprehension and production, then the large social interaction possible in these courses may prove to be very valuable for language learning, correction, feedback, and evaluation in distance educational environments and will no doubt be a subject for future research.

Gamification has come a long way and its potential for educational applications was evident since its arrival. This concept is related to the use of the mechanics of amusement present in most games in other contexts, so that people adopt similar positive attitudinal aspects as they do when playing. Without going back too far in time, we can mention some classic publications dealing with the use of gamification techniques, such as the texts by Deterding et al. (2011), Huotari and Hamari (2012), and Zichermann and Cunningham (2011). In education, it makes the most of the psychological predisposition of people at play to make "boring" coursework (as language coursework is quite often perceived to be) more attractive, which in turn, is believed to directly improve learning. This field of research is still becoming established, although some articles have been published, such as Reinders (2012), Sykes et al. (2012), and Blake (2013). Cross-fertilization is, however, not that rich with LSP, where there is still considerable scope for research.

Perhaps one of the most active areas of educational technologies is that of mobile learning, and specifically in the context of the research related to this book, MALL (Mobile Assisted Language Learning), including augmented reality. The trend of Internet access from mobile devices is steadily increasing with almost 40 % of all access coming from smartphones and tablets (comScore 2013). This figure reflects a change in people's habits of accessing knowledge and information away from desktop and portable computers toward the use of handheld computing devices. Hence, it is reasonable that the scope for using such devices for language learning is being actively researched. Although mobile applications have been around for a lot less time than digital games or the Internet itself, there is already a large number of publications dealing with theoretical and practical aspects of MALL, ranging from journal papers (Arrigo et al. 2013) and book chapters (Kukulska-Hulme 2012) to monographs, such as those by Díaz Vera (2012), Zhang (2012), and Facer and Abdous (2011), the latter with a focus on FLT within the context of mobile learning. Regarding the application of MALL for LSPs, the possibilities are great since professionals and academics are known to be regular mobile users and also travellers. The frequent change of environment can enrich the learning process since it naturally forms part of the functionality of smartphones and other similar mobile devices. Example publications in this area include Arnó (2012), Arús-Hita et al. (2013) and Bárcena et al. (2013). As for augmented reality, as a way to supplement real world events with additional information (for example, Liu et al. 2010 and Specht et al. 2011), it also holds great promise for language learning, as mobile devices become smaller and more integrated into our clothes and everyday items.

In conclusion, this monograph is likely to be one of the first comprehensive volumes to combine LSP issues with the use of technology. Given that, as we have seen, the future of technological innovations in the LSP context is very promising, it is evident that there is great scope for further volumes on these questions in the near future.

References

Arnó, E. 2012. The role of technology in teaching languages for specific purposes courses. *The Modern Language Journal* 96: 89–104.

Arrigo, M., A. Kukulska-Hulme, I. Arnedillo-Sánchez, and G. Kismihok. 2013. Meta-analyses from a collaborative project in mobile lifelong learning. *British Educational Research Journal* 39(2): 222–247.

Arús-Hita, J., P. Rodríguez-Arancón, and C. Calle-Martínez. 2013. A pedagogic assessment of mobile learning applications. In *Proceedings of ICDE 2013, Mobilizing Distance Education*, UNED, Madrid.

Barcena, E., E. Martín Monje, and T. Read. 2013. Mobile learning and social networks: A socially sensitive proposal for the development of oral professional English capabilities. In *Proceedings of ICDE 2013, Mobilizing Distance Education*, UNED, Madrid.

Beetham, H., and R. Sharpe (eds.). 2013. *Rethinking pedagogy for a digital age: Designing for 21st century learning*. London: Routledge.

Bennett, S., A. Bishop, B. Dalgarno, J. Waycott, and G. Kennedy. 2012. Implementing Web 2.0 Technologies in higher education: A collective case study. *Computers and Education* 59(2): 524–534.

Best Web 2.0 Applications For Education. http://larryferlazzo.edublogs.org/2012/07/10/the-best-web-2-0-applications-for-education-in-2012-—-so-far

Blake, R.J. 2013. *Brave new digital classroom: Technology and foreign language learning*. Georgetown: Georgetown University Press.

comScore.2013.http://marketingland.com/report-nearly-40-percent-of-internet-time-now-on-mobile-devices-34639

Deterding, S., D. Dixon, R. Khaled, and L. Nacke. 2011. From game design elements to gamefulness: Defining gamification. In *Proceedings of the 15th international Academic MindTrek conference*, 9–15.

Díaz Vera, J.E. 2012. *Left to my own devices: Learner autonomy and mobile assisted language learning*. Bingley: Emerald Group.

Edudemic. http://www.edudemic.com/best-web-tools/

Effective Web 2.0 Tools for the Classroom. https://sites.google.com/site/educationalweb20tools

Facer, B.R., and M. Abdous. 2011. *Academic podcasting and mobile assisted language learning: Applications and outcomes*. Hershey: IGI Global.

Friedman, S. 2012. As it happens: The added value of synchronous web 2.0 communication tools in second language and culture courses. In *Proceedings of INTED2012*, 4465–4472.

Garrett, N. 2009. Computer assisted language learning trends and issues revisited: Integrating innovation. *The Modern Language Journal* 93(s1): 719–740.

Geser, G. 2012. Open educational practices and resources: The OLCOS roadmap 2012. *Revista de Universidad y Sociedad del Conocimiento* 4(1): 1–9.

Hilton III, J., D. Wiley, J. Stein, and A. Johnson. 2010. The four 'R's of openness and ALMS analysis: Frameworks for open educational resources. *Open Learning* 25(1): 37–44.

Huotari, K., and J. Hamari.2012. Defining gamification – A service marketing perspective. In *Proceedings of the 16th international Academic MindTrek conference 2012*, 17–22.

Kukulska-Hulme, A. 2012. Language learning defined by time and place: A framework for next generation designs. In *Left to My Own Devices: Learner Autonomy and Mobile Assisted Language Learning. Innovation and Leadership in English Language Teaching, 6*, ed. J.E. Díaz-Vera, 1–13. Bingley, UK: Emerald.

Liu, T.Y., T.H. Tan, and Y.L. Chu. 2010. QR code and augmented reality-supported mobile English learning system. In *Mobile multimedia processing*, 37–52. Berlin: Springer.

McAuley, A., B. Stewart, G. Siemens, and D. Cormier. 2010. *The MOOC model for digital practice*. www.elearnspace.org/Articles/MOOC_Final.pdf

Papadima-Sophocleous, S., and C. Yerou. 2013. Using wikis in an English for specific academic purposes (ESAP) context: University students' perceptions and reflections. *Teaching English with Technology* 13(2): 23–54.

Pilgrim, J., and C. Bledsoe. 2013. The application of Web 2.0 Tools for literacy education. In *Technological tools for the literacy classroom*, ed. J. Whittingham, S. Huffman, W. Rickman, and C. Wiedmaier, 27–44. Hershey: IGI Global.

Read, T., and E. Bárcena. 2013. MOOCs and open higher education: The case of UNED. In *Proceedings of Ikasnabar 2013, the 6th International conference on open education and technology*, ed. G. Palazio. Leioa: Publishing Service of the University of the Basque Country.

Reinders, Hayo. 2012. *Digital games in language learning and teaching*. Basingstoke: Palgrave MacMillan.

Sadaf, A., T. Newby, and P.A. Ertmer. 2013. Exploring factors that predict preservice teachers' intentions to use web 2.0 technologies using decomposed theory of planned behavior. *Journal of Research on Technology in Education* 45(2): 171–196.

Saurabh, S., and A.S. Sairam. 2013. Professors – The new YouTube stars: Education through web 2.0 and social network. *International Journal of Web Based Communities* 9(2): 212–232.

Specht, M., S. Ternier, and W. Greller. 2011. Mobile augmented reality for learning: A case study. *Journal of the Research Center for Educational Technology* 7(1): 117–127.

Sykes, J.M., J.E. Liskin-Gasparro, and M.E. Lacorte. 2012. *Language at play: Digital games in second and foreign language teaching and learning*. London: Pearson Education.

Wang, S., and C. Vasquez. 2012. Web 2.0 and second language learning: What does the research tell us? *CALICO Journal* 29(3): 412–430.

Zhang, F. 2012. *Computer-enhanced and mobile-assisted language learning*. Hershey: IGI Global.

Zichermann, G., and C. Cunningham. 2011. Introduction. In *Gamification by design: Implementing game mechanics in web and mobile apps*. Sebastopol: O'Reilly Media. xiv.

FSC
www.fsc.org
MIX
Papier aus verantwortungsvollen Quellen
Paper from responsible sources
FSC® C105338

If you have any concerns about our products,
you can contact us on
ProductSafety@springernature.com

In case Publisher is established outside the EU,
the EU authorized representative is:
Springer Nature Customer Service Center GmbH
Europaplatz 3, 69115 Heidelberg, Germany

Printed by Libri Plureos GmbH
in Hamburg, Germany